TRICKY DICK AND THE PINK LADY

TRICKY DICK

AND

THE PINK LADY

Richard Nixon vs.
Helen Gahagan Douglas—
Sexual Politics and the
Red Scare, 1950

GREG MITCHELL

RANDOM HOUSE ⌂ NEW YORK

Grateful acknowledgment is made to the following for permission
to use previously published and preexisting material:

THE ESTATE OF RICHARD M. NIXON: Excerpts from items from the
Richard M. Nixon Pre-Presidential Papers housed at the Richard
M. Nixon Library & Birthplace. Reprinted by permission of the
Estate of Richard M. Nixon.

FRANCES COLLIN, LITERARY AGENT: Excerpts from letters and other
unpublished writings by Helen Gahagan Douglas. All unpublished
material reproduced here by permission of Frances Collin, Agent for
the Estate of Helen Gahagan Douglas.

THE RICHARD M. NIXON LIBRARY & BIRTHPLACE: Excerpts from notes
contained in the speech files and various letters and memos by
Richard M. Nixon housed at the Richard M. Nixon Library &
Birthplace. All material reprinted by permission of the Richard M.
Nixon Library & Birthplace, Yorba Linda, California.

Library of Congress Cataloging-in-Publication Data
Mitchell, Greg.
Tricky Dick and the Pink Lady / Greg Mitchell.
p.   cm.
Includes bibliographical references and index.
ISBN 0-679-41621-8
1. Nixon, Richard M. (Richard Milhous), 1913–1994.   2. Douglas,
Helen Gahagan, 1900–1980.   3. Electioneering—California—
History—20th century.   4. Anti-communist movements—California.
5. California—Politics and government—1850–1950.   6. United
States. Congress. Senate—Elections, 1950.   I. Title.
E856.M57   1997
324.973´0918—dc20   96-43670

Random House website address: www.randomhouse.com
Printed in the United States of America on acid-free paper
24689753
First Edition
Book design by Jo Anne Metsch

FOR BARBARA

Fear hath a hundred eyes that all agree
To plague her beating heart . . .

—WORDSWORTH

Acknowledgments

I wish to thank the Harry S. Truman Library Institute and the Carl Albert Center at the University of Oklahoma for providing visiting scholar grants to aid my research. I would also like to express my appreciation to archivists Dennis Bilger, Liz Safly, and Sam Rushay at the Truman Library and John Caldwell, formerly at the Albert Center.

I am particularly indebted to two other fine archivists who went out of their way to assist me. They are Susan Naulty at the Richard Nixon Library in Yorba Linda, and Fred Klose, formerly at the National Archives and Records Administration in Laguna Niguel. Among other archivists who assisted me through thick and thin the following stand out: Ned Comstock at the University of Southern California's Cinema and Television Library and John Ahouse at U.S.C. special collections; Craig St. Clair at the *Los Angeles Times* Archives; Nicole Bouche at the Bancroft Library (University of California at Berkeley); Linda Hanson and Mary Knill at the Lyndon Johnson Library; and Sam Gill at the Academy of Motion Picture Arts and Sciences' Margaret Herrick Library.

Dozens of individuals contributed invaluable reflections, insights, and advice—or provided shelter on my many visits to California. I'd especially like to thank Bill Blum, Ed Cray, Ralph de Toledano, Mary Helen Douglas, Lyn Goldfarb, Mary Ellen Leary, Gina Lobaco, and Ingrid Winther Scobie.

Finally, much gratitude to my agent, Sarah Lazin; my editor, Ann Godoff; assistant editor Enrica Gadler; and associate copy chief Beth Pearson, for their wise and steadfast work.

Contents

Preface

America at mid-century experienced a year like no other. It has been called savage, traumatic, a time of crisis—"the year it all fell apart." Events within and beyond our control in 1950 would fix the nation on a perilous path for decades. The Korean War began, the Communists completed their takeover of China, and the United States sent its first military advisers to Vietnam. President Harry S. Truman, responding to the Soviets' first atomic explosion, announced that the United States would develop the hydrogen bomb. A secret document known as NSC-68 promoted a fateful surge in the Pentagon budget. Alger Hiss was convicted, and Julius and Ethel Rosenberg were arrested. Hard-line anticommunism had won a wide audience following World War II, but only in 1950 did it threaten to provoke hysteria. Senator Joseph R. McCarthy launched his anti-Communist witch-hunt, and the movie-industry blacklist began in earnest after the Hollywood Ten went to jail.

Would militant anticommunism prove to be a passing phenomenon or a permanent fixture? It had produced Red-scare headlines yet in 1948 "failed as a partisan issue," Stephen Ambrose has observed. The Cold War was already established, but Cold War politics remained in its infancy.

Then, in 1950, several campaigns for U.S. Senate seats promised to put Cold War politics to the test. In California, two prominent and attractive members of Congress, Richard M. Nixon and Helen Gahagan Douglas, swept to victory in June primaries, then squared off in what was destined to become one of the most significant, notorious, and lamented election contests in the nation's history. Douglas attempted to become only the fourth woman ever elected to the U.S. Senate. Nixon considered the race a stepping-stone to higher office.

She was a progressive Democrat, he a moderate Republican. She was effervescent, he was intense. She was wealthy, a famous actress from the East; he was an attorney of moderate means from Whittier. She declared that Communist sympathizers posed no serious threat to America; he had just helped send Alger Hiss to jail. Helen Douglas called him Tricky Dick. Richard Nixon referred to her as the Pink Lady.

When the campaign ended, the career of one of the most impressive women ever to appear in American politics was over. Victory, on the other hand, would catapult the equally exceptional Richard Nixon to the vice presidency and ultimately to the White House. Out of politics for good, Douglas quickly shed the Pink Lady label, but Nixon would forever remain Tricky Dick. A generation of liberals would never forgive him for what he allegedly did to Helen Douglas.

In 1973, as the Watergate nightmare unfolded, a popular bumper sticker appeared in California. DON'T BLAME ME, it read, I VOTED FOR HELEN GAHAGAN DOUGLAS.

There have been dozens of volumes about Richard Nixon's life and presidency and one biography of Helen Gahagan Douglas, but *Tricky Dick and the Pink Lady* is the first book on the 1950 Senate campaign. There is a reason for this. Until now, little primary-source material on the Nixon campaign has surfaced. The prepresidential papers that Nixon deeded to the federal government contained mysteriously little on the 1950 race. This was consistent with Nixon's longtime approach. Over the years, he wrote less about his encounter with Helen Douglas than about any other major episode in his life, including Watergate, so it was easy to imagine that he had purged some of the files he eventually turned over to the National Archives. Whenever he did discuss 1950, he generally limited himself to a few words disputing the common perception that he had unfairly Red-baited Helen Douglas into oblivion. The Democrats attacked her first, he asserted, and when the fall campaign began, *she* smeared him, and he was forced to respond by exposing her left-wing voting record. "I never questioned her patriotism," he explained. Biographers friendly to Nixon often accepted this argument.

Then, near the end of 1992, an official at the National Archives in Laguna Niguel, California, discovered thousands of documents locked in an old trunk. Among them were several boxes of material on the 1950 Senate race that had been deeded to the government by Nixon (perhaps by mistake) years before. Two weeks later I examined the papers before they were even processed. Included were many revealing letters and memos that had been written by Nixon and by campaign manager Murray Chotiner, providing at last an inside look at their campaign. This material appears in print for the first time in this book.

A year after the discovery at Laguna Niguel, I became the first researcher to use the archives at the Richard M. Nixon Presidential Library and Birthplace in Yorba Linda, several weeks before its official opening. I found there additional Nixon letters from 1950 and other newly available campaign material.

In contrast, the extensive Helen Gahagan Douglas Papers, at the University of Oklahoma's Carl Albert Congressional Research and Studies Center, have been available for years. I spent considerable time there, at the Harry S. Truman Library in Independence, Missouri, and at other archives, and interviewed several dozen veterans of the 1950 campaign, including Robert Finch, Samuel W. Yorty, Edmund G. "Pat" Brown, McIntyre Faries, Ralph de Toledano, Alan Cranston, Frank Mankiewicz, Patrick J. Hillings, Mary Ellen Leary, Florence "Susie" Clifton, Ken Chotiner, Dick Tuck, Philip Dunne, Allen Rivkin, Diane Baker, and Mary Helen Douglas, the daughter of Helen Douglas.

Now, at last, one can judge, based on ample evidence, the accuracy of the revisionist view that Nixon had "the cleaner hands" in the 1950 campaign, as Nixon biographer Jonathan Aitken recently put it.

Fate may have compelled me to write this book. One of my earliest childhood memories is walking back and forth on the sidewalk in front of my upstate New York home in the autumn of 1952 waving a sign that read I LIKE IKE. Richard Nixon was Eisenhower's running mate that year and my parents, rock-ribbed Republicans, admired him a lot. On a family visit to the White House a few years later we happened to pass within a few feet of Vice President Nixon in a hallway, and he waved happily to us. Then, in 1960, I took Nixon's side in a junior high school debate on the presidential race. I won the debate on points, and passed out Nixon-Lodge campaign buttons, but to no avail: The class voted 22–2 for John F. Kennedy. Still, I stuck with Nixon, and took his loss in the November election very hard.

So Richard Nixon and I go way back.

·   ·   ·

Tricky Dick and the Pink Lady in some ways serves as a sequel to my book *The Campaign of the Century: Upton Sinclair's Race for Governor of California and the Birth of Media Politics.* The anti-Sinclair crusade in 1934 introduced publicity and advertising techniques that shaped the modern political campaign. Sixteen years later, Richard Nixon and Murray Chotiner drew on 1934's anti-Communist theme, refined the publicity techniques (and introduced them to a new medium, television), and took campaign trickery to another level. One of Douglas's supporters told her just after her defeat, "I hope you haven't forgotten the Sinclair campaign, as all the mud they didn't throw then, they have done so now. . . ." Many of the notable characters introduced in *The Campaign of the Century* reappear in *Tricky Dick and the Pink Lady,* including William Randolph Hearst, Earl Warren, Cecil B. DeMille, Westbrook Pegler, Eleanor Roosevelt, Louis B. Mayer, Joseph L. Mankiewicz, and very briefly, Upton Sinclair. None of the small snatches of dialogue in this narrative is "re-created"; it appears exactly as transcribed in the correspondence, oral histories, and memoirs of the participants.

As one of its main themes, this book profiles Helen Douglas at a time when a woman running for office and serving in Congress faced even more obstacles than she does today. Douglas was one of only nine congresswomen, but she was more than that. She was, as a leading Democratic official put it, "the pioneer female activist in the Congress." The columnist Drew Pearson observed that a "lady Congressman is supposed to be demure, winsome, and follow the leadership of the males," but Douglas was "as smart as she is beautiful" and had "chucked all this folderol aside." More than one commentator remarked that Helen Douglas was the first woman who had the ability and the stature, not to mention the beauty, to be a viable presidential candidate—that is, if she won in November 1950.

"Some day there will be a woman President," Helen Douglas declared. "Women couldn't do worse than men have done." *Tricky Dick and the Pink Lady* explores the status of women in postwar politics, the way Douglas was viewed by both men and women, and the way gender, perhaps as much as Cold War politics, played a crucial role in her defeat in 1950.

After Helen Douglas lost, more than forty years passed before California elected a female senator—and then, as if to compensate, it selected two.

Accounts of the Nixon-Douglas campaign have tended to focus on "dirty tricks" and other foreshadowings of Watergate. *Tricky Dick and the Pink Lady* explores that terrain but also places the 1950 Senate race in the context of its era and reveals its significance, not just in the careers of Richard Nixon and Helen Douglas, but in the emergence of Cold War politics in the United States.

What has long been overlooked is the role the Nixon-Douglas race played in helping to set a divisive and rigid agenda for forty years of election campaigns. Until 1950, candidates rarely campaigned primarily on an anti-Communist platform, and when they did, they usually lost. When challenging Truman in 1948, Thomas E. Dewey pressed the anti-Soviet issue only sporadically and criticized fellow Republicans who called for repressive new measures to control subversives. In early 1950, conservative columnist David Lawrence warned Republicans that they could not win elections that year on "charges and innuendoes about Communism." But that November the success of Richard Nixon and several other candidates for the U.S. Senate, such as Everett McKinley Dirksen in Illinois, suggested that making Soviet aggression and the alleged Communist threat at home crucial campaign issues could pay off politically. Richard Nixon would call the 1950 elections "the most crucial" in history.

Although the results of the 1950 elections were ambiguous, Republican and Democratic leaders alike *interpreted* the outcome as a victory for McCarthyism and a call for a dramatic surge in military spending. For this reason and others, Red-baiting would haunt America for years, the so-called national security state would evolve and endure, and candidates would run and win on anti-Sovietism for decades, until the fall of the Soviet Union.

By studying the overall climate of 1950, however, this book tries to avoid simplistic denunciations of McCarthyism—and characterizations of the Douglas-Nixon contest as "Beauty and the Beast." It attempts to illustrate how dramatic events and legitimate fears helped shape public opinion, electoral politics, blacklisting in Hollywood, and loyalty investigations in almost every walk of life. As Nixon himself reflected many years after the campaign, "It was a hard, tough campaign at a hard, tough time." James Warburg, the New York banker, put it another way in a letter to Douglas after the election, claiming that she had lost simply because "we are living in a crazy time."

Since the end of World War II, the United States has experienced two years of absolute trauma, Tom Wicker asserted in his Nixon biography. One year was 1968, the other was 1950. "American politics, like all sectors of American life," Stephen Ambrose has observed, "was attempting to adjust to the realities of the atomic age and the cold war." Considering the events—Korea, atomic spies, Soviet belligerence, and all the rest—it is little wonder that strident anticommunism developed a following in America during 1950. It was not Nixon "who created the widespread sense of fear,"

Ambrose added, "although he surely managed to profit from it." It was this kind of year:

- Police in Columbus, Ohio, warned teen clubs to be suspicious of new members "whose background is not an open book." Officials in Mississippi tried to break up the state's Communist Party, which had exactly one member. A New York woman was granted a divorce solely on the grounds that her husband was a Communist.
- Howard Hughes, as head of the RKO studio, devised a simple test to weed out Communists: He asked one director after another to make a film called *I Married a Communist*. If a director turned it down, Hughes considered him Red.
- A short circuit in the New York City subway caused a stampede of one thousand passengers, who believed that World War III had started. In Brooklyn, when four sewer covers blew off, thousands panicked, certain an atomic bomb had exploded, and three were injured. A Gallup poll revealed that Americans overwhelmingly favored a law requiring everyone to wear a name tag, which would also indicate blood type, in case of nuclear attack.

Although the witch-hunt in Hollywood began in 1947, it quickly stalled, and only reached its turning point in 1950, when several prominent writers and actors volunteered to name names to save their careers. It was the beginning of what one member of the Hollywood Ten called "government by stool pigeon." The embrace of loyalty oaths within the movie industry reflected the overall "temper of the times," *The New York Times* observed, adding that just a year earlier "liberal protest would have been vociferous."

The 1950 campaign transpired during boom times in California. The 1950 census showed that while the population of the country had grown by almost 15 percent in the past ten years, California had surged by almost 55 percent. "World history records no other purely voluntary migration of such size," Governor Earl Warren commented. One report called it nothing less than a substantial redistribution of the population of the United States.

There were, of course, negative effects of such rapid growth. Shortages in housing, fuel, and water appeared, and a low, gray pall, soon to be known as smog, settled over Los Angeles, a symbol of trouble in paradise. Still, California remained its exuberant, trend-setting self, "stumbling pell-mell to greatness without knowing the way," Carey McWilliams (one of the state's leading writers) observed.

More than ever, politics in California was impossible to predict. Since the end of World War II, seven million notoriously independent Californians had been joined by three and a half million new residents with little political allegiance. Nowhere was McCarthyism more evident. All state employees had to sign a loyalty oath or resign. J. Edgar Hoover claimed that there were exactly 6,977 Communists working underground in California. The *Los Angeles Times* advised readers not to assault antiwar activists because "Reds are used to that. Get his name and address and phone the FBI."

So when Sheridan Downey—Upton Sinclair's running mate in 1934—announced his decision not to run for reelection to the U.S. Senate in 1950, leaving the field open for Richard M. Nixon and Helen Gahagan Douglas, anything could happen, and nearly did.

TRICKY DICK AND THE PINK LADY

Tricks, Deceptions, and Wondrous Visions

wo Hollywood screenwriters, former members of the Communist Party, flew east to face imprisonment for contempt of Congress. Seventy-three professors at the University of California fought dismissal for failing to sign a loyalty oath. The owner of KFI, a radio and television station in Los Angeles, ordered his two hundred employees to endorse a similar oath. Only one KFI worker, a registered Republican, refused on principle, denouncing not only her boss but coworkers who "chose to see no further than today's loaf of bread." The mayor of Los Angeles, meanwhile, called on all citizens to notify the police of any neighbors they considered politically tainted. "You will do no injustice by reporting all you know," the mayor explained. "The information conveyed to the police need not be more than a suspicion." In this atmosphere of vigilance and fear, Californians went to the polls on June 6, 1950, to nominate two candidates for the U.S. Senate, setting the stage for a sensational election contest that fall.

As polls opened on primary day, political "dopesters" went "stir-crazy" trying to predict the results, the *Hollywood Reporter* observed. With California's population surging it was impossible to predict how the new arrivals would vote. At midafternoon, Helen Gahagan Douglas, the Democratic front-runner in the Senate race, received a telegram from actress Greta Garbo that read, "Helen—Tonight or Never. God bless you." *Tonight or Never,* a Broadway hit, had catapulted Helen Gahagan to stardom in 1930 and introduced her to future husband Melvyn Douglas, who later appeared opposite Garbo in *Ninotchka*.

Garbo must have sensed her friend's need for a boost on primary day, for the campaign had been painful and exhausting. The outgoing Democratic senator, Sheridan Downey, had announced that Douglas did not have "the fundamental ability and qualifications" to replace him and accused her of giving "comfort to Soviet tyranny." Privately, an associate had advised Downey that Douglas was "a self-seeking, highly perfumed, smelly old girl," adding, "I don't believe in sending women to the House of Representatives or to the U.S. Senate either." A San Jose newspaper reported that if not exactly Red, she was "decidedly pink." Westbrook Pegler, the syndicated columnist, cataloged her female deficiencies: her inattention to serious duties and her willingness to be nothing more than a "fluttering satellite" of the far left wing of her party. On top of that, fraternity boys at the University of Southern California had sprayed seltzer at her during a campus rally.

Perhaps the most distasteful personal attack, however, came from the state's leading political writer. Kyle Palmer of the *Los Angeles Times* had criticized her Democratic rival, Manchester Boddy, for running a colorless campaign with "too much dignity" but advised that he "might still defeat the lady if he tried—in a political sense, of course—to slap her around a bit." And so as the race tightened, Boddy charged that a "subversive clique of red hots" was attempting to take over the Democratic Party, and he accused Douglas of harboring "communist sympathies."

But it was the newspaper he published, the Los Angeles *Daily News,* that first put into print a new nickname for Helen Douglas. "The Pink Lady," the *Daily News* called her.

Through it all, Douglas had remained confident, and with some cause. She was intelligent, articulate, and attractive, one of only nine female members of Congress, the best-dressed woman in public life (according to the Fashion Academy in New York), and the first prominent actor to run for high office. "I know I am going to win," she informed a national Democratic leader. Most of the party leaders in California, however, opposed her. They didn't like the idea of having a woman in the Senate "with whom they can't make deals," she charged. "In the House it is all right since it is like having a feather stuck in your hat, but it is not all right in the Senate." She had fought back, campaigning furiously, barnstorming by helicopter— the first time this had been done outside Texas. An editorial cartoon portrayed her in a football helmet, stiff-arming male politicians. Another, under the title IF A BODY MEETS A BODDY, pictured Douglas and Boddy blocking each other's path, with the caption "Coming through the rye, should the Body or the Boddy let the other by?"

Tall and stately, Douglas was the number-one glamour girl of the Democratic Party, a writer for a New York newspaper observed. On the campaign trail, however, she had little time for "feminine necessities" such as getting her hair and nails done, according to the reporter, and she had already put on ten pounds, munching on candy bars to keep up her energy and consuming cakes baked for afternoon teas. Another writer observed that a woman running for the Senate has problems that never bother a "bald-headed candidate." A man goes straight to bed at night after a final speech, but a woman "has to get a shampoo at midnight. She has to go to bed with her head in a towel to dry while she sleeps." Douglas also had to contend with the demands of two children at home. "But mother!" her eleven-year-old daughter, Mary Helen, had recently implored. "Why must you work so hard? Why can't you stay home and go swimming with me?"

When Douglas visited Santa Clara, a local columnist revealed that she had arrived for a campaign appearance right on time, "sufficiently remarkable in any woman." She looked young for her age, which was forty-nine, and the former opera diva and Hollywood star did it without the usual artifice of makeup, retouched hair, or "trick millinery." From this, the columnist concluded that she was interested "in persuading the minds of her audience, not in charming them off their feet." Still, the political attacks on the candidate grew harsher, and she was too busy defending herself from attacks by Democrats to go after her likely Republican opponent, Congressman Richard M. Nixon. Yet she told her San Diego organizer, "You know, what happens to me personally isn't very important. But that pipsqueak [Nixon] has his eye on the White House and if he ever gets there, God help us all."

Close to primary day, Douglas assured her mentor, Eleanor Roosevelt, that Boddy's Red-baiting was so excessive "it helped us." In San Francisco near the end, she led a march of women carrying grocery baskets up Market Street to protest the high cost of living. A local newspaper published a photo of a radiant Douglas surrounded by the huge crowd under the headline NEVER UNDERESTIMATE THE POWER OF A———. Over the radio, Douglas confidently proclaimed, "Money alone never has won and never will win an election."

Unlike the Democratic front-runner, Richard Nixon, standing first in line to cast his ballot in his home precinct on primary day, was already looking ahead, knowing he was a winner twice over. The savvy young congressman had not only sewn up the Republican nomination for the U.S. Senate, but he had also thrown the Democratic contest into last-minute turmoil with one brilliant stroke.

His campaign committee in Whittier, under the direction of attorney Murray Chotiner, had sent 68,500 leaflets to registered Democrats in en-

velopes emblazoned with the words AS ONE DEMOCRAT TO ANOTHER! It was
true that California's cross-filing laws allowed Nixon to run in the Democratic primary, but he had little hope of winning, and in any case he was not
a Democrat. The campaign material failed to disclose his party affiliation, referring to him simply as Congressman Nixon, "The Man Who Broke the
Hiss-Chambers Espionage Case." One photograph showed the thirty-
seven-year-old candidate in his living room on Honeysuckle Lane in Whittier entertaining his wife, Pat, and his two young daughters with a puppet.
Another pictured him standing bare chested in the South Pacific during
World War II, pith helmet in hand. This photo had been sent to Nixon recently by a former navy buddy, and the candidate had passed it along to
Murray Chotiner with the suggestion that it be used in a campaign flyer
under the heading STRIPPED FOR ACTION. Veterans of the war, "seeing such a
shot, would know that I did not have so-called 'soft duty,' " he explained.
Chotiner used the photograph but rejected Nixon's title for it.

The mailing to Democrats was intended not so much to win votes in the
primary but to attract converts for the general election, when Nixon would
need them. It might have passed without public notice if not for one over-
sight: Included on the mailing list was Will Rogers, Jr., son of the famous
humorist and a former Democratic congressman from southern California.
Rogers turned over the material to Manchester Boddy, and on primary eve
the Los Angeles *Daily News* ran a picture of the "viciously false circular. . . .
How far," the newspaper asked, "can a Republican candidate go in misrepresenting himself as a Democrat?"

The same day, a full-page advertisement sponsored by a Democratic
committee appeared in several papers under the heading WARNING TO ALL
DEMOCRATS. It showed a cartoon Nixon emerging from a barn, holding a
pitchfork full of hay (labeled CAMPAIGN TRICKERY) that he intended to feed
to a Democratic donkey. "What manner of candidate is this," the copy read,
"who will use the United States mail in an attempt to delude Democrats
into believing he is one of them?"

The most enduring aspect of the ad was its attempt to provide a pet name
for the Republican candidate. Political opponents, poking fun at his Pumpkin Papers detective work in the Alger Hiss case, had once christened him
Dick Tracy, but the name did not stick. Now the Democrats tried again.
"Look at 'Tricky Dick' Nixon's Republican Record," the ad implored. It
had a certain ring.

This kind of name-calling did not surprise or trouble Nixon. In his final
statewide radio address on primary eve, he continued to bait the Democrats,
calling on Californians to "forget blind partisan politics and vote as Ameri-

cans" who opposed the policies of President Truman. Nixon had de-nounced the administration's "socialistic program" and often tried to link Truman, indirectly, to American Communists. A few days before the pri-mary, he told a *Chicago Tribune* reporter, "The commies really don't like it when I smash into Truman for his attempted coverup of the Hiss case," adding "the more the commies yell, the surer I am that I'm waging an hon-est American campaign."

As Californians voted on June 6, President Truman sent a letter to a Veter-ans of Foreign Wars official complaining that all this "fuss" over which po-litical groups a person belonged to gave him a pain in the neck. "I'd be willing to bet my right eye," he added, "that you yourself and I have joined some organization that we wish we hadn't. It hasn't hurt me any and I don't think it has hurt you any." But how would American voters respond to Red-baiting—and more delicate forms of anticommunism—between June and election day? After a feverish few months and then a lull, signs pointed to renewed political clamor.

Tension had been building for years. With the Soviets tightening their grip in Eastern Europe and a newly Republican Congress promising to root out Communists in America, President Truman in 1947 had created a con-troversial loyalty program. It mandated background checks on two million federal employees, who could be dismissed if an inquiry found reasonable grounds for believing them "disloyal" to the government of the United States. An invigorated House Un-American Activities Committee investi-gated Communists in the federal government and in Hollywood. The fol-lowing year the journalist Whittaker Chambers testified before HUAC that an old friend, Alger Hiss, a top State Department official, had once belonged to the Communist Party.

Then, in 1949, a series of unexpected events set off shock waves. Whit-taker Chambers, under the patient guidance of Richard Nixon, accused Hiss of working for the Soviets. The Communist forces of Mao Tse-tung seized virtually all of China and drove Chiang Kai-shek's Nationalists off the mainland to Taiwan. (Republicans asked rhetorically, "Who lost China?") In September, the Soviets exploded their first atomic bomb. No longer did America have a monopoly on the ultimate weapon. The Soviets still had no means by which to deliver a weapon over U.S. territory, but the writing was on the wall, and Americans could read it. "This is now a differ-ent world," a prominent U.S. senator warned.

On January 21, 1950, a jury in New York found Alger Hiss guilty of per-jury. Soon Senator Karl Mundt called for every town in the country to form local committees to carry out "vigilante action to combat Communism." A Justice Department employee named Judith Coplon was convicted of espionage. Mao Tse-tung and Joseph Stalin met in Moscow to negotiate a mutual defense treaty. The Chinese, meanwhile, contemplated invading Taiwan and aiding a North Korean plan to liberate South Korea. On January 31, President Truman dramatically announced that the Soviet menace had compelled the United States to build an even more devastating nuclear weapon, the hydrogen bomb.

Then, on February 2, 1950, British physicist Klaus Fuchs was arrested for passing atomic secrets from the Manhattan Project to the Russians. An Atomic Energy Commission official called it "one of the blackest" moments in U.S. history. Exactly one week later Senator Joseph R. McCarthy of Wisconsin delivered a groundbreaking speech before a women's group in Wheeling, West Virginia.

Until that day, McCarthy's national reputation as a Red hunter was nil; he was just another midwestern senator named Joe. But he had decided to do something about that, and to do it, he would borrow the words of Richard Nixon, a well-known anti-Communist. Nixon, in a recent speech before Congress on the Hiss case, had charged President Truman with "failure to act against the Communist conspiracy" and treating "Communist infiltration like any ordinary political scandal," allowing the enemy to "guide and shape our policy." McCarthy's remarks at Wheeling would draw heavily, sometimes word for word, from Nixon's address. In addition, he accused Secretary of State Dean Acheson of traitorous actions aimed at assisting Soviet subversion. "I have here in my hand," McCarthy said, waving a sheet of paper, "a list of names [of reputed Communists] that were known to the Secretary of State and who nevertheless are still working and shaping the policy of the State Department."

When reporters demanded proof, McCarthy faltered; the evidence was always in another briefcase. Truman declared that the senator might be "the greatest asset the Kremlin has." Asked whether he felt he had libeled McCarthy, Truman replied, "Do you think that's possible?" Privately, he referred to McCarthy as "a ballyhoo artist" who would have little impact. Communist Party membership in the United States had already fallen to roughly forty thousand, half its high-water mark, but McCarthy kept up the attack. Nothing, he said, could stop him from driving the "egg-sucking phony liberals" and the "Communists and queers" out of the State Department.

McCarthy took his case to Congress, where most of his Republican colleagues embraced him. (One senator said, "Joe, you're a real SOB. But sometimes it's useful to have SOBs around to do the dirty work.") The Democrats scheduled hearings, figuring they would tear him to shreds and stop the inquisition in its tracks. Knowing he needed stronger proof, McCarthy called on his friends for help. Congressman Richard Nixon passed along HUAC files while warning that McCarthy should not overstate his case or claim that any of the research was new; instead, he should let the facts speak for themselves. "You will be in an untenable position if you claim that there were umpteen, or however many, card-carrying Communists in the State Department, because you cannot prove that," Nixon advised. "On the other hand, if you were to say that there were so many people whose records disclosed Communist-front affiliations and associations—this you can prove."

J. Edgar Hoover supplied FBI data (and also opened a secret file on McCarthy). William Randolph Hearst lent the senator a couple of investigative reporters. Former Communists who had named names before Congress came forward with new suspects, but the information they provided was old or unreliable, and the hearings went badly for McCarthy. Hard-drinking and undisciplined, he seemed the wrong man to be in the right place at the right time. *Life* magazine ridiculed "the McCarthy lynching bee." Henry L. Stimson, the former secretary of war, observed that Joe McCarthy was not trying to get rid of Communists in government; he was "hoping against hope that he will find some." President Truman predicted that the American people were not going to be fooled by "the Republican approach to the election."

But McCarthy, sensing that many Americans were behind him, fought on, at least partly because he was receiving hundreds of dollars a week from fans around the country to finance his investigation, cash he simply stuffed into his pocket. Admirers claimed that whatever his faults, Joe McCarthy had the courage of his convictions. The writer Richard Rovere, however, observed that "if a man has no convictions, he can scarcely draw courage from them." A full-page *Washington Post* editorial warned that "the Capital has been seized and convulsed by terror."

Back in McCarthy's home state, a spectacular incident drew national attention. On May 1, Russian soldiers took over the small town of Mosinee, Wisconsin, pulled the mayor (dressed in his pajamas) out of his house, confiscated all firearms, imprisoned clergy in a stockade, seized all businesses, and forced restaurants to serve customers only soup and bread. The Russian invaders were soon exposed as local American Legionnaires out to teach their neighbors a lesson. Unfortunately, the mayor, a bit rattled, suffered a heart attack the following day.

McCarthy, meanwhile, roared ahead. He had become, in Rovere's words, "an engine of denunciation." The senator lectured around the country, and when he spoke in California, Richard Nixon asked God to "give him the courage to carry on." Songwriters composed tributes to him. Then, on June 1, just five days before the California primary, opposition came from a surprising source: Margaret Chase Smith of Maine, a moderate, low-profile Republican and the only woman in the U.S. Senate.

The flinty Smith had bucked the party line before, supporting civil rights measures and federal aid to education. Initially intrigued by McCarthy's charges, she now believed he was perpetrating a hoax. So she drafted a "Declaration of Conscience," persuaded six other Republicans to endorse it, and read it on the floor of the Senate while McCarthy sat three seats away. She warned that the current climate of "fear and frustration" could result in "national suicide." Without naming McCarthy, she added, "I am not proud of the way we smear outsiders from the floor of the Senate. . . . I don't want to see the Republican party ride to political victory on the four horsemen of calumny—fear, ignorance, bigotry and smear."

The speech was hailed by the Democrats and many in the media. But conservatives rose to McCarthy's defense, and the senator angrily referred to Smith and the cosponsors of the declaration as "Snow White and the Six Dwarfs." The dissident Republicans indeed lacked a powerful leader and were isolated in their own party. McCarthy had grown so intimidating that most of the cosponsors of the declaration quickly distanced themselves from it. Only Smith and Wayne Morse of Oregon held firm.

So Joe McCarthy had withstood a woman's scorn and now, having survived, might even flourish. The signal to Richard Nixon as he prepared to take on Helen Gahagan Douglas was unmistakable.

Adding to the drama, the uncertainty, and the national significance of the Nixon-Douglas contest was California's emergence as the second most important state in the Union. Anyway, this was how John Gunther, in his recent best-seller, *Inside U.S.A.,* had figured it. California, he explained, was "the most spectacular and most diversified American state . . . so ripe, golden, yeasty, churning in flux . . . a world of its own . . . at once demented and very sane, adolescent and mature. . . . No one can easily put salt on its tail."

The population, exactly one hundred years after the territory entered the Union, had hit ten million, leapfrogging California over Illinois and Pennsylvania to reach the number-two slot, behind New York, and promising a gain of six to eight congressional seats. Los Angeles was now the third largest city in the country, and the most sprawling. Many counties, and cities such as San Diego, doubled in population between 1940 and 1950. Experts had earlier predicted that natural limitations—starting with a lack of water—would soon put a brake on immigration. Now they forecast that the state's population might reach the unfathomable figure of twenty million by the end of the century. Part boast, part warning, it was in any case "something for the nation to ponder," Carey McWilliams wryly noted.

The world's largest subdivision had opened in April 1950, with more than seventeen thousand homes waiting to be built on thirty-four thousand acres at Lakewood ("Tomorrow's City Today"), outside Los Angeles. Each house sold for ten thousand dollars or less, with easy terms, especially for veterans on the GI Bill. It was the American dream in stucco. The first day the houses went on sale thirty thousand Californians, most of them young and blue-collar, showed up to take a look.

More than ever, California percolated with youthful spirit and a sense of possibility. The building boom promised both high profits and profound corruption. Social services strained to the breaking point as thousands of new arrivals streamed into schools, hospitals, and inevitably, prisons. It might lack cultural and social integration, but California could not be stopped. It was, as Carey McWilliams described it, "bursting at its every seam. It is tipping the scales of the nation's interest and wealth and population to the West, toward the Pacific."

California was a state divided in two—culturally, economically, and politically—at the Tehachapi Mountains, with the cool, tranquil sophistication of San Francisco competing with the feverish, sun-drenched energy of Los Angeles. San Francisco was the Baghdad of the West, Paris on the Pacific. Los Angeles was "Iowa with palms," full of religious cultists and crackpot economists, the "incoherent, shapeless, slobbering civic idiot in the family of American communities," according to Westbrook Pegler. San Francisco was built high while L.A. spread wide; one suffered fog, the other smog. San Franciscans had roots and tolerated diversity; Angelenos were generally rootless and retained middle-American values.

But the contrasts hardly stopped there. California was highly urbanized yet almost absurdly rich in agriculture. It generated more new jobs *and* had the highest unemployment rate in the nation. It depended on water but had precious little of it. Seemingly a land of opportunity, it was actually dominated by large landowners, oilmen, a handful of newspaper publishers, and moguls who controlled its water and power. Labor and management had been at war for decades, with violence on the waterfront and vigilantism in the fields. The beauty and bounty of California's farms obscured much squalor. More than a decade after *The Grapes of Wrath,* the plight of tens of thousands of migrant farmworkers, now mainly Chicano, remained frightful. John Gunther felt California contained the most sophisticated and the most bigoted sections of society. It had "a zest for direct action and a tradition of going to extremes. . . . If either Fascism or Communism should ever smite this country," he wrote, "it is more likely to rise first in California than in any other state."

Politically, the state in 1950 was also split, with a U.S. senator from each party and a moderate governor who enjoyed bipartisan support. Democrats dominated party registration but more often than not lost elections. Californians were ahead of the rest of the country in their disdain for political parties. By 1950, at least one third of them either enrolled as independents or voted that way. The decline of political machines was a legacy of Hiram Johnson and the Progressives, who had enacted in California such procedures as the direct primary, the initiative, the referendum, and the recall. California also allowed cross-filing. A candidate could compete in each party's primary; an alarming number won both races. With the decline of the parties, California politics was dominated by lobbyists, public relations wizards, and newspaper editors. It was no mystery why that new breed of kingmaker—the political consultant—first emerged in California in the 1930s to fill the vacuum left by the party boss. Garry Wills would later observe that "a special campaign style was bound to emerge in California. . . . Where party loyalty is comparatively insignificant, the 'image' of the candidate must be stressed."

Behind the Republicans stood many powerful industries—oil, railroads, and Pacific Gas and Electric; boom-driven financial institutions and real estate interests; the Associated Farmers and the Merchants and Manufacturers Association (both fiercely antiunion); the Los Angeles Chamber of Commerce; the California Fruit Growers Exchange (marketers of the Sunkist brand); and a very active American Legion in a state with more veterans than any other. Organized labor, meanwhile, rallied to the Democrats' side. In no other state had unions been so fiercely political for so long.

Carey McWilliams in 1949 identified California as essentially "a freak, a trend-setter, the great exception." Yet in many ways, it was postwar America in microcosm, with an expanding middle class, a severe housing and school shortage, racial problems, and a growing reliance on the automobile. California had all this and Hollywood, too. McWilliams detected a "golden haze over the land—the dust of gold is in the air—and the atmosphere is magical and mirrors many tricks, deceptions, and wondrous visions." And nowhere in 1950 was this more evident than in the atmosphere of electoral politics.

As they visited friends on primary day, Richard Nixon and his pretty wife, Pat, radiated happiness and confidence. Dick Nixon appeared certain to win more than 90 percent of the Republican vote, and Manchester Boddy had already bloodied the likely Democratic winner. Nixon knew that his campaign against Helen Douglas would be well managed and well financed, and the most grueling period was already past: his travels up and down this cruelly distended state in a yellow wood-paneled station wagon, journeying fifteen thousand miles to deliver more than six hundred speeches in fifty counties. And that was for a one-sided primary contest. The rest of the campaign would be a war; it would be for all the marbles; it would pit him against a strong, worthy, but highly vulnerable candidate (a woman no less)—meaning, in political terms, it would be challenging, fascinating, possibly even fun. "There is only one way we can win," Nixon had vowed. "We must put on a fighting, rocking, socking campaign."

California would also host the most closely watched governor's race in the country: two-term incumbent Earl Warren against young James Roosevelt, FDR's son. The survivor would become a favorite in the 1952 presidential race (Harry Truman had privately decided not to run for reelection). The winner of the state's Senate contest would no doubt be considered for the second spot on a ticket. A boomlet for Douglas for vice president at the 1948 Democratic National Convention "heralded what may happen sooner than we think, even possibly in 1952," *The Washington Post* had observed, and Nixon was clearly a hot prospect on the other side.

"Mrs. Douglas takes wholeheartedly after the Administration's program," Richard Nixon remarked on primary day, "one hundred percent plus, including such things as socialized medicine." That evening, Nixon and his family checked the early returns at City Hall in downtown Los Angeles, then celebrated at election headquarters on the second floor of the Garland Building over on West Ninth Street. His vote of more than 740,000 exceeded even his high expectations as his two minor GOP challengers mustered less than 35,000 between them. More significant, however, was Nixon's tally in the Democratic column: more than 300,000 votes. This suggested that his attacks on Truman and other Democrats as unwitting allies of the Soviets had paid off and should be pressed even more intensely in coming months.

"I welcome Mrs. Douglas as an opponent," Nixon announced. "It won't be a campaign of personalities but of issues." Douglas would have to reveal where she stood on those issues, "or," he added ominously, "I'll do it for her."

Most of Nixon's advisers felt that Douglas would be a formidable foe; she was as brave and as energetic as their man, with twice the charisma. For the record, Nixon concurred, calling her "a colorful, aggressive, vote-getting candidate" who had long been underrated by the "wise boys" of politics. But privately, he and campaign strategist Murray Chotiner felt otherwise. If

Senator Downey had run for reelection, the outcome, they believed, would have hinged on farm issues, not on the Communist threat. But that all changed with Downey out. Nixon and Chotiner wanted Helen Douglas to win the nomination because her liberal politics played into the freedom-versus-socialism theme they had already decided would dominate the campaign. "There's no use trying to talk about anything else," Nixon told his northern California chairman, "because it's all the people want to hear about." This was sure to become a self-fulfilling prophecy.

During their travels across the state that spring, Nixon and Douglas had rarely crossed paths. Douglas, aware of her rival's talent as a debater, avoided joint meetings. One day, however, they appeared separately in a small town in the north. Nixon's aide Bill Arnold went out to hear what she was saying, came back, and reported to his boss. This was during a phase when Douglas, angered by Nixon's gibes, sometimes lost her composure and referred to him as a "peewee" who, like Joe McCarthy, was trying to get people so scared of communism they would be afraid to turn off the lights at night.

When he heard what she had said, Nixon muttered, "Why, I'll castrate her!" That would be literally impossible, Arnold pointed out. "I don't care," Nixon responded, "I'll do it anyway!"

As a woman, Helen Douglas was particularly vulnerable to charges that she lacked the toughness to oppose the Communists. But Chotiner reminded his candidate, "You can't get into a name-calling contest with a woman. The cost in votes would be prohibitive." Still, Nixon would later admit that Douglas's emergence on the Democratic side "brightened my prospects considerably."

On primary night, Helen Douglas, dressed in a simple black dress—but still movie-star radiant—joined her mostly female staffers at her Los Angeles headquarters. She had won a solid victory, defeating Boddy by a two-to-one margin and rolling up more than 150,000 votes in the GOP primary. Her supporters, true believers, responded with whoops and hugs, as if she had already won the election. She asked much, sometimes too much, of her aides, but they remained devoted to her. Some of them felt that the voters (particularly women) admired what Douglas stood for, and she was a fabulously vibrant campaigner, so there was no way she could lose. Red-baiting had ultimately failed Boddy, so Nixon would not dare revive it.

The candidate's personal satisfaction on primary night was marred by an uncomfortable moment at headquarters involving a male volunteer, a Greyhound bus driver who demanded a private conference with her. She soon discovered that he was more interested in sexual favors than political favors. Douglas knew that the passions of a campaign often become sexually charged but still faulted herself for not recognizing the bus driver's agenda earlier.

Before returning to the home she shared with her children and husband in the hills high above Los Angeles, she stopped at several local campaign headquarters. Paul Ziffren, the well-known attorney and one of her chief fund-raisers, finally drove her home, and Douglas, all business, asked him to make sure to thank Eleanor Roosevelt and others for their help. Then she prepared to catch a few hours' sleep—alone. Her husband was on the road, appearing in a play called *Two Blind Mice,* which had opened in New York, Philadelphia, Washington, D.C., and now Chicago. A comedy about a forgotten government agency, the Office of Seeds and Standards, the play promised to keep him out of California for the entire campaign.

Unlike many of her supporters, Douglas knew she was far from a shoo-in. Simple arithmetic told her that Nixon's combined vote in the GOP and the Democratic primaries exceeded one million, whereas hers did not quite reach nine hundred thousand. This in itself was not fatal, for the Democratic turnout would likely soar in November. But there was something more troubling. For nearly four years, she had observed her colleague Richard Nixon at close range in Congress, and she knew him to be smart, dynamic, daring, a formidable speaker—and out to win at almost any cost. A reporter for a Democratic paper called him "Whittier's tall, dark and handsome gift to the Republican party." Now she had received a letter from a member of Students for Douglas at the University of California at Berkeley. Nixon had spoken at Sather Gate, and the student was surprised to hear him give a "magnificent" speech. "He is one of the cleverest speakers I have ever heard," he warned:

> The questions on the Mundt-Nixon bill, his views on the loyalty oath, and the problem of international communism were just what he was waiting for. Indeed, he was so skillful—and I might add, cagey—that those who came indifferent were sold, and even many of those who came to heckle went away with doubts. . . . If he is only a fraction as effective [elsewhere] as he was here you have a formidable opponent on your hands.

The student added that Nixon based his entire campaign on foreign policy and "would like nothing better than to draw you into a dispute with him over communism. On that question, I venture to say, he is rhetorically impregnable, but the rest of him is all Achilles' heel. Hit him on the home front, and hit him hard."

The letter was remarkably astute. Douglas, in reply, told the student that his report corroborated what she had heard from others. "I think you are quite right," she observed, "and will act accordingly." As Helen Douglas retired on primary night, she knew that if she let her gifted opponent call the shots in this campaign she had no chance of becoming just the fourth woman ever elected to the U.S. Senate.

The Gal from Cal

At her hillside home on Senalda Road just north of the Hollywood Bowl, Helen Douglas received congratulatory telegrams from many admirers, among them screenwriters Philip Dunne and Allen Rivkin, two of her Hollywood fund-raisers. "We are proud of you and glory in the opportunity you have to be the only Democratic woman in the Senate. . . .You will be one of the best 'men' there, however," observed India Edwards, a national party leader. Another prominent Democrat told her he hoped "all the disem-Boddyed votes will be yours in November." But Manchester Boddy, while sending his regards, failed to offer his endorsement.

Reporters speculated that President Truman, protecting his right flank, would abstain from campaigning for Helen Douglas and other liberal Democrats. The day after the primary, Douglas sent a telegram to the White House. "You can be assured we have only just begun to fight for your program," she told the president but at this point did not request his help. In reply, Truman wished her "every success" in the fall and told her she could count on the party to "do everything possible" in her behalf, although he did not indicate what contribution, if any, *he* would make.

Still, Helen Douglas told a friend in Chicago that she had no doubts about winning the election. To do it, however, she would have to keep up a wearying transcontinental pace, juggling campaign, congressional, and family duties, flying between California and Washington with occasional side trips to Chicago and other cities to meet briefly with her husband. Often her family would be in four places at once: daughter in L.A., son in Washington, husband on the road, wife in the air. This was nothing new; in fact, it had been the norm for Helen Douglas since she entered politics. Even before running for office she had stepped lively. (She referred to her family as the *Go*-hagans.) It was this spirit and reckless enthusiasm, this quest for new challenges and adventures, that even her detractors found most appealing about her.

Raised in Park Slope, Brooklyn, in a prosperous, Republican, and socially prominent Scotch-Irish family, Helen Gahagan from an early age displayed a rebellious streak and a love for the spotlight. Her father, Walter Gahagan, was a civil engineer whose company built bridges and tunnels and later dredged the land for New York's airports. He was argumentative yet warm and generous and taught his children the eternal verities, such as "your word is your bond," "don't make excuses," and (this struck Helen most powerfully) "don't talk about it, do it." He urged his children to analyze every problem carefully, decide on a course of action, and not worry about the consequences. Many years later Douglas would admit that Adlai Stevenson was correct in saying that emotion drove her, but "so did the rooted values I learned from my parents."

With two older brothers and a younger sister and brother, Helen learned to fight to be heard and later compared her formative years to *Life with Father.* She grew accustomed to "strong, opinionated men" and "to arguing with them without feeling threatened." Helen insisted on doing anything her brothers did, including boxing, but soon learned that she most enjoyed the attention that came from acting in school plays and performing with the debating team.

At the age of fourteen, she cut classes at the all-girls Berkeley Institute to lend her talents to Liberty Bond drives. This adventure ended when her mother, Lillian, caught her delivering one of her dramatic pitches on the steps of the New York Public Library with a group of Broadway stars behind her. Obsessed with the theater, Helen never cared for academic studies and did poorly in school. A "free spirit" and "a goddess," according to a college friend, she dropped out of Barnard College to audition for acting jobs against the wishes of her father, who believed an uneducated woman was destined to be nothing more than a breeding machine.

"I know anything I really want, anything, I can get," Helen told a friend. "I just have to want it enough." The theater was one of the few professions where women and men received nearly equal treatment, and a talented actress could become financially independent. Walter Gahagan had ordered his wife, a former schoolteacher and store manager who dreamed of singing opera, not to seek work outside the home, but she instructed Helen that marriage and a career were not incompatible.

Through luck and intense study, Helen Gahagan became an overnight sensation on Broadway at the age of twenty-two and, with Helen Hayes and Katharine Cornell, one of the leading lights of the New York stage in the 1920s. She was tall, at five foot seven, and graceful. She had a rich, cultured voice and, according to a leading critic, was one of the best at "reproducing the patrician style." Gilbert Seldes predicted a "brilliant future." George Abbott called her a "strange classic beauty"—oval faced, big boned, statuesque. In Heywood Broun's estimate, she was ten of the most beautiful women in the world rolled into one. For Helen, the transition from the Gahagan household to the theater—from being the center of an admiring family to the star of the stage—"must have seemed both easy and natural . . . the applauding audiences must have seemed rather like a constantly expanding family circle," Carey McWilliams later commented.

But typically, she soon grew restless with Broadway. Perhaps hoping to fulfill her mother's ambition, she left the theater and took voice lessons with the aim of becoming an international opera star, and nearly succeeded. She performed *Tosca* and *Aïda* across Europe but could not quite overcome her late start; failing to become an overnight success again, she returned to the theater, and critics rejoiced. Describing the Helen Gahagan of this period, a longtime friend called her "a force of nature, one of those rare human beings in whom life focuses itself, so that there is something irresistible about them, as about a great wind or a charge of electricity. . . . Her effect on other people is something like that of a very potent cocktail." She was a "creature of passionate preferences, ardent and loyal, warm as sunlight is."

Although she dated such actors as Tyrone Power, Sr., she remained unwed past her thirtieth birthday. She appeared "lush" and "sultry," one friend commented but was actually something of a "puritan" and told friends she never expected to marry or have children. Then, appearing in the David Belasco production *Tonight or Never* in 1930, she fell in love with her costar, the handsome, intelligent, blond-haired Melvyn Douglas. They played a love scene so convincingly playgoers would stop them on the street and tell them the only decent thing they could do was get married.

They were an odd match. Douglas was Jewish, distant from his family, and divorced. He was refined, an intellectual, while Gahagan as a young woman was (by her own admission) "an essentially hysterical person." A onetime follower of socialist leader Eugene V. Debs and an admirer of Clarence Darrow and H. L. Mencken, Douglas had an interest in politics and the outside world that the extraordinarily self-centered Gahagan thoroughly lacked.

(She would not ride second class in trains "because the people smell" and refused to take buses or subways.) But they shared an interest in music; his father was a concert pianist. "I've seen many romances in the theater," David Belasco calculated, "but none so fine, so old-fashioned and honest."

Soon the two were wed. Much against the custom of her time, Gahagan kept her maiden name, even offstage. Defiantly, she told a reporter that she would not be cooking and sewing for her husband. "Anybody can roast chicken. . . . But I won't be that kind of wife . . . I'm going to be the most devoted, loving wife in the world," she vowed. "But never a housewife!"

Shortly after the wedding, Douglas received his first movie contract, and the couple moved to Los Angeles. Gahagan started to drift professionally. She was far from Broadway and had little interest in movies. She acted in road shows on the West Coast and in a play that had a short run in New York and in 1933 gave birth to the couple's first child, a son they named Peter.

Two years later she finally gave Hollywood a chance, choosing an odd vehicle: a big-budget RKO science-fiction film based on H. Rider Haggard's *She,* costarring Randolph Scott. Gahagan would play the regal goddess of the kingdom of Kor who preserves her life by standing in an eternal flame. Finding the script "ghastly," she rewrote several of her lines. Then, when shooting began, she was dismayed to discover that the director considered her "too mental" and planned to make her a sex object, outfitting her in a chiffon robe and no undergarments. She rebelled, however, when he asked her to pose in a bra and panties. Her husband commented that she had "got into the high-powered sex-appeal class quickly." He wrote, "I hope, Miss Gahagan, it doesn't give you any bacchanalian ideas, at least not until I arrive."

The film, later a cult classic, received mixed reviews when it opened, praised for its special effects and lampooned for its script. One reviewer, at least, observed that Gahagan invested her character with the "wisdom of the centuries." Turning her back on Hollywood, Gahagan returned to singing, giving recitals in the United States and concerts across Europe, where she witnessed firsthand the terrifying ripples of the rise of Hitler.

About this time, Gahagan and Douglas, shunning Beverly Hills, built their ranch house on Senalda Road. Rimmed by eucalyptus trees on three hilly acres, it had wood paneling, large windows, fine light, and a gorgeous view of Los Angeles from a long balcony—and of course a small swimming pool. In some ways, Gahagan lived the life of a Hollywood star, with cooks and servants, two Cadillacs, and furs. (Westbrook Pegler would poke fun at the house's "sensual" bedroom lined with "peach colored mirrors" from floor to ceiling.) But the couple found the atmosphere in Hollywood "cheesy," as

Mel put it, and took little part in the social scene, preferring to stay home and read.

Away from Broadway, disengaged from opera and disenchanted with film, Gahagan might have retired from the public stage to live the life of a doting mother and wife of a movie star, but she would not settle for that. She was "bored stiff with Hollywood," according to a friend, and she did not like being eclipsed by her husband, whose movie career was thriving (he would soon star in *Ninotchka*). Once again, in 1937, she jumped into a challenging new field, seeking expression and attention—this time in politics.

At first, Gahagan merely watched as her activist husband cofounded a Hollywood anti-Nazi league and a pair of anti-Franco organizations. He became a leader in the state Democratic Party, helping to elect Sheridan Downey as senator in 1938. He campaigned for Franklin Roosevelt and became the first actor to serve as a delegate to the Democratic National Convention. Slowly, under her husband's tutelage, Gahagan became socially conscious, particularly in regard to the legion of rural poor in Depression-era California. In 1938, several weeks after the birth of her daughter, Mary Helen, she visited migrant camps, hosted fund-raisers for farmworkers, and organized a Christmas party for five thousand needy children. She relentlessly quizzed expert friends, such as Carey McWilliams, economist Paul Taylor, and his wife, photographer Dorothea Lange.

Not to be outdone by her husband, she became an activist in the Democratic Party. Her love and talent for acting could be expressed in public speaking, which also provided the applause she craved. Listeners were enchanted by a voice that allowed her consciously or unconsciously to endow her words "with an intense vigor and musical warmth that make them persuasive," according to one observer. Her daughter would later refer to this as her "great skill at illustrating the text." Politician was just another difficult role to master. Her husband encouraged her on this path—he probably had little choice—but not without fearing the family upheaval it might bring.

Quickly, she forged a friendship with role model Eleanor Roosevelt, and the Douglases were invited to the White House as overnight guests. Following custom, Gahagan and Douglas were assigned adjoining rooms. Lonely in the big Lincoln bed, Gahagan asked her husband to join her for the night; in the morning, he went back to his room and roughed up the bed to make it appear he had slept alone. Soon afterward the First Lady stayed with the couple in Los Angeles, and Gahagan took her on a tour of migrant camps.

With friends in high places—on top of wealth, good looks, and a sharp tongue—Helen Gahagan soon became the top Democratic woman in California, supplanting veteran activists who would never forgive her for it. This was another overnight success. She was at the forefront of a new generation of postsuffrage women who entered the political arena without apology. A New Deal official who met her at this time came away with "a sense of wonder at Helen's display of energy—at the physical, emotional and mental drive of this beautiful and glamorous person." She became a voracious reader. An old friend, describing her unusual method of acquiring knowledge, observed, "She doesn't bother much with logical processes, she just wraps herself around an idea more or less in the way an amoeba wraps itself around a bit of food, a good nourishing way of absorbing information. . . ." (Years later Gahagan explained this process to her daughter: "When you dig into a problem you will learn what you need to know, you will learn how to solve it, you'll stumble upon authenticity and the people with the answers.")

When her husband joined the army in 1942 and was sent to India, Gahagan immersed herself ever deeper in politics. Characteristically, she soon grew weary of organizing and searched for a new path. In 1944, encouraged by Franklin and Eleanor Roosevelt, she announced for Congress as a kind of carpetbagger, after renting an apartment in the Fourteenth Congressional District in Los Angeles, an inner-city enclave. FDR told Vice President Henry Wallace that he wanted Gahagan to offset the Republican congress-woman from Connecticut, Clare Boothe Luce, who also had a famous husband (Time, Inc., founder Henry Luce). Wallace replied that Gahagan was smarter than Luce, and her heart was in the right place, too. Soon reporters were calling them the glamour gals of their respective parties and portraying them as arch rivals. Gahagan called this talk "nonsense and an insult to the American people."

At first, the novice politician refused to campaign under her married name, but finally, convinced that her husband was the star of the family, she agreed to be known henceforth as Helen Gahagan Douglas.

Helen Douglas faced a hard fight in her first political race. At her first important press conference, at the Democratic National Convention, gossip columnist Earl Wilson asked her how much she weighed. Many blacks resented the outsider, believing that their assemblyman, Augustus Hawkins, an able Democrat, would have run and won had Douglas stayed out.

Ed Lybeck, with help from his wife, Ruth, and organizer Florence "Susie" Clifton, managed the campaign, and he knew the district well. Lybeck was a droll, unassuming liberal, an ex–New Yorker who had worked on Al Smith's campaigns, a writer of widely published detective stories. He brought Douglas down from her home in Outpost Estates to take walking tours of the gritty district and attend dozens of "house meetings" (a practice she continued after the campaign). Help from old Hollywood friends like Walter Huston, Ronald Reagan, and Eddie Cantor helped overcome Republican Red-baiting. At one campaign function she introduced a startled friend to Rita Hayworth.

Douglas won in November, and Franklin Roosevelt told her, "You are going to be a real Congressman, not just a beautiful cloak model to outdo the Luce woman." Eleanor Roosevelt let her room at the White House until she found a house in Chevy Chase. When Douglas took office as only the third woman from California to serve in Congress, her son was eleven, her daughter was six, and her husband was still away at war. The kids were looked after by twenty-five-year-old Evelyn "Evie" Chavoor, a daughter of Syrian immigrants. She had worked for the Douglases in Los Angeles as a nanny and secretary and now served as Helen Gahagan Douglas's political aide-de-camp and household organizer in Washington. In letters from the Pacific, Mel urged his wife not to overdo her usual hard work. She had always been an "alive and fascinating" and "absorbing sort" of person, but now she had developed "real stature," he wrote, and it "is a very thrilling thing to see and to feel." But he missed "the beautiful thing we have."

Ironically, Helen Douglas, a blue-blooded celebrity married to a Hollywood star, would represent an astonishingly diverse district that included slums, the city's skid row, and all of South Central L.A. Her constituency was at least one-quarter nonwhite. She described the district this way:

> In the north-west corner of the district, we have Hollywood Junction; that is as close as I get to Hollywood. From there, we go down through a large home-owning area, through the heaviest apartment-house belt in the city, through the so-called Wilshire District, through the Civic Center and the downtown business district, through a heavy concentration of Spanish-speaking citizens, through China City and Little Tokyo, and on into the 62nd Assembly district which contains the largest Negro community west of Chicago. That's the 14th California district; more cosmopolitan than Hollywood—and very hard to fool. I love it.

Campaigning in the district, Douglas finally rode streetcars—to show she was just folks—but had to ask which end to get on. She seemed oblivious to danger, often picking up hitchhikers in rough parts of town while wearing a fur. Occasionally, she burst out with patronizing statements. Introduced at an African-American church, she greeted the applause with "I just love the Negro people!" She once wrote an article for *Negro Digest* entitled "If I Were a Negro." (If she were, she would ally herself "with liberals of all faiths, all shades.") Critics in the press referred to her as La Douglas, but her fans called her "our Helen."

On top of everything else, Douglas was responsible for child rearing, sometimes close at hand, other times from across the country. She often packed her children off to school in the morning (after braiding her daughter's hair), something few congressmen had to do. One day, Mary Helen called her mother at work and demanded a new pair of pajamas and *not* something ordered out of a catalog or selected by an aide. "Pick out some pretty ones your very own self and bring them home with you tonight," she pleaded. Douglas reportedly left her Capitol Hill office early that day to go shopping.

Douglas once spoke, with some anguish, about the problems all working women with husbands and children endure. A wife and mother who served in Congress faced the additional problem of long absences from home, she added. This required personal sacrifice "not only on her part, but on the part of her husband and children." Was it worth it? For herself, the answer was yes, but only as long as she was able to inject the "special viewpoint" and "special knowledge" of women "in the great decisions which Congress is called upon to make."

Being a woman in politics was hard enough. Women had been allowed to vote in every state for only twenty-five years, so running for office was rare indeed. Helen Douglas, because of her celebrated background, theatrical oratory, stunning good looks, and passionate commitment to progressive issues, caused a stir in Congress. Washington was prepared for her beauty, according to one correspondent, but surprised by "her brilliance, in short, her brains." Her eight female colleagues embraced her; some men despised her, others wanted to get close to her. The press dubbed her the Gal from Cal.

Douglas tried to look businesslike. On the floor, she wore little makeup, pinned her hair up in a modified bun, and favored conservative suits. Still, she was often surrounded by "attentive male colleagues," according to one writer. Another reporter, recalling Clare Luce's comment that no woman over forty retains her glamour, observed that Douglas, at forty-four, "still knocks them dead when she speaks in the House, her chestnut-brown hair smartly coiffed and her tailoring impeccable. You wouldn't believe she had risen at seven, pulled a household together, supervised the dressing, breakfasting, and getting-off-to-school of two children, and driven as fast as the D.C. law allows to her office."

When she was named to several best-dressed lists—in the company of celebrities like Elizabeth Taylor and Rosalind Russell—and her beauty was constantly compared with Luce's, she complained, "Congresswomen's ideas should rate above their clothes and their looks. Why all this emphasis on the sexes anyway, in a serious thing like government?" A Douglas associate later commented, however, that the congresswoman cultivated an "aura of glamour" and "was on stage a great deal of the time . . . she knew how to use her body, to use her face, to use her whole 'get-up' to make her point." Evie Chavoor claimed that some of Douglas's colleagues didn't take her seriously because she "had been an actress," then laughed and corrected herself—"she *still* was an actress." Another supporter observed that when Douglas "got in trouble, she could rely on her dramatic talents to help."

It soon became apparent that Douglas was a quick learner, and she even earned the praise of some of the hawkish members of the House Foreign Affairs Committee, as well as her new mentor, Lyndon B. Johnson of Texas. "Helen has really been in the smoke-filled rooms," one Democrat commented, "and that's the first time that's happened with any woman." She spoke proudly of doing her homework on the issues. Many of her colleagues, however, hated her politics or her "very excitable" style (as one put it). They called the wing where she and several other liberals had offices Red Gulch. Nobody could deny her "brains, wit and courage," but Southern Democrats "have no use for Mrs. Douglas because of her outspoken support for civil rights," *The Atlanta Journal* commented.

But there was another reason she would not become an effective member of Congress in a lawmaking sense: She did not have the temperament for it. Bold and impatient, eager for applause and quick results—forever the rebel—she consciously chose the role of what one writer has called "idealistic harasser . . . goader . . . self-appointed whip . . . demagogue." She had no interest in statutory details, and her "sense of propriety . . . baffles and infuriates the menfolk of the House," a California reporter observed. Her colleague Chet Holifield noticed that she "wouldn't have anything to do with the lobbyists." In love with her own voice, she was long-winded even by congressional standards. Accustomed to getting what she wanted, she refused to ingratiate herself with colleagues. "She was not a team player," a friend explained. "She was Helen Douglas." She loudly hissed a colleague on the floor of the House—the powerful John Rankin of Mississippi—when he blamed many U.S. casualties in World War II on the ineptitude of Negro soldiers.

In short, Douglas rejected the notion that "a little bit of flattery and you can get a woman to go your way. . . . I looked with a jaundiced eye on whatever was said to me and proceeded to do whatever I was going to do." As a result, she could not claim credit for passing a single piece of legislation. Ed Lybeck admitted that she "could not have gotten a bill passed mak-

ing December 25th a holiday." But as an advocate, a spokeswoman, a light-
ning rod—often a court of last resort—she had few peers. With only a
handful of allies, she railed against an atomic arms race, opposed Truman's
loyalty program, and defended victims of HUAC. Lybeck referred to her as
"a god-damned good stubborn bull-headed proselytizer." She would drive
herself to exhaustion, rest up in a hospital for a few days, then return to the
battle.

Douglas also put her civil rights pieties into practice, becoming the first
white member of Congress to hire a black secretary: Juanita Terry, a quiet,
efficient young woman, the daughter of a prominent constituent. (One of
Douglas's staffers, who hailed from the South, promptly quit.) Then she
took steps to integrate the House cafeteria, a bold move that black congressmen, like Adam Clayton Powell, Jr., had not undertaken. She was not
unaware of the political advantages. At least a year before the 1950 election,
Lybeck had suggested she hire a "Negro girl." It was "silly," he advised, to remain vulnerable to the "lily-white office sneer. And our good friends
among the Negroes would really enjoy it. . . ."

Even Douglas, however, did not attempt to infiltrate the many chambers
in the House that were off-limits to women. But the essential Douglas was
on display the day her Democratic colleague Mary Norton tried to speak in
favor of a fair-employment bill. Southern Democrats repeatedly interrupted
Congresswoman Norton with points of order, then retreated to an all-male
enclave just off the floor. While Norton's face was turning red, Douglas rose,
rushed to the men's den, flung open the door, and exclaimed, "If you'd *ever*
get on the side of God there isn't anything we couldn't do!"

Westbrook Pegler complained that the former actress's "cheesecake glamour" had "turned to senescent Limburger." But her combination of femi-
nism, idealism, and personal magnetism created loyal staff members (all
female) and political volunteers. A reporter observed that Evie Chavoor did
not have a life of her own, but "she doesn't seem to mind." One associate
compared being with Douglas to "warming one's hands at a glowing fire."
Some claimed she lacked a sense of humor, a reporter observed, adding,
"She has it, but the crusading zeal obscures it most of the time." Aides joined
her in uproarious games of bridge and charades at her home.

Strain was beginning to show in the Douglas marriage, however. Mel,
back from the war, had resumed his career in Hollywood and New York—
in any case, away from Washington. He told a reporter that his home often
resembled the proverbial smoke-filled room, and it had been years "since we
had a strictly social party." He joked, perhaps uneasily, about becoming a
"vice-presidential consort" or "Second Lady of the land." The children split

their time between two cities, two parents. Speaking of her parents, Mary Helen later explained, "There was no question they loved to be together, but they took such delight in their work they could enjoy being on their own. They didn't need to feed off each other."

Douglas's landslide victory in her 1948 race suggested that she could hold her congressional seat for as long as she wanted. She received more money from labor than any other candidate for Congress and easily fended off Red-baiting, partly because the Communists were attacking her for supporting the Marshall Plan and snubbing Henry Wallace's race for president. She was, in addition, the brightest star to emerge from Hollywood's circle of liberal activists. If she did remain in Congress for a few more years, she would shoot up the seniority ladder on the Foreign Affairs Committee, where a woman never before had exerted significant influence. Already that panel's fourth ranking member, she had a fair chance of heading it some day. From that perch, she could run strongly for the Senate in '56 or '58. Ed Lybeck described this strategy as concentrating on "keeping you in the House and . . . suddenly everybody would wake up and realize that you were the outstanding law-giver in this part of the woods and why the hell weren't you a Senator?"

Helen Douglas, however, was growing restless in the House and eyed a Senate race way ahead of schedule. She was "frustrated, furious, and heartsick" (she said) at the inability to push social legislation through Congress without making crippling compromises. Her experience at the Democratic National Convention in 1948 fed her national ambitions. After she delivered a major address, delegations in several states floated her name for vice president. Urged to squelch such talk, she refused on grounds that "it would be a great honor to the women of this country to have a woman's name placed in nomination."

Ego played a strong part, of course, but so did the rightward drift and the growing vulnerability of Sheridan Downey. He had come to prominence as Upton Sinclair's running mate in the 1934 race for governor of California. Sinclair's left-wing End Poverty in California (EPIC) movement had helped the two candidates—dubbed Uppie and Downey—capture the Democratic primary in a landslide, but a sensational dirty-tricks campaign by their opponents (initiating new media and advertising techniques) denied them the election. Downey became a champion of the Townsend Plan and other pension schemes for the elderly and in 1938 won election to the U.S. Senate. But by the mid-1940s, while maintaining a mainstream New Deal record on national programs, he began to side with corporate interests on important California issues. Douglas privately accused him of selling his soul to oil magnates and agribusiness tycoons. Westbrook Pegler hailed him as a "repentant undercover Republican."

In early 1949, shortly after beginning her third term in Congress, Douglas seriously contemplated a challenge to Downey. Her musings inspired, and were inspired by, letters from admirers around the state. Typical was a fan from Alameda who claimed to speak for working people and the small businessman, praising her "uncompromising and unflinching fight" for the common man. Some of Douglas's aides started calling her Senator.

Many political pros, as much as they liked her, felt pessimistic. Some warned she simply could not win because none of the key elements—party leaders, funders, voters as a whole—were ready to support a woman for the Senate. Labor groups and Democrats in Washington valued her influence in the House so much that they opposed a long-shot race for the Senate. She had a large group of idolators in the south but lacked support in the north. Her acolytes let their "admiration and worship" overcome common sense, India Edwards felt. As vice chair of the Democratic National Committee, Edwards had known several capable congresswomen who had tried for the Senate, and each had failed. Because so few women had served in the House, the ones who did developed an inflated sense of their significance, she believed.

An African-American leader in San Francisco sounded out local support and reported that many Democrats were "flattened" by what he termed the "unorthodoxy" of her candidacy. Another activist warned that party leaders considered her a "good showman but not a good politician," surrounded by a "little coterie" of advisers. A longtime supporter considered her myopic in believing that "if she latched onto an issue, that everybody else was automatically interested in it, believed in it, and wanted to hear about it. . . . She asked for trouble, a little bit unnecessarily."

Even Ed Lybeck and Evie Chavoor were apprehensive. Lybeck was well aware of her political liabilities, which he memorably described as being "a traitor to her class," "the wrong sex politically," anti-Catholic (for opposing Franco in Spain), and in the eyes of many a "nigger lover." Oddly, he felt that "the hardest thing about Helen was selling her to women"—and for this reason used photos that downplayed her beauty. On top of all that, he feared she would not raise enough money and would "commit suicide with no dough." But he knew that she wished to "alleviate the boredom" caused by the slow pace of the House, and he told her, "I'd rather lose you in a hell-bending race for the United States Senate than lose you just because you got bored." If she did make the race she should not be afraid to draw on Hollywood celebrities, he advised. Someone to make speeches who was a "stellar attraction on his own" would be ideal—someone like Ronald Reagan, for example.

Evie Chavoor was already overwhelmed handling Douglas's congressional and personal business. With Melvyn away most of the time, she essentially served as Helen's spouse. Adding a Senate race—a "keg of dynamite," as Chavoor put it—to the agenda seemed impossible. "She's a complex gal," she told Ruth Lybeck, "and you can only change her way of doing things only a little and only after a struggle."

Douglas's congressional colleague Richard Nixon was taking the same sort of soundings for a Senate race. Already the two were being matched as potential rivals. A veterans' magazine endorsed both of them, for Douglas was a liberal with "some conservative ideas" and Nixon a conservative with "some liberal tendencies." Douglas got such a kick out of it she sent a rare note to Nixon along with the magazine. "Dear Richard," she wrote, "Have you seen this? I thought it would amuse you. Sincerely, Helen."

The moment of truth for Helen Douglas came in August 1949. She had just completed a tour of reclamation projects and migrant camps in the Central Valley with Dorothea Lange and Paul Taylor. This fired her determination to punish Downey for turning his back on the farmworkers' plight. She planned to peg her campaign to a key California issue, known as the 160-acre limit. Decades ago liberals had passed laws that limited state-financed irrigation to farms of no more than 160 acres. This was meant to give the small farmer a chance to survive in a state dominated by agribusiness. But now the two-billion-dollar Central Valley Project was creating new irrigation channels, and land barons were fighting for a repeal of the 160-acre limit, often referring to it as a socialist conspiracy. Among those who said this was that old populist Sheridan Downey.

When Congress recessed, Douglas headed for Vermont to spend a few weeks, all too rare, with her husband, who was between films, and the children. As state chairman of Americans for Democratic Action, Mel remained politically committed, but he feared that the Senate race would adversely affect both his marriage and his wife's ability to care for the children. Yet the family had overcome similar obstacles, and so he would support any decision she made. Helen dreaded giving up a safe House seat, but unlike most of her advisers she was confident she could defeat Downey. She decided to enter the race—an intuitive decision, not a wholly rational one, "just going, hell-bent for election," as a friend later characterized it.

Aware of what was about to transpire, state Democratic leaders tried to strike a deal—with Downey, to retire and accept a federal judgeship, or with

Douglas, to wait for 1952 and a clear field against GOP Senator William Knowland. Neither accepted.

John B. Elliott, a party leader and oil entrepreneur, had never previously supported Douglas. "He didn't want to see a woman elected when there were perfectly good men candidates available," she observed of the man known as Black Jack. One of her close friends later revealed that Black Jack inspired the normally tactful Douglas to "let go" in private conversation. Douglas said she hoped that when Elliott died he would go to heaven and get his wish—all the oil he ever wanted, "so much that he drowns in it!"

But now Black Jack told her, "I want to be your friend." To prove it, he invited her to a meeting with top newspaper publishers and informed her she could have anything she wanted if she would only change her position on "the tidelands." Vast new reservoirs of offshore oil, recently discovered near California, were now managed by the federal government. Naturally, the oil companies wanted control shifted to the state legislature, where they had enormous influence. So far Washington had resisted the move despite the pleas of California moguls like Edwin Pauley, who once told President Truman he could "raise $300,000 from oilmen" for the Democratic Party.

After listening to Elliott's offer, Douglas promptly delivered a ten-minute lecture to his friends on the necessity of opposing Standard Oil and maintaining federal control over the tidelands. Elliott subsequently became "an implacable enemy" and, Douglas noted, "put all his rage and resources into fighting me."

Douglas announced her candidacy on October 5, 1949, billing herself as a "people's candidate," and established her primary headquarters in the Broadway Arcade Building on South Broadway in Los Angeles. She predicted that she would be Red-baited throughout the race because of her passionate support for civil rights, the small farmer, low-cost housing, Social Security, arms control, and peaceful coexistence around the globe. She justified her candidacy by insisting that Knowland and Downey were both in thrall to Republican businessmen. She, on the other hand, had no obligation to any "special interests."

At this point, Ed Lybeck bowed out as chief statewide strategist, arguing that his strength was local politics; privately, he lamented her decision to run because he feared she would lose. His departure pleased those Douglas insiders who felt he was too rough edged and parochial for a high-profile race. Ruth Lybeck would oversee the campaign in the south, and Harold "Tip" Tipton was named overall campaign manager and chief of the San Francisco office. Publicity would be handled by Bob Sill, a former newspaperman who had worked for movie studios and once promoted a Helen Gahagan play.

Hiring Harold Tipton, a Glendale native, had been suggested by Paul Taylor, his former economics professor at Berkeley, despite the fact that his only work in campaign management had been on behalf of Washington congressman Hugh Mitchell. "I'm scared to death," Tipton privately told Mitchell, "but ain't showing it." The only explanation he could give for Douglas's enlisting an outsider like him was that things were "so screwy in this state." He was appalled that some Douglas aides proposed getting her message across in lengthy treatises and others wanted to use comic books. "Personally," he commented, "I'm bored by both." He closed by asking Mitchell to tell Douglas that "generally speaking I know what I am doing." Helen Douglas, in other words, was not in the most capable political hands.

Media commentators found the Douglas challenge fascinating. Herb Caen, the *San Francisco Examiner* columnist, called her "the would-be Senatoress." A writer for the San Francisco *News* declared that the 1950 campaign was now a "dilly double feature," and Earl Warren and Jimmy Roosevelt would "have to work like cra-a-azy to hold top billing." A cartoon in that paper showed Douglas throwing a flowery hat into the senatorial ring, where it landed next to the statesmanlike top hat of Sheridan Downey. Tristram Coffin, the columnist, referred to her as "the gushy Democratic congresswoman" and, like most other observers, declared Downey the favorite. Across the ideological spectrum, however, she received positive reviews on her physical appeal. "She is quite an attractive female," observed a San Diego newspaper. "Red smear around the mouth and all. Nicely bobbed hair, with a boy's parting on one side; blue eyes and a fitting black dress. Trim, well turned out for a Hollywood actress." The *San Francisco Chronicle* recalled that in Congress, "she got the long, low whistles formerly reserved for Rep. Clare Boothe Luce." Some reporters speculated on how much weight she might gain on the rubber-chicken circuit.

Douglas admirers were ecstatic. "There were a lot of people who loved Helen, and who really cared because she cared about the things they cared about," Evie Chavoor recalled later. So if one person lost interest or wasn't able to perform a particular task, "fifty-seven others would be there to take over." Eleanor Roosevelt, after cohosting a fund-raising tea for Douglas in New York, explained in her newspaper column that when a woman "has done credit to all women by her public service, she should receive the support of women beyond the limits of her own state."

Ed Lybeck hinted at a reason for Douglas's popularity when he explained to Evie Chavoor why she had become such an effective speaker on the radio. The congresswoman had lowered and modulated her tone, he wrote, so that now she was coming off the radio "in a black lace negligee. Intimate, is the word." If she could get on enough stations, he added, "she can be elected to ANYTHING." *Pageant* magazine placed Douglas twelfth on its annual list of the most influential women in the United States.

The Douglas announcement also pleased Richard Nixon, who believed that if Downey won the primary, he would be weakened by the congress-woman's attacks—and if Douglas won, she would be easier to beat than the male incumbent.

Claiming to welcome the contest, Downey challenged Douglas to de-bate, an offer she spurned. He called her an "extremist" as donations flooded his campaign office. "Oil money came in here on railroad gondolas," one Democratic fund-raiser recalled. "They would *shovel* it off. Not literally, of course, but they had no end of money." To defeat Douglas, money was "*vi-olently* spent," he added. Kyle Palmer, in the *L.A. Times*, mocked the rabble-rousing Helen Douglas and referred to her as "a scolding woman . . . not at all averse to campaign brawling. . . . There are a few male demagogues scat-tered around here and there, but HGD has no female challengers for her su-premacy in that category. She's tops."

Suddenly, however, in March 1950, Downey quit the race, citing doctor's advice; he was suffering from peptic ulcers. The cause and effect were murky indeed. A Downey speechwriter later claimed that the senator felt he could lick Douglas but quit after a poll showed he would likely lose to Nixon.

Sheridan Downey threw his support to an unlikely late entrant in the race, another lapsed Progressive, Manchester Boddy, publisher of the Los Angeles *Daily News*. Bill Malone, the state Democratic leader, offered Douglas his support (political and financial) in return for control over patronage in northern California, but she refused, and the party machinery quickly backed Boddy. Black Jack Elliott would cochair Boddy's campaign, hauling oil money behind him. Clearly, Douglas had no intention of withdrawing from the Senate race even though her stated goal of removing the incum-bent had already been achieved, for Boddy had proclaimed that he would carry on Downey's work.

Only recently Boddy had praised Helen Douglas as "one of California's great women" and "one of its ablest representatives," but when he entered the Senate race he depicted her as "pink" or a "red-hot" and linked her to Vito Marcantonio, the left-wing congressman. She recognized the long-term implications. Boddy, like Downey, was stockpiling ammunition for Nixon to fire later.

Once Boddy established himself as a credible candidate, money arrived in bulk. His campaign managers said they expected to spend two hundred thousand dollars just in the last two weeks of the race. When Downey weighed in with his charge that Douglas had given "comfort to Soviet tyranny," Boddy's election seemed plausible. To meet the threat, Douglas campaigned ever more furiously, alarming her staff, who feared she would collapse at any moment. A San Diego organizer who drove her around the city was amazed at her ability to rest between stops and then awaken on cue, "always alert" and able to make a good impression.

At first, money was tight. Eleanor Roosevelt's party in New York attracted book publisher Bennett Cerf, actresses Lillian Gish and Myrna Loy, newspaper publisher Barry Bingham, and members of the Carnegie and Bloomingdale families and raised fifty-seven hundred dollars. In a letter of thanks to Roosevelt, Douglas revealed that she had received offers of "big money" but refused to take them because they were "conditioned on a slight reversal of my thinking on certain subjects." Friends, including *New Republic* editor Michael Straight, took out an ad in a New York City newspaper, calling for donations.

Slowly, labor organizers rallied to her side, and screenwriters Allen Rivkin and Philip Dunne and others made headway for her in Hollywood. Paul and Mickey Ziffren threw one fund-raising party after another, trying to make up for Democratic defections. Admirers floated campaign slogans, such as "I don't love no Boddy and no Boddy loves me." To combat what she called a newspaper blackout, Douglas took out small newspaper ads in which she chatted amiably to voters. Many women took the reins of the local campaigns. Elinor and Ed Heller, two leading Democratic organizers in the north, went their separate ways in this race, with Ed backing Boddy and Ellie supporting Douglas. (Had she done otherwise, she later explained, "I would have been a traitor to the first woman who was running statewide.") A professor at Mills College, a women's school, told the congresswoman, "If I had my choice of being given a permanent teaching job in political science or of having you in the U.S. Senate I would choose the latter without hesitation."

As a campaigner, Douglas was terrific in small groups, but with larger audiences she continued to be plagued by one crippling fault: an inability to come to a point and quit. Never afraid of the spotlight, able to sound convincing on nearly every subject (because of her acting ability), she let her speeches go on and on. "You throw me into a pond and I'll come up talking," she once confessed. Helen Lustig, her San Diego coordinator, and other organizers sometimes stood at the back of an audience, frantically giving her the cut-off sign—to no avail. Douglas had "so much to give that she couldn't stop," Lustig rationalized.

Evie Chavoor complained that Douglas thought she could educate the whole state on issues like the 160-acre limit. "And she would stand there in the sun by the hour talking about the water," Chavoor recalled, "and I would say, 'For God's sake Helen, that's enough.' " Ellie Heller was even more blunt. "The only one I knew in politics who made longer speeches was Hubert Humphrey!" she remarked. "She had no terminal facilities . . . her audiences would start to wander away from her."

The candidate also had a tendency to demand as much (or more) from her helpers as she expected from herself. "She is a wonderful gal but you can stand only so much evangelism," Harold Tipton told a friend. "She is a swell candidate but too intense—swell for voters and audiences—tough on associates." Evie Chavoor once complained that her boss was "always scolding me . . . she fairly shouts and I have to tell her I'm standing right next to her." But Douglas, she explained, always apologized quickly.

Throughout the spring, Helen rarely saw her husband and children. Mel was on the road with *Two Blind Mice,* and according to a press report, one of Chavoor's principal tasks was "to arrange the timing of their daily phone calls." On one occasion, desperate to see each other, if only for a few minutes, they arranged a meeting at New York's La Guardia Airport. A newspaper photo of them there appeared under the headline BUSY PATHS CONVERGE. Helen had managed to attend Melvyn's opening nights in Philadelphia and New York but was upset about having to miss the premieres in other cities. When Paul Sifton of the United Auto Workers went backstage to meet her husband in Detroit, the actor's first words were "What's the latest news about Helen's campaign?"

Douglas complained to a friend that campaigning was "rugged business. . . . There seems never to be a peaceful moment. The routine in Washington is mild by comparison, believe me." She told another friend that she was proud that the campaign was doing so well on so little money, "a tour de *force,* believe me—just plain elbow grease and a lot of good will has brought us this far along." According to an article, she responded this way to her daughter's request that she take a break from campaigning and play with her: "But, dear, this is important. This is for democracy. We've got to show the world it works!"

Her husband's letters offered support and advice. "I miss you and hope you are not beating yourself to a pulp," he wrote in late April. "Call me when you can." Later he sent along a few small campaign donations from friends. "I'll keep plugging," he declared. "Don't kill yourself. Love to yourself and the kids." Around her neck, for luck, she wore a Gahagan heirloom, a locket that held pictures of Melvyn, their two children, and Melvyn's son from his first marriage.

Her husband wasn't the only one worried about her health and safety. Helen had brought to California politics an exciting but somewhat dangerous campaign innovation, borrowed from her friend Lyndon Johnson, who had used it successfully in his close race for the Senate in 1948: hopscotching across the state by helicopter. The *San Francisco Chronicle*'s longtime political reporter, Earl Behrens, who thought he had seen it all, flew around in the copter with her and reported that she had "pioneered a new method of campaigning today." It perfectly suited her temperament, nearly allowing her to be in two places at once, and in the most theatrical style. Instead of pulling into town unheralded in a clunky, dusty station wagon, she would alight from the heavens like a modern-day Valkyrie in a sleek, noisy, and dust-producing chopper. No longer bound to street corners, she could land at a train station, on top of a building, in any empty park or farmer's field or ball yard. One day she took off and landed nine times in widely scattered areas of northern California. When she descended in San Rafael, her local organizer, Dick Tuck, dubbed the vehicle the Helencopter, and the name stuck.

The campaign had leased the small two-seater from Republican businessmen in Palo Alto who hoped she would help their helicopter company land a military contract. It was painted white with DOUGLAS FOR SENATOR printed on one side. Through a loudspeaker next to the cockpit she would announce her impending arrival and attract a crowd. On one occasion, her printed schedule called for her to land at a train station, and so, risking life and limb, she ordered the pilot to bring the plane down right on the platform. "Let's show them we aren't afraid," she said. After managing to land, they were informed that *of course* they were supposed to land on an adjoining field. Another time, on the way to Stockton, pilot Harry Watson (a Republican who had no intention of voting for her) realized he was lost. Spotting a farmer on a tractor in an open field, he swooped down, hovered, and asked for directions.

The helicopter had no roof, leaving pilot and candidate exposed to the elements. Sometimes Douglas tried to tie up her hair with what a reporter described as a "green thingamajig," but it seldom helped. Another writer revealed that she had to wear nylon slips with "straps that will give and seams that'll hold when she swings into a helicopter." A Nixon supporter who attended a Douglas landing in San Fernando watched with amazement as she emerged from the copter even before the rotors stopped turning. On her way to a formal occasion, she was wearing a long black dress, black gloves up to her elbows, and a black hat with a rose in it—but her hair was an absolute mess. The windblown look didn't seem to bother Douglas, who usually dressed elegantly if simply and used a minimum of makeup. It did bother some women, however; they were often heard to remark that they found the campaign by copter "unladylike" in the extreme.

Local Republican officials sometimes refused to grant her permission to land within town limits, claiming safety concerns. When this happened in San Rafael, Dick Tuck pointed out that a few months earlier the mayor had allowed Santa to land in town. Modesto refused a copter landing but OKed a Junior Chamber of Commerce request to allow a member to ride a bull through the streets to publicize a rodeo. "Even in towns where the Republican reactionaries won't let her land downtown, she can still get the crowd she wants by buzzing around for a while," a San Francisco reporter pointed out. "Yup, the candidates have pretty much given up the airplane."

Across the country, politicians and commentators took note of Douglas's bold experiment. A columnist in Washington observed that now a candidate could descend from the sky "like Heaven's own gift to the dear pee-pul." But he warned that crowds might get chopped like "sausage meat" because they rush forward when the copter lands, forgetting the rear propeller. "And one accident," he pointed out, "can lose a candidate more votes than his sensational air arrival can possibly win him." But Douglas told a New York reporter of her love of helicopter travel: "It's like sitting in a rocking chair in the sky, as near as I can imagine to using your own wings." Her only problem was that she couldn't nap in it.

On May 16, three weeks before primary day, Douglas delivered a noontime speech from atop a trailer on the street in front of the University of Southern California library. The school's Skull and Dagger honor society was holding an initiation that day, and some of its members and pledges, dressed only in tuxedo jackets, undershorts, and top hats, rode atop a hay wagon crisscrossing the campus. Either by design or chance, they came across the political rally, and as they neared the speaker, some of them sprayed seltzer and tossed hay on the candidate and shouted and ranted as she tried to speak. A scuffle broke out between one of the hay riders and another student.

Douglas took off her coat, which was soaked with seltzer, brushed the hay out of her hair, and tried to make light of the attack. "I don't know what I was squirted with," she complained, "but I hope it wasn't beer—I hate beer." She also said, "Boys will be boys," and "I didn't mind the shower a bit. I only wish I had something to squirt back." An Associated Press account also tried a humorous approach: "She wasn't even pledged to the fraternity, but Congresswoman Helen Gahagan Douglas got the works in this initiation." The university took the incident seriously, however. The USC president apologized for the disruption, claiming the stunt was "unpremeditated but went beyond the bounds of gentlemanly conduct."

Some in the Douglas camp suspected that the Nixon campaign, which had strong ties to Young Republicans at USC, was behind the incident. A history professor who was present suggested that two young Nixon activists, Joseph Holt and Patrick Hillings (both recent USC graduates), had directed the prank from the edge of the crowd, but hard evidence never materialized. Tom Dixon, Nixon's radio announcer, later conceded that generally the candidate knew about everything going on in his name. "If someone threw paint on Helen Douglas he knew about it," Dixon affirmed. Douglas, in any case, was conciliatory, sending a telegram to the student newspaper expressing her "deepest appreciation" to the student body "for their sportsmanship and gallantry following Tuesday's incident."

Helen Douglas made one exception to her rule against sharing the stage with her opponent, a fabulous debater, and when it was over she vowed she would never make that mistake again.

In May, the two spoke at the Press Club in San Francisco. The affair was off-the-record, and descriptions of what happened differ. In the most common account, Nixon took an envelope out of his pocket and read a letter that had come with a donation to his campaign—from none other than Eleanor Roosevelt. Members of the audience apparently gasped or applauded in delight while Douglas's face betrayed her shock and dismay. Then Nixon explained, "I, too, was amazed with this contribution—amazed, that is, until I saw the postmark: Oyster Bay, New York." *This* Eleanor Roosevelt was closely related to that great Republican, Theodore Roosevelt. In another account, Nixon did not come clean about the contributor, leaving his opponent and the audience to figure it out afterward. In any case, Douglas would later recall feeling "bewildered," as if she'd been "put . . . in a ridiculous position." When it was her turn to speak, she gave a very poor account of herself.

A few days later, in a note to the Nixon campaign committee, Murray Chotiner observed that Manchester Boddy had failed to attend the Press Club debate, and "Mrs. Douglas now wishes she had not shown either."

Nevertheless, after her smashing primary victory in June, Douglas told friends she was thoroughly "optimistic" about her chances that fall. Although Nixon had piled up more votes in the primary the Democrats retained a huge edge in registration. Sheridan Downey would endorse her if Harry Truman asked him to. And, she believed, "the worst" of the Red-baiting and campaign tricks was surely over.

Presidential Timber

While Helen Douglas paused to lick her wounds after a rugged primary, Richard Nixon plunged into the general election. A day after sweeping to victory, Nixon and Murray Chotiner paid an unannounced call on Edwin Pauley, the oilman, in his Los Angeles office. Harry Truman had once said that he felt "a very strong fondness" for Pauley, and no wonder. As a national party leader, Pauley had played a central role in persuading FDR to put Harry Truman on his ticket in 1944. Later Truman nearly appointed him undersecretary of the navy and viewed him as a potential secretary of defense—"I wanted the hardest, meanest son of a bitch I could get," he explained—but Pauley's oil background scuttled those plans. Wouldn't it be wonderful now if Pauley used his influence to persuade the president to stay out of California in the coming campaign?

The oilman had endorsed Manchester Boddy in the Democratic primary, so he was ripe for recruitment. He had raised hundreds of thousands of dollars from oil interests around the country for previous candidates, and Nixon gave him the respect he deserved, soliciting his advice on key issues. Pauley replied that he wouldn't think of telling the Republican Party what to do but promised to "discourage my friends" from voting for Douglas. Although the oilman did not offer financial backing at this time, Nixon's eyes (Pauley observed) "lit up" with appreciation—and, no doubt, anticipation. Two days later Nixon's political director, Bernard Brennan, confided to another campaign operative that his candidate had met with several Boddy backers and now expected "considerable support from those people."

At headquarters downtown, Chotiner perused the final primary returns and discovered with pleasure that his candidate had edged Douglas in total balloting in every large city and county across the state, with close to a one-hundred-thousand-vote bulge in Los Angeles. "Searching my memory of past campaigns—and I have been in a few of them—I can honestly say that never before has there existed such a spirit of friendly teamwork and real enthusiasm," he told his associates. But the Nixon team knew that the primary had been a cakewalk and that the Democratic opponent inspired just as much devotion on the other side.

In Helen Douglas, Richard Nixon confronted a woman who would not bend easily to his wishes. This was nothing new for Nixon. He was enormously shy around women, could barely look one in the eye, but he was used to dealing with women who sometimes stood up to him. This had been the case with the three most important women in his life—his mother, his college sweetheart, and his wife—and he had made extraordinary attempts to win the affection of each. Nixon did not seek, or need, to accomplish *that* in the case of Helen Douglas, but his difficulties with stubborn women in the past no doubt resonated in his carefully planned drive to humble his Democratic opponent.

His mother, Hannah Milhous Nixon, was a puritanical, cool if loving Quaker. It was to her, not to his explosive father, that young Richard was attached. By all accounts, he was a determined, extremely smart boy living in the shadow of his ebullient older brother, Harold. Perhaps because of his quiet and sensitive nature, Richard "needed" her more than his four brothers did, Hannah Nixon once said. To him, she seemed incredibly tough. For one thing, she had bucked the wishes of the Milhous family in marrying crude Frank Nixon.

Her husband worked hard to make a success of various business enterprises, first in Yorba Linda (where Richard was born) and then in nearby Whittier, finally succeeding with a grocery store. Contrary to the myths Richard later spun, the family rarely lived in poverty. There was love in the house—between husband and wife, parents and children—but also a good deal of shouting and spanking, courtesy of Frank. Hannah never yelled at the boys but "burned inside," she later confessed (a tendency passed on to her second son). Richard inherited from his dad a love of politics and debating, but he confided in his mom. He counted on her to smooth things over with Frank and to make him feel wanted, which she usually did. He feared his father's physical abuse, but he also dreaded his mother's stern lectures; when he did wrong, he preferred a spanking from Frank to a speech from Hannah. One of his brothers once described their mother as the "judge" and their father as "the executioner."

Richard later acknowledged his family's "reticence about open displays of affection" and admitted that he had acquired it. His mother, he reflected, "never indulged in the present day custom, which I find nauseating, of hugging and kissing her children or others for whom she had great affection. . . . I can never remember her saying to any of us 'I love you'—she didn't have to!"

When Richard was in his early teens, his older brother Harold contracted tuberculosis, and Hannah moved to Arizona with him for the better part of three years in an attempt to alleviate the illness (which eventually killed him). Richard resented being abandoned, but how much it affected his behavior is uncertain. Some have asserted that it caused him to grow socially isolated and angry and unsteady with women. Others concluded that his political ambition was a sublimated drive to earn the devotion of his mother. Bryce Harlow, later a close friend, speculated that as a child he was "hurt very deeply by somebody . . . so badly he never got over it and never trusted anybody again." The result, he added, was that "Richard Nixon went up the walls of life with his claws."

At Fullerton Union High School, Richard (now Dick) was a top student, a scrappy football player, a skilled orator and debater. He had what was viewed as a slightly unhealthy drive to be number one at everything, and losing his first race for office—for senior class president—pained him deeply. An awkward dancer, he rarely dated and seemed inordinately dismissive of the opposite sex. One female classmate recalled that he "hated girls" and made faces at them, "but he didn't seem to mind arguing with us." After finishing near the top of his class, he was invited to apply to Harvard and Yale, but his family could not afford the tuition, so he enrolled close to home, at little Whittier College. This no doubt contributed to his long-simmering and sometimes self-destructive resentment of Ivy Leaguers and East Coast intellectuals.

The contrast with young Helen Gahagan, the dilettante, could not have been sharper. She had earned poor grades in high school yet was socially and financially equipped to attend exclusive Barnard College—only to skip many classes and ultimately drop out. Richard Nixon, on the other hand, made the most of his limited opportunities. He threw himself into activities at Whittier, becoming class president, ace debater, and a star in school plays, all while earning top grades. Many years later he explained his extraordinary drive this way: "What starts the process really are laughs and slights and snubs when you are a kid. . . . But if you are reasonably intelligent and if your anger is deep enough and strong enough, you learn that you can change those attitudes by excellence, personal gut performance, while those who have everything are sitting on their fat butts." He still rose nearly every morning at four o'clock to shop for produce for his father's market.

Despite his smallish frame he scrimmaged with the football team, refusing to quit even after absorbing poundings. Nixon later revealed that he admired, and learned more from, his college football coach, Wallace "Chief" Newman, than from any other man aside from his father. Coach Newman, he explained, "had no tolerance for the view that how you play the game counts more than whether you win or lose. He used to say, 'Show me a good loser and I'll show you a loser.' "

As a debater, he was "merciless," according to one teacher. Another observer marveled at his ability to keep an opponent off-balance, always "using that ace in the hole. . . . He would so fluster the other speaker with his steady attack that his opposition would become emotional and stop thinking clearly." Nixon did have one thing in common with Helen Gahagan: He loved the stage so much that his drama coach believed he might head for Broadway or Hollywood after college. He was "at home on the platform," the teacher said, and "got a thrill out of getting to an audience." It was his first experience "in the arena," an expression (borrowed from Theodore Roosevelt) he would later use to describe the place where he spent most of his life.

Nixon met his first girlfriend, Ola Florence Welch, in a high school play, and their relationship continued throughout college. Ola was far more carefree and fun loving than he and liked to dance, and they often argued over politics. Like Hannah Nixon, Ola Florence was opinionated; she admired Franklin Roosevelt, whom Nixon detested. After four years, they broke up. He stubbornly courted her for another year, but ultimately she jilted him and married another man, who was, she explained, more "fun." Later she would wonder whether Nixon was only "playacting" affection for her. "I never really knew him . . . he was a mystery," she added.

Finishing second in his college class, Nixon received a scholarship to Duke University Law School in September 1934. At Duke, he studied ferociously and never dated, earning the nickname Gloomy Gus, but won his second election race, for president of the law school bar association. He also participated in a break-in of the dean's office to find out who had placed first in his class (alas, he finished third).

After earning his degree and failing to secure a position with the FBI in Washington, Nixon returned to Whittier to practice law. He became active in civic clubs, those in-bred launching pads for local politicians, and as early as 1940 considered running for the state assembly. While performing with a community theater group, he met, and immediately fell in love with, a slender young schoolteacher with reddish golden hair named Thelma "Patricia" Ryan. An aspiring actress popular with men, Pat was far more worldly than Richard. She had worked at a hospital in the Bronx and then lived in Los Angeles while attending USC as a business major. She had also toiled as a movie extra at MGM and RKO, and in 1935, the same year Helen Gahagan starred in *She,* Pat Ryan had a small speaking role (later cut) in *Becky Sharp.* Discouraged by the studio caste system—and disgusted with the notion of casting-couch auditions—she set her sights on a career in education. Although she enjoyed teaching at Whittier High School, she found the town far too provincial and fled to Los Angeles every weekend.

Meeting Richard Nixon onstage, Pat Ryan was not impressed. As in his previous relationship, he would have to be the aggressor. One of their fellow actors later remarked, "If anybody ever had a mind of her own, she did." (Pat was a registered independent.) Nixon was so intent on wooing her he even drove her home from her dates with other men. Slowly, she came to appreciate his fine mind and his "drive . . . he was going places and he always saw the possibilities," and in June 1940 they were wed. Like Helen Gahagan, Richard Nixon married a former costar.

When World War II broke out, Nixon took a job with the Office of Price Administration in Washington, D.C., and in 1943 enlisted in the navy. (About half of all draft-eligible Quakers elected to go off to war.) Assigned to the South Pacific, he worked in a supply unit, never seeing combat but witnessing its brutal effects on injured and mutilated GIs. He also evolved into a daring, world-class poker player.

Returning to Washington after the war, he was immediately drafted by a handful of Whittier businessmen to run for Congress against the popular progressive Jerry Voorhis. It was a long shot. Even Republicans admitted that Voorhis was a decent man and a hardworking legislator. But when the recruiters, led by bank manager Herman Perry and advertising salesman Roy Day, assured him that they could raise enough money to make it feasible, Nixon accepted. He promised an "aggressive, vigorous campaign" to expose Voorhis's "particular brand of New Deal idealism." While inexperienced in politics, young Nixon was a war veteran, a go-getter, an attractive alternative to the plodding, middle-aged Voorhis.

Pitching his candidate to party activists, Roy Day exclaimed, "This man is salable merchandise." Day kept after him to look women in the eye at campaign appearances, or "they won't think you're telling the truth." He also advised him that "nice guys and sissies don't win elections." Crucially, Nixon earned the support of the kingmakers at the *Los Angeles Times,* and the vast majority of other local newspapers followed suit. Money came from oil companies and such Hollywood activists as Louis B. Mayer and Mendel Silberberg. Pat Nixon threw herself into the campaign with relish, perhaps for the last time.

By now, Nixon was a confirmed anti-Communist. Winston Churchill's recent warning that an Iron Curtain had fallen across Europe profoundly influenced him. Contrary to legend, however, communism was "not the issue at any time in the 1946 campaign," he later asserted. "Few people knew about Communism then, and even fewer cared." Although the Cold War had begun, fear and hatred of the Soviets, our wartime allies, were still somewhat submerged. No candidate could run strictly on anticommunism (as Nixon would do four years later) and win; and Republicans, in any case, had plenty of other issues, such as high taxes and inflation, to hurl at a Democrat like Voorhis, who was out of step with his increasingly conservative district.

Still, a little Red-baiting could go a long way, and Republicans across the country used it to threaten the Democratic majority in Congress. From the start of the campaign, Nixon repeatedly pointed out that Voorhis had belonged to the Socialist Party in the early 1930s and charged that his voting record in Congress was "more Socialistic and Communistic than Democratic." The turning point in the campaign came, however, when Voorhis agreed to a series of debates. Nixon scored heavily when he falsely charged that his opponent had been endorsed by a "Communist-dominated" political action committee. One of his college debating partners recognized the same tactics, the use of "half-truths" and "innuendoes," that Nixon had mastered years before. Approaching Nixon after a debate, he asked, "Why are you doing this?" Nixon, still high from his victory, replied, "Sometimes you have to do this to be a candidate. I'm gonna win."

In the closing weeks of the campaign, anti-Voorhis smears circulated widely, none directly linked to Nixon headquarters and therefore all the more effective. One rumor warned that international Jewry was using Voorhis and other political leaders, such as Helen Douglas, to "destroy Christian America." The weekend before the election, many voters answered their phone to hear a stranger ask, "Did you know that Jerry Voorhis is a Communist?" and then hang up.

When it was over, Nixon had won a smashing victory. A few months afterward he reportedly confided to a former Voorhis aide that "of course" he knew his opponent "wasn't a communist. . . . I had to win. That's the thing you don't understand. The important thing is to win."

Republicans took control of Congress in 1947, and true to his word, Nixon attempted to undo the Voorhis–New Deal legacy. He opposed rent control and tax cuts for low-income groups. He voted against additional money for education, Social Security, public housing, and public power projects while supporting antitrust exemptions and tax reductions for business. He fought foreign aid to countries friendly with the Soviets. None of this, however, distinguished him from most of his Republican colleagues. What would set him apart, and would bring him to national attention, was his decision to focus his energies on rooting out domestic communism.

First, he landed a spot on HUAC, which, under the new GOP leadership, immediately went after Communist infiltration of the government and Hollywood. With Karl Mundt, he drafted a bill requiring Communists and Communist front groups to register with the Justice Department, and it passed the House before sinking in the Senate. His big break arrived, however, when *Time* magazine editor Whittaker Chambers came forward to identify former State Department official Alger Hiss as a onetime Communist. Nixon was not responsible for producing the witness, but his dogged faith in the rather unsavory Chambers enabled him to take credit for breaking the Hiss case. (Chambers later revealed that Nixon's "somewhat martial Quakerism" amused and heartened him.) Most spectacularly, he displayed for newsreel cameras the so-called Pumpkin Papers, several rolls of microfilm of classified documents that Hiss had allegedly passed to Chambers, who hid them in a pumpkin on his farm. Whatever the political benefits, Nixon sincerely believed in Hiss's guilt.

Then, in July 1949, Nixon suffered an unexpected setback when a federal case in which Hiss was accused of perjury resulted in a hung jury in New York. Recognizing a threat to his political career, Nixon condemned the verdict and questioned the judge's "fitness to serve on the bench." He also hinted that the White House had fixed the case to avoid a humiliating defeat. To Nixon's relief, prosecutors quickly moved forward with a second trial.

Like Helen Douglas, Richard Nixon had become a national figure only to find that his patience with the pace and the protocol of the House of Representatives rapidly wore thin. Douglas faced many obstacles in attempting to gain influence in Congress: her gender, her liberalism, her flamboyance. Nixon faced none of these drawbacks and in fact had much in his favor, especially the public image he had built while investigating alleged Communists. But he confronted one huge barrier: Democratic control of Congress and the White House, which might not end any time soon. As he easily won reelection in 1948, the Democrats regained a majority in Congress and soon he started thinking about running for the Senate in 1950.

His aide Bill Arnold considered him "a restless soul," but personal ambition played a large role in Nixon's decision as well. Like Helen Douglas, he could have held on to his safe seat in the House while making even more of a national name for himself. More than a decade younger than Douglas, he had even more reason to mark time, but he knew that if he wanted to advance to the Senate—and he did—his options were narrow. He wouldn't think of challenging his friend William Knowland in 1952, and there was no reason to think the senator would be ready to retire in '58. That left Sheridan Downey's seat, which would be up for grabs in 1950. Downey was still fairly popular, particularly since his swing to the right had gained applause from many Republicans (including Nixon himself). If Nixon did not take Downey on now, he would have to wait until 1956 to go after that seat. And he didn't want to wait that long. Some of his friends suspected that he hoped to be running for *president* by '56.

Early in 1949, after just two years in the House, Nixon began sounding out friends and supporters about a Senate run, telling them the House "offered too slow a road to leadership." He didn't want to be part of "a vocal but ineffective minority." If he failed in a race for the Senate, he would happily return to Whittier and practice law. Like Helen Douglas, he discovered— perhaps to his surprise and certainly to his chagrin—that nearly everyone discouraged him from running, believing he could not beat Downey and was foolish even to think about giving up a safe seat in Congress, especially since he was already a national figure. Yet it was the very notoriety he had gained in the Hiss fight—"publicity on a scale that most congressmen only dream of achieving," he reckoned—that spurred his ambition, for he feared he would never achieve such prominence and popularity again.

To him, that meant the time was ripe for a Senate race. When Herman Perry, one of the men who helped launch his political career in 1946, argued against making the effort, Roy Day took Nixon's side, explaining, "When your star is up, that's when you have to move." Like Helen Douglas, Nixon was naturally reckless, a gambler. It came with the territory—California. Knowing they live in an exceptional state, Californians have always had a sense of "being lucky," Carey McWilliams once observed. But Nixon also had the foresight to recognize that he would have few serious rivals for the GOP nomination.

Still, he felt uncertain. In the late spring of 1949, he discussed the matter with Bernard Brennan, a forty-seven-year-old L.A. attorney who had worked on campaigns for Earl Warren and Thomas Dewey. He told Brennan that he recognized "the hazards" involved, but he added bravely: "I will say, however, I have never been insistent on 'sure-fire' deals. If I thought there was a good fighting chance to make the race and win, I would be inclined to take it."

Within weeks, he had received promises of support from key Republicans in the south, including Asa Call and Roy Crocker, who had raised money for him in previous campaigns. Call, director of Pacific Mutual and a prime mover in downtown L.A. for decades, once boasted that over the telephone in an hour or so "we could always raise enough money to run a campaign" from a list of about fifty people. McIntyre Faries, the state's GOP national committeeman, also helped, although he considered Nixon "a bit of a boy debater and a little cold." Then Nixon made a successful journey to San Francisco to line up financial help in the north.

On the train back to Los Angeles, Nixon told insurance man Frank Jorgensen, that he had made up his mind—"We're going to go"—and he wanted Jorgy to run the campaign with other veterans of his previous races. Jorgensen protested that he lacked the experience to manage a statewide race and proposed naming two L.A. attorneys to run the show. One was Bernie Brennan. The other was Murray Chotiner, who had worked part-time for Nixon in '46, a "pretty agile" fellow with "good political sense," in Jorgensen's estimate.

"All right," Nixon replied a bit reluctantly. "You make your deal with him." When they got back to L.A., Jorgensen offered to pay Chotiner $12,500 to manage the primary race (under the overall direction of Brennan), with the promise of a larger fee for the fall campaign. Jorgensen knew the forty-year-old Chotiner as a loose cannon who ran roughshod over subordinates and frequently alienated his clients. "He had the habit," Jorgensen later explained, "of . . . tramping on them. He'd move ahead. He'd just leave wreckage behind him, but he would get the job done." He made clear that he expected Chotiner to follow their organizational plan. "If you do not follow the plan, just pick up your hat and go home," he instructed. "Do we understand this?"

"I understand it," Murray said, to Jorgensen's relief.

No one, Nixon included, knew quite what to make of Chotiner. He came from a broken home but had finished law school at the age of twenty. Despite that quick start, he was known as a police-court lawyer, his practice consisting mainly of defending bookmakers. As a political field-worker, he had helped elect several Republican candidates but had failed in his own race for state assembly. He promoted Earl Warren's election in 1942, but when he went to Warren for a few favors in return, the governor threw him out of his office and never had anything to do with him again. Chotiner was bright but ruthless, not only an opponent's worst enemy but his own. His law office, which also housed his campaign-management firm, was in the Fox Wilshire Building in Beverly Hills, but his manner and even his appearance—short and chubby with slick but thinning hair—was that of a small-time operator.

But this was deceiving. In law, as in politics, he could go for the jugular, but, as his son Ken later explained, he was "always well-prepared, and saw the big picture so he was able to counter an opponent's moves."

A disciple of Clem Whitaker, the nation's first freelance political consultant, Chotiner had been hired by Roy Day to provide publicity for Nixon's run against Jerry Voorhis in '46. He worked only part-time on that campaign since he was also helping Bill Knowland retain his Senate seat (often by smearing his Democratic opponent, Will Rogers, Jr.). Pat Nixon despised Chotiner and asked her husband to fire him, but he decided that Murray's "hard-line, street-smart political advice was more important to him than his wife's objections," their daughter Julie later revealed. It was Chotiner who conceived the tactic that turned the campaign around, suggesting that Nixon start attacking Voorhis as a tool of the left-wing labor PACs. Now, three years later, Chotiner would attempt to jump-start Nixon's Senate race.

"Sometimes I loathed Murray Chotiner—we all did," Adela Rogers St. Johns, a Democrat for Nixon, confessed many years later. "He was a brute in many ways. But never, never, was he cold or indifferent." He was "violent," "hot," but always focused on "NIXON, NIXON, NIXON."

The writer Garry Wills explained the Chotiner-Nixon link a little differently. Nixon, he said, "wanted tough guys around him to even the odds. . . . He was always trying to unlearn the niceness his mother had taught him with the help of people he hoped were bad enough for the job. . . ." Wills called this the conflict between Nixon's "natural sweetness and this diligently acquired meanness."

Besides attracting political pros and major funders Nixon also gained the crucial early support of Kyle Palmer of the *Los Angeles Times.* Over lunch at the Biltmore Hotel, Palmer warned that he was "a damn fool" to run against Downey, but if he did, California's newspaper "axis" would support him. Indeed, the *Times,* the *San Francisco Chronicle,* and the *Oakland Tribune* quickly endorsed Nixon, propelling most of his GOP rivals right out of the race. (Nixon considered the Biltmore lunch so significant that decades later he could still recall what he ate—a hot tamale with beans on the side.) In his column, Palmer praised Nixon to the sky while condemning Douglas for spreading "class hatred and social antagonism."

A Republican from Downey, California, meanwhile told the candidate he was the first man of "Presidential timber" to show up since Teddy Roosevelt.

Many women headed local Nixon offices but the key operatives were men. Nixon inspired the crucial, untiring advocacy of a new generation of spirited and very conservative young men, many of them converted Democrats—rah-rah types formerly active in campus politics. Recent USC Law School graduate Pat Hillings had first approached Nixon seeking HUAC files on student groups at the college. Then he worked as a paid Nixon aide for several months. Finally, he announced his plan to run for the House seat his mentor was relinquishing, proclaiming himself "A Young Man Who Is Going Places." Insurance agent Joe Holt, twenty-seven, son of a major Nixon funder and president of the state Young Republicans, became field director of the Senate campaign. Other key advance men included Walter "Buzz" Forward, president of the Young Republicans in San Diego, and Jack Drown, a magazine distributor in Long Beach.

Two other young men made important contributions. One was Herb Klein, a soft-spoken reporter from Alhambra who wrote material for the Senate campaign (as he had done for the '46 House campaign) and served as press adviser. The other was Robert Finch, the handsome former Occidental College student-body president and national chairman of the Young Republicans who had met Nixon while working for another congressman in Washington. Nixon had impressed him by backing the Marshall Plan when conservative Republicans were pressuring him to oppose it. Bob Finch had also met Helen Douglas and considered her "bright as hell" but knew that in this campaign "being a woman was clearly a negative."

Among other young Nixon fans were recent UCLA graduates John Ehrlichman, and H. R. "Bob" Haldeman (son of one of the candidate's chief funders). Each had been involved with the loyalty-oath debate and other hot-wire issues of campus politics. Ehrlichman later explained his "counterespionage" operation—helping the dean of students identify campus radicals.

Murray Chotiner did not want to curb the enthusiasm of the young activists, but he would not let them run wild. He sent a friendly letter to Pat Hillings, for example, protesting some of the language he had used in a Young Republicans statement. "Congressman Nixon," Chotiner explained, "refers to the present administration as moving toward 'state socialism'— and I think that is more desirable than the phrase 'socialist-*labor* government.' We have enough of a fight ahead as it is without taking on labor unnecessarily." Chotiner also suggested they quit denouncing the "welfare-state" since "a sincere concern for human welfare is a commendable thing."

To get the campaign rolling, Bernie Brennan and Asa Call turned to a Committee of Twenty, leading businessmen who each contributed one thousand dollars to a secret fund that would never be reported to the state election board. Things went so smoothly that some campaign leaders started to look beyond the Senate race. Mac Faries told one potential contributor that the Nixonites "think and have thought since the start that he was Presidential material and we expect to make him President. He could be President." Pledges quickly reached thirty thousand dollars, and Nixon officially launched his Senate campaign on November 3, 1949.

In his announcement—a speech so cogent it was reprinted in its entirety on campaign leaflets—Nixon recalled the "political miracle" he had achieved three years earlier in upsetting Jerry Voorhis. Now he faced "an even greater task," for the 1950 election "will be the most crucial in our nation's history." The advocates of "State Socialism" who had captured the Democratic Party wanted to turn America into another England, where "it is an offense to give your neighbor a pitcher of milk" or "repair your own home with your own hands." Once these types of programs "are voted in we cannot go back."

> Right here let me take off the gloves and get down to some political brass tacks. First, we must recognize once and for all that the time is past when the Republican or any other party can win an election by "playing the angle," pussy-footing on the issues, or compromising on principle for the sake of gaining votes. We will win only if we deserve to win, and we shall deserve to win if—without double-talk or hedging—we squarely meet the great issue which is before the American people at this time. That issue is simply the choice between freedom and State Socialism, make no mistake about that. They call it planned economy, the fair deal, or social welfare. It's still the same old Socialist baloney any way you slice it.

He warned it would be a tough fight. The Democratic opposition, he asserted, "will be well-financed. A huge slush fund is even now being wrung from the hands of workers for the purpose of opposing any candidate who will not take his orders from a clique of labor lobbyists in Washington." Nixon noted that there was "only one way to win. We must put on a fighting, rocking, socking campaign, and carry that campaign directly into every county, city, town, precinct and home in the State of California."

As was his custom, Nixon chose to involve himself in even the most trivial campaign discussions and decisions. He frequently reviewed strategies and dictated instructions to his aides. He advised Chotiner, for example, that "we must constantly remind ourselves that our goal is to get before as many non-Republican groups as possible without endangering our chances for the Republican nomination." On his frequent travels, he scribbled notes on pads of paper or hotel stationery such as these: "publicity—idea man essential. . . . Better handling of volunteer groups . . . need better contact with local editors. . . . Campaign strategy meetings—draw in bigger people." He sent along a new photograph to be used in campaign literature: Nixon and his family on the living room carpet engaged in what he called the "great American past-time of reading the Sunday funny papers." For his part, Chotiner wrote very exacting, never chatty memos to Nixon and other campaign officials, often with instructions to his secretary to "cc" Kyle Palmer at the *Los Angeles Times.*

The young congressman promised a new kind of campaign: not the gray, morally upright posture of Earl Warren and other older Republicans but the no-holds-barred approach of a young battler. Bernard Brennan described these qualities as "virile," "red-blooded," "aggressive," "fearless," "honest." He advised Nixon campaigners not to dwell on the candidate's youth but rather on his "hard-hitting, fighting ability . . . his new approach to campaigning, etc." A Nixon campaign pamphlet revealed that he "takes a sixteen-hour work day in stride, and still has time for his family, who are very close to his heart." Fulton Lewis, the national radio commentator, did his part, hailing Nixon as a "young, tough, toe-to-toe slugging veteran campaigner who . . . has made a brilliant record in the House . . . he fights it out on the issues, instead of compromising with a lot of me-too talk."

A key moment in the campaign came very early. Nixon's considerable support might not have meant much if the second Hiss trial (with a new judge presiding) had ended with an acquittal. If that had happened, Nixon "would be vulnerable to charges of witch-hunting," Stephen Ambrose later commented. But on January 21, 1950, Nixon got the guilty verdict he desperately needed. "This conspiracy," he quickly charged, "would have come to light long since had there not been a definite . . . effort on the part of certain high officials in two Administrations to keep the public from knowing the facts." He pleaded for a new offensive to root out Red sympathizers in government. Soon reprints of his triumphant speech in Congress following the Hiss verdict were mailed to seven thousand newspaper editors at taxpayers' expense; since it was drawn from the *Congressional Record,* the congressman could frank it. Hearst papers in Los Angeles and San Francisco and throughout the country reprinted parts of the speech on their front page under Nixon's byline.

Reviewing this call for a new crackdown on Communists, I. F. Stone warned of "turning the whole nation into a vast jail with J. Edgar Hoover as its turnkey. Behind Nixon's proposals there advances the shadow of the police state." Someone sent a clipping of Stone's statement to the candidate

with a note that Hollywood fund-raiser Mendel Silberberg believed that
this would be "the line taken against you in California in the campaign."
Less than three weeks later, in Wheeling, West Virginia, the little-known
senator from Wisconsin, Joseph McCarthy, made his first headline-grabbing
speech promising to expose Communists in the U.S. State Department.

Nixon's road show opened in early April, and like Helen Douglas's helicopter barnstorming it featured a mode of transportation that would enter
California campaign lore: the bright yellow, wood-paneled, 1949 Mercury
station wagon, or woody, license-plate number 80A3255, equipped with a
loudspeaker and 120-watt amplifier, on loan from car dealer Henry Kearns
in Alhambra and driven by a man named Ace Anderson. Soon the sight of
Richard Nixon standing on the roof or the tailgate, microphone in hand,
would become familiar in small towns from one end of the state to the
other. According to the candidate's office, he made thirty-nine "station
stops" (as the Nixonites termed them) at street corners during just the first
two weeks of the tour. In a letter to local organizers, Murray Chotiner described the visits this way:

> The car will stop at some suitable place in a particular community. The driver
> of the car will play a couple of records to attract a crowd, and Dick will then
> make a five or ten minute informal talk to those who gather. The purposes of
> this type of campaigning are:
>   1) To get away from the orthodox campaign of only speaking at banquets
> and to our own people;
>   2) To reach, and talk to the people;
>   3) To get maximum publicity on the type of campaign that Dick will be
> waging particularly since he promised that he will carry the campaign into
> every community in the state.

While the candidate spoke, his wife circulated among the crowd, passing
out plastic Nixon thimbles printed with the words SAFEGUARD THE AMERI-
CAN HOME. "One human interest story which I think could be used in regard to the campaign trip," Nixon wrote Chotiner, "is the fact that Pat not
only goes along for the scenic effect but that she also goes as my secretary . . . she is an accomplished stenographer."

No town or potential audience was too small, and Chotiner had ordered
that it be arranged for Nixon to "meet the people on 'Main Street,' such as
barbers, druggists, clerks etc." Before or after the talk, the candidate would
cruise the sidewalks, shaking hands, barge into shops and restaurants to greet
sales help and customers, visit the local newspaper office, appear on radio

programs. Now that Sheridan Downey was out of the race, he could concentrate his fire on Helen Douglas and her "phony" stands on tideland oil,
power, and water, and the 160-acre limit on farm irrigation. He also singled
out his opposition to Truman's national health-insurance plan, claiming it
would lead the country "down the road to state socialism." But nearly everywhere he spoke—at rodeos, Rotary Club lunches, and big-city ballrooms—
he discovered, in the question-and-answer period, that people most often
asked about the Hiss case or the latest charges by Senator McCarthy.

Back at his office in Whittier, meanwhile, his congressional district staff
sent out another ninety thousand reprints of his Hiss speech. The bulk went
to Democrats while others were targeted at specific professionals, such as
Realtors, doctors, and attorneys. The copies mailed to newspapers around
the country received a good response, Nixon told one of his supporters.
Dorothy Cox, the candidate's secretary, sent two thousand copies of the
HUAC pamphlet *100 Things You Should Know About Communism* to the state
American Legion and even offered to frank envelopes for the organization.
With little GOP opposition, Nixon could pursue Democratic crossovers
without risk. Chotiner believed that even if his candidate didn't win the
Democratic primary, a large vote in that column would throw the Douglas
campaign into a tizzy and discourage some of her funders.

Nixon outlined each street-corner talk in pencil on yellow paper. The
notes for station stops in Taft and Bakersfield read: "Can't tell you everything
I believe but: a) don't believe in wild promises you can't keep—I tell the
truth, b) Better life for average guy . . . grew up in a store . . . reduce your
taxes . . . reduce your prices, c) chance for small business, d) Chance to
live—no place for Commies in gov't—let them go abroad—never seen one
who wanted to go. . . ." The first drafts of major speeches were written by
others, such as Bill Arnold, but Nixon revised them heavily. Like Helen
Douglas, he heard criticism that his speeches were too long, and unlike his opponent he sharpened them considerably as the campaign wore on. He also
made use of what he called confidential data on local newspapers, compiled
by Pat Hillings, as well as profiles of "local dignitaries" he could hurriedly
study as he pulled into town. Still, he maintained a "grave, deliberative" style,
often wearing a "troubled frown," Mary Ellen Leary observed in the San
Francisco *News.*

After a few days of station stops and other appearances, Nixon sent a
memo—typically detailed—to Murray Chotiner and his publicity manager
in the north, Harvey Hancock. Among other things, he suggested that
"whenever possible, get local business men and plants to let out their employees for a few minutes to attend the street meeting. . . . Make it clear to

all chairmen that when I am taken [into a shop] *I am to meet everybody in the establishment, not just the ones they happen to know, or the bosses.* Otherwise, I think such visits may do more harm than good." He offered one more bit of sage advice. He had noticed that Warren's people often recruited Democrats to cochair the campaign in largely Democratic areas, and Nixon believed his people should do the same.

Later he sent Chotiner aide Ruth Arnold a memo appealing for no more late-night appointments (because he had breakfast meetings almost every day) and asking that his hosts be sent a standard form of introduction. "All along the line, those who introduce me are constantly referring to the manner which I was selected as a congressman [in 1946]. This is old stuff and not effective. The introduction should be brief and should relate particularly to my present national prominence and experience."

By this time, the Nixon campaign coffers were flush, but driving for more Democratic votes cost a lot of money. Another few thousand dollars would be helpful, even if it came in a questionable way: through Nixon's first association with a so-called bagman.

A month before the June primary, the candidate besieged Owen Brewster of Maine, head of the Republican Senate Campaign Committee, requesting a five-thousand-dollar donation. The committee had the cash, but there was one problem: It was prohibited from playing favorites in a primary; it could not fund candidates who faced even token opposition. But Nixon was relentless, so Brewster reluctantly borrowed five thousand dollars in his own name from a Washington bank to make the loan. But how to advance it and cover his tracks? The senator chose as his conduit Henry "the Dutchman" Grunewald, known variously as a lobbyist, a gambler, an influence peddler and a "fixer," and the deal was done. (Grunewald's role as Nixon bagman would not be revealed until 1952.)

As primary day neared, Nixon won the editorial support of an overwhelming majority of newspapers across the state, many of which barely mentioned the Democratic candidates. The San Francisco magazine *Argonaut* declared that "a new champion has arisen on the American political stage . . . Nixon could be the Moses to lead [the GOP] into the promised land. . . ." A survey of media coverage commissioned by Chotiner revealed that the *Paso Robles Journal* had announced that Nixon would be "a good running mate for Eisenhower in 1952." The same survey praised a Petaluma newspaper for virtually reprinting a profile of Nixon sent over by the candidate's office. Of the *Los Angeles Times*, it was simply noted, "Gave everything."

A man in Pasadena wrote Nixon expressing alarm at the press depictions of Helen Douglas as the Pink Lady. Recalling the campaign against Jerry Voorhis in 1946, he asked, "Have you started another whispering campaign?"

By all accounts, the high point of the campaign—"one of the greatest thrills of my political career," Nixon later commented—was a rally at the Long Beach Municipal Auditorium close to primary day, attended by a feverish crowd of more than two thousand. A small band of pro-Douglas unionists marched outside while Nixonites taunted them with cries of "Go back to Russia!" The sound system of the yellow Mercury was put to good use, blasting out a recording of "If I Knew You Were Comin' I'd've Baked a Cake," delighting the Nixon advocates.

In a closing series of radio broadcasts, Nixon's announcer, Tom Dixon, introduced the candidate as "California's brilliant young congressman, the man described by Washington's best-known news correspondents, columnists and radio commentators as the most outstanding prospect to appear on the national scene in many years." On June 6, Nixon's landslide in the GOP primary, along with his strong showing among Democrats, did nothing to diminish this luster.

Judas Goats and
Red Pepper

T wo days after the California primary the banner headline in the *Los Angeles Examiner* screamed, NIXON, DOUGLAS, IN BITTER ROW. Nixon, already on the attack, had charged that Douglas "violently fought" attempts to expose Communist infiltration of the U.S. government. Douglas had responded by calling her opponent "a man who has a record of consistent opposition to the general welfare." The press, both national and local, predicted a dramatic fight to the finish. "Big political guns from both parties will be trained on California's final Senate race in November," a wire-service dispatch disclosed, and President Truman would likely "hit the whistlestops."

Republican leaders targeted the Nixon-Douglas race as one of the GOP's two must-win contests. (The other pitted Scott Lucas, the Senate majority leader, against Republican challenger Everett Dirksen in Illinois.) *The Christian Science Monitor* congratulated California voters for giving the nation a grandstand view of a big state choosing between "two divergent political approaches," which it identified as "middle-road" versus "left-liberal." Both candidates were "Americans of good stock . . . both deeply grounded in national traditions, opposed to Russian communism," but Douglas had a social conscience patterned on the FDR model, "championing the people against big money interests."

Near the close of the primary contest, Douglas had charged that the California press had ignored her campaign, but she predicted that "they'll have to print the news about me the day after the primaries. There will be no way to ignore the fact that I've won the nomination." Indeed, this came to pass, but not necessarily to her advantage. The California papers predicted an almost apocalyptic contest—"fireworks (A-bomb sized)," as one put it—but those expressing an early opinion all backed Nixon. The *Los Angeles Times* affirmed its earlier endorsement when it noted that the election of Helen Douglas "could serve no purpose other than to afford her and her left-wing following greater opportunity to spread their doctrine of class hatred and social antagonism." The local Hearst papers also supported Nixon. One of them called Douglas a "red radical" and identified "a clear choice between an American progressive and a siren in a 'beautiful' red dress. . . . Manchester Boddy was a sacrifice to the pinko lady of the hustings."

Two days after the primary, Drew Pearson, in his syndicated column, reported that an unnamed California politico had just asked one of the major wire services whether it had on file any photographs linking Helen Douglas to Moscow or to fellow travelers, such as singer Paul Robeson. According to Pearson, the wire service could find only one "Moscow" photo—and sent to California a picture of Douglas presenting an award to *New York Times* reporter Warren Moscow.

In the days following the California primary Democrats partial to Douglas expressed concern about her prospects. Paul Jacobs, writing in the *New Leader,* observed that she was in the fight of her life against a "handsome young man" who "cannot be underestimated as a vote-getter. . . . Energetic and personable, he looks and acts like the hero of a story that might appear in the *Ladies Home Journal,* in which a young lawyer, usually called Derek or Lance, takes on a political campaign as a crusade and smashes through to victory." Nixon, he predicted, would have ample funds, "a smear machine" at his disposal, and a generally supportive press. One of the few papers favoring Douglas, a small weekly in L.A., condemned "little Nixie Nixon" and complained that the *Los Angeles Times* was now calling Douglas "red hot."

A leading Democratic activist warned Douglas that the Nixon effort would likely exceed dirty campaigns of the past. She knew that in 1946, Nixon had tried to catch Jerry Voorhis off guard and force him to respond to false accusations. *He's not going to throw me off track,* she vowed to herself. *I'm going to talk about what I want to talk about.*

Her friend Alan Cranston, a former quarter miler at Stanford, now a home builder in Palo Alto, had succeeded Cord Meyer, Jr., as head of the United World Federalists and was about to move to New York. A longtime Democratic activist, Cranston admired Douglas's odd blend of glamour and down-to-earth qualities. He advised her to appeal to minority groups, noting the growing influence of Asians, Chicanos, and blacks in California, and suggested she emphasize strengthening the United Nations and preventing an atomic arms race. If anyone could overcome the obstacles facing a woman running for the Senate, she could, he believed.

Like the policeman in *The Mikado,* the lot of the California Democratic organization was not a happy one, the San Francisco *News* declared. The party's preferred candidate had lost in the Senate race, and it didn't care for James Roosevelt. The newspaper offered a solution: Democrats should take a walk in the top races and concentrate on electing Edmund G. "Pat" Brown, its mainstream candidate for attorney general. Another moderate Democrat, Assemblyman Samuel Yorty, was delighted with Douglas's primary run, for it cleared the way for him to take her seat in Congress. Still, he hoped Douglas would lose to Nixon and he was confident she would. A lobbyist for a big utility had told him that when she was dubbed the Pink Lady, "that's the end of her."

But Helen Douglas remained upbeat. She was particularly pleased with a telegram from Senator Claude Pepper, recently defeated by Congressman George Smathers in the Democratic primary for the U.S. Senate in Florida—the year's first political contest that hinged on anticommunism. Applying the Pink Lady smear in a deeper hue, Smathers had dubbed his opponent Red Pepper. (*Time* magazine poked fun at Smathers's use of code language, claiming that he had accused Pepper of being an "extrovert" who "practiced nepotism" and had a sister who was a "thespian.") Replying to Pepper's telegram, Douglas told him that she had waged the rest of the campaign "for you, Claude. . . . I was fighting with renewed vigour against all the vicious, wicked things that were said and done against you in that campaign." She wanted California to show the rest of the country that "the failure of the voters in Florida to support a great public figure, was only an isolated instance of political nearsightedness." She could not have known that after Pepper's defeat, Richard Nixon had called Smathers and asked, "How'd you do it?"

Three days after the California primary, famed screenwriters Dalton Trumbo and John Howard Lawson were dramatically hustled off to jail, the first of the so-called Hollywood Ten to exhaust their legal appeals in attempting to overturn contempt citations issued by Congress in 1947. Eight colleagues who had also refused to divulge whether they were members of the Communist Party faced sentencing later in the month. The case had already reverberated in the California Senate race. Richard Nixon, who helped lead the fight in Congress for issuing contempt citations, frequently pointed out that Helen Douglas was among the handful who voted against the sanctions. On the defensive, Douglas explained that she had not campaigned in support of the Ten but had merely protested the methods employed by HUAC to subjugate them. Clearly, this was a fine point Nixon would not let slide for long. Communist subversion in Hollywood did not loom as a factor in many Senate campaigns, but it would obviously shadow the California contest. Anything involving the movie industry was a local issue in this state.

On the surface, however, it was business as usual in Hollywood. There was an early buzz over Billy Wilder's *Sunset Boulevard,* due to open in August. Marlon Brando, after his screen debut in *The Men,* was a hot commodity, with Elia Kazan's movie version of *A Streetcar Named Desire* in production. Katharine Hepburn and Humphrey Bogart agreed to star in John Huston's *The African Queen.* A movie based on Irving Stone's *Lust for Life* was planned, with Jose Ferrer scheduled to play van Gogh. Stanley Kramer was trying to get Kirk Douglas to star in *High Noon.* Hedda Hopper reported that young Elizabeth Taylor, about to appear in the sequel to her current hit, *Father of the Bride,* had "lost weight and is glad of it." MGM embarked on Mervyn LeRoy's *Quo Vadis,* likely to be the most expensive film ever made, at around six and a half million dollars. Orson Welles was reported to be making a picture in Paris titled *The Unthinking Lobster,* about a fat, stupid Hollywood film producer named Meyer. Howard Hughes, who had taken over RKO two years before, seemed to have "an aversion" to going onto the lot, visiting only once "and then at midnight and alone," according to the *Hollywood Reporter.*

Frivolity reigned, but below the surface, Hollywood worried. Television, still in its infancy, was already keeping moviegoers at home, cutting into profits. What would happen when half of all families, instead of one in ten, owned a TV set? Yet there was something equally threatening for the movie industry to ponder. After two years of relative quiet regarding Communists in Hollywood, another noisy, accusatory period was clearly approaching. This did not bode well for Helen Douglas, for she retained strong ties to liberal Hollywood through her personal and political friends and her marriage to an outspoken movie star. Because of her theatrical speaking style, she reminded listeners of her acting career every time she spoke on the radio.

The previous year the California State Senate's Un-American Activities Committee, chaired by Jack Tenney, charged that many Hollywood-related figures, including Helen Douglas, were "within the Stalinist orbit." Others named were John Huston, Fredric March, Lena Horne, Orson Welles, Dorothy Parker, Danny Kaye, Gene Kelly, Charles Chaplin, Gregory Peck, Vincent Price, Clifford Odets, Pearl Buck, and Lillian Hellman. Several of the accused responded quickly, and none too favorably. "If they don't cut it out I'll show them how much an American can fight back, even against the state if the American happens to be right," Frank Sinatra warned. Katharine Hepburn, on the other hand, "refused to dignify" Tenney's charges with a reply, according to a spokesperson. She had suffered in Hollywood ever since supporting Henry Wallace for president in 1948.

Douglas, already contemplating the Senate race—and sensing that much more of this was coming her way—had decided to meet the charges head on. In doing so, she set a dangerous precedent for herself. "I've never been able to make up my mind whether he [Tenney] is a crackpot or the instrument of those special interests which seek to destroy liberalism in America," she said. "Whichever he is, Mr. Tenney is undermining our form of government when he attempts to make people believe that liberal and Communist are synonymous."

The Tenney charges soon fell flat. A year later, however, just before Douglas won the primary, the Motion Picture Alliance for the Preservation of American Ideals, a broad-based group headed by John Wayne, renewed the attack, calling for a "complete delousing. Let us in Hollywood not be afraid to use the DDT on ourselves. We don't need much of it." The movie industry had better move fast, the group warned, because Congress had reportedly compiled a list of one hundred "subversive Communists" in Hollywood and was likely to move on them during the coming year. The *Los Angeles Times* praised the Alliance while finding it "strange that many motion picture executives have no sympathy with this effort."

Then, on primary day in California, Dalton Trumbo and John Howard Lawson left Los Angeles for incarceration in the East. Arriving at La Guardia Airport in New York on June 7, Trumbo told supporters, "We are angry and resentful in having to go to jail but I don't see how we can do otherwise in all conscience." The next morning at Pennsylvania Station admirers hoisted the two left-wing writers onto their shoulders and carried them to the train that took them from New York to Washington. At the federal courthouse attorney Martin Popper cited letters of support from George Bernard Shaw, Albert Einstein, and others. Arguing for probation, he declared that the jailings represented a threat to the Bill of Rights and the free expression of "ideas, opinions and associations." Lawson and Trumbo had already suffered enough, the attorney added, having been blackballed in Hollywood for nearly three years; they were family men, with wives and children to support.

The judges, however, sentenced them each to a year in prison and a one-thousand-dollar fine, the heaviest penalty possible. The two writers were then handcuffed, herded into a prison van, and taken to the city jail to await transfer to the federal prison in Ashland, Kentucky. It was a day few in Hollywood believed would ever come. "Before the Ten actually went to the pokey, nobody believed anybody was going to jail," Robert Kenny later reflected. Now that the courts had thoroughly endorsed the notion that an individual's political beliefs were fair game for congressional investigators—and a reasonable basis on which to deny employment—an inquisition in Hollywood could begin in earnest.

The crusade against the Hollywood Ten was rooted in the long-simmering labor wars within the movie industry. Union activists had been accused of pro-Communist leanings since the early 1930s, and this only intensified following World War II. Many of the liberals, including Melvyn Douglas, had joined anti-Fascist or civil rights committees that later appeared on lists of suspected Communist fronts. At the same time, a secret Communist Party chapter thrived in Hollywood.

In the spring of 1947, Congressman John Rankin of Mississippi, a segregationist and noted anti-Semite, called for a purging of Communists in the film industry. A few months later HUAC subpoenaed forty-seven witnesses, identifying nineteen of them as likely to be "unfriendly," most of them writers. Dalton Trumbo suspected three motives: to destroy trade unions in Hollywood, to halt left-wing political activity, and "to remove progressive content from film."

When the hearings opened in October, chaired by J. Parnell Thomas, several witnesses, including actors Gary Cooper and George Murphy, took the stand to denounce the Red infiltration of Hollywood. Ronald Reagan, president of the Screen Actors Guild, revealed how left-wingers raised funds and won friends in Hollywood but argued against outlawing the Communist Party, believing "democracy is strong enough to stand up and fight against the inroads of any ideology." Walt Disney, who had served as an informer for the FBI since 1940, testified that the Cartoonists' Guild of America was dominated by Communists who hoped to one day turn Mickey Mouse into a fellow traveler. Adolphe Menjou drew applause when he announced, "I am a witch-hunter if the witches are Communists."

Congressman Richard Nixon questioned witnesses only briefly, for he had little expertise or interest in the entertainment business. He pointedly asked Jack Warner, however, whether his studio had ever made a movie showing the evils of communism. No, Warner confessed, but he promised to make one very soon. Later, when Louis B. Mayer of MGM was asked whether he was making any anti-Communist pictures, he replied with a chuckle, "I think the one we are going to start shooting promptly."

Then some of the Unfriendly Nineteen were called to the stand. As a group, they had made a crucial decision. They knew the committee would ask each whether he ever belonged to the Communist Party. And, indeed, many of them were or had been CP members. Should they answer the question truthfully or lie or not answer it at all? They decided to refuse to answer the question, citing not the Fifth but the First Amendment—freedom of speech—implying the right to remain silent when asked about fundamental personal beliefs and political affiliations. The committee did not go for it. "This is the beginning of concentration camps in America!" Dalton Trumbo shouted as he was hauled away.

With that, HUAC called off the rest of the hearings, with only eleven of the Unfriendly Nineteen having been called. The eleven included several of the well-known writers—Trumbo and Lawson, Lester Cole and Ring Lardner, Jr.—and director Edward Dmytryk. The committee felt it had proved its point and recognized that bullying did not play well with the public. Indeed, polls suggested that at least half of all Americans felt the HUAC hearings were unnecessary and that the witnesses should not be punished, for Communist activities in Hollywood were not much to worry about. Still, as Carey McWilliams soon pointed out, the committee had conducted a form of psychological warfare on the American people, for "what was done to the Ten served as a warning to all."

At the start, the Ten—the eleventh witness, Bertolt Brecht, fled to Germany after the hearings—gained considerable support from colleagues (such as John Huston, Frank Sinatra, Lucille Ball, Melvyn Douglas, and Judy Garland) and other liberals who were unaware that eight of the ten *were* linked to the Communist Party. Studio boss Louis B. Mayer, who was concerned mainly with the bottom line, said that whether his employees were Communists or not didn't matter—if they could write good scripts, they were good Americans. Eric Johnston, president of the Motion Picture Association of America, announced, "I will never be party to anything as un-American as a blacklist."

In November 1947, however, Congress voted to cite the Ten for contempt. Richard Nixon and Helen Douglas, as usual, took opposite sides on the issue, Nixon speaking passionately in favor of the action and Douglas among the daring group of seventeen representatives who voted against the move. She called the Hollywood hearings "a tragic farce." Although she personally wished the Ten had answered all questions to "clear the atmosphere," she nevertheless condemned the trampling of individual rights. And she denounced HUAC for telling the studios "what kind of pictures they should make. I am opposed . . . to communistic propaganda on the screen, but I am equally opposed to movies becoming dedicated to the spread of reactionary propaganda."

Congressman Rankin, unimpressed by the opposition, read off a list of additional Hollywood suspects, among them Danny Kaye, Eddie Cantor, and Edward G. Robinson, all of whom had Anglicized their Jewish names. "There is another one here who calls himself Melvyn Douglas," he added, "whose real name is Melvyn Hesselberg."

The following month the Hollywood Ten were indicted by a grand jury. With that, support began to dwindle, particularly in Hollywood, where the studios looked unfavorably on anyone campaigning in their behalf. (Humphrey Bogart now called his initial support "ill-advised, even foolish . . . impetuous.") An audience in Chapel Hill, North Carolina, reportedly threw stones at a movie screen in a theater showing a film with Katharine Hepburn, a supporter of the Ten.

At a meeting in New York, fifty leaders of the industry capitulated to the Red hunters and agreed that they would never employ anyone suspected of being a Communist—and promptly discharged the five members of the Hollywood Ten then under contract. Essentially, the Ten were to be sacrificed to establish the anti-Communist credentials of industry leaders, to prevent boycotts, and to protect popular left-wing (but not Communist) actors and actresses from feeling the heat. Dore Schary, a top movie producer and crusading liberal, opposed the firings but explained that he went along with them because he was faced with "supporting the stand taken by my company or of quitting my job. . . . Anyway, I like making pictures." Studio bosses, Lillian Hellman wrote in a prophetic article, were frightened men, "and you pick frightened men to frighten first. Judas goats, they'll lead the others, maybe, to the slaughter for you. The others will be the radio, the press, the publishers, the trade unions, the colleges, the scientists, the churches—all of us."

Trumbo and Lawson stood trial first, as a test case, and the two were found guilty of contempt of Congress in April 1948. During the appeals, some of the Ten found work abroad or wrote in the United States under pseudonyms; others just went broke. Still, the movie studios refrained from extending the blacklist while the Hollywood Ten cases worked their way through the courts. The studio czars, meanwhile, responded to the call of Congressman Richard Nixon to make films that would warn Americans about the evils of communism. This was one type of "message" film looked on with favor.

Soon shoddy little films like RKO's *I Married a Communist* and Republic's *The Red Menace* arrived in theaters to tepid public response. "We'd be in a hole if we didn't have Lassie," an MGM official told Lillian Ross of *The*

New Yorker. "We're sure of Lassie. Lassie can't go out and embarrass the studio. Katharine Hepburn goes out and makes a speech for Henry Wallace. Bang! We're in trouble. Lassie doesn't make speeches." Another executive explained how self-censorship worked. "It's automatic, like shifting gears," he explained. "I now read a script through the eyes of the D.A.R. [Daughters of the American Revolution], whereas formerly I read them through the eyes of my boss." William Wyler, the director, said he feared Hollywood would produce no more films like *The Grapes of Wrath.* "In a few months," he predicted, "we won't be able to have a heavy who is an American."

Lawson and Trumbo lost one appeal after another. Trumbo's agent suggested that he might be able to clear his name and get off the blacklist if he presented himself to right-wing columnist Westbrook Pegler and confessed his sins. Trumbo refused, noting the absurdity of a Jew begging an anti-Semite like Pegler for forgiveness, and fired the agent. In May 1950, the U.S. Supreme Court upheld the convictions by a vote of 6–2 (Justices Hugo Black and William O. Douglas dissenting), meaning the Ten would likely be sent off to prison in June. Ben Margolis, attorney for the defendants, declared that the Supreme Court had given "legal sanction to witchhunting, political blackmail and McCarthyism," and he placed the responsibility for this on President Truman, who had recently appointed two conservative justices to the top court. The same day it doomed the Ten the Supreme Court refused to review the case of writer Howard Fast and ten other members of a left-wing group that had failed to turn over certain records to HUAC. Two weeks later Dalton Trumbo and John Howard Lawson were behind bars.

With that, the legal saga of the Hollywood Ten was ending, but politically it was just beginning. With the test case settled to their liking, emboldened HUAC staff members now spoke of launching a follow-up investigation that would clean all the Red trash out of Hollywood—and finally establish blacklisting on a serious scale.

Even before facing HUAC-alumnus Richard Nixon in the general election, Helen Douglas had to explain her position on the Hollywood Ten to often hostile reporters and Democratic voters. "I took my stand in defense of the principles of justice," she revealed, not in defense of Hollywood or "any individual's behavior" before HUAC. Even worse for Douglas, the jailing of Trumbo and Lawson was likely to discourage liberal activism and fund-raising in Hollywood. The candidate could take heart from the fact that in 1948, sixteen of the seventeen members of Congress who had voted against the contempt citations had won reelection anyway. But that was before Russia got the bomb, before Alger Hiss was convicted, before Joe

McCarthy produced his famous list—before the Hollywood Ten started going to jail. Douglas knew that Nixon was certain to challenge her on this issue long before November. And if she was really unlucky, a new wave of blacklisting would wash over Hollywood, forcing her to take positions likely to hurt her, again.

After the June 6 primary, while Helen Douglas rested, the Nixon team met to discuss strategy. The next weekend, eighteen Nixonites from all regions of the state, plus their candidate, attended a retreat at a ranch near Santa Barbara. The discussions must remain "confidential," campaign chairman Bernard Brennan informed the guests in advance.

Nearly all the Nixon advisers were veteran Republican leaders—business owners or lawyers, middle-aged or younger, decent and respectable white Protestants, and overwhelmingly male—with mainstream political views. They certainly weren't out to lead an anti-Communist crusade. Their cause was simply to elect Dick Nixon, a man they believed, quite rightly, was the brightest and most attractive GOP candidate to emerge in years. They differed somewhat from his grassroots volunteers; for starters, many of *them* were women. In addition, a fair number of these local activists backed Nixon mainly because of his aggressive role in nailing Alger Hiss, and they expected him to continue to put anticommunism at the top of his agenda. A rancher from Los Gatos typified this view. When he wrote a letter congratulating Nixon on winning the primary, he added, "Now let's get rid of the communistic vermin."

At the Santa Barbara retreat, the Nixon top brass focused on nuts and bolts—finance, organization, scheduling—but also on issues and tactics. Nixon played the central role in nearly every discussion, no matter how trivial.

Some advisers thought the candidate had sounded the anti-Communist theme long enough; it was a volatile subject and severely polarizing. Senator McCarthy, for example, seemed to be the hero of the media one week and a demon the next. As far back as mid-March, one top adviser had warned that "too much emphasis on the Red situation will make you look like an Old Maid looking under the bed too frequently!!" And besides, voters were more interested in issues relating to agriculture and jobs and labor, which Helen Douglas would emphasize. Campaign officials advocated taking a poll to find out which local issues the public cared most about.

But Nixon disagreed. He felt that emphasizing what he called un-American activities had served him well and that he should continue to ride that horse. On the campaign trail—in fact, everywhere "outside so-called intellectual circles," as he once put it—he still got his strongest response when he talked about the Hiss case. Longtime Nixon stalwarts might be sick of the subject, but many new recruits had "pledged their support as a result of the case." Other issues may be just as important, but in Nixon's experience the average citizens didn't particularly want to hear about them. What they wanted to hear about was the Communist threat.

This fit in well with Murray Chotiner's number-one campaign principle: Keep your opponents on the defensive by ignoring their charges, and make them respond to *your* issue. He advocated a "stop and drop" campaign. Chotiner would finagle a copy of Douglas's campaign schedule and send Nixon field-workers ahead of her. They would supply local activists and journalists with fresh allegations that she would have to answer when she arrived. Another plan was to organize "flying squadrons" of Young Republicans who would attend Douglas rallies and heckle her, "just to embarrass the candidate," as one Nixon associate described it.

Rather than conduct the campaign in Douglas's arena, domestic politics, they would try to lure her onto Nixon's turf, the Red menace at home and abroad. Already they were compiling research on Douglas's political affiliations and voting record that might call into question her opposition to communism. One particular piece of evidence appeared most promising. L. W. Jeffery, secretary of the Republican Senatorial Committee in Washington, had sent Bill Arnold of Nixon's staff a fateful memo "comparing the votes" of Helen Douglas and Vito Marcantonio.

Widely considered the most left-wing member of Congress, charismatic Vito Marcantonio had been elected on the American Labor Party ticket in New York City. Manchester Boddy had linked him to Douglas in the primary but had not bothered to compare their voting records. But L. W. Jeffery did, and found 247 occasions during the past several sessions of Congress when Douglas and Marcantonio had voted alike and only 31 times when they voted differently. This should not have been surprising. Douglas generally voted the Democratic Party line, as did Marcantonio. Yet the sheer number of joint votes, taken out of context, might paint her Red by association.

Bill Arnold had passed the Jeffery memo along to Nixon with the notation that he was "holding this for later use."

All this was in keeping with Murray Chotiner's emphasis on denigration. Although party activists often claim they don't want a negative campaign, deep down they know that "if you do not deflate the opposition candidate before your own campaign gets started, the odds are that you are going to be doomed to defeat," he believed. "Because, if we like it or not, the American people in many instances vote against a candidate, against a party, or against an issue, rather than for a candidate or an issue or a party."

The other major tactical issue settled at Santa Barbara concerned a subject new to all of those present: how to campaign against a woman. Few women had appeared as candidates in the first half of the century, and even fewer had been elected, so there was no book on how to treat, or defeat, them in a campaign. The Nixon men would have to improvise. Prescott Bush, who had just defeated a female candidate in the GOP Senate primary in Connecticut, admitted that he was "afraid of women who are pithy and sharp and sarcastic at times. . . . I mean, I don't know how to deal with them, because I've always been trained, and trained myself, to be deferential to them, and I don't know how to deal with them when they respond differently."

Even if a woman candidate was the political equal of a man, still a dubious assumption, she was *different*. This view of women in or out of politics was typical for the time. Many men—Republican or Democratic, conservative or liberal, wealthy or working class—did not believe women belonged in top levels of government or in other traditionally male realms. A bank president from Turlock had put it concisely in a recent letter to Nixon: "Women have no business in Congress." Yet male voters could be persuaded to make exceptions in certain instances, as they had in Helen Douglas's three campaigns for her House seat.

"Now we have a woman who is running in opposition," Frank Jorgensen, the self-titled "ramrod" of the Nixon operation in southern California, told his comrades at the ranch. "I've learned enough in politics to know that the average woman in politics reasons with her emotions rather than her head." This attitude fed the idea of keeping up a steady attack on their opponent and waiting for her emotions to get the best of her when she attempted to respond.

Nixon himself did not disagree with this. A key aide later said that the Republican candidate had "a total scorn for female mentality." Another said that he considered women "an extra appendage, a different species." Pat Nixon would later reveal that she could hardly recall her husband ever paying a woman a compliment, "except to remark on her hat." But now the candidate argued for carefully modulating his approach. There could be no "cattiness" or any explicit suggestion that Douglas was underqualified because of her gender. Yes, Nixon was pleased that Douglas, and not Boddy, was his opponent. She was more vulnerable politically, and she would not be taken seriously by many men and by some women. But he knew he would have to be circumspect in his attacks, or he might seem to be bullying her. ("I knew that I must not appear ungallant in my criticism of Mrs. Douglas,"

Nixon would later record in his memoirs.) In that sense, at least, running against Douglas would be harder than taking on any male candidate.

Privately, however, Nixon and some of his associates sometimes mocked Douglas in sexist or sexual terms. One official, for example, typed out the following note and attached it to a Douglas campaign leaflet showing her carrying a market basket: "Suggestions for renaming the picture: 1) All that remains is the cheesecake. 2) True or falsie." But there could be none of that in public.

"Politics in the United States ceased being a stag party over thirty years ago," Perle Mesta, U.S. minister to Luxembourg, said in 1950. Yet reporters and others in Washington often treated congresswomen merely as trophies, as aberrations, sometimes as objects of ridicule. What they wore, how they set their hair, and which cologne (if any) they favored sometimes seemed more significant than anything they said or did. Congresswomen were still "looked on in many places as sufficiently odd to warrant a place in a zoo or museum," Helen Douglas commented early in 1950. The press dubbed a veteran congresswoman from Massachusetts the Lass from Mass.

A woman first came to the House in 1917, three years before full suffrage, when Jeannette Rankin, a social worker, was elected in Montana. A Republican and a pacifist, she became famous for voting against U.S. entry into World War I and in 1941 cast the only vote against the declaration of war on Germany and Japan. (Rankin ran twice for the Senate, both times unsuccessfully.) During the 1920s and '30s, the House averaged about five female members every term, in a total membership of around 435. Prior to Helen Douglas's election in 1944, thirty-one women had served in the House; but only four lasted more than four years, and even fewer rose to leadership positions. Women had long been active in politics and social causes, but had no experience as candidates or legislators to fall back on. Altruism did not carry one very far in the electoral arena. One trailblazing congresswoman left office declaring, "Politics is man's business."

The first female U.S. Senator, Rebecca Felton of Georgia, age eighty-eight, was appointed in 1922, but she served just two days. The second woman senator, Hattie Caraway of Arkansas, was selected to fill her late husband's seat in 1931 and was later elected and reelected in her own right. She served with little distinction, however, and lost her seat to J. William Fulbright in the primary race of 1944. Four other women entered the Senate, three through appointment; none served more than a year.

A high-water mark was reached in 1945, with eleven women in the House and one in the Senate. This was a particularly impressive group. Besides Helen Douglas, it included Clare Boothe Luce (the actress and writer),

Chase G. Woodhouse (a professor of economics and a state official), Jessie Sumner (a judge), and Emily Taft Douglas (a League of Women Voters leader and wife of Senator Paul Douglas). Two years later all but Helen Douglas were gone, having either retired or been defeated at the polls. In 1949, the small complement of women on Capitol Hill reached ten: five Republicans, five Democrats.

Most of these women were fundamentally different from those serving before World War II, who often gained their seat by appointment after their husband died or retired. The majority of the second generation of women came to prominence or won election primarily on their own. They were a varied lot. The group in 1950 included a former judge, a schoolteacher, and the wife of a corporate president. Their dean was Mary Norton of New Jersey, a longtime force on the House Labor Committee. The senior Republican, Edith Nourse Rogers of Massachusetts, was the first woman whose name was attached to a major piece of legislation. She preferred wearing suits on the floor of the House to "blend in"; a dress sticks out "like a sore thumb," Rogers explained.

The steely Margaret Chase Smith of Maine had been elected to the House in 1940, after her husband, a congressman, fell ill and died. Reelected three times (with strong support from women's groups), she won a Senate seat in 1948, thus becoming the first woman to enter the Senate by election, not appointment. Still, she was often depicted stereotypically: as overly emotional and prone to change her mind. When she dared speak out against McCarthyism on June 1, 1950, Westbrook Pegler complained that she "took advantage of the special privileges of her sex"—her "feminine prerogatives."

The women legislators declared themselves the equal of any male but also drew on female qualities to emphasize how they were different. "War to women, to most women, is never an adventure," Helen Douglas asserted, adding that the world would be closer to peace if half the members of Congress were women, "our best women." Many of the congresswomen emphasized that as homemakers they knew better than men the effects of high prices and inflation. Douglas in particular encouraged women not to be intimidated by politics. "Government is only housekeeping on a large scale," she quipped.

Judging the ten female legislators of 1949 as a whole, one columnist called them mostly "outstanding," adding that their male colleagues "will admit that, on the average, the female House members have better records than the males." Why? "One reason is: they've got to be good," he explained. Isolated on the Hill, they must "stand on their own ground and fight their own battles. Often they have to fight their own party organizations. . . . It's a good bet there will be more of them as time goes on."

But how many more and how soon? Three decades after the passage of the Nineteenth Amendment, women represented less than 2 percent of the lawmakers on the Hill. Although they were slowly gaining respect, most politicians outside Washington still acted "as if women had no brains, that they weren't capable of anything more than a seven-year-old child could do," India Edwards, vice chairman of the Democratic National Committee, complained. Only two women had ever served as a governor. The number of women serving in state legislatures reached a peak of 234 in the mid-1940s—about five per state—but slipped back as men returned from military service. This retreat came at a time when women, for the first time, outnumbered men in the United States, both in the census tallies and on the voter-registration rolls. Since the end of the war, commentators had predicted an upsurge in female officeholders to reflect the new demographics and the growing participation of women in politics, but by 1950 the breakthrough had not yet occurred. Women may have outnumbered men, but they were only a little more likely to vote for one of their own. Like most men, many of them felt a wife's place was in the home.

What did occur, however, was a more intensive wooing of the "distaff vote" or the "petticoat vote" (as it was known) by candidates of both parties. They did this on the stump and by supporting legislation that was friendly to women. Helen Douglas herself had sponsored measures mandating equal pay for equal work, establishing a minimum wage for telephone operators, and permitting tax deductions for working women who hired housekeepers.

Party activists, who had always welcomed female volunteers to perform menial tasks, now sought more female candidates. But they did this, according to one analyst, not out of a sense of fairness but for the sake of image; the party that appeared to be more open to women at the top might corral more of their votes right down the line, for as a reporter observed, the first loyalty of women activists "appears to be to the party and then to their sex."

To emphasize the double standard that still existed in judging women as politicians, one of Helen Douglas's aides told her, "Where the average run-of-the-mill Congressman pulls something at least once a year that belongs strictly in the comic strips, you can't EVER do it [or] ten thousand people, including all the trained seal columnists, will jump up and scream that's what you get for putting a woman in office. . . ." Later, when Douglas announced for the Senate, a Sacramento newspaper declared that if California ever elected a woman to that body, "she ought to be the outstanding woman on the Pacific political horizon. She ought to be so gracious and so able that she will reflect credit on her sex, and make it inestimably easier thereafter for other able and efficient women to be elected to the national political scene." But Helen Douglas, the editorial pointed out, was "a disciple of the rough and tumble school of politics"; she represented a "seething" congressional district, and therefore her nomination "would be a calamity."

Outside Congress, the female members would often gather at testimonial teas or to be photographed for magazine articles on the new breed of political ladies, but they did not form a women's caucus or anything like it. Eager to be respected by their male colleagues on their own merits, they never met as a group to discuss common goals, issues, and strategies. Margaret Chase Smith proudly explained that "women did not function as women but as members of Congress." The only perk a female Senator needed was a *wife,* she declared.

Douglas, in a major address early in 1950, advised women to enter politics "as individuals, not as women." They should have neither extra burdens nor preferences placed on them because of their gender. "There is not much gallantry in politics," she explained, "and it may be a good thing." It might take a long time, she lamented, for women to make up even one quarter of Congress, but that time would certainly arrive. To get there, women must be "willing to compete on an equal basis with men and expect no favors. They must neither ask nor give quarter. They must have principles, based on knowledge and understanding of their own, and not be the mere shadows of someone else. Given this," Douglas concluded, "women will take their proper place in the public life of America, and the nation and the world will be the better for it."

While the Nixon campaign, in the aftermath of the primary, rushed along, Helen Douglas resisted, knowing that almost five months remained until election day. This had always been her pattern: frantic activity followed by total bed rest. An old friend once confided that she did not know anyone who enjoyed "the supine posture" more. Helen's energy "tends to collapse suddenly when the need for it is over," the friend explained. "There is no gradual wearing; one moment she is intensely alive, the next she isn't there at all. If you take the trouble to look you will find her lying flat on her back somewhere in profound and utter relaxation."

Also, unlike her opponent, she had many domestic duties to attend to, among them arranging for household help for the summer in both Los Angeles and Washington and planning for camp and other vacation activities for sixteen-year-old Peter (mainly in Washington) and eleven-year-old Mary Helen (mainly in Los Angeles). Nixon's wife took care of things like that. Douglas's husband was still half a continent away.

Friend and mentor Lyndon Johnson told Douglas he was "proud" of her. Returning to Washington from a check-up at the Mayo Clinic, Johnson wrote Douglas that her primary win was the happiest news he had heard in a long time, "perhaps since November 1948," when he was elected to the Senate. "Of course, I know nothing of California politics, but reading the weathervanes as well as I can from this distance, it seems clear to me that a favorable wind is blowing for you." A few days later Douglas thanked "dear Lyndon" for his help, observing that "as a reader of weathervanes, I am sure you are expert," and promised to call him when she got back to Washington.

Douglas had been close to Johnson since her start in the House. While quite different in many ways, politically and personally, the two shared a flamboyant, crusading spirit and a New Deal optimism. Johnson, who came to the House in 1938 and was close to Speaker Sam Rayburn, was a good fellow to know and only too eager to show the vivacious Douglas the ropes. The Texan, his friend George Reedy later remarked, was "terribly vulnerable to women. . . . He would pour out his soul to them in nothing flat. They all reminded him of his mother."

Helen Douglas spent a lot of time in Johnson's congressional office or at his side in the corridors, and he often visited at her home. Some of Johnson's associates strongly suspected that their relationship had become rather too intimate, with Melvyn Douglas often away. A Douglas congressional aide later confirmed that Johnson surely "made passes" at Helen—because "he made passes at everyone, even me." But she doubted Douglas had any sexual escapades on Capitol Hill; the congresswoman's devotion to her husband and children remained strong.

Johnson and Douglas had, in any event, an almost playful relationship. On one occasion she sent him a brief, congratulatory letter: "Just saw the latest report on you in the newspapers. HURRAH! HURRAH! HURRAH!" In reply, he said he was impressed by the "length and dignity" of that letter.

When Johnson was elected to the Senate (after winning his primary by a razor-thin margin) in 1948, Douglas told him that she and Mel were "expecting great things of you now. . . ." Douglas, however, did not agree with Johnson's conservative position on many civil rights and labor issues. One of her associates would refer to him as "an SOB" for embarrassing Helen in his 1948 race—getting her to drum up trade union support for him and then delivering an antilabor speech. Johnson, for his part, would later call Douglas "an emotional girl . . . [who] often said and did things that I didn't approve of" but added that she was "basically our kind of a person."

Yet Lyndon Johnson, little known in California, could not help Douglas much in her Senate race. The Democrat whose imprimatur the candidate craved was President Truman. Several California Democrats had implored Truman to denounce Boddy's "smears" during the primary, but he had referred all such requests to the Democratic National Committee. The president's popularity, which had bobbed up and down, seemed to be on the rise, yet he continued to draw barbs, like the one offered by radio comedian Fred Allen, who in early June confessed that the president "still reminds me of the guy who stepped in to watch the grocery store while the boss was away." Of course, this was the humble quality that many people liked about Truman.

It was hard to get a read on Truman's view of women in politics. Unlike Franklin Roosevelt, who had an activist wife at his elbow, Truman "had never known any professional women," India Edwards once observed. Thanks to Edwards, he had appointed many women to commissions and other secondary posts, among them the first female U.S. district court judge, but he had named no women to his cabinet. Edwards nearly persuaded him to appoint a woman to the Supreme Court, but the president told her that the other justices protested that a woman would disrupt their work habits.

Emma Guffey Miller, a Democratic leader from Pennsylvania, wrote Truman in 1950 at the request of several women who wanted him to press the issue of equal rights. They believed this would help swing the vote to Democratic candidates in several close contests. But his reply gave Miller "a solar plexus blow," she confided to Edwards. In his brief note, the president had expressed his appreciation for a "continued interest in the equality of men and women" but hastily added, "It has been my experience that there is no equality—men are just slaves and I suppose they will always continue to be." Miller told Edwards she was shocked that Truman would respond to a serious query with a "facetious slap in the face," and she was worried "about what such an attitude will do to the party in states like Maryland and Connecticut where only a few thousand votes mean defeat or victory."

Privately, some Democratic activists counseled Truman to stay out of California. The *Los Angeles Times* claimed he had been warned that Helen Douglas and James Roosevelt were political "liabilities." In addition, Truman could not campaign for Douglas without also stumping for Roosevelt, and he detested Jimmy for encouraging Eisenhower to challenge him for the Democratic presidential nomination in 1948.

There was an additional complication, which an oil executive from Oakland relayed to Truman on June 9. Earl Warren, he pointed out, had always run independent campaigns. This year, if he followed form, Warren would not endorse Richard Nixon. But if Truman came to California, the governor (easily the most popular political figure in California) would no doubt throw his weight behind Nixon, with disastrous results for Douglas. And there were other considerations.

Alfred Cohn of Los Angeles informed the White House that Nixon "will have a world of oil money. That's the big source of political money out here and they know how to spend it." All in all, Truman's involvement in the race, he advised, would not help the party, the Democratic candidates, "and most important of all, himself."

Six days after Dalton Trumbo and John Howard Lawson surrendered, another spectacular jailing proved Richard Nixon prophetic, thus boosting his chances for election. Back in February, after the arrest and confession of Klaus Fuchs, the British physicist who gave Manhattan Project secrets to the Soviets, Nixon had called for a full congressional investigation "to find out who may have worked with Fuchs in this country." Arthur Krock, in *The New York Times,* observed that the Fuchs case "had an impact and a powerful one" on the entire Truman administration, since it opened the president to new charges that he was lax on subversion. After the Hiss case and then the Fuchs confession, there was a kind of hysteria over Soviet spying in the United States. Among the scientists under renewed scrutiny by the FBI was J. Robert Oppenheimer, who had directed the Manhattan Project but later ruffled feathers by opposing the hydrogen bomb project. In May, an informer told California's Tenney Committee that in 1941 she and her husband had attended a meeting of Communist Party leaders at Oppenheimer's house in Berkeley.

The FBI was certain Fuchs had not acted alone. It badly needed more arrests and would soon have them. On June 15, agents seized a twenty-eight-year-old machinist in New York and accused him of passing classified material to the Russians. He was David Greenglass, a former member of the Young Communist League. The FBI said that while working with the Manhattan Project at Los Alamos in 1945, Greenglass had supplied top-secret information to chemist Harry Gold, who had served as the intermediary between Klaus Fuchs and the Soviets. Gold was already in custody.

Investigators believed that Greenglass, who quickly confessed his crimes, would lead them to other members of the spy ring. Following this trail was crucial for U.S. intelligence agencies, which had been excoriated by Richard Nixon and others for allowing the "secret of the A-bomb" to slip into Soviet hands. Greenglass, according to the FBI, explained his actions this way: "I felt it was gross negligence on the part of the United States not to give Russia the information about the atomic bomb [in 1945], because she was an ally." But the stockily built spy said more than that: With little prompting, he implicated his wife, Ruth Greenglass, and his brother-in-law, Julius Rosenberg.

From Harry Gold's confession, the FBI had already suspected Rosenberg's involvement in the spy ring. Agents had been tailing him for days but did not know whether he was the ring's mastermind or messenger boy. They wanted to find out which—in either case, he could lead them to others. So, at eight o'clock on the morning of June 16, the day after the Greenglass arrest, three agents visited the thirty-two-year-old Rosenberg at the apartment he shared with his wife, Ethel, and two young sons in a modern high-rise building on Manhattan's Lower East Side. Rosenberg, who ran a small machine shop, took the news of Greenglass's arrest calmly. He refused the agents' request to search the apartment but agreed to accompany them to their headquarters for questioning. "What would you say," an agent inquired, "if we told you your brother-in-law said you asked him to supply information to the Russians?"

"Bring him here," Rosenberg replied. "I'll call him a liar to his face." Then he called a lawyer, who advised him to exit the FBI office quickly, since he had not yet been charged with anything. With that, Rosenberg put down the phone, bowed to the agents (in a mock farewell), and walked away a free man.

Richard Nixon responded to the Greenglass arrest by stressing the rising threat of Communist subversion. J. Edgar Hoover had revealed on June 9 that more than half a million subversives, a "potential fifth column," resided in the United States. Of this number, nearly 10 percent were Communist Party members—exactly 6,977 in California—often living underground. Many were engaged in spying operations far more extensive than anything attempted by the Nazis, the FBI director charged. Now Nixon elaborated, warning of a "reign of terror if we ever cross swords with Russia." American Communists, he added, had been trained in sabotage, instructed to seize military arsenals and contaminate food supplies—"a virtual blueprint for revolution."

War Fever

A week after the California primary Helen Douglas returned to Washington and on June 20 paid a visit to President Truman. Emerging from the White House, she predicted she would win in November but was evasive on the question of whether the president promised to actively support her. In a letter to a friend, however, she revealed that both Truman and Democratic National Committee chief William Boyle had "laid down the law to the key Boddy supporters," ordering them to return to the fold and back her. "This is going to make a great difference," she reckoned. Then she added: "Boyle will come to California and I am sure the President will. He said he would if he was convinced it would be helpful."

Four days after meeting with Helen Douglas, Harry Truman flew to his home in Independence, Missouri, for a short vacation. Late that evening he was about to retire for the night when the telephone rang. It was Dean Acheson, the secretary of state, back in Maryland. "Mr. President," he said, "I have very serious news. The North Koreans have invaded South Korea."

Acheson had just received a cable from the U.S. ambassador in Seoul reporting that North Korean infantry had crossed the 38th parallel, the border that had divided the two sectors since 1945, and had already overrun at least one city. All signs indicated an "all-out offensive," the ambassador asserted. Acheson, in response, had requested a meeting of the UN Security Council even before calling the president. Truman said he would fly back to Washington immediately, but Acheson advised him to sit tight and await further developments. Truman then suffered a rare night of little sleep.

Early the following afternoon, with the North Koreans continuing to advance, Truman returned to Washington, for an emergency meeting with military and diplomatic advisers. Only three weeks had passed since Truman boasted that the United States was closer to securing "a permanent peace" than it had been for five years. Now, in the limousine ferrying them from the airport, he suddenly told Acheson, referring to the North Koreans, "By God, I am going to let them have it."

But if an American response was a fait accompli, a question remained: What sort of response? Diplomatic or military? If military, would it be confined to supplying armaments to the South Koreans or to providing air and naval support, or would it mean deploying U.S. troops—less than five years after the end of World War II?

Korea, of course, had been a powder keg ever since the defeat of Japan and the convenient if tragic division of the country. At first a line across the peninsula at the 38th parallel was merely used to mark occupation zones: To the north, the Japanese army would surrender to the Russians; to the south, to the Americans. But quickly the zones became institutionalized, with a pro-Soviet (totalitarian) government in the north and a pro-American (totalitarian) government in the south. South Korea, largely agricultural but with twenty million citizens, had twice the population of its highly industrialized neighbor, and its leaders hoped to send its army north one day and reunite the nation.

By 1950, all U.S. troops had been withdrawn from the south, and despite frequent clashes along the 38th parallel, high U.S. officials, such as Dean Acheson, downplayed the danger and did not include Korea on a list of vital American interests. Many of these officials had contempt for South Korea's dictator, Syngman Rhee, and his notoriously brutal police. Rhee, who had spent much of his life in America (and had earned a doctorate from Princeton), had long promised, and delayed, free elections, finally succumbing to U.S. demands and scheduling a vote for May 30, 1950. The results were embarrassing to say the least; Rhee's opponents easily took control of the national assembly. Worse, this came at a time when the North Koreans, emboldened by the Communist victory in China, were advising the South Koreans to depose Rhee and promote reunification. It even seemed possible that Rhee, like Chiang Kai-shek, would have to flee his country. As much as the United States loathed him, it did not favor that resolution. Now the attack from the north had restored Rhee's full authority in the south. The invasion, I. F. Stone soon observed, gave him "a sudden respectability."

At the Blair House meeting, Truman learned that his advisers agreed with his inclination to strike back. General Omar Bradley said, "We must draw the line somewhere." Dean Rusk, from the State Department, warned that an all-Communist Korea would be "a dagger pointed at the heart of Japan." All assumed, based on fragmentary evidence, that the Soviet Union directed and sponsored the invasion, probably to test U.S. resolve and possibly as a prelude to a similar move somewhere in Europe. Truman concluded (he later revealed in his memoirs) that if the Communists "were permitted to force their way into the Republic of Korea without opposition from the free world, no small nation would have the courage to resist threats and aggression by stronger Communist neighbors." The Cold War apparently was ending; an era of heated conflict between Soviet and U.S. proxies was surely about to begin.

By this time, the UN Security Council had voted unanimously to condemn the North Korean assault and called for an end to hostilities. Russia, for once, was in no position to veto the measure, its ambassador having walked out months earlier to protest the UN's refusal to unseat Nationalist China.

The following evening, with the North Koreans still advancing, Truman ordered U.S. naval and air support for the South Koreans under the direction of General Douglas MacArthur and his headquarters in Tokyo. At the same time, he issued three other directives that would have equally far-ranging effects: a dramatic increase in U.S. aid (including military advisers) to the French in Vietnam; a buildup of U.S. military forces in the Philippines; and a vow that the U.S. Navy would protect the Nationalist Chinese on Taiwan from any assault from the mainland. Still, Truman's generals opposed sending troops to Korea, with Omar Bradley arguing that no matter how many he sent, MacArthur would demand more. The South Korean ambassador to the United States said, "We don't expect American soldiers to give their lives for us."

On June 27, as the North Koreans captured Seoul, Syngman Rhee fled south, and Truman (after gaining overwhelming support from congressional leaders) announced the start of direct U.S. air and naval strikes. The United Nations voted to endorse the action, the first time it ever sanctioned a military course. Intervention had already begun, but the UN's move allowed the United States to claim wide international support.

Convalescing from a heart seizure at his home in Beverly Hills, William Randolph Hearst ordered editorials charging that the United States had been "caught napping" in Korea, just as it had been in the last war. "Being caught napping," he added, "is a U.S. custom." Support for the president from the American media and the public appeared fairly solid, however. The press did not challenge the official story: The North Korean invasion, ordered by Moscow, had been a complete surprise and was unprovoked—and if the United States did not take a stand, one domino after another would soon topple, starting perhaps with West Germany. A *New York Times* reporter observed that the march across the North-South Korean border appeared similar to the attacks that Hitler used to make—"to feel out the opposition." A few Republicans accused Truman of creating a war to win seats in November, but most muted their criticism. "We've got the rattlesnake by the tail," one key Republican observed. "The only way to get rid of him is to hit him hard on the head and the sooner the better."

Few journalists questioned whether the invasion really came out of the blue. This indeed was a sensitive question for the White House. If the invasion was a surprise, it represented an embarrassing failure of U.S. intelligence. And if it wasn't, one had to wonder whether the Rhee cabinet or the White House actually wanted a confrontation with the North Koreans. Hanson Baldwin, the esteemed *New York Times* military reporter, cited U.S. documents noting "a marked buildup by the North Korean People's Army along the 38th Parallel beginning in the early days of June." Other scattered intelligence reports had warned that an attack from the north was imminent.

The United States, in any case, was acting now, and the mood of America, so tense and fearful just forty-eight hours earlier, now shifted to one of pride and excitement—a war fever. "We have drawn a line, not across the peninsula, but across the world," intoned Edward R. Murrow. "We have concluded that Communism has passed beyond the use of subversion to conquer independent nations and will now use armed invasion and war." At a press conference, however, Truman denied that the United States was at war, preferring to use the term "police action."

Then, in the early morning of June 30, the president received a message from General MacArthur asserting that only the use of U.S. combat forces would prevent a rapid Communist victory in Korea. Truman later claimed that this was the hardest decision he made as president, for there was no telling how the Soviets and the Red Chinese would respond. But characteristically, he made it immediately. MacArthur would get his troops. Later that day he wrote in his diary: "Must be careful not to cause a general Asiatic war."

When war broke out, Richard Nixon had just returned to California to address a Veterans of Foreign Wars convention. For days, he had little to say about the conflict and Truman's response to it. Understanding what was happening and why in a part of Asia few knew or cared about before was difficult for any American. Nixon had the additional difficulty of figuring out how the issue might play in the California Senate race. It could break either way for him or perhaps spin off in multiple directions, depending on the flow of events. America, no doubt, would rally around the flag, and the flag was being carried by a Democratic president whose popularity would probably get a boost. Criticizing any military decision Truman made over the next several weeks would be hard, particularly since Nixon fully endorsed the U.S.-UN intervention. Only if that commitment flagged or the war effort soured could a Republican strongly attack the president (and, by extension, other Democrats) on this issue.

On the other hand, the Red aggression in Korea could only fuel fear and hatred of Communists, especially since many young American soldiers were likely to die at their hands. And even if some of his aides disagreed, anti-communism was *his* issue, Nixon knew. Many Americans now agreed that Communist sympathizers in the United States should be closely watched, even quarantined, if not prosecuted. In mid-June, the Red-scare tactics of Senator McCarthy and other extremists were flagging. Now the war in Korea put them right back on track.

Nixon was no McCarthy; blacklisting and loyalty oaths made him uncomfortable. But his anti-Communist credentials were impeccable, and after June 24 he could say, in reference to Korea, "I told you so"—while remaining supportive of the U.S. president directing the war effort. "It happens that I am a Quaker; all my training has been against displays of strength and recourse to arms," he said in one speech. "But I have learned through hard experience that, where you are confronted with a ruthless, dictatorial force that will stop at nothing to destroy you, it is necessary to defend yourself by building your own strength."

Helen Douglas strongly endorsed Truman's decision to intervene in Korea. Nearly everyone except Vito Marcantonio did, and it must have pleased her to stand with the vast majority for a change on such an issue. But the war, many of her aides sensed, would make her Senate race even more difficult, for Red hunting in California and throughout the country would likely grow more fervid and less disciplined. If the war did not end quickly and decisively for the American side, Truman would be accused sooner or later of inviting the Communist assault. And that time would probably arrive before the fall election.

Responding to this uncertainty, Douglas went on the attack. A friend in San Mateo had reminded her that in January of that year, Nixon had voted to kill a sixty-million-dollar aid package for South Korea—and funding had been denied *by a single vote.* Douglas, stung by Nixon's early assaults on her patriotism, now charged that this vote showed "the failure of so many to understand the communist threat in the Far East." In fact, it may have "influenced the communist decision to strike now in Korea."

Douglas was prone to zealotry and overstatement in the heat of battle, and she knew it. "My Irish always works overtime," she once confessed, "when I am operating on impulse." Facing a former debating champ who had promised a "rocking, socking campaign," Douglas would do well to take the offensive only if she had her ducks in a row. In this case, she did seem to have the goods on her opponent vis-à-vis Korea. But there were mitigating circumstances, as Nixon and his allies in the press quickly explained. Conservatives, at the urging of the China Lobby, had opposed the Korean aid bill in January largely because it did not also include money and armaments for Chiang Kai-shek's regime. And indeed, Nixon and others ended up ordering the money for Korea just three weeks after the first vote, when aid for Taiwan was added to the bill. It was hard to believe that this three-week delay encouraged the North Koreans or had any material effect on South Korea's defenses.

In a written statement, Bernard Brennan responded coolly but effectively, denouncing Douglas's "campaign of vicious lies." His candidate's voting record showed his support of military assistance to resist Communist aggression "on every occasion." Douglas, on the other hand, had denied aid to Taiwan and "consistently opposed actions by Congress and the President to stop the spread of Communism." Brennan cited a number of examples: Douglas contested military aid to Greece and Turkey, opposed a loyalty program for federal employees, and (on fourteen occasions) voted against appropriations for HUAC—in every case joining Congressman Vito Marcantonio, "the notorious Communist party-liner from New York City." Brennan vowed to let Californians decide between the two candidates entirely on the basis of "their records as members of Congress. We propose to present those records to the voters during this campaign EXACTLY FOR WHAT THEY ARE, without distortion or misrepresentation. WE WILL KEEP THE RECORD STRAIGHT—AND THE TRUTH SHALL PREVAIL!!"

A few days after war came to Korea, a 213-page paperbound book entitled *Red Channels* landed on the desks of editors and executives in New York City. Ed Sullivan had revealed in his syndicated column that a "bombshell will be dropped into the offices of radio-TV networks, advertising agencies and sponsors this week with the publication of *Red Channels,*" and those who took the trouble to skim its contents recognized that Sullivan for once had not exaggerated. For *Red Channels* (subtitled *The Report of Communist Influence in Radio and Television*) provided the raw material for a wave of blacklisting finally to begin in earnest throughout the entertainment industry.

Behind the new book stood a trio of former FBI agents, Theodore Kirkpatrick, Kenneth Bierly, and John G. Keenan, all young men in their thirties. Since 1947, their American Business Consultants, Incorporated, located on West Forty-second Street in New York, had periodically published a four-page report called *Counterattack: The Newsletter of Facts to Combat Communism,* which exposed evidence of Communist infiltration overlooked by the mainstream media. The three men—partly funded by Alfred Kohlberg, the millionaire businessman and lobbyist for Chiang Kai-shek—also served as freelance Red hunters, charging employers in various industries five dollars to investigate whether so-and-so on their payroll was a Communist or fellow traveler. "The way to treat Communists is to ostracize them, . . ." *Counterattack* affirmed. "It's the only DEED that will prove you believe what you say about them."

At first, however, few heeded the call, and the three men tempered their accusations after Fredric March and his wife, Florence Eldridge, sued them for slander. But in 1950, in the wake of Senator McCarthy's revelations, the *Counterattack* crew, with the help of former naval intelligence officer Vincent Hartnett, decided to lay it on the line, excavate everything from their files on famous entertainers, and publish it for the first time in the form of a book that could be widely distributed, even sold over the counter. The result was *Red Channels,* which featured on its cover a huge hand, glowing red, about to seize a microphone (which was already leaning to the left). In his introduction, Hartnett observed that Communists "now rely more on radio and TV than on the press and motion pictures . . . to transmit pro-Sovietism to the American public." He charged further that a blacklist was already in place, but it was being used by Red sympathizers against anti-Communists.

The heart of the book was a massive, alphabetical index of 151 suspicious characters and the alleged Red fronts they had once belonged to. Some of these groups had disappeared more than a decade earlier; many others expired with the end of World War II. One suspect had somehow managed to join forty such organizations; others made the list for belonging to just one. Some of the names were routine—you couldn't throw this kind of party without inviting Lillian Hellman or Dorothy Parker. But other names were relatively new and raised eyebrows: playwright Arthur Miller; conductor

Leonard Bernstein (he earned seventeen citations); composer Aaron Copland; stripper Gypsy Rose Lee; actors Jose Ferrer, Jack Gilford, Burgess Meredith, Lee J. Cobb, and John Garfield; actresses Judy Holliday, Jean Muir, Ruth Gordon, and Uta Hagen; comedians Zero Mostel and Henry Morgan; author and anthologist Louis Untermeyer; folksinger Pete Seeger; radio commentators William L. Shirer and Howard K. Smith—and so on.

As the writer Stefan Kanfer would observe, "Every man's past was amber in which all discretions lay preserved." Fortunately for Helen Douglas, however, her husband's name and past affiliations with left-leaning groups were notably absent.

The listings in themselves accomplished nothing. Punitive action was needed, and it would come only, the creators of *Red Channels* observed, if "freedom-loving" readers "*act* on the information." Readers could pen letters of protest to the sponsors of radio and TV programs written by or starring *Red Channels* listees; they could write to the networks and to the advertising agencies that customarily hired the talent on behalf of the networks. To fan the flames still higher, *Counterattack* warned:

IN AN EMERGENCY
IT WOULD REQUIRE ONLY THREE PERSONS (subversives):
    one engineer . . .
    one director . . .
    one VOICE before a microphone
TO REACH 90 MILLION AMERICAN PEOPLE
    WITH A MESSAGE

Within days of *Red Channels*'s emergence, hundreds of protest letters began arriving at the offices of ad agencies, corporate sponsors, and radio and TV stations across the country.

It was the most terrifying moment in the history of the Washington Gridiron Club roasts. One evening in late June, reporters and other guests meeting in the ballroom of the Statler Hotel had just sat down to dinner when the doors flew open and a dark, heavyset, slightly balding man around forty years of age burst in carrying a revolver, a rifle, a machine gun—and a slingshot. Members of the audience gasped, some in horror but most in recognition. The gunman suddenly threw away his weapons and held out a baby's diaper. "I'll never let *that* go," he declared. "That's my cloak of immunity." With that, a musical group started a number, and the intruder broke into song, spoofing a recent Bert Williams tune:

"Somebody lied,
Somebody lied, dear, dear;
Some say there is no evidence,
While others say it's clear. . . ."

The guest of honor had arrived: Joseph R. McCarthy, the increasingly controversial Republican senator from Wisconsin. The onlookers applauded vigorously, perhaps in relief. Many of them had never taken Joe McCarthy seriously. There was some comfort in recognizing that he might not take himself seriously either.

The Gridiron roast came at an uncertain time for McCarthy. He had ridden a roller coaster since making his famous February 9 speech in Wheeling. When *The New York Times,* in a June 24 article, reviewed the past four months, the headline said it all: MCCARTHY UP TO NOW—NONE OF HIS CHARGES HAS BEEN PROVED BUT NO CONCLUSION IS IN SIGHT. The same day, Freda Kirchwey, editor of *The Nation,* provided her own summary, which included a definition of something called McCarthyism: "slander masked as testimony, protected by privilege, and broadcast as fact." President Truman privately predicted that McCarthy would eventually be thrown out of the Senate for telling lies. A more positive assessment was provided by the Gallup Organization: A poll showed that 43 percent of all Americans felt McCarthy's crusade was "a good thing," and 31 percent felt he was "doing harm." Nearly two thirds of all Americans believed there was "something" to his charges.

Red scares, of course, were nothing new in the United States. Anticommunism had characterized American life for more than three decades, but only periodically, as in 1950, did it become a paramount political and social issue. The first Red scare, from 1919 to 1920, followed the Bolshevik victory in Russia. Fear of immigrants and aliens—"foreign influences"—importing Communist views spread rapidly. A. Mitchell Palmer, attorney general, ordered his investigation unit, led by J. Edgar Hoover, to build dossiers on left-wing groups and their leaders, a list that soon contained more than two hundred thousand entries. Without any evidence of criminal activity, thousands of aliens suspected of Communist sympathies were rounded up in the so-called Palmer Raids, jailed, or expelled from the country.

During the 1930s, desperate social conditions created by the Great Depression caused a surge in Communist activity, little of it out in the open. The Communist Party in the United States had gained thousands of new members and was unquestionably gaining influence in many labor organizations. This sparked the formation in the late 1930s of legislative panels to investigate subversive activities. The first HUAC, led by Congressman Martin Dies of Texas, established a list of over one thousand pro-Communist organizations, including labor unions, political groups, and even the Boy Scouts of America (for promoting "international understanding"). It was Dies who introduced techniques later embraced by Joe McCarthy, leaking information to the press to defame suspects and linking individuals to Red fronts with which they had only the most tenuous connection. Phrases used by Dies committee members later became part of the McCarthy lexicon: "I hold in my hand," "soft on communism," "coddling Communists." (Jack Tenney's so-called Little HUAC in California gained similar notoriety.)

For a time, Dies was the darling of the press and drew wide public support. In 1940, Congress passed the Smith Act, which outlawed the advocacy or abetting the overthrow of the U.S. government "by force or violence." Not only actions but also words could now be considered seditious. But then World War II intervened, the Soviets became our allies, and defeating the Germans and the Japanese took precedence over Red hunts.

When the war ended, however, and U.S.-Soviet relations deteriorated, concern about domestic communism again appeared. Americans resented that they had destroyed German and Japanese fascism at a terrible cost and now had to worry about Soviet expansion and infiltration. J. Edgar Hoover fed the fears, claiming Red subversion of unions, movies and radio, schools, publications, and—yes—the federal government. By his count, there was exactly one Communist for every 1,814 Americans. This did not seem like much, but he pointed out that at the time of the Bolshevik revolution there was one Communist in Russia for every 2,771 people. This comparison was cited over and over. Many top officials, including the secretary of labor, called for outlawing the Communist Party.

At this moment, in 1947, President Truman took a fateful step, which, according to one writer, "codified the association of dissent with disloyalty and legitimized guilt by association"—and led inexorably to the rise of Joe McCarthy. Attempting to deflate Republican charges that the government had been infiltrated by Reds, Truman issued on March 21, 1947, executive order 9835, initiating the first federal loyalty program. The action came nine days after the president announced (as part of his call for military aid for Greece and Turkey) what became known as the Truman Doctrine, stating that it is the policy of the United States to help "free peoples" everywhere stand up to Communist aggression. Isolationists in Congress and other war-weary Americans had questioned the nature of this commitment. Truman could hardly hope to gain overwhelming support for intervention without appearing to stand up to communism at home.

The president no doubt had his eye on the political calendar, too. In another year, he would be running for reelection, and the Republicans were poised to club him on the Communists-in-government issue. Clark M. Clifford, a top Truman adviser, would later comment that the loyalty issue had been "manufactured," and there "was no substantive problem. . . . We never had a serious discussion about a real loyalty problem. . . . It was a political problem. Truman was going to run in '48, and that was it. . . ." The president, in fact, believed (as he wrote in a letter) that the United States was "perfectly safe so far as Communism is concerned—we have far too many sane people." The essence of loyalty, in any case, is devotion *freely* given.

Now, however, three million federal employees faced dismissal if investigators judged them "disloyal" to their government. Dossiers compiled by HUAC and the FBI provided evidence, and the attorney general was ordered to draw up a definitive list of Communist front groups. The measure was fraught with dangerous imprecision. Disloyalty was broadly defined. It could be found in blatant acts, such as sabotage or espionage, but also in "sympathetic association" with groups that the attorney general held to be "totalitarian, fascist, Communist or subversive." Dismissal would not take into account whether the employee was engaged in a sensitive national security job or worked as a clerk in the Agriculture Department. Workers could be fired for something they did or simply because they had a spouse or a close relative friendly with a Communist front—or they might be let go for heavy drinking or sexual indiscretions that left them vulnerable to foreign agents. What constituted suspicious political activity was highly subjective, of course. Advocating civil rights for Negroes often set off alarms. In other words, ideas as well as overt acts could be penalized. Even worse, the accused had no right to confront their accusers or even know exactly what the charges were and who had made them.

In addition to an assault on civil liberties, Truman's move was a tragic political blunder. Instead of assuring Americans that he had a minor problem under control, the president lent credibility to the fears of some, spurring on (rather than silencing) the right-wingers on HUAC. He would now also have difficulty rejecting on moral or civil libertarian grounds the call for even more onerous background investigations and loyalty oaths (which his executive order in fact inspired). In his 1948 election campaign, Truman defended what he called "the most loyal civil service in the world"—the same workforce he was subjecting to a rigorous loyalty test. Carey McWilliams would complain that "few observers have been willing to admit that

McCarthyism is a direct outgrowth of the President's loyalty program. The parentage . . . is unmistakable. . . ." Truman had "given the sanction and prestige of his office to the very doctrine which he now seeks to disavow. The President does not believe in witches, but . . ."

After operating for more than two years, the Review Board had dismissed only 201 employees (and half of those cases were still under appeal). Not one instance of espionage had yet been proved, but that hardly meant the program had little punitive affect. Thousands of accused federal employees had gone through months or years of suffering; many others were kept jittery wondering whether they were next. The apparently reassuring results so far—no spies uncovered—only caused conservatives to charge that the Truman administration's standards for disloyalty were, well, un-American.

Still, by 1949, the steam seemed to be going out of the federal inquisition. HUAC, which had earlier probed Communists in government and in Hollywood, suddenly pulled in its horns. Democrats had seized control of Congress again, and HUAC, under its new chairman, John Wood, acted more responsibly, even earning reluctant praise from Helen Douglas.

Then, in February 1950, Senator McCarthy, visiting West Virginia, waved around a sheet of paper, which was probably blank but was said to contain the names of Communists in the State Department, and all hell broke loose again. Revived, loyalty oaths soon spread to state and local governments, to factories and offices, to schools and trade unions. In Indiana, professional wrestlers had to take the oath, and in California, amateur archers. F. O. Matthiessen, the noted critic, committed suicide in March 1950, shortly after appearing before a Massachusetts legislative committee investigating communism. "As a Christian and a Socialist believing in international peace, I find myself terribly oppressed by the present tensions," he wrote in a farewell note. Even the American Civil Liberties Union succumbed. Its board of directors decided to insert in its legal briefs a clause declaring the organization's opposition to communism. What Carey McWilliams recently called a "symptom of insecurity" had become a national obsession, and "the more we yield to the anti-Communist hysteria," he warned, "the more we minimize the differences between democracy and Communism."

But now, in late June, after riding high for weeks, Senator McCarthy was in eclipse again—for once, not because of his actions but on account of events he could not control. The war in Korea had unified all Americans against the Communist menace, and the senator's name and face were driven off the front pages.

McCarthy told a friend that "the war situation makes it difficult to continue the anti-Communist fight effectively—at least temporarily." Why only temporarily? "I am inclined to think that as the casualty lists mount and the attention of the people is focused on what actually has happened in the Far East, they can't help but realize there was something rotten in the State Department. . . . I still think this [Communist subversion] is going to be the major issue this fall. . . ." If it wasn't, neither Joe McCarthy nor Richard Nixon had much of a political future.

In the days following the U.S. intervention in the Far East, Helen Douglas continued to publicize her opponent's ambiguous stand on Korean aid, not recognizing that this wouldn't fly. Stridently, Douglas denounced Nixon's "whining . . . alibiing and distorting" his votes on Korea. She asked members of the press to resist "printing the campaign drivel emanating from my opponent's headquarters" concerning this issue. But the newspapers stood up for Nixon. "In none of her characterizations on the legitimate stage," columnist Kyle Palmer wrote in the *L.A. Times,* "was she more arresting than in her recent outburst against Communism and Communists. She made news just as the man who bit the dog made news: It was new and different."

Palmer was nothing if not consistent. He had been the kingmaker of Republican politics in California since the 1930s. Short, cynical, curly haired, bow tied, and pushing sixty in 1950, he was known by friends and enemies alike as Mr. Republican or the Little Governor. When candidates came by the *L.A. Times* or his table at Perrino's to pay him a visit, it was known as "going to kiss Kyle's ring." He felt that telling candidates what to do was improper, but he expected them to follow his "advice." Asked what happened when they didn't, he replied, "They got into trouble . . . political trouble." Palmer once advised Richard Nixon to smile when he clobbered an opponent—and apparently Nixon took the instruction to heart.

The *Times* was only one third of the press axis that virtually dictated the rise and fall of countless Republican politicians in a state where the party machinery was practically dead. Political editors at the *Oakland Tribune* and the *San Francisco Chronicle* followed the dictates of their publishers (Joseph Knowland and George Cameron, respectively). When he started, Palmer heeded the directives of the owner of the *Times,* Harry Chandler, but when Harry's son Norman took over, Palmer was pretty much left to do what he wanted. Other political editors also lacked Palmer's experience, his forum (he wrote articles, columns, and editorials), and most important, his inclination to play the part of power broker—to nakedly, even proudly drop the guise of objective reporter. Palmer's idea of balanced coverage was reflected in his public explanation that even though his newspaper opposed Helen

Douglas "from time to time, as space allows, news accounts of what she has to say and what she is doing will be published."

Asked how far a political editor should go in assisting a candidate, he said, "Try and get him to make speeches and statements that will help him." For Richard Nixon in 1950, as for many others, he went even further, advising the candidate on many matters and writing some of his speeches and radio talks. In 1934, Palmer had played a crucial role in helping the hapless Frank Merriam defeat Upton Sinclair in the gubernatorial race. In 1948, he did a little more for Earl Warren, assuring him a spot on the national ticket as Tom Dewey's running mate.

Palmer privately called Helen Douglas "a delightful woman, a very beautiful woman, and a pretty good politician." But he considered Nixon a kind of dream candidate: clean-cut but a gutter fighter with "an old head on young shoulders," as he put it. Nixon was the best tactician he'd ever seen and also "intellectual." Without the journalist's promise of support, Nixon may have never run for Congress in '46 or for the Senate in '50. Palmer promoted, and was on friendly terms with, Earl Warren, Bill Knowland, and even a Democrat, Pat Brown, but only Nixon sought his views with such devotion, and vice versa. They had an almost father-son relationship.

Now Palmer accused Nixon's opponent of acting more like a "comedienne" than "her more accustomed role as a star in the tragic dramas":

> To what extent her sudden turn to the right will benefit Mrs. Douglas' political fortunes is problematical. She has been long identified with leftist leadership and leftist aims. Some aspects of her voting in the House of Representatives placed her toe to toe with Communist sympathizers. She has been highly praised in some quarters by the native Reds, and she should not be pained or astonished if a certain degree of skepticism creeps into conjectures concerning the reasons for the seeming rift that has developed between her and her erstwhile admirers.

Nixon, on the other hand, "has never deviated from a set course since he first was elected. He will meet Mrs. Douglas on the major issues, and issues will decide the Senatorial race. Douglas has a little of the best of it in glamour, but when it comes to issues, Nixon has the lady at a disadvantage."

Murray Chotiner, meanwhile, just sat back and marveled. Was it possible that Helen Douglas was going to do exactly what he wished: attack Nixon's strengths—foreign policy and anticommunism—instead of exploiting his weaknesses? The Republican candidate wasn't taking anything for granted, however. He wrote Kyle Palmer a note calling the journalist's latest anti-Douglas column "right on the nose." But, he warned, "there is too much of a tendency in our ranks to be over-confident. When I get out there I intend to do everything I can to dispel such an attitude because I believe we are going to have to put on an all-out campaign to win."

And what would be the character of that campaign? Nixon left little doubt in his reply to a letter from a Republican businessman in San Diego who had assailed him for joining twenty House colleagues in signing a Declaration of Republican Principles. The declaration called on GOP candidates to abandon purely negative attacks on the Democrats and instead campaign on a positive platform. Now Nixon assured the businessman that he did not intend to "play down" the Communist issue. "On the contrary," he added, "I based my primary campaign for the Senate in large part on my disapproval of the Truman socialistic program, and on the necessity for ridding the government of communists and communist sympathizers. I shall conduct my general election campaign in the fall," he added, "in the same fashion."

Photostats Will Be Prepared

Candidates running hard against communism continued to chalk up impressive victories in 1950. Smathers had defeated Pepper in Florida, and then, on the day war broke out in Korea, Willis Smith topped the incumbent senator from North Carolina, Frank Graham, in a Democratic runoff (assuring his election in November). Smith had linked Graham, former president of the University of North Carolina and a well-known liberal, to Communist front groups; one newspaper claimed that the challenger had "out-McCarthied McCarthy." As in the Florida contest, race was also a factor, with Graham (like Claude Pepper) tarred as an integrationist. But clearly a trend was building. Never had so many candidates in so many states run so strongly on anti-Communist issues—and in the two most important races so far, they had won. Many others besides Richard Nixon were now following this path, including Everett Dirksen in Illinois, Wallace Bennett in Utah, John Marshall Butler in Maryland, and to a lesser extent, Prescott Bush in Connecticut.

Nixon had asked George Smathers for advice on how to paint Helen Douglas a deeper shade of pink. Nixon's office, meanwhile, received many unsolicited tips. A supporter from Los Angeles, for example, wrote that when she lived in Hollywood prior to Helen Douglas's election to Congress she "often heard of her being present and addressing Communist meetings." A writer for *Human Events* magazine named Edna Lonigan now worked full-time for his campaign in Washington, investigating such reports, as well as Douglas's voting record. That Nixon should be interested in this information was understandable. More surprising, he or his secretary often responded *personally* to the tipsters, sometimes seeking additional material. Here, as in all areas of the campaign, Nixon was intimately involved.

And so when a woman from Iowa informed him that Douglas was not the real name of Helen's "Red" husband and wondered whether he had legally changed his name, a Nixon secretary informed her that, indeed, Melvyn Douglas's "birthright surname" was Hesselberg. A reporter from the *Sacramento Union* alerted Nixon that a friend knew where to find a picture of Helen Douglas lunching with left-wing labor leader Harry Bridges at a hotel in that city. Did he want to use it? Two days later Nixon himself replied: "I am interested in seeing it. . . ."

The tips went beyond communist issues. Sam L. Collins, speaker of the California State Assembly, told Nixon that he had asked a committee to investigate charges that a certain bank in Los Angeles had never made a loan to a member of "the African race." Helen Douglas was reputedly a director of the bank. If all this was true, it would certainly knock off her "halo." Nixon immediately responded: "I would very much like to obtain any information. . . . I am convinced that it is going to be necessary to get the true facts about our opponent before the public. . . ."

Sometimes he took the lead in the investigations. He asked a state senator from Riverside County to send him a "complete report" concerning Helen and "Melvin" Douglas from the files of the Tenney Committee, which had investigated Communist activities. "I understand they have some material which is not in the files of the Committee on Un-American Activities in Washington," Nixon explained. A few days later the legislator informed Nixon that he had requested all material on the couple and suggested the candidate make full use of any voting connection between Helen Douglas and Vito Marcantonio. He asked Nixon to provide voting records and photostats of "family origin," explaining that she was "bound to be sympathetic with her people." (It was becoming common knowledge that Douglas was married to a Jew.) Nixon passed the letter along to his aide Bill Arnold with this note scrawled on the bottom: "Send him the vote record I prepared . . . and tell him photostats will be prepared as soon as possible."

Helen Douglas would not officially open her campaign until September, but organizing and strategizing continued throughout the summer. Her campaign would be aimed at the grass roots, but Nixon was strong on that

level as well and would be much better financed despite the Democrat's significant edge among labor unions. More than Nixon, Douglas would need
top-drawer support on the hustings.

As Douglas wished, President Truman came to Los Angeles in mid-July,
but only for about six hours and not to campaign for her, although they appeared together at an official function. Afterward she wrote the president a
personal letter praising his "courageous and far-sighted leadership" in arranging the United Nations response in Korea, which proved "that collec-
tive security can be made to work." A Truman aide revealed, however, that
the president would be staying in Washington indefinitely, keeping an eye
on Korea.

Yet Truman attempted to be useful in another way, or so he claimed. After
Douglas won her party's Senate nod, she was entitled to represent the state
on patronage matters. So when there was a vacancy on the federal bench in
California, she drew up a list of liberal candidates for Truman to consider
recommending to the Senate—but she had a hard time getting the president to discuss the matter. One day, to her dismay, she learned from White
House aide Matthew Connelly that Truman had nominated William M.
Byrne, a man she knew nothing about, for the judgeship. Connelly said that
the president had done this to help her campaign. How could that be true?
she asked. Connelly explained that Byrne was a Catholic and a friend of the
powerful (and politically conservative) archbishop of Los Angeles, J. Francis
McIntyre. Truman wanted Douglas to phone the archbishop and take full
credit for the nomination, a move that would presumably help her with
Catholics throughout the state.

Instead, Douglas called her friend Paul Ziffren to ask what she should do.
She "certainly" was not going to lie and tell Archbishop McIntyre she was
for Byrne. In fact, she suspected that Byrne was the candidate of Ed Pauley,
the Los Angeles oilman close to Truman (and, lately, to Nixon). "Now, what
do you think I should do, Paul?" she asked.

"Did you say that the President has *already* sent over Byrne's name to the
Senate?" Ziffren asked. "Well, Helen, I would suggest you call the archbishop."

Apparently, she never did; and McIntyre would work miracles for Nixon.

With Truman limiting his direct involvement in the race, Douglas pressed
for help from other notable Democrats, such as her friend Lyndon Johnson
and House leaders Sam Rayburn and John McCormack. If they couldn't
make personal appearances, they might tape commercials for radio or television. Claude Pepper, now a lame-duck senator in Florida, offered to come
to California and do anything to help, "from ringing doorbells to speaking."

"I want you to know, Helen," he added, "that we've just got to save you. I know with your intrepid leadership and indomitable courage and power, these wicked people cannot destroy you as the champion of our cause." He was concerned that his defeat would have an "adverse effect" on other liberal candidates, fearing that with the success of the "Red Pepper" smears in Florida, others would employ the same tactics against other liberals.

His concerns were well founded. Senator Karl Mundt of South Dakota had sent Nixon something for his "ammunition kit": a forty-eight-page booklet that had "contributed substantially to the gratifying" defeat of Pepper. It was called *The Red Record of Senator Claude Pepper,* and it included several pages listing Communist fronts Pepper was allegedly affiliated with, accompanied by photostats of key documents and letterheads provided by a former FBI agent in Jacksonville. "You will notice on many of the photostats of this book," Mundt added, "that the name of Helen Gahagan Douglas is close to that of one Claude Pepper." Mundt asserted that one reason this booklet proved effective was because it claimed not to be a political tract but "simply a factual document taken exclusively from the printed records and made available to the citizens of Florida. . . . [It] made these presentations just almost impossible to refute," adding that "if Helen is your opponent in the fall that something of a similar nature might well be prepared by some other former FBI agent with access to the official records. . . ." He promised to impart to Nixon, the next time they met, how the booklet was financed and distributed and other "interesting information."

Voters in California, like those in Florida and North Carolina, would likely prove receptive to such material. Communist subversion had given the state a serious case of the nerves, exacerbated by new fears of nuclear attack. With the explosion of the first Soviet atomic device in September 1949 and the assumption that the Russians were working on a hydrogen bomb, terror spread. In Los Angeles, the Disaster Council disseminated a report entitled "What to Do Before, During, and After Atomic Bomb Attack." It advised, among other things, to wear "a hat with brim to protect the face" but claimed "the occurrence of radioactivity after a blast is slight." Angelenos should not panic and try to flee in cars, for there "is danger of starvation in the surrounding deserts."

RCA Victor and Columbia Records withdrew from circulation a recording, "Old Man Atom," by the popular Sons of the Pioneers following complaints from anti-Communist groups that the lyrics followed the Kremlin's "peace line." The song, a talking blues, warned that "all men may be cremated equal" by the atomic bomb and asked people to choose between "peace in the world or the world in pieces." To no avail, the songwriter argued that he was merely following the Washington line—that atomic war would be a catastrophe.

NBC radio announced a series of dramatic presentations on the bomb to begin in July, beginning with *The Quick and the Dead* (starring Bob Hope and Helen Hayes). In the film *The Flying Saucer,* American officials suspected that UFOs were actually a Soviet aircraft "designed for one purpose—to carry an atomic bomb." (*Pravda,* on the other hand, identified flying saucers as merely American spy planes—which, it turned out, was in many cases true.) Entrepreneurs began peddling backyard bomb shelters and "decontaminating agents." Real estate ads touted buildings and homes that would stand up well under nuclear attack. A promoter in upstate New York offered to store sensitive corporate records in an abandoned iron mine. The *Saturday Review* published a letter from Upton Sinclair revealing that he wished to transfer five hundred cartons of his papers from a fireproof storeroom in California to an underground vault at a library in a remote part of the country so they might survive a nuclear attack.

Atomic scientists urged a massive civil-defense program, but federal officials tended to downplay the danger. A government-funded booklet, *How to Survive an Atomic Bomb,* declared that most of the danger of radioactivity was "mental." That this "fallout stuff" might cause cancer was "absolutely false." The most important thing in the midst of an atomic attack was to keep calm: "Lots of people have little tricks to steady their nerves at times like that—like reciting jingles or rhymes or the multiplication table."

Subscribing to the notion that an apocalyptic offense was the best nuclear defense, the U.S. military expanded its atomic strike force. The Strategic Air Command under General Curtis Le May now commanded 868 aircraft, almost one third of them modified to drop atomic bombs. On June 6, 1950, as Californians voted in the state primary, General Le May, from SAC headquarters in Nebraska, directed a simulated first-strike attack on the Soviet Union, which he called Sunday Punch, involving more than one hundred planes dropping unarmed nuclear-type bombs over air bases scattered across the country. An internal report described this "first realistic test" of a first strike as a resounding success.

America's desperate attempt to invent a thermonuclear or hydrogen bomb continued. In the wake of military activity in Korea, fear expressed after President Truman's January approval of the H-bomb project was nearly forgotten now. A group of respected atomic scientists, while recognizing the danger of Soviet advances, had questioned building a new order of weaponry that would "provide the means to exterminate whole populations." Hans Bethe, the physicist, asked, "Can we, who have always insisted on morality and human decency between nations as well as inside our own country, introduce this weapon of total annihilation into the world?" But when the scientists' appeal had no effect, some of them, including Bethe, went to Los Alamos to work on the "super," hoping that it would prove impossible to develop.

Helen Douglas, always in the forefront of arms-control activities, received dozens of letters from constituents asking her to stop the super project somehow. But Douglas, knowing the fight was hopeless, replied with platitudes about learning "to live together" and "improving the science of human relations." America had chosen the path to an arms race instead of the path to arms control. Russia had done the same.

There was no guarantee, to be sure, that the super could be built. Technical problems remained. Expecting the best, Washington moved ahead with budgetary allocations for a massive increase in the nuclear-testing program. Starting in January 1951, according to projections, the military, which had previously conducted its tests in the Pacific, would start setting off bombs above ground in Nevada, which were sure to send radioactive clouds over America. Hans Bethe warned that H-bombs would poison the air with the radioactive isotope carbon 14, which "has a life of 5,000 years." At Los Alamos, officials discussed "the probability that people [downwind from the Nevada test site] will receive perhaps a little more radiation than medical authorities say is absolutely safe," according to the minutes of one meeting.

There was little public or media criticism of bringing the bomb tests home or threatening the Soviets with nuclear annihilation. A Gallup poll in July 1950 revealed that 77 percent of the public advocated using the bomb in any future world war. Another Gallup survey found 28 percent of Americans in favor of using it in Korea.

That the United States should seek security by relying on genocidal weapons was rarely questioned even as the arms race led to a world of "total insecurity," as social philosopher Lewis Mumford put it. Reverend Norman Vincent Peale, in a 1950 book, urged readers to "develop the habit of not talking about our anxieties and worries." The historian Paul Boyer would later reflect: "The shift in attitudes toward the atomic bomb that culminated in 1950 runs like a fault line through the culture, nearly as visible as the one caused by the Hiroshima bombing itself. . . .The dread destroyer of 1945 had become the shield of the Republic by 1950. America must have as many nuclear weapons as possible, and the bigger the better, for the death struggle with communism that lay ahead."

. . . .

While Helen Douglas scrambled for money and outside help, Richard Nixon sensed that in his case contributors wouldn't have to be asked twice. In mid-July, he kicked off his fund-raising push with a letter to key businessmen, including Robert Bell (of Packard Bell) and Charles Ducommun (of Ducommun Metals), who had donated to his primary run and now were expected to give again. Nixon observed that it was essential to understand "that we have a hard battle on our hands this fall." The White House had called this race one of its "top objectives," so Douglas's campaign would be "extremely well financed," and many national figures would come to California to campaign for her.

At the same time, Nixon accepted an invitation from former president Herbert Hoover to attend the fabled midsummer encampment at Bohemian Grove, staged by the private men's club. A. C. "Bert" Mattei, an oil company president and chief GOP fund-raiser in San Francisco, advised Nixon to stay "as long as possible." The men-only retreat amid the redwoods outside that city, known for its high-level chitchat and fraternity-like games and skits, always attracted business and political leaders, usually of a conservative bent. Among the members or guests set to attend this year were radio personalities Lowell Thomas and H. V. Kaltenborn, insurance man James Kemper (who had expressed keen interest in Nixon's campaign), *Newsweek* columnist Raymond Moley, GOP national chairman Guy Gabrielson, University of California president Robert Gordon Sproul, and Columbia University president Dwight D. Eisenhower, the retired general who was already the object of speculation concerning the 1952 presidential race. Nixon had never met Eisenhower, but privately, after the GOP debacle of '48, he swore that the Republicans needed to nominate someone of Ike's stature to win in '52.

Arriving at the Grove on July 20, Nixon checked in to Hoover's unit, known as the Cave Man Camp. In this exclusive setting, the Republican candidate was just another guest, and one day he had to sit near the end of a long table while the featured speaker of the day, General Eisenhower, sat in the place of honor. Eisenhower, tired of his role as college president, had been raising money around the country in behalf of a group called the American Assembly, attacking "collectivistic ideas" and the country's lack of military preparedness.

Since the outbreak of war in Korea, Eisenhower itched to return to an official leadership role in Washington or Europe. Privately, he considered Harry Truman "a fine man" who, "in the middle of a stormy lake, knows nothing of swimming." In his diary, Ike disclaimed political ambitions but never quite ruled out a run for office. The latest Gallup poll showed that in a trial heat he was favored over Truman in 1952 by a two-to-one margin.

But was he a Republican or a Democrat? No one seemed to know. White House aides enjoyed the Republican infatuation with Ike, believing the general would inevitably declare himself a Democrat and leave the GOP high and dry for '52.

At the Grove, Nixon felt Ike was in "enemy territory," an East Coast moderate in the company of mainly California conservatives. He drew hearty applause only when he endorsed the University of California loyalty oath. He seemed deferential to Hoover but not obsequious, Nixon noted. Later, around the campfire, some of the men kicked around Eisenhower's chances for the presidency. Most were impressed with what Nixon later called his "personality and personal mystique." Still, many agreed that he had "a long way to go before he would have the experience, the depth, and the understanding to be President," according to Nixon.

With Congress still in session, Nixon could not stay long at the Grove. By this time, however, his fund-raising activities were in high gear, aimed at nothing less than soliciting and spending more money than had ever been circulated in a Senate race anywhere.

There was so much money available in California that the Nixon team could have ignored outside contributions. As far back as January, party offi-cials in Washington (after polling some fat cats in California) had told Nixon that he would be able to raise all the funds he needed at home. Busi-ness was still booming in California, and "practically all the big men in both San Francisco and Los Angeles [were] Republicans," Mac Faries, the state's GOP national committeeman, later observed.

Nixon's support cut across all industries and institutions, north and south. Backing came from Dean Witter (founder of the brokerage house), Stephen Bechtel (the builder), and Justin Whitlock Dart (president of Rexall Drug and Chemical). There were bankers (Howard Ahmanson, W. W. Crocker), a real estate tycoon (Colbert Coldwell), industrialists (J. D. Zellerbach, Charles Ducommun), millionaire car dealers (Henry Kearns and Harry Haldeman), an actor (George Murphy), and a movie czar (Louis B. Mayer). From agri-business, there was Robert Di Giorgio, nephew and likely heir of Joseph Di Giorgio, California's fruit king and owner of the largest winery in the country, among many other holdings. Notoriously antiunion, the Di Giorgios had fought off attempts of their workers to unionize, withstanding a lengthy strike in 1947–48 (which ended when its leader was shot in the head).

Also on board were Walter Haas, Jr. (a Levi Strauss heir), oilmen Henry Salvatori and Richard Rheem, and San Francisco Chronicle publisher George Cameron. Especially close to Nixon was C. Arnholt Smith, the freewheel-ing banker and founder of the conglomerate Westgate, who had financial interests in everything from tuna boats to taxi cabs and was known as Mr. San Diego. Many of these men, who tended to be quite conservative, had long been cool to the moderate Earl Warren but were downright enthusiastic about young Nixon, for both ideological reasons (they, too, were strongly anti-Communist) and business concerns (they liked the candidate's stand on tax cuts, oil and land development, and other measures). So it was Nixon, not the governor, who received most of this Republican money.

There was so much of it, and so little of it needed to be reported, that the Nixon campaign committee decided on July 21 to open two separate accounts at the Security–First National Bank of Los Angeles: one specifically for the campaign, another as a "trust" account for purposes undefined.

Even with all this money, contributions to Nixon were strongly encouraged from outside the state, particularly from archconservative Texas tycoons, such as H. L. Hunt, Clint Murchison, and Hugh Roy Cullen, but also from anti-Communist Democrats. Dana Smith, chairman of Nixon's finance committee, drafted a solicitation letter aimed specifically at the outsiders. "There is a major political battle on here in California in which your personal interests are very much at stake," the letter began. It assured these strangers that they "would like and respect" Nixon if they knew him; he was the man who "broke" the Hiss case while being "always careful to avoid the smearing of innocent people":

> He is a firm believer in the American way of life and the free enterprise competititve system. On the other hand, his opponent has consistently opposed in Congress the efforts to eliminate Communists and their sympathizers from the Government, has voted with Vito Marcantonio almost always in following the Communist line in matters pertaining to our national defense. She goes all the way with the Administration on all of its various efforts to substitute Socialism for our American freedoms.
>
> . You can see that the issue is squarely drawn here, and that all right thinking people should be glad to support Nixon's candidacy whether they are Californians or not. A defeat for Nixon would be a serious blow to the future of our country and to your personal interests. . . . Nixon's opponent is, of course, getting substantial contributions from Labor Union channels and we very much hope that people like you will be willing to give us some help to offset this situation.

One of the most unexpected outside donations, however, came from an individual who did not need an invitation, and it was hand-delivered to Nixon's Washington office shortly after the primary—by the young Democratic congressman from Massachusetts, John F. Kennedy.

Like Nixon, Kennedy had come to Congress three and a half years earlier and had served on the Education and Labor Committee. Their offices
were not far apart in the back of the House Office Building, an area known
as the attic, and they maintained cordial relations. Each recognized that the
other was a hot prospect in his party. Though both were ex-navy men (the
sinking of Kennedy's PT boat in 1943 had occurred not far from where
Nixon was stationed in the South Pacific), the two had little of substance in
common socially or culturally. Nixon both envied and resented Kennedy's
wealth and connections.

Politically, however, they were not continents apart. They agreed, for example, on the threat of communism. Kennedy had voted to continue funding HUAC and favored the latest version of the Mundt-Nixon
internal-security bill. Like Nixon, he strongly hinted that Truman's policy of
vacillation had led to "losing" China and inviting Communist advances in
Korea. He favored aid to Franco's Spain and vast increases in the Pentagon
budget. Both congressmen felt that organized labor had grown too powerful. Earlier that year, upon receiving an honorary degree at Notre Dame,
Kennedy had warned of the "ever expanding power of the Federal government" and "putting all major problems" into the all-absorbing hands of the
great Leviathan—the state. Each man craved higher office, but Nixon's ambition burned even brighter than Kennedy's, if that was possible.

Like Nixon, Kennedy had ambivalent feelings about Joseph McCarthy.
His father, Joseph P. Kennedy, the former ambassador to Great Britain, had
placed him in a difficult position by striking up a close relationship with the
Roman Catholic senator from Wisconsin. Always more conservative than
his son, Joe Kennedy had turned rabidly anti-Communist, donating money
to McCarthy for his investigations and introducing the senator to such
friends as Francis Cardinal Spellman. Shortly after the California primary,
McCarthy flew to Cape Cod for a weekend at the Kennedy compound.
Jack Kennedy knew McCarthy well; his sister Pat even dated him. Jack liked
Joe personally but distrusted him politically.

On his visit to Nixon's office, Kennedy presented his colleague with a
personal check from his father for one thousand dollars. A former movie
executive, Joseph Kennedy was no stranger to California politics, and despised the brand of liberal activism embraced by Hollywood actors and
writers. He had no use for Helen Douglas and a great deal of admiration for
Richard Nixon.

"Dick, I know you're in for a pretty rough campaign," Kennedy observed, "and my father wanted to help out." But what did the young
Kennedy think? "I obviously can't endorse you," he explained, "but it isn't

going to break my heart if you can turn the Senate's loss [that is, Helen Douglas] into Hollywood's gain."

Describing the visit to Pat Hillings, Nixon exclaimed, "Isn't this something?"

It is uncertain whether this gift marked the elder Kennedy's only contribution to the Nixon cause. Nixon aide Bill Arnold deposited the one-thousand-dollar check into the campaign account, but neither it nor any further Joseph P. Kennedy donation would be listed in financial records of the campaign. These records show, however, that another of Joe's sons, Robert F. Kennedy, then attending law school at the University of Virginia, contributed an unspecified sum.

Decades later, in his memoirs, longtime Massachusetts congressman Thomas P. "Tip" O'Neill claimed that Joe Kennedy once told him that he had contributed $150,000 to Nixon's campaign in 1950, "because he believed she [Douglas] was a Communist." In the same conversation, Kennedy reportedly said he donated nearly the same amount to George Smathers's crusade to defeat Claude Pepper in Florida.

If money from the East Coast were a priority in her campaign, Helen Douglas might have taken the advice of her friend Lorena Hickok and spent a few private moments with financier Bernard Baruch. Hickok, long-time confidante of Eleanor Roosevelt now working for the Democratic Party in New York, suggested that Douglas allow Daisy Harriman to set up a personal meeting with Baruch. "You know he's a fall-guy for any attractive woman," Hickok reported. "Nasty old man. Only, so far as I know, he really isn't nasty about it. He just likes 'em." But Douglas, though desperate for funds, was too proud for that. "Of course," she replied, "it would be wonderful to get some money out of Barney Baruch, but if it means I have to be present in order to get it, I am afraid it is out."

Hoping to offset Nixon's financial advantages, the Douglas campaign moved quickly but quietly to mobilize the liberal Hollywood crowd. With the Democratic candidate's background, one might assume she had the movie industry in her pocket, but this was far from the case. Liberals, in fact, were a minority in Hollywood, and no longer a very noisy minority. Since the Hollywood Ten case, they had grown less active in organizations that could be construed as leftist—including the Democratic Party—and less free with donations. Many were now giving only to mainstream charitable groups and religious funds. Douglas needed their financial and organizational support but not in a way that would draw public attention. So her friends, at least for now, would have to keep a low profile.

Republicans still dominated the industry's front office, and they loved Richard Nixon. Twentieth Century–Fox, for example, had volunteered the use of a staff photographer to take his official campaign photos. For raising funds, the Republican candidate could count on such studio heavyweights as Mendel Silberberg, MGM's chief attorney and GOP insider—"Our man Friday around Hollywood," in Mac Faries's estimation—as well as the actor John Wayne. George Murphy, who earlier that year had flirted with the idea of running for Helen Douglas's seat in the House, headed the Hollywood Republican Committee; other officers included Walt Disney, writer-director Charles Brackett, director Leo McCarey, and actors Robert Montgomery, Ginger Rogers, and Adolphe Menjou.

Douglas, on the other hand, was represented by relative small fry: Beverly Hills tax attorney Paul Ziffren and screenwriter Allen Rivkin. Ziffren had come to town in 1943 at the age of thirty, and although he had worked on a couple of local campaigns and Truman's reelection run in 1948, this was his first big statewide contest. He was close to Douglas, but he had not intended to work intensely on her race until a number of other supporters drifted away when the Red-baiting intensified. It was Allen Rivkin, however, who would solicit the rank-and-file writers and actors. Rivkin had been active in the liberal wing of the party since the Sinclair race in 1934 and was a founder of the Screen Writers Guild. Although not top ranked in his field, he had written or cowritten some well-known films, including *The Farmer's Daughter; Joe Smith, American;* and *Till the End of Time.* He was a relatively safe character for Douglas to be associated with, for he was staunchly anti-Communist and had attempted to prevent a left-wing takeover of the Screen Writers Guild.

Following the primary, Rivkin wrote Douglas "You're a cinch, kid," and promised to "try to round up my gang." His gang, the Citizens Committee for Candidates, had collected more than thirteen thousand dollars for the primary, of which five thousand dollars was distributed to Douglas. Among its members were producers Dore Schary, Lew Wasserman, and Hal Wallis; directors Mervyn LeRoy, Billy Wilder, George Cukor, Vincente Minnelli, and Otto Preminger; writers Albert Hackett, Sidney Sheldon, and Philip Dunne; and actor-performers Frank Sinatra, Groucho Marx, Gene Kelly, Danny Kaye, George Montgomery, Dinah Shore, and Ronald Reagan.

Rivkin also took dead aim at a much broader group, the Hollywood Democratic Committee, which included such top-echelon industry figures as Edward G. Robinson, Bette Davis, James Cagney, Walter Wanger, Joan Crawford, Judy Garland, Fritz Lang, Joseph L. Mankiewicz, and many others. John Huston, Myrna Loy, and Eddie Cantor had already contributed, but Gregory Peck had turned Douglas down cold. Sam Goldwyn and Joseph Schenck were among the few top executives who expressed any interest in the race, but they had failed to help so far.

Helen Douglas also relied on Rivkin for advice on whether to accept the creative help of volunteers from Hollywood whose political ties might come back to haunt her. When one screenwriter offered to work for her following the primary, she notified campaign manager Harold Tipton that while he was a good writer he might be "too far over to the left." She suggested that Tipton check him out with Rivkin. (At least one Communist Party member, screenwriter Paul Jarrico, had already written a speech for her.)

Her strongest asset in Hollywood, however, was her husband, a popular figure despite a love-hate relationship with the movie industry that periodically drove him back to the theater. He was still starring in *Two Blind Mice* in Chicago, but he continued to advise his wife via telephone, as well as contribute some of his own money to the cause at crucial moments. Still, Mel would be missed, and not only because his absence meant that throughout the grueling campaign Helen would be a single parent. Among other things, he was incisive, levelheaded, and experienced in California (and Hollywood) politics. One of Helen's top aides referred to him as the "strongest" and "brightest" person around her.

And their separation, no doubt, would continue to spark rumors in the press of an impending divorce. They were reportedly (as one gossip columnist put it) "saving a headline for after the November elections." Responding to the divorce rumors, Melvyn had sent the following wire to columnist Sheilah Graham: "Nothing is further from the truth, now or in the future." But that didn't stop the stories, which only added to the continuing whispers concerning Melvyn Douglas's real name (what *was* he hiding?) and his Jewishness.

Helen, however, remained upbeat about the coming campaign. She wrote an old friend that she would not let Nixon set the agenda for the race and promised to have her staff compile a comparison of the two candidates' voting records to show "what's at stake. . . . He really isn't a very good fellow—he's very dangerous." And she confidently exclaimed, "It is sure to be a good and rough [campaign] and that is the kind I like. We will win if everyone does his part."

Helen Gahagan as she appeared in *The Cat and the Fiddle.*
(Courtesy the Albert Center/University of Oklahoma)

Gahagan in her only Hollywood film, *She*.
(Courtesy the Albert Center/University of Oklahoma)

Anti-Douglas poster from
her first campaign, creating a
"carpetbagger" image.

Helen Gahagan
Douglas *(far
right)* with
Eleanor
Roosevelt
(second from left)
and fellow
congresswomen
from the 79th
Congress.
*(Courtesy the Albert
Center/University
of Oklahoma)*

With husband
Melvyn Douglas,
around 1947.
*(Courtesy the Albert
Center/University of
Oklahoma)*

In 1950, Douglas arrives
for takeoff as a pioneer
helicopter campaigner,
an idea borrowed from
Lyndon Johnson.
*(Courtesy the Albert
Center/University of
Oklahoma)*

Richard Nixon on the unending campaign trail during the primary.
(Courtesy the Nixon Library)

On the radio, with Pat looking on.
(Courtesy the Nixon Library)

With the soon-to-be-famous "woody" station wagon.
(Courtesy the Nixon Library)

Roy Day was summoned to the rescue in October.
(Courtesy the Nixon Library)

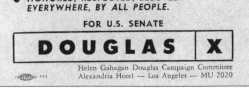
Nixon and Douglas campaign flyers during the primary race sought bipartisan support.

DOUGLAS-MARCANTONIO VOTING RECORD

Many persons have requested a comparison of the voting records of Congresswoman Helen Douglas and the notorious Communist party-liner, Congressman Vito Marcantonio of New York.

Mrs. Douglas and Marcantonio have been members of Congress together since January 1, 1945. During that period, Mrs. Douglas voted the same as Marcantonio **354** times. While it should not be expected that a member of the House of Representatives should always vote in opposition to Marcantonio, it is significant to note, not only the great number of times which Mrs. Douglas voted in agreement with him, but also the issues on which almost without exception they always saw eye to eye, to-wit: Un-American Activities and Internal Security.

Here is the Record!

VOTES AGAINST COMMITTEE ON UN-AMERICAN ACTIVITIES

Both Douglas and Marcantonio voted **against** establishing the Committee on Un-American Activities. 1/3/45. Bill passed.

Both voted on three separate occasions **against** contempt proceedings against persons and organizations which refused to reveal records or answer whether they were Communists. 4/16/46, 6/26/46, 11/24/47. Bills passed.

Both voted on four separate occasions **against** allowing funds for investigation by the Un-American Activities Committee. 5/17/46, 3/9/48, 2/9/49, 3/23/50. (The last vote was 348 to 12.) All bills passed.

COMMUNIST-LINE FOREIGN POLICY VOTES

Both voted **against** Greek-Turkish Aid Bill. 5/9/47. (It has been established that without this aid Greece and Turkey would long since have gone behind the Iron Curtain.) Bill passed.

Both voted on two occasions against free press amendment to UNRRA appropriation bill, providing that no funds should be furnished any country which refused to allow free access to the news of activities of the UNRRA by press and radio representatives of the United States. 11/1/45, 6/28/46. Bills passed. (This would in effect have denied American relief funds to Communist dominated countries.)

Both voted **against** refusing Foreign Relief to Soviet-dominated countries UNLESS supervised by Americans. 4/30/47. Bill passed 324 to 75.

VOTE AGAINST NATIONAL DEFENSE

Both voted **against** the Selective Service Act of 1948. 6/18/48. Bill passed.

VOTES AGAINST LOYALTY AND SECURITY LEGISLATION

Both voted on two separate occasions **against** bills requiring loyalty checks for Federal employees. 7/15/47, 6/29/49. Bills passed.

Both voted **against** the Subversive Activities Control Act of 1948, requiring registration with the Attorney General of Communist party members and communist controlled organizations. Bill passed, 319 to 58. 5/19/48. **AND AFTER KOREA** both again voted against it. Bill passed 8/29/50, 354 to 20.

AFTER KOREA, on July 12, 1950, Marcantonio and Douglas and 12 others voted **against** the Security Bill, to permit the heads of key National Defense departments, such as the Atomic Energy Commission, to discharge government workers found to be poor security risks! Bill passed, 327 to 14.

VOTE AGAINST CALIFORNIA

Both recorded **against** confirming title to Tidelands in California and the other states affected. 4/30/48. Bill passed 257-29.

VOTES AGAINST CONGRESSIONAL INVESTIGATION OF COMMUNIST AND OTHER ILLEGAL ACTIVITIES

Both voted **against** investigating the "whitewash" of the AMERASIA case. 4/18/46. Bill passed.

Both voted **against** investigating why the Soviet Union was buying as many as 60,000 United States patents at one time. 3/4/47. Bill passed.

Both voted **against** continuing investigation of numerous instances of illegal actions by OPA and the War Labor Board. 1/18/45. Bill passed.

Both voted on two occasions **against** allowing Congress to have access to government records necessary to the conduct of investigations by Senate and House Committees. 4/22/48, 5/13/48. Bills passed.

ON ALL OF THE ABOVE VOTES which have occurred since Congressman Nixon took office on January 1, 1947, **HE has voted exactly opposite to the Douglas-Marcantonio Axis!**

After studying the voting comparison between Mrs. Douglas and Marcantonio, is it any wonder that the Communist line newspaper, the Daily People's World, in its lead editorial on January 31, 1950, labeled Congressman Nixon as "The Man To Beat" in this Senate race and that the Communist newspaper, the New York Daily Worker, in the issue of July 28, 1947, selected Mrs. Douglas along with Marcantonio as "One of the Heroes of the 80th Congress."

REMEMBER! The United States Senate votes on ratifying international treaties and confirming presidential appointments. Would California send Marcantonio to the United States Senate?

NIXON FOR U. S. SENATOR CAMPAIGN COMMITTEE

NORTHERN CALIFORNIA	CENTRAL CALIFORNIA	SOUTHERN CALIFORNIA
John Walton Dinkelspiel, Chairman	B. M. Hoblick, Chairman	Bernard Brennan, Chairman
1151 Market Street	820 Van Ness Avenue	117 W. 9th St., Los Angeles
San Francisco—UNderhill 3-1416	Fresno—Phone 44116	TRinity 0661

◄■► 111

The Pink Sheet: A stroke of luck, or genius, at the printing plant.

The Douglas comic book: Not much competition for the Pink Sheet.

Flyer from the final days promising prizes for people who answer the phone with "Vote for Nixon."

Douglas with supporters in the closing days of the 1950 race.
(Courtesy the Albert Center/University of Oklahoma)

Tell Nicky to Get on This Thing

Helen Douglas considered the state Young Democrats convention in late July reason enough to leave Washington and fly to Los Angeles, but perhaps she regretted it later. During the Saturday-night dinner, actor Keenan Wynn, midway through his routine, objected to being heckled by a delegate who had apparently downed a few drinks. Wynn asked for a spotlight to be trained on a raucous section of the crowd. Surprisingly, it focused on the spot where Helen Douglas and her party were sitting. As Douglas vacated her seat, Wynn walked up and threatened to punch the unlikely suspect, her campaign manager, Harold Tipton, but in the nick of time he was informed that the actual heckler, a fellow from Bakersfield, had been found in a tier of seats below. So Wynn walked over there and slugged the offender, knocking him out of his chair. Then, after apologizing, he resumed his act.

In her speech to the convention, Douglas went on the attack, knowing she was among friends. She now knew that Nixon intended to link her closely to Vito Marcantonio, although her opponent was still being cagey about it. One Douglas supporter, a prominent L.A. attorney, had advised that it was "ridiculous to have a candidate of Helen's stature get up on a platform and deny that she is a 'Red' or a radical." What she could do, however, was try to steal some of Nixon's thunder by again pointing out that he had voted with Marcantonio in opposing Korean aid. Douglas also planned to fight fire with fire by suggesting that on domestic issues conservative Republicans, not liberal Democrats, were the ones doing the dirty work of the Soviets, such as halting projects intended to provide cheap electricity. "Those persons who opposed public development in the last five years," she charged, "have been among the most effective saboteurs of our national strength that the Communists could hope to enlist. I nominate for the Order of Stalin those Republicans and private power executives who . . . have obstructed the development of this vital source of energy."

The speech pleased most of the youthful delegates, but its overstatement and strident tone would not serve the candidate well in most other settings. Once again she revealed her insecurity, not her strength, in venturing onto Nixon's political turf. She could never hope to be widely considered as fierce a foe of communism as the man who broke the Hiss case. Every time she flirted with name-calling she not only opened herself to further assault but also lost some of her hard-won dignity. Yet in the cauldron of the summer of 1950, few could blame her for continually attempting to affirm her anti-Communist credentials. It was a gamble either way. If she ignored Nixon's charges and then plummeted in the polls, she would forever wish that she had fought back and met the attacks head-on.

The Nixon campaign was indeed readying a full-throttle attempt to tie Douglas to Vito Marcantonio. A central figure in this effort was Edna Lonigan, who worked out of Nixon's Washington office, systematically scouring every statement or association Douglas had ever made. Lonigan told Nixon she hoped to produce something along the lines of the *Red Pepper* booklet that Senator Mundt had sent him. To that end, she kept four large files on Douglas, labeled "Biography," "HGD and the Fronts," "Congress," and "Fifth Column," and subfiles on specific subjects, such as foreign and domestic policy, Korea, and political action committees. One folder was headed "Her Policy—Whose Policy? She Read the Lines—Who Wrote Them?" Lonigan was also collecting visuals for the booklet, including a picture of Stalin rubbing his hands and smiling, a wonderful non sequitur.

The file on fronts contained an impressive collection of photostats, letterheads, party invitations, and conference agendas on which Douglas's name appeared, plus a ten-page description of her connections to such groups as Consumers Union and the League of Women Shoppers (cited by HUAC as a Communist front). A paragraph written by Lonigan for use in the proposed booklet read: "Does this mean Mrs. Douglas is a Communist? It doesn't matter. If she knows these fronts are pro-Communist, then she gave aid and comfort to the enemy." Her note on labor PACs indicated that one unit was part of a subversive Communist campaign to convert the U.S. Congress "to its totalitarian program . . . the Fifth Column Triumphant." The biography file included this tidbit on Douglas: "11/1/29 returns from

Europe. Studied under Russian singing teacher Mme. Cehanovska. 'I am her product, I hope to make her proud.' "

On July 25, Lonigan sent Nixon a memo informing him that she had completed an examination of past issues of *The New York Times, The CIO News,* and the *Daily Worker.* She found "practically nothing" in the way of direct quotes by Douglas that cast the candidate in a pinkish light, "but it is very clear that the pattern of her public comments conformed exactly with whatever was uppermost in the party line at the time." Lonigan was "most curious" about Douglas's odd interest—for a woman—in atomic energy and "extremely curious" about her appointment to the House Foreign Affairs panel in 1945, which coincided with the period when "the Communists were moving their Hisses up to higher places in foreign policy." She reported that a certain congressman friendly to Nixon would "see if he can get any clues" about that. A little later, in another memo, Lonigan informed Nixon that the Communists were trying to seize the GOP and had already "taken it over in New York."

Lonigan was also in touch with a network of "researchers" around the country. She had asked the managing editor of the Brooklyn Roman Catholic diocese newspaper, the *Tablet,* to check into the background of Douglas's father, Walter Gahagan. All the editor could report was that he was "a self made man" and his "reputation was good." Lonigan was more impressed, however, with a lengthy letter from one Hunter Lovelace of Los Angeles, and she forwarded it to her boss. After presenting a long list of Melvyn Douglas's early Communist-front activities, Lovelace asserted that he was "morally certain" he was a Red "in spirit" as late as 1944, while serving in the Army in Burma. What was his proof for this? A young man who lived in Lovelace's apartment building, a "fellow traveler," had served directly under Douglas in the war "and devoutly admires him."

At about this time, Nixon received a very different letter—from Vito Marcantonio. This was not as bizarre as it seemed. Nixon and Marcantonio were friendly foes on the Hill. Each knew where the other stood on practically every issue, and each granted the other grudging respect for sticking to his principles. Marcantonio was wrong about nearly everything, Nixon believed, but sincere and not a political opportunist.

Back in January, when the second Hiss trial was coming to a close, Nixon happened to be in New York with another California conservative, Congressman Donald Jackson, and he invited *Newsweek* writer Ralph de Toledano to join them for drinks at the Essex House. After a couple of cocktails, Jackson said jokingly, "Why don't we invite Marc up?"

"He won't come—he's a Communist!" de Toledano declared, laughing.

But Nixon was all business. "Watch," he said and walked over to a telephone. A half hour later Marcantonio showed up at the hotel with a babe on either arm, sat down, and began drinking and chatting with the Republicans. Nixon later told de Toledano that it was all a "gag" but reiterated that Vito was "a nice guy." Perhaps if Douglas had a photograph of that meeting, she might have been able to make headway on the Nixon-Marcantonio link.

As it was—irony of ironies—Marcantonio appeared to favor Nixon over Douglas in the Senate race. Nixon told Frank Jorgensen that Vito had said to him, "Dick, do you want me to work for you or against you?" Nixon recognized, of course, that the latter would produce more votes for him in November. When Marcantonio learned that someone was tabulating the number of times he and Helen Douglas had voted alike, he reportedly told a Nixon associate, "Tell Nicky [Nixon] to get on this thing because it is a good idea." The source of Marcantonio's dislike for Douglas was unclear. Possibly, he resented that she had become a national hero of the left without spending years in the trenches as he had. There was stronger evidence that he had problems with her gender, commonly referring to her as "that bitch." On one occasion, he found himself standing next to Nixon, waiting to cross a busy street near the Capitol. After looking around to make sure no one was eavesdropping, he whispered, "I hope you beat that bitch out there in California."

Now, well into the campaign, Nixon received a friendly note from Marcantonio accompanying a copy of a letter he had just sent to Manchester Boddy. In a recent L.A. *Daily News* editorial, Boddy had urged voters in New York to turn Marcantonio out of office. In his letter, Marcantonio assured Boddy that his reelection was a question the people in his district would decide for themselves. "However," he added, "the people have already acted on you. . . ."

Nixon could hardly contain himself: This was just too rich. He sent a copy of the letter to a friend with the notation "I thought you'd get a kick out of this." He also sent a copy to Kyle Palmer of the *L.A. Times.* "I thought it was such a good laugh," he told him, "that it ought to be shared with somebody. . . ." Palmer must have been sorely tempted to share it with his readers, but he resisted.

Another influential California newspaperman also volunteered his support for Nixon. William Randolph Hearst's opinion of Helen Douglas had changed only for the worse since 1940, when he had described her emerging political views as "softly suffused with pink, like the sky at morning, when tenderly touched by the rosy fingers of the dawn." Now eighty-seven and virtually confined to bed in his Beverly Hills home, Hearst remained involved in his newspaper empire, but only sporadically, when he was lucid.

In his then recent book *Inside U.S.A.,* John Gunther had called Hearst a "preposterous old aurochs" with declining influence in California who seldom promoted candidates but "rather, . . . tries to knock off opponents by shouting 'Red.' " In the present campaign, however, Hearst's papers had also taken a positive approach, slanting coverage in Nixon's direction even more radically than the *Los Angeles Times* did. Nixon was "youthful," "vigorous," "dynamic." On those rare occasions when a Hearst reporter mentioned Helen Douglas, she was invariably referred to as "the former actress." This had to hurt her campaign, for Hearst's *San Francisco Examiner* reported the highest circulation of any paper in the north, and the circulation of his sensationalist papers in L.A., the *Examiner* and the *Herald-Express,* ran close behind that of the staid *Times* in that city.

Now W.R. offered the Nixon campaign the services of John Clements, his publicity chief. More to the point, Clements also directed the publisher's so-called Communist Program, an elaborate investigative unit that created files on suspected subversives and passed them along to politicians the newspaper magnate favored, such as Nixon and Joe McCarthy. Clements also had the connections to help raise money from conservatives, but he brought more to the campaign than a dislike of communism. A Nixon associate later revealed, "He couldn't stand ladies," including Helen Gahagan Douglas.

There was, however, at least one important journalist who favored the female candidate. Mary Ellen Leary, the San Francisco *News's* political reporter, was thrilled that a woman was running for the Senate, but she kept these feelings out of the paper. As a Nieman fellow in 1946, Leary had invited Douglas to speak at Harvard. The congresswoman had arrived ill prepared after a difficult day in Washington and had given a lackluster talk. At the time, she also needed "a new hair job," the reporter noted. Now Leary watched Douglas take the stage at outdoor, evening appearances, wearing a cloak, the wind blowing back her hair, looking "like a Hollywood star." When a crowd exploded with applause, Leary had to remind herself not to get carried away with adoration.

The empathy was understandable, for Leary's minority role in her newsroom was akin to Douglas's position in the House. Most newspapers in California hired exactly one female reporter and usually assigned her to a "woman's beat," writing fluffy features. But the *News,* a Scripps–Howard paper, was more liberal than most and allowed the Stanford-educated Leary to cover politics. From the start, her male peers warned that she could not expect to have the "same relationship" they enjoyed with politicians, a cozy one built on drinking or playing cards. It took her two years to discover that she was routinely excluded from dinner parties where politicians, lobbyists, and reporters mingled, and she was furious when Governor Warren kept her off invitation lists. On balance, however, she felt she benefited from a more "healthy" relationship with her subjects and believed that as a woman she "listened better" and got more out of them in interviews.

For Nixon, whom she covered extensively in 1950, Leary felt what she later described as "instinctive dislike and distrust." He struck her immediately as "a manufactured person . . . anointed by a cabal of businessmen, his personality implanted." She also sensed that his campaign manager, Murray Chotiner, was a political trickster, and so she started looking for evidence of misdeeds.

In late July, Chotiner sent all Nixon volunteers a "special bulletin" describing strategies for the coming months. Among other bits of advice, he urged that they seek Democratic support and thereby refrain from criticizing Democrats as a whole. "Let us remember," he explained, "that Dick Nixon's opponent is Mrs. Douglas, NOT the Democratic Party."

There was no question, however, who was in charge of the campaign. The candidate took "ahold of the reins, and once he had them he drove the horses," according to one insider. He also worked on his own speeches. "Nixon knew what he wanted to say," Roy Day recalled. "We'd throw in some ideas." The candidate approached all these tasks with grim seriousness. Nixon's radio announcer, Tom Dixon, discovered that Murray Chotiner, "for all his evil twists and turns," was nevertheless a much warmer person. Chotiner would "make jokes," he noted. "I can't remember Nixon laughing at anything."

Richard Nixon, in truth, was a perfectionist, which had certain liabilities in a statewide political race. The time for the candidate to be intimately involved in details was about to end. "Dick, you can either be the candidate or the manager," Chotiner finally told him. "You can't be both. A candidate's job is to think and to speak. You must go out and make speeches and get votes, and let us make the other mistakes!" By now, the symbiotic relationship between Nixon and Chotiner was apparent to in-house observers. Chotiner considered his candidate a political genius and gave him his all. In turn, in the caste system that was the Nixon campaign (few aides got close to the candidate), Chotiner was the only adviser "Dick ever really listened to," another associate noted.

"Uncle Herman" Perry, one of Nixon's original promoters in Whittier, found the campaign's increasing insularity troubling. He sent his friend Dick Nixon a letter listing twenty-eight observations and complaints. A high-ranking member of the team was "more interested in a cocktail" than in talking strategy, he revealed; a valued adviser refused to work "on account of Chotiner," who had been rehired for the finals "without the consent of [the] Finance Committee." Perry concluded by hinting that he would quit the campaign—and warned that Nixon would lose the race if he did not keep his campaign on a "grassroots level."

Among the many visceral issues expected to throw the two California senatorial candidates into heated conflict that fall was a final showdown on the old Mundt-Nixon internal-security act. In 1948, Nixon had authored, with Karl Mundt of South Dakota, a bill that called for the U.S. attorney general to draw up a list of suspected Communist Party organizations and front groups and require their members to "register" with his office or face severe penalties. The bill easily passed the House but ran into criticism from moderates in both parties and in the press, and it was shelved by the Senate.

Now, two years later—after Hiss and Fuchs, after McCarthy, after Korea—it was back with a vengeance. Polls showed that the public, by a three-to-one margin, favored forcing Communists to register. Nixon and Mundt reintroduced the bill, revised slightly and cosponsored by many others. The American Legion and the U.S. Chamber of Commerce led a lobbying campaign in support of it, and the stage was set for a dramatic confrontation, for President Truman had long opposed Mundt-Nixon. Besides emphasizing the civil libertarian aspect and the possible threat to labor unions and liberal groups, Truman had practical objections. Such measures, he said, would drive the Reds even deeper underground, preventing surveillance and FBI infiltration, thus causing a greater danger than it curbed.

But by the summer of 1950, the White House recognized that the only way to turn back Mundt-Nixon and avoid a resounding Democratic defeat in the November elections was to propose a tough measure of its own. Many Democrats up for election in November pleaded for a Truman bill that would shield them from charges of being soft on communism. "As a result of the Korean situation and the general tenseness, the Congress is in a mood to pass very drastic legislation indeed," White House aide Stephen J. Spingarn warned the president on July 20. The following day Spingarn reported signs of tension "bordering on hysteria" across the land. The city council in Birmingham, Alabama, for example, had just outlawed the Communist Party and had given the Reds and anyone found to be "in voluntary association or communication" with them forty hours to get out of town or face arrest.

Westbrook Pegler, the controversialist, had been escalating his attacks on left-wingers all summer. He cited his friend Congressman Nixon as a source for his assertion that America was facing a "reign of terror." Pegler advocated that the authorities round up all suspected Communists and all known fellow travelers and place them in concentration camps. Sure, some innocent people would suffer, but Pegler cited the example of the Japanese interned during World War II: Most were harmless, but the United States had to protect itself from the few who were dangerous.

Soon Pegler upped his penalty for Red plotters. Concentration camps were too good for these scum. "The only sensible and courageous way to deal with Communists in our midst is to make membership in a Communist organization or covert subsidies a capital offense," he declared, "and shoot or otherwise put to death all persons convicted of such." In their trials, "circumstantial evidence . . . should be admitted and given the most earnest consideration." He added: "I could not be damaged by a charge that I was a Communist or a fellow-traveler. Nobody would believe it. The same can be said of any loyal American. Embarrassment begins to appear as the charge is levelled at persons who have given grounds for such remarks. . . . People don't get called Communists without any reason at all."

The internal-security bills in Congress were not much saner, Spingarn observed in his memo to the president, likening them to "police state methods of the Soviets and the Nazis." But since "it is difficult to beat something with nothing," he suggested that Truman send Congress and the American people a message outlining new measures to combat communism that would strike a delicate balance between protecting the security of the nation and the rights of its citizens. Spingarn and two other advisers met with the president the following day to press this proposal. Truman observed that civil liberties had not been threatened so profoundly since the Alien and Sedition Acts of 1798, and a lot of good people on the Hill who "should know better" had been "stampeded into running with their tails between their legs." He revealed that he had decided to veto Mundt-Nixon or any other legislation that "adopted police-state tactics and unduly encroached on individual rights," and he promised to keep this pledge, "election year or no election year."

So the showdown was set. Truman at least had the advantage of not having to face the voters himself that fall, when the issue would come to a boil. Helen Douglas, a prominent opponent of Mundt-Nixon, had no such luxury, and California, if anything, was ahead of the country in clamoring for a crackdown. Hearst's *Los Angeles Examiner* had just called for the arrest of all alleged Communists in California and internment "in remote detention centers—perhaps in Wyoming. For the situation WITHIN the United States with respect to Communists is much worse than the situation OUTSIDE the United States."

. . .

Two suspected California Communists had already been incarcerated back East. With Dalton Trumbo and John Howard Lawson in prison, the fate of the rest of the Hollywood Ten was a mere formality. At the conclusion of his trial, Ring Lardner, Jr., responded with one of his most eloquent statements, asserting that there was "only a minor difference between forcing a man to say what his opinions are, and dictating what those opinions should be." Then he and Lester Cole were shipped to federal prison in Danbury, Connecticut.

To their delight, they learned that one of their fellow prisoners was J. Parnell Thomas, the former HUAC chairman, who had recently been convicted of taking kickbacks from friends and relatives he had placed on his congressional payroll. "What luck!" Lardner told Cole. "There's got to be a way, a dozen ways, to make the bastard miserable." Several weeks passed at Danbury before Cole had a confrontation with his former nemesis. Thomas's job at the facility was to gather eggs and clean out the chicken coops. One day, Cole was out in the field near the chickens, cutting hay with a scythe, when Thomas yelled through the barbed-wire fence, "Hey, Bolshie, I see you still got your sickle. Where's your hammer?"

"And I see you're still picking up chickenshit!" Cole reportedly replied.

Back in Hollywood, John Wayne, speaking for the Motion Picture Alliance for the Preservation of American Ideals, called on the Los Angeles City Council to require the registration of all Communists. Harry Warner offered to pay all expenses if any Reds at his studio wished to emigrate to Russia. A B'nai B'rith publication identified an "amazing disproportion of Jewish talent" on lists of subversives. "The cry of 'Clean out the Jews' is no longer whispered in studios," it warned. "It is becoming more and more audible."

In the wake of the Hollywood Ten sentencings and the release of *Red Channels,* rumors of a new federal inquisition spread. Movie personnel with political pasts wondered whether a blacklist had been instituted and whether they were on it—and if they were, how to get off. They had several options: ignore the threat and wait for a formal inquiry; publicly refute any charges or listings that had appeared; quietly meet with any panel or person who might offer "clearance" and if necessary provide names of others guilty of political indiscretions. In the Dark Ages, witches had been forced to sit on hot irons until they recanted. Now, Carey McWilliams observed, "we use steam, and the pressure of steam."

The most terrifying thing for director Joseph Losey was watching friends "succumb" and "seeing all protest disappear. Because if you did protest, you'd had it." It was hard for any individual to stick to principles, gauge the danger, or judge whether the whole thing was good or bad for Hollywood. "What am I going to do?" producer Sam Goldwyn asked a friend. "My best writers are in jail. How can I do a decent picture? But I'm telling you, I wish they'd be hanged."

Freelance Red-baiting had appeared in Hollywood even before *Red Channels* emerged in New York. Since 1949, a local Red hunter named Myron Fagan, who cowrote one of Humphrey Bogart's early films, *A Holy Terror,* had circulated a series of oversize booklets entitled *Red Treason in Hollywood, Documentation of the Red Stars in Hollywood,* and the like. They were printed on cheap paper and sold for a buck, and their inside front covers contained testimonials from J. Edgar Hoover, Adolphe Menjou ("Great work!"), Ed Sullivan, and Hedda Hopper ("I'm all for you"), among others. Fagan described himself as a disgruntled writer and director who couldn't get his anti-Communist plays produced because the "kings of Hollywood were pals and appeasers of Joe Stalin." Communist "stormtroupers" such as Edward G. Robinson, Groucho Marx, and Melvyn Douglas controlled the Screen Actors Guild despite the efforts of such "loyal Americans" as Ronald Reagan and George Murphy.

Like *Red Channels,* the heart of the publication was a listing of "pals and helpers and agents" of Soviet communism, along with the challenge "Sue me if it ain't so!" Fagan awarded each celebrity from one to five stars based on how Stalin might grade his or her usefulness. Earning five stars were Melvyn Douglas, Charlie Chaplin, Humphrey Bogart, Katharine Hepburn, Edward G. Robinson, Lena Horne, Philip Dunne, Gregory Peck, Dore Schary, John Huston, and for good measure, Upton Sinclair. Others won fewer stars: Sinatra (four), Bette Davis (three), Billy Wilder (one), and Sterling Hayden and Keenan Wynn (one-half each), and so on. Yet a measure of Fagan's ineffectiveness could be found in an early-1950 volume, when his strongest boast was that he caused Gregory Peck to lose a speaking engagement in Dublin, Ireland.

That all began to change in the summer of 1950, however, when some of those listed in the Red-baiting bibles began to run—or plead—for their professional lives. First to crack, apparently, was forty-six-year-old screenwriter Richard Collins. He was one of HUAC's Unfriendly Nineteen who had not been called to testify in 1947 despite being a serious student of Marx and a key Communist Party functionary. He may have escaped the fate of the Hollywood Ten, but like the other Unfriendlies he didn't avoid the wrath of the studio bosses and had done little work in Hollywood ever since. By 1950, he had drifted away from the CP, ashamed of having bullied others within the party for years—"I was a son of a bitch, a miserable little bastard," he later reflected. So one day he called the FBI and said, "I'm Richard Collins and I'd like to come down and see you." And he went. At first, he spoke only generally about party activities, without naming names that hadn't already surfaced, but clearly he was on the path to full disclosure. He also offered to put the FBI in touch with others who were ready to step forward.

Second in line was the hulking young actor Sterling Hayden. Unlike Collins, he had been a fringe member of the CP, but by 1950 he feared that his rising career—he had just appeared in *The Asphalt Jungle*—would soon stall because of his alleged Red ties. He also needed to maintain his income: He owned a fifty-foot boat, he was renting Jane Withers's Bel Air home, and his wife was expecting their third child. When the Korean War broke out, he realized he might be called to serve and then would be confronted with the question of whether he had ever been a member of the party. If he lied and said no, he faced perjury charges; if he said yes, his career was dead. So he sought the advice of lawyer Martin Gang, who specialized in "clearing" marginal Communists.

He also began seeing a therapist known for helping patients come to terms with coming clean. Hayden told the therapist that Gang had suggested he write J. Edgar Hoover a letter admitting he once belonged to the party and then hope his honesty counted for something. But the actor was worried. "The FBI isn't going to let me off the hook without my implicating people who never did anything wrong—except belong to the party," he told the therapist. He explained that what he really wanted to do was take out a two-page ad in the trades, admit he was a Red, and then say, So what?

"Why not do it?" the therapist asked.

"Because I haven't the guts, that's why. Maybe because I'm a parlor pink. Because I want to remain employable in this town. . . . Because when it comes time for the divorce I'd like to be able to see my children. . . . That's why."

So Hayden allowed his lawyer to send the letter to Hoover on July 31. The lawyer revealed that a certain unnamed young man "in a moment of emotional disturbance" had joined the CP for a period of six months in 1946 and since then had had no contact with any Communist-affiliated group. "While it must be admitted that a mistake was made in 1946," Gang disclosed, "it does appear that justice requires some method by which one mistake does not . . . prevent our client from earning a living." And then the key offering: "He is perfectly willing to submit to any interrogation or examination by the Federal Bureau of Investigation so that the organization may be convinced of his sincerity and of the truth of all the statements related herein." His client would then like to refer potential employers to the FBI, which could notify them "that there was no reason for not employing" him.

Two weeks later Hoover thanked Gang for his generous offer but informed him that bureau policy forbade trading "a clearance to any person" for information. He suggested, however, that some good might come out of the young man's contacting the FBI office in Los Angeles and providing details of his party membership and "the nature of the party activities during that period." After a few more sessions with his therapist, Hayden decided to visit the local FBI office and if necessary finger other former party members.

One of those who left the country in 1950 rather than face the coming crackdown was writer Gordon Kahn, another of the Unfriendly Nineteen who had escaped the HUAC hearings three years earlier. Kahn packed his bags one night while his wife was away and bribed his way across the Mexican border. His wife found out he had fled when she received a letter from him from Mexico explaining that HUAC was rumored to be readying a second round of hearings and that his name was surely at the top of the list of suspects. To avoid FBI surveillance, she could send him letters in care of a Mexican family.

If J. Edgar Hoover had little time for Sterling Hayden, it was understandable. His agents had returned to the apartment of Julius and Ethel Rosenberg on Manhattan's Lower East Side, almost one month to the day after their first visit. This time they searched the place, and this time they placed Julius under arrest, handcuffed him in view of his two young sons, and hauled him away. Ethel Rosenberg asked the agents to produce a search warrant and allow her to call her attorney. In their report they would refer to this request as "typical Communist remonstrance."

The front-page headline the following day in *The New York Times* read FOURTH AMERICAN HELD AS ATOM SPY. Julius Rosenberg, charged with conspiracy to commit espionage, was kept in prison on $100,000 bail. Hoover asserted that Rosenberg had "aggressively sought ways and means to secretly conspire with the Soviet Government to the detriment of his own country." His arrest came after his brother-in-law, David Greenglass, provided additional incriminating testimony against him, including details about Julius's offer a few weeks earlier to help David flee the country to avoid arrest.

Julius Rosenberg, a child of Jewish immigrants and the slums of the Lower East Side, had received a degree in engineering in 1939 from City College of New York, where he had been active in left-wing groups, particularly in support of the Loyalists in Spain. Later he served as a civilian engineer with the Army Signal Corps but was fired in 1945 for concealing his membership in the Communist Party. After the war, he set up a machine shop on Houston Street in Manhattan, where Greenglass joined him as a partner.

Only a sketchy description of the conspiracy, based on statements by Harry Gold and Ruth and David Greenglass, was released to the press. Anatoli A. Yakovlev, a diplomat at the Soviet consulate in New York, had allegedly forged an alliance with young Julius Rosenberg during World War II. In 1944, Rosenberg persuaded Greenglass, a machinist working with the Manhattan Project, to pass secrets to the Russians, including a sketch of the atomic bomb and the names of other project personnel. In June 1945, Yakovlev gave Harry Gold—the courier who had collected atomic secrets from Klaus Fuchs—five hundred dollars and told him to go to New Mexico and exchange it for information from Greenglass.

Every suspect in the spy ring going back to Klaus Fuchs had quickly confessed, and the FBI hoped Rosenberg would be no different, especially under the pressure of a possible death penalty. But Julius was not speaking, except to declare his innocence. His wife, however, *was* talking, despite her attorney's suggestion that she keep a low profile. The morning after her husband was seized, she invited the press to their comfortable, three-room apartment, where photographers snapped pictures of the tiny, smiling, dark-haired woman in a flowery dress drying dishes in her kitchen. "Neither my husband nor I have ever been Communists, and we don't know any Communists," she said, disingenuously. "The whole thing is ridiculous." Ethel did not know what a jam she was in. Her brother David had told the FBI that Ethel knew about Julius's efforts to recruit him as a spy.

On August 11, four weeks after the arrest of her husband, Ethel Rosenberg testified before a grand jury in lower Manhattan. While walking across Foley Square in front of the courthouse, two FBI agents stopped her and escorted her to the bureau's office in a building nearby. A little later she was arraigned on espionage charges and also held on $100,000 bail.

The evidence against Ethel was not extensive, however. Greenglass had placed her in the room on several occasions when he and Julius discussed spying, but his statements were largely uncorroborated. The Justice Department's primary interest in Ethel rested on the likelihood that in return for leniency she would confess her rather minor sins—and her husband's more substantial ones—and identify the real brains behind the spy ring. Ethel seemed disoriented during her first hours in the Women's House of Detention, but unlike her brother she did not crack. Neither did Julius, even after the incarceration of his wife, who, like him, faced execution if convicted.

Two weeks later, the Rosenbergs appeared in court and pleaded innocent to all charges.

. . .

In early August, the truly unthinkable occurred. Westbrook Pegler, too, was accused of aiding and abetting the Communists. Pegler had been spewing invective, often with brilliant turns of phrase—the man was a stylist—for more than twenty years. Once he seemed quaintly reactionary, journalism's self-styled "last angry man," but now his single-minded assault on the labor movement, Eleanor Roosevelt, and other liberal institutions struck most observers as slightly deranged. Literary critic Clifton Fadiman, accused by the columnist of being a Communist, replied that if he could arrange additional life insurance to provide for his family he would kill Pegler and go willingly to the electric chair. Pegler's language had become increasingly violent. Average citizens were not simply advised to oppose labor strikes; he asked them to join strikebreakers in "batting the brains out of pickets." He couldn't even write about cats getting stuck up in trees without demanding that they get blown to pieces for causing so much trouble. One of the few national figures he never bad-mouthed, however, was Richard Nixon, the hero of the Hiss case. Nixon, in turn, kept in touch with "Peg" (as he called him).

But now Pegler himself was in trouble with superpatriots. On August 1, his column began, "The futility of the Korean war cannot be concealed and there is no sensible course for the United States but to save as many of our men and as much of equipment as we can and get out." He argued that few Americans had any interest in the Far East and were unwilling to make sacrifices for "a total war effort. . . . We just haven't got what it takes or anyway we are not willing to put out what it will take." Isolationism was the answer: "I say let's get home and let's build up the United States. And let's lock up in concentration camps in positions most inviting to Soviet bombers all the Communists and fellow-travelers in the United States."

Some newspapers refused to print the column; others mocked the writer in their editorials. L. M. Birkhead, director of a right-wing group called Friends of Democracy, fired off a letter to Attorney General J. Howard McGrath, asking him to prosecute Pegler for sedition. The *New York Post,* which admitted to loathing Pegler, nevertheless stood up for his right to be heard. Punishing him for his words, the *Post* said, "is as foolish and dangerous as W. Pegler's frequently-voiced desire for the suppression of those who disagree with *him.*"

The news from Korea, in any case, continued to be nearly all bad. U.S. troops, slow in arriving, had made little impact and had suffered shockingly high casualty rates, in the range of 20 to 30 percent as the retreat continued. The Americans had been thrust into an alien land, where they were fighting on the side of allies they never knew they had. The heat and rain were oppressive; dysentery raged. And worse—they were losing. Ed Murrow tried to broadcast some of these truths from Tokyo, but CBS radio refused to relay them to U.S. listeners, fearing they might hurt the war effort.

On July 30, General Curtis Le May was ordered to send an atomic task force to the Pacific for possible use over Korea. Ten B-29 bombers would be outfitted with unactivated atomic bombs, which could be armed on Guam and ready for use under orders from the White House. The American public knew nothing about this, as President Truman had remained silent on the question of using atomic weapons against the North Koreans. As it happened, only nine bombers would make the trip. On the night of August 5, one of the B-29s crashed on takeoff at an air force base east of San Francisco. More than a dozen people were killed, and the shell of the bomb exploded, spreading mildly radioactive uranium across the airstrip.

The United States may have been fighting in Korea under the flag of the United Nations, but it was fighting largely alone, and General MacArthur was completely in charge of what Truman persisted in calling a police action. Now MacArthur demanded thirty thousand more troops; a week later he doubled the order. Only the odd failure of the Soviets to throw their own troops and best weapons into the battle kept the war going as long as it did. And why didn't they do this? "Generalissimo Stalin can kick us into the sea in Korea if he really wants to," Hanson Baldwin observed in *The New York Times,* but Uncle Joe knew he "might well regret it later."

With the outcome uncertain and public opinion running against further U.S. intervention, Truman was almost, but not quite, in a helpless position. There were fundamental measures he could propose that might put the country on a kind of permanent wartime alert for the first time and enable America to confront the Communists not just in Korea but elsewhere (even everywhere) in the world, not just this year but in years or decades to come.

Back in April, the National Security Council had sent the president NSC-68, a top-secret report on America's overall military posture. At a time when Truman was proclaiming a new era of peace, and Democrats and Republicans alike supported cuts in defense spending, the report's conclusion came as a shock: America, despite all its strengths, stood in its "deepest peril." Defense cuts, necessary to balance the budget and hold down taxes and inflation, had gone too far, robbing the nation of military power to back up its professed policy of "containing" the Soviets. The United States, in essence, was a paper tiger. Even its nuclear hegemony had ended, and the Russians, the report said, were likely to achieve nuclear parity by the mid-1950s. The solution? A massive military buildup—tripling the Pentagon budget for starters.

The purpose of NSC-68, Dean Acheson would later admit, was to "bludgeon the mass mind of 'top government.' " But Truman, for the moment, resisted its call and put the report on the shelf. The nation that spring did not appear to be on the verge of a shooting war anywhere in the world, and many Americans, no matter how much they feared Communist subversion at home, embraced isolationism when it came to global affairs.

But now that there was war in Korea, Truman had to rethink his opposition to NSC-68. Had his defense cuts encouraged Communist aggression? Increasingly, the press criticized the president's failure to keep America militarily prepared. Several Republicans called for the resignation of Defense Secretary Louis Johnson. The turning point came at a mid-July Cabinet meeting when Dean Acheson revived the call for a profound shift in budget priorities to accommodate enormous military outlays. A few cabinet officers raised concerns about the impact of new taxes and a militarized economy's long-term effect. But Truman quickly concurred with Acheson and scheduled for July 19 an historic speech to the American people—the first nationally televised presidential address.

That night, Truman stood at a lectern in the White House with a U.S. flag in the background. Reviewing his performance, a *New York Times* writer observed that for "the first time in a period of national emergency, the person at home not only heard the fateful call for sacrifices to preserve his freedom, but also saw the grave expressions of the President as he explained to the country what it would mean. In millions of living rooms . . . history was personalized last night. . . . In the close-up 'shots' his jaw was firmness itself. . . . There were both the reassurances and the increased understanding that come from being told the worst on a face-to-face basis and from seeing the added gesture which so often gives life and meaning to the spoken word."

Truman appealed for emergency military appropriations that would nearly double the present Pentagon budget, with further increases slated. "We shall have to maintain larger forces for a long time to come," he warned. It was NSC-68 under another name. He confessed that this would mean higher taxes, consumer shortages, and sacrifices for all Americans, but he expressed confidence that as a nation they would be up to a task—halting Communist aggression wherever it appeared—that might take years to accomplish.

Public response was positive. A White House analysis of incoming mail noted that not one person who saw the speech on television voiced an objection, suggesting that the new medium made viewers feel like insiders, "a part of their government." From Congress and the media, Truman won bipartisan support. Senator Lyndon Johnson hailed Truman's "excellent blueprint" but said he preferred going "much further, much faster." *The Washington Post* correctly identified this as a turning point for the country. "What this means," it declared in an editorial, "is that the United States will no longer temporize with aggressive communism. . . . If the Korean Reds should abandon their insane venture tomorrow, this country would still have to expand its armed forces to minimize the danger from other possible outbreaks of aggression." But it was Arthur Krock of *The New York Times* who identified the unsettling implications:

> The normal process of civilian life in the United States [will be] subordinated to the acquisition of military power for the foreseeable future. . . . The generation too young for service in World War II was given notice that it must grow to maturity under a military economy if it is to survive and remain free. The President did not state the case in these depressing terms, but they are implicit in the requests he made . . . and in the later requests he foreshadowed.

One month after her strident speech to the Young Democrats, Helen Douglas attempted to focus and moderate her earlier charges in her second major address of the summer. Once again she would be among friends, at the national convention of the Oil Workers International Union in Long Beach. Douglas usually had this sort of audience eating out of her hand. Men were intoxicated by her charm and enthusiasm, her femininity and accessibility. "Of course, you like Helen intellectually," one of her labor supporters said, "and in addition . . . you can't help but like her not only for her points of view. I think all men liked Helen as a lovely woman. . . . We regarded her as a lady, as an angel, as someone whom we admired and loved in the general sense of that word. And this meant that she had a strong personal following, as well as a strong ideological following." He admitted that for male political activists "there was a little extra zing" to working with women.

Long Beach would be a typical bravura Douglas performance. Ill with a cold and fever, she rejected Evie Chavoor's request that she cancel the appearance. She lay down—her favorite position—in the backseat of the car as Chavoor drove her to the engagement. Revived, the candidate gave a strong and overlong speech. The oil workers sent a sheaf of roses up to the platform, and she started all over again. As always, she displayed a wide vocal range and used pauses, silences, and melodramatic inflections for emphasis. Douglas reserved her harshest statements not for Republicans in general but for the specific figure of an "irresponsible, demagogic . . . political madman who . . . lent aid and comfort to Communist plotters throughout the world"—Senator Joseph McCarthy. She did not equate Nixon with him but merely asserted, vaguely, that "McCarthyism has come to California" and wisely left it at that.

Attempting to place herself in the rational center, Douglas raised domestic issues popular with unionists and other Californians—jobs, the minimum wage, slum clearance, tenant farming—and said she trembled to think of "the gyrations" by Republicans they would be forced to witness that autumn. This time, when she brought the Communist issue into the domestic arena, she did so in a positive way, asserting that what the Reds were most afraid of was not Cold War rhetoric but "the economic power of this Nation. . . ." Ever more hawkish on Korea, she declared that the nation was fighting not only "to defend the new little republic of South Korea" but "also to prove to the Soviet Union that any further aggression by its satellites or itself will also meet with immediate resistance." This was, for the moment, relatively safe political ground.

Finally, Chavoor tugged on her sleeve and whispered, "Enough already." The union president then affirmed the group's support, declaring that Californians simply could not afford to be represented by two Republicans in the Senate. Quoting from Deuteronomy, he said, "Thou shalt not plow with the ox and the ass together." William Knowland, he said, was the ox and Nixon the ass. At last, Douglas walked out to her car and collapsed, for a moment.

One of Nixon's top organizers, Jack Drown, had secretly attended the gathering, and his notes were later typed up and sent to his candidate.

Hard as she tried, Helen Douglas couldn't quite shake the desperate impulse, born of resentment and necessity, to turn the tables on Nixon. A few days after the Long Beach speech, she returned to Washington and sent a note by messenger to her friend Drew Pearson over on Twenty-ninth Street, asking him to compare Nixon's Red-baiting—through manipulation of the media—to Joe McCarthy's. Would Pearson write a column linking the two Republicans' "pattern of attempted suppression of the true facts" and "interference with freedom of the press"?

It was still risky to pick on Joe McCarthy, however. Senator Millard Tydings's subcommittee, dominated by Democrats, had cleared former State

Department consultant Owen Lattimore and others on the list of sus-pects—and had charged McCarthy with creating a "fraud and a hoax . . . perhaps the most nefarious campaign of half-truths and untruths in the history of this republic." But when the report reached the floor of the Senate, it sparked one of the most violent debates in the chamber's history.

At first, Republicans merely tried to table the report; Democrats refused to comply or shouted them down. With that, ultraconservative senator Ken-neth Wherry ordered subcommittee attorney Edward P. Morgan off the floor. When Morgan refused to go, Wherry walked over to him and shouted, "You dirty son of a bitch!" Then he threw a wild punch that struck Morgan in the shoulder. The two men were separated before a brawl could break out.

The words spoken on the floor were nearly as violent. Tydings called McCarthy a charlatan and compared him with the town dunce. He said that Senator William Jenner, one of McCarthy's allies, was the real traitor, for having voted against NATO and the Marshall Plan, thus inviting Soviet ag-gression. Jenner responded by accusing Tydings of conducting "the most scandalous and brazen whitewash of treasonable conspiracy in our history." When the Senate voted to accept the Tydings report, it did so along parti-san lines. Marquis Childs, the columnist, asserted that McCarthyism should be consigned to the "garbage heap of history," but he added, "that is proba-bly a vain hope."

No minds, apparently, had been swayed by the Senate investigation. That left McCarthy free to carry on his campaign. As he had predicted, the United States had got bogged down in Korea, and as the bodies of slain American boys started arriving back home, public criticism of the war and the blunders that allegedly caused it rose, fanned by people like Joe McCarthy, who accused Truman's top aides of delivering Korea on a platter to the Soviets.

Running for the Cyclone Cellars

Murray Chotiner believed that a brief (if intense) six- to eight-week election campaign should be "sufficient." Any longer, and "you wear out your candidate and your workers." Voters, he felt, are simply "not ready to receive campaigning in advance of eight weeks before the election." Nixon, therefore, would not officially begin his race until September 18, nearly two weeks after Douglas's scheduled start. It was an approach that conserved resources and emanated confidence—as if Nixon were the incumbent. But Chotiner also cherished starting a campaign "with a bang" and so made plans for Nixon to hop by airplane from one end of the state to the other on launch day—a "simultaneous opening . . . the first time this has been done"—and lay down withering fire against his foe everywhere he went. After that, the campaign would concentrate on the ten largest counties, where 80 percent of Californians lived. Nixon explained to a supporter that he had spent a lot of time in the "outlying" areas during the primary campaign to become better known, but now he would go "where the votes are."

In the weeks leading up to the launch, however, the Nixonites were hardly idle. They already had Douglas on the defensive and didn't want to give her a chance to steady herself before their candidate took to the stump. The maneuverings took many forms and directions.

Chotiner strongly believed in mobilizing committees of prominent members of the opposing party. The present campaign offered almost infinite possibilities in this regard, for many Democrats opposed Douglas on principle (on the basis of her politics or her gender). A number of Boddy Democrats, under pressure from the state and national party, followed Will Rogers, Jr., into the Douglas fold, but many refused to go. One of them was George Creel, the California writer and political activist best known as Woodrow Wilson's propaganda chief during World War I. Creel was still labeled a Democrat although for years he had often voted Republican. This switch began in 1934, when he organized Democrats to support a Republican for governor after Upton Sinclair won the Democratic primary.

Now, sixteen years later, Creel (with Chotiner's help) created a similar network to oppose Douglas. Sheridan Downey, who as Sinclair's running mate in 1934 had lost partly due to Creel, would be the hidden hand behind the committee. A top Nixon organizer would later say of Creel, "We didn't have to recruit him." Still, the Nixon committee appreciated his volunteerism—and paid him an unreported sixteen thousand dollars to keep up the good work.

Chotiner also focused on advertising, which could play a dual purpose: promoting Nixon and inspiring the vast majority of California newspapers to slant news and editorials in his direction. He favored small ads over full-pagers, for the big ads made voters "think that you are spending too much money for the campaign." The trick was to spend a phenomenal amount of money without appearing to do so. Chotiner had learned other trade secrets from Clem Whitaker, California's first great campaign manager. (Whitaker was then in Chicago with partner Leone Baxter managing the American Medical Association's drive to halt Truman's national health-insurance plan.) One ploy was to ask each newspaper for its advertising rates at an early date, suggesting that the campaign would provide ad revenue later, which in turn assured positive coverage of the candidate. After Murray finalized a budget, he would pay *in advance* for an entire series of ads, further encouraging the papers to "kind of lean your way," as a Nixon manager slyly commented. The same principle was applied to radio and television ads.

Sometimes the Nixon campaign simply arranged for favorable coverage without bothering to buy advertising. Bernie Brennan boasted that he had "made a deal" with the publisher of a local Italian American weekly that would result in favorable news stories and editorials "in all of the issues of his newspaper." Brennan asked a local organizer to get in touch with the publisher "to see that we get the best advantage of our investment."

Chotiner also believed strongly in outdoor advertising. Many corporations had long made a practice of turning over thousands of their billboards to Republican candidates. They merely had to be asked. On August 11, Elwood Robinson, a leading ad man and member of Nixon's finance committee in Los Angeles, informed the assistant to the president of Union Oil that his candidate wanted up to half of the company's billboards, if that wouldn't interfere with its ad campaigns too much. He hoped that Union Oil, "in the interest of good government," would agree that Nixon needed the billboards "more than you do."

The corporations sometimes donated the billboards without charge, a political contribution that would not be reported in any meaningful way. In other cases, the campaign was expected to pay for the loan. In this instance, Robinson offered to send a check from the Nixon campaign committee to Union Oil's ad agency—Foote, Cone and Belding—so that the money would not be traced to the oil company.

Chotiner didn't really care what the boards looked like. "The billboards we have used in our campaigns have been the worst designed you can imagine," he once said. All that mattered was getting "the name of the candidate" out there with very little additional copy. So the Nixon billboards, which had been going up at a blistering rate all summer, often just said ELECT CONGRESSMAN RICHARD NIXON U.S. SENATOR, perhaps with the slogan "On Guard for America." One billboard materialized over the border in Tijuana, to catch the weekend tourist trade.

Nixon's fund-raising, meanwhile, continued apace. An internal survey of key supporters listed, among others, both Joseph and Robert Di Giorgio ("contributed, raised money"), Cecil B. DeMille ("contributed, aided in lining up movie people"), and Howard Jarvis ("sent thousands of letters to businessmen"). In late August, the Nixon finance committee met for one of the last times. From here on out, action, not talk, would be the policy.

The finance committee included Chotiner, Jorgensen, Brennan, and Herman Perry. John T. Garland, brother-in-law of L.A. Times heir Norman Chandler and owner of the Garland Building, had again arranged space for campaign headquarters on the second floor of his office building in downtown L.A. Finance chairman Dana Smith—an attorney in San Marino and heir to a lumber fortune—had been a Nixon partisan since 1946. Also on board, uncredited, was Asa Call, "the man who called more shots for businessmen in Los Angeles than anybody else," according to Mac Faries. Then there was Mendel Silberberg, the Hollywood lawyer, who had once raised fifty thousand dollars from movie people in a single day.

The Nixon men agreed there was sufficient cash on hand to meet immediate needs. But they were concerned about paying back certain loans and knew expenses would increase as soon as the campaign shifted into high gear. They were also afraid that the Republican Party's fund-raising efforts, which they would share in, might fall short. The truth was a lot of conservative GOP donors couldn't stand Earl Warren and didn't want to hand him a nickel, but they might be induced to give heavily to Nixon. So the finance committee decided on a Nixon-first strategy, soliciting major donations earmarked for their candidate. Asa Call helped woo several big California oil executives who were (he explained) "disenchanted" with Warren.

Nixon backers, meanwhile, besieged GOP national committeeman Mac Faries for an unreasonably fat slice of the party's pie. He understood—they were "young and full of energy"—but he held them at bay. Full coffers or not, Nixon was in for a tough autumn, Faries believed, because Douglas was a "smarter woman and had more ability than most people thought—a liberal but a good American."

Besides the anti-Warren Republicans, the committee identified two other prime "classes of prospects." First were Democrats who had "no use for the 'pink lady,' " as Dana Smith put it. They could contribute to the pro-Nixon Democratic group by sending checks to Smith, who would funnel the money to George Creel. Second were out-of-state funders. Someone pointed out that Senator Robert Taft was sucking a lot of money out of California, so Nixon should not be shy about casting a wide net. In a follow-up memo to committee members, Dana Smith concluded, "The time of the campaign is now upon us when it is necessary to get the money in fast and in substantial amounts."

As the campaign kickoff neared, the urgency felt by Nixon fund-raisers was reflected elsewhere in the organization, most apparently in the effort to paint Douglas pink. Research had to be completed and all of the facts, quotes, opinion, innuendo, and slander boiled down and distributed long before election day.

A Nixon researcher in his San Francisco office submitted to Bill Arnold four pages of citations from *People's World,* the Communist Party newspaper, concerning the woman he referred to as "Hesselberg, Helen—true name." He also sent along a file of similar listings but warned that the Communist newspaper "so rarely follows up its advance notices that you cannot expect to get anything much on what she said at a meeting, or to know definitely whether she actually attended the meetings." Edna Lonigan, meanwhile, had submitted to Nixon's secretary in Whittier, Dorothy Cox, a dummy for the proposed booklet that might do to Douglas what a similar document had done to Claude Pepper—that is, destroy her. But it was unclear when, if ever, it would be published. Such crude Red-baiting might work in Florida but backfire in California.

More promising was the purely factual approach provided by the Douglas–Marcantonio vote analysis. No one could claim it was unfair to scruti-
nize and publicize an opponent's record; candidates had always done this.
And Douglas was nothing if not consistent in her voting patterns. The latest Americans for Democratic Action ratings found her voting "correctly"
on fourteen of fifteen key bills (and Nixon voting correctly on just one).
That was fair game—and trouble enough for Douglas.

What was unfair was the context. Most of the votes on which Douglas
sided with Marcantonio pertained to routine domestic legislation, supported by the administration, a majority of other Democrats, and some Republicans. There were times, to be sure (particularly relating to HUAC),
when Douglas and Marcantonio were joined by few colleagues. But in the
vast majority of cases, they simply voted together as mainstream New Dealers. In fact, on many foreign policy votes, they were abetted by Republican
isolationists, such as Robert Taft and Kenneth Wherry, who could hardly be
accused of harboring Communist sympathies. Murray Chotiner would later
admit, in discussing this aspect of the 1950 campaign, that "you can take any
vote and you can find that a man as conservative as Bob Taft voted the same
way as Marcantonio for different reasons."

But if the picture of the relationship between Douglas and Marcantonio
was highly distorted, the evidence could not be questioned: The votes were
on the record; make of them what you will. Exactly how many times *had*
Douglas and Marcantonio voted alike in recent years, and more important,
how many of those instances could Lonigan and other Nixon researchers
identify by Labor Day? Counting continued at a feverish pace, for now
there was no doubt that a document based on the final number would soon
emerge as a centerpiece of the fall campaign.

One day in August, left-wing labor lawyer Lee Pressman, under the careful
prodding of Congressman Richard Nixon, finally named several names for
the benefit of a HUAC panel convened in New York City. Walter Goodman, in his book *The Committee,* later compared Pressman's performance to
that of a woman who, not wishing to be considered unchaste, makes her
suitor wait twenty-five minutes—before jumping into bed with him. Still
dissatisfied, Nixon decided Pressman was not "coming clean." That night
the congressman and reporter Murray Kempton found themselves in the
same hotel in New York City and fell into conversation until the wee hours.
Nixon told Kempton that he was about to officially launch his campaign
against Helen Gahagan Douglas. He hated to end her career on Capitol Hill
so abruptly, he explained with apparent sincerity, because he respected her
so much—but he had to do it.

. . .

Like Richard Nixon, many Republicans running for Senate seats emphasized the Communist threat, sometimes to the point of obsession. This strategy had already played a major role in defeating incumbents Claude Pepper
and Frank Graham. A third liberal Democrat fell in August: Idaho senator
Glen Taylor, Henry Wallace's running mate in the 1948 presidential race. A
Democratic challenger called him a "dupe" of the Communists, and a leading Idaho newspaper reprinted selections from the now infamous *Red
Record of Senator Claude Pepper* that linked him to Communist front groups.
Taylor denounced the "smear techniques" but lost the primary nonetheless.

Accordingly, many senators running for reelection planned to "shelve the
domestic issues," *The New York Times* reported in early August, "and talk almost exclusively about the battle against communism." In the closely
watched campaign in Illinois, conservative Everett Dirksen, a former congressman, challenged Scott Lucas, the Democratic leader in the Senate. Bolstered by Joe McCarthy's six visits in his behalf, Dirksen painted Lucas as soft
on communism and seemed poised to earn an upset, if he could gain enough
votes downstate to overcome the Cook County machine. McCarthy called
a vote for Dirksen a "prayer for America."

Also making headway was John Marshall Butler in Maryland, who benefited from Millard Tydings's desperate and, in the end, unsuccessful attempt
to stop Joe McCarthy in his tracks. Tydings was a four-term senator, a conservative Democrat difficult to attack from the right, but Butler was doing
it with the active support of McCarthy. Campaigning in Maryland, Mc-
Carthy called Dean Acheson "the procurer of pinks and punks in the State
Department." He also supplied Butler with files, funds (including ten thousand dollars from oilman Clint Murchison), research support, and a scandal
sheet called "From the Record" that contained all the dirt on Tydings he
had managed to excavate. The strongest piece of evidence was a photo of
Tydings apparently chatting with former U.S. Communist Party boss Earl
Browder. It was actually a composite—a current photo of Browder meshed
with a 1938 shot of Tydings.

Another GOP challenger campaigning largely against communism, Wallace Bennett, appeared to have Senator Elbert Thomas on the run in Utah.
Bennett called Thomas the "darlin' of several un-American organizations."
Republicans distributed an anti-Thomas newspaper produced outside the
state that carried headlines like THOMAS PHILOSOPHY WINS RED APPROVAL.

Connecticut was another battleground, with two Senate seats contested.
Democratic incumbent Brien McMahon seemed relatively secure, but
William Benton, who had just been appointed, faced a tough foe in con-

servative Prescott Bush. Joe McCarthy made three visits in behalf of the Republicans but drew only modest crowds in a state known for its moderation. The patrician Prescott Bush considered McCarthy crude and insincere, just a political "gambler."

Perhaps the most critical race was under way in Ohio, where Senator Robert Taft, a favorite for the '52 GOP presidential nomination, attempted to hold off Joseph T. Ferguson by Red-baiting his chief supporters, big labor groups. The CIO's PAC, he declared, was oriented toward socialism, and although it may have purged many of its Communist members, "it still uses Communist techniques." The Truman administration, Taft charged, had "strange pro-Red sympathy" and had "practically invited" the North Korean invasion. Like Helen Douglas, Ferguson responded by pointing out several instances when his Republican opponent voted with Vito Marcantonio. Thanks to a tip from Truman aide Ken Hechler, he distributed widely a legitimate photo—not a composite—of Robert Taft standing with Earl Browder at an American Youth Congress rally in the late 1930s. Hechler advised, rather dubiously, that this was "one way to answer the charges of 'guilt by association.' "

To assist its candidates running on the Communist issue, the Republican National Committee produced a booklet called *Red Herring and Whitewash.* It charged the Truman administration with "appeasement, obstruction, evasion, softness, and apathy in the face of imminent danger to national security." Local candidates had been using such language for months; now the national party was throwing fat on the fire. "The association of the Democrat Party with Communism," the booklet declared, "has been of such long standing that the fellowship has ceased to seem strange and has become familiar. . . . The red brand of Communism has been stamped on the Democrat record. Whitewash can not hide it. . . ."

While Nixon fund-raisers hit pay dirt, the Douglas drive flagged as September approached. Thousands of dollars in small donations were pouring in, but the large donors were apathetic, sometimes hostile. One newspaper reported the "romantic news" that "fickle" state Democratic leader Bill Malone had "kissed and made up" with Helen Douglas. But it was clear to Douglas that many reliable Democratic donors were reluctant to sponsor her and might even be funding Nixon. Paul Ziffren reluctantly hit up his Hollywood clients who were leery of Douglas but would contribute to her out of loyalty to him.

Apart from finances, campaign organizing appeared to be going well, although compared with the Nixon juggernaut it was amateurish in many respects. Douglas "did have loyal people working for her," according to Ellie Heller, her key supporter in the north, but she didn't think Helen "was any administrator or organizer at all. She was a personality person . . . willing to devote all her energy."

Both Helen Douglas and James Roosevelt were buoyed by the news that his mother would visit California after Labor Day. Contrary to what her son suggested to the press, ER had not volunteered to come to California. "He [Jimmy] insists that I come out to speak for him and for Helen, which seems a mistake to me but I have agreed to go," she told her daughter without explaining why she thought it was a mistake. Because everyone already knew where she stood? Or because she feared, in the present illiberal atmosphere, she might do more harm than good? "Jimmy is discouraged I think. . . . It will be hard for any Democrat to win this year, because of Korea," she reckoned.

The refurbished Mundt-Nixon bill, now sponsored by Senator Pat McCarran and Congressman John Wood, was about to come up in the House. The vote appeared certain to be lopsided and in Richard Nixon's favor. As his aides suggested, President Truman had proposed several modest new measures to slow the bill's momentum. But it was too late, and the president's heart wasn't in it anyway. He declared that Communists would never make much headway in the United States and that current measures—such as his loyalty program—were sufficient to control the situation with just a few refinements.

The stage was set for a showdown over the McCarran bill, now known as the Internal Security Act of 1950. (Truman referred to it as "the Mundt-Nixon bill as revised by Senator McCarran and made a little worse.") Its final provisions went beyond requiring Communist groups and those affiliated with them to register with the attorney general. Once registered, individuals would be barred from defense- or military-related jobs. Front groups would have to reveal all sources of funds; names of their members could be released to the public; and all of their printed literature had to be labeled "Communist in origin." Arresting and deporting left-wing aliens would become much easier, and the United States could bar from entering the country any visitors or immigrants who had ever belonged to an organization advocating totalitarianism.

In late August, debate over the bill raged on Capitol Hill. When Helen Douglas entered the House chamber, Sam Rayburn privately implored her not to make any major mistakes in the coming weeks. He glanced at Nixon, who had already taken his seat. "Take that young man out in the finals," he instructed. "His is the most devious face of all those who have served in Congress in all the years I've been here." Knowing he had the upper hand on the McCarran vote, Nixon was relaxed, even jovial. Douglas would later recall watching him "laughing and talking" with his allies. Returning to her office after a futile effort to corral votes, she told her staff, "It's down the tubes!" Then she called her campaign headquarters in Los Angeles to issue a kind of storm warning. "You know what I'm going to do," she told Ruth Lybeck.

"Yes, Helen," Lybeck replied, worried but proud, "we know."

"Okay," Douglas added, "just wanted to tell you because you know what this might mean."

"We're prepared," Lybeck answered.

The next day as the roll call began, Douglas's Democratic colleagues from California whispered to her that she really ought to back the bill. It was going to pass anyway, so her vote meant nothing; and everyone would understand that she was up for election. "Anyway, Truman will veto it," one advised.

Her friend Chet Holifield told her he was voting against it, "but I'm not running for the Senate against Nixon." If she voted no, he advised, "you won't be able to get around the state fast enough to explain." Nixon would "beat your brains in." She knew Holifield and the others were right but said little. Then she cast one of only twenty nay votes on the measure—joined, inevitably, by Vito Marcantonio—as opposed to 354 on the winning side.

That afternoon she met several Democrats for lunch in the House dining room at a corner table presided over by John McCormack. "How does it feel to be a dead statesman, Helen, instead of a live politician?" one of them joked. "Just fine," she replied.

Back in the chamber, Republicans paid tribute to the man who had in a sense started it all, Richard Nixon. A dozen in all put their feelings for their colleague on the record, thanking him for his tireless service in combating communism and predicting his victory in the coming election. Helen Douglas returned from lunch in the middle of all this and smiled gamely at her rival, hoping the crisis had passed.

The following day she took the floor. She explained that she wanted spies and traitors rooted out and prosecuted but there were numerous laws already on the books to accomplish this. She would support closing any loopholes but would not sacrifice the liberty of the American people "on an altar of hysteria erected by those without vision, without faith, without courage, who cringe in fear before a handful of crackpots and their traitorous Communist cronies." The country was fighting for freedom and democracy in Korea and would no doubt triumph, but that victory "would be hollow if, in winning, we sacrifice our own freedom and democracy."

Two days later *The New York Times* declared that the new bill "represented a potentially serious threat to American civil liberties." *The Washington Post* echoed Douglas's plea for faith in "the good sense of the people and in the vitality of American institutions." Many other editorials disagreed, however, and the California press in particular hailed the House and mocked Douglas for being part of such a tiny minority. "It is hard to understand Mrs. Douglas," a Long Beach paper observed. "The only conclusion we come to is that she is a sincere 'pink.' " George Rothwell Brown, the Hearst columnist, observed that as the roll call proceeded most of the Democrats "were running for the cyclone cellars," recognizing that "it is no longer regarded as smart—or politically safe—to be pinko." The woman he called La Gahagan was "in a frightful dilemma. Her record for feminine consistency was at stake."

The kind of Communist controls called for by the McCarran bill were new, but loyalty oaths had come to government, to corporate America, to colleges, and to radio and television months before, and by the summer of 1950 they seemed to be headed for Hollywood. In her column, Hedda Hopper quoted a movie-business insider who favored an industry-wide oath. She added: "And those who aren't loyal should be put in concentration camps before it's too late." Cecil B. DeMille decided that the Screen Directors Guild (SDG), which he had run for years, would be the first Hollywood craft union to institute a loyalty oath. Y. Frank Freeman, vice president of Paramount, had told him that this would have a steamroller effect; all the other movie-industry guilds and unions would go along, and "steel, coal and other industries would follow suit."

Only one roadblock stood in DeMille's way: the newly elected president of the SDG, Joseph L. Mankiewicz, who had moderately liberal political views and was known to oppose loyalty oaths. Mankiewicz had emerged as a powerful figure, having won Academy Awards earlier in the year for writing and directing *A Letter to Three Wives,* and having just finished shooting a promising picture called *All About Eve.* Still, DeMille expected Mankiewicz to follow his wishes, just as Joe's predecessors had.

C. B. DeMille may not have been the most reactionary man in Hollywood, but he was probably the most influential. He had thrown his weight behind numerous right-wing causes, and his DeMille Foundation for Americanism kept files on the political affiliations of his peers (information he leaked to HUAC and other investigative bodies). He even urged that the

SDG members, at the close of shooting every film, file a report listing everything the director had learned about the politics of anyone connected with the project. This report would remain on file for other directors to consult before doing any hiring.

Fearing that Mankiewicz might oppose any move to adopt a loyalty oath, DeMille put the measure to a test while the SDG president was in Europe. He called the guild's board members together on August 18 to propose a new bylaw that would make signing an oath—declaring nonmembership in the Communist Party—mandatory for all present and future SDG members. "A tremendous principle has to be acted upon here," DeMille announced. "The question we are asking is, are you on the American side or on the other side? There are members of the guild on the other side and we all know that. . . . It is a wonderful thing, the Screen Directors Guild leading the procession of planting the stars and stripes. . . ." The board then sent SDG members a ballot seeking their views on this matter. The vote came back overwhelmingly in favor of adoption, but the result was fatally compromised by the fact that the ballots had been numbered so that the board could identify how each member voted.

When Mankiewicz's boat docked in New York on August 23 he was greeted by a herd of reporters—and a batch of telegrams from SDG members protesting the new bylaw and the open balloting that confirmed it. Several directors pointed out that in the present climate few could risk voting against a loyalty oath even if they adamantly opposed it. They pleaded with Mankiewicz to at least call a meeting at which the oath could be explained and debated. He refused to make a strong statement one way or the other until he returned to Hollywood. *The New York Times* observed that no organized opposition to the oath was expected, even though certain directors abhorred it (and "asked not to be quoted by name, admitting that they feared the consequences of dissent"). This reflected the temper of the times, the newspaper noted; a year earlier "liberal protest would have been vociferous."

Hollywood conservatives hailed DeMille's move. Frank Freeman congratulated the SDG board members on their "overwhelming victory," adding that he hoped it would be "a forerunner of a movement that all other crafts, guilds and unions will join. I am sure the boys fighting in the armed forces in Korea will be glad to join in saying to all of those members of the SDG who have taken such a forthright stand, 'We are fighting here and we are delighted to know you are fighting at home.' Let us all join together to eradicate Communism from within our borders."

This was too much for Mankiewicz. On August 30, he intimated that, indeed, he opposed the oath and warned, "I won't pull in my horns."

. . .

Fear and tension thickened at the University of California as the August 25 meeting of the state Board of Regents neared. The fate of some thirty-one full-time faculty members who had not signed the university's loyalty oath would be decided here. At a meeting two months earlier, 157 other UC employees (mainly nonteachers) had been discharged. But all eyes rested on the faculty dispute, for both real and symbolic reasons, and because among the nonsigners were many prominent academic figures. The UC controversy had become a national cause célèbre, and its resolution would help determine the future of college loyalty oaths elsewhere.

The UC controversy also threatened to become an issue in the California Senate race, although Richard Nixon so far had struck a relatively moderate stance on it. Communists should not be allowed to teach, he believed, but he advocated finding some grounds for compromise, as it would be "a tragedy if large numbers of teachers left." Helen Douglas bluntly declared that the oath was "not consistent with our American tradition of freedom of speech and thought" and would destroy academic freedom. Meanwhile, inspired by the regents' action, many private employers in California instituted their own loyalty oaths.

Among the regents, Earl Warren had come around to the antioath side. Three of his children currently attended the university, and he claimed that he had no fear that they would be exposed to "a Communist faculty." UC president Robert Gordon Sproul, who had initiated the oath the year before, now opposed it. But these two popular moderates had not been able to win a majority to their side.

With more than forty thousand students on eight campuses, the University of California was the nation's largest school and one of its best. It had plunged into the loyalty-oath quagmire in January 1949, after the regents of the University of Washington ousted two tenured professors who had admitted membership in the Communist Party. A week later the legislature in California passed a resolution, written by Jack Tenney, commending the Washington decision and pointedly sent it to Robert Sproul. At the time, the legislature was considering fifteen repressive anti-Communist bills, also proposed by Tenney, including one mandating a loyalty oath for all teachers. The message out of Sacramento was that UC administrators had better institute their own oath, or the state would do it for them (and, by the way, also cut their budgets).

So Sproul, against his true beliefs, proposed that the university demand that each of its employees affirm that he or she was "not a member of the Communist Party or under any oath or a party to any agreement or under any commitment that is in conflict with my obligations. . . ." Unexpectedly, the UC faculty revolted. Teachers at both Berkeley and UCLA overwhelmingly rejected the existence of the oath (although most said they would sign it to save their jobs). Among the objections: The oath substituted a political test for academic qualifications; it compromised tenure and destroyed academic freedom; and it undermined the safeguard against self-incrimination. Addressing the regents, one of the nonsigners, German-born medieval scholar Ernst Kantorowicz, reminded them, "It is the 'harmless' oath that hooks; it hooks *before* it has undergone those changes that will render it, bit by bit, less harmless. Mussolini Italy of 1931, Hitler Germany of 1933, are terrifying and warning examples for the harmless bit-by-bit procedure in connection with politically enforced oaths."

Then, in February 1950, the regents (with strong support from the press) notified the faculty and employees that they would have to sign the oath that spring or face dismissal. Even the leading proponent of the oath, John Francis Neylan, admitted it was "not worth the paper it is printed on" since Communists could simply lie and sign it anyway. Neylan even admitted privately that he would not sign the oath himself. Faculty members overwhelmingly continued to oppose the oath, with support (including promises of financial aid for discharged professors) coming from twelve hundred distinguished colleagues around the country, including Albert Einstein, Reinhold Niebuhr, and J. Robert Oppenheimer. Some active in opposing the oath met secretly and refused to speak over university phone lines, fearing wiretaps.

Many other state universities, also dependent on public financing, followed UC's example, whereas private institutions, such as Harvard, resisted. Loyalty oaths were quickly adopted by public school systems in big cities and small towns across the country. HUAC, in addition, sent letters to eighty-one colleges and high schools demanding the names of the textbooks they used.

As weeks passed, the heretics who refused to sign the UC oath dwindled from several hundred to seventy-nine, partly out of fear of dismissal.

On June 23, the regents voted to discharge 157 academic assistants and other employees who had not signed the oath (as well as six professors) and to decide the fate of the other 73 faculty nonsigners later in the summer.

Soon the ranks of the nonsigners had fallen to thirty-nine. Patience on all sides was running out. "While American youth is being conscripted to die fighting Communistic barbarism in Korea and elsewhere," the *San Francisco Examiner* complained, "it is proposed to accord to thirty-nine professors and assistant professors . . . the privilege of defying a simple regulation to protect the institution which is engaged in research vital to national defense." No wonder another eight nonsigners suddenly took the oath, reducing the number of holdouts to thirty-one. "The real question," the *Los Angeles Examiner* editorialized the day before the August 25 showdown, "is whether educators, under the cloak of academic freedom, shall be free to poison the minds of American youth with the fallacious doctrines of a foreign despotism."

The final battle would be bitterly fought among the regents, but not so much over potential subversion as over actual power. "No Regent has ever accused a member of the faculty of being a Communist," one of the pro-oath regents admitted. An antioath regent exclaimed, "There is no longer an impugning of those individuals as Communists. It is now a matter of demanding obedience. . . ." With that, the regents voted 12–10 to dismiss the thirty-one nonsigning professors.

Four days later, on August 29, Bernard Brennan launched the opening salvo of the Nixon campaign—still almost three weeks before the official kickoff. He did it with relish, which surprised some of his associates, who considered him such a kindly gentleman. ("It was hard for me to align him with the skulduggery that went on," Nixon radio announcer Tom Dixon later commented.) The campaign director released a statement charging that Douglas supporters were trying to "cast their actress candidate in a new role of foe of Communism" when "her record as a member of Congress discloses the truth about her soft attitude toward Communism." In fact, she had "voted 353 times exactly as has Vito Marcantonio, the notorious Communist Party–line Congressman from New York."

Although an enormous effort went into counting those votes, Brennan claimed that "the import of the votes is more significant than their number." He analyzed some of them: Douglas and Marcantonio against HUAC, against requiring Communists to register with the attorney general, even against investigating how Russia had allegedly managed to purchase sixty thousand U.S. patents. Had the two prevailed in denying aid to Greece and Turkey, "these two countries would now be behind" the Iron Curtain. Brennan concluded his statement with a flourish often cited by the press in the days ahead:

How can Helen Douglas, capable actress that she is, take up so strange a role as a foe of Communism? And why does she, when she has so deservedly earned the title of "the pink lady"? Perhaps she had just heard of the chameleon that changes color to suit conditions, or perhaps [she] had decided pink isn't becoming any more, or at least while we are in a bloody war with Communism. If Helen Douglas in her new role can divert enough Californians from her record, she can be elected Senator, and the Communist *Daily Worker* will have one of its heroes in the body of Congress which passes on the nation's foreign policy.

If this "red-hot broadside" was any indication, the Senate contest would be "a sizzling one," the *Los Angeles Times* declared, and then it reprinted the entire press release. A San Francisco paper praised Brennan's ability to ignore the beauty of Nixon's opponent, observing that he "has been looking at the record instead of Mrs. Douglas. Nothing like politics to hype up your will power!"

Far from finished, Brennan notified Herman Perry at Whittier headquarters that fifty thousand reprints of a *Reader's Digest* condensation of *Seeds of Treason* could be purchased for two thousand dollars. The best-seller on the Hiss case by Ralph de Toledano and Victor Lasky offered a heroic portrait of Nixon. Brennan wanted copies in his state and unveiled a plan to have someone else pick up the tab. It seems that General Motors had purchased 150,000 reprints and circulated them among their employees across the country. Perhaps the corporation would make a similar "contribution" in California "to do something for the cause." Brennan claimed he could furnish legal opinions that such a corporate "service" did not amount to a political contribution.

Obviously, Perry's inquiries on the book went well, for three days later Murray Chotiner notified Brennan that he expected the *Seeds of Treason* reprints to be made available shortly—not in quantities of fifty thousand but in quantities of five hundred thousand.

Yet Richard Nixon was not leaving all the work to others. Perhaps he sensed that soon he would have to sacrifice the remarkable attention to detail he had exercised so far. The candidate continued to write notes to himself and to his aides. On a sheet of lined yellow paper, for example, he scribbled:

Douglas.
Votes (against UnAmerican Activities and Security Legislation).
Similarity to Marcantonio Vote Record.
100% P.A.C. Vote Record.
Resolution on Withdrawal from China (5 Down 1 to go).
I.P.P. write-in candidate.
Support of Wallace in 1944.
"Daily Worker" Editorial.

Nixon had just received a letter from Mac St. Johns, son of his good friend Adela Rogers St. Johns, the famed Hearst reporter. A fellow named Bill Burke had told Mac that if he received some dirt on Helen Douglas, he would pass it along to "Catholic papers and magazines." But Burke wanted a personal okay from the candidate. Nixon immediately offered approval.

"I would suggest," Nixon wrote to St. Johns, "that you start passing information to Bill Burke on Douglas just as soon as it is available in the campaign office. . . . I believe that a fact sheet showing a comparison between the voting records of Douglas and Marcantonio is now available, and that other pieces of literature are in the process of preparation." He also suggested publicizing Douglas's vote against the McCarran bill, "particularly in Catholic circles."

A few days later, on September 2, Nixon told Bill Arnold that someone had just informed him that Douglas was the only member of Congress "who defended the Yalta agreement at the time it was announced. Will you please get this speech and bring it along?"

The same day, Nixon sent Arnold a startlingly detailed memo asking him to "please check" eight important sources related to smears against Douglas. It started with "1. Get the reference which shows that Douglas is connected with the Civil Rights Congress" and "2. Check the reference to her in 'The Red Decade' by Eugene Lyons." Nixon also wanted Arnold to do the following: search for a 1944 article alleging that Douglas had received $954 from a left-wing PAC; find a pair of People's World articles listing her as a speaker for, or sponsor of, two front organizations; locate a 1944 newspaper quote by Mother Bloor, the Communist heroine, praising Douglas; and identify in The New York Times of April 1, 1945, a reference to Douglas as "one who uses and is used by Communists." Arnold hopped right on it, contacting reporters and other sources, including Edna Lonigan.

At about the same time, Nixon asked Murray Chotiner to publicize widely Douglas's vote on the McCarran bill. On September 5, Chotiner asked campaign publicity chief Charlie Bowen not only to "play up" the Douglas vote (and her partnership with Marcantonio) but also to "point out the Democratic leaders who voted for the bill. In short, Mrs. Douglas did not vote as a Democrat or a Republican, but as a member of a small clique that has voted against American security." The campaign office also prepared one-page statements to be released by dozens of special interest committees—one might call them front groups—it had helped establish throughout the state. A doctors' group would charge, for instance, that Douglas was "a proponent of socialized medicine," while veterans would assert that "she has been a Communist 'coddler.' "

A local Nixon organizer, meanwhile, conceived a publicity campaign around the magic number 354. Why 354? The Douglas-Marcantonio rejection of the McCarran bill had now been added to the previous count of 353 votes the two representatives shared. In a stroke of luck, 354 also reflected the number of House members who had voted for the McCarran bill. The organizer wanted to plant that number indelibly in the public mind, much as advertisers had done with such products as Raleigh 903 cigarettes. He suggested "Douglas 354" as a campaign slogan.

Douglas fought back weakly. Her beleaguered, largely untested campaign staff released a statement boasting, "We have not put a statistician to work determining how many times either Mr. Nixon or Mrs. Douglas voted on any number of routine and inconsequential bills the same way that Vito Marcantonio did." But on the single most important vote, regarding Korea, Nixon and Marcantonio had voted together. This approach managed to confirm the sinister nature of voting with Marcantonio—and used an ineffectual, now discredited example to boot. A Nixon biographer would later comment, "When compared with the surgeons of the Nixon camp, Mrs. Douglas's operators performed like apprentice butchers."

Such attacks seemed just to roll off Nixon's back. A San Francisco newspaper observed that "trying to out-Nixon Nixon on this issue" was indeed difficult, for he "really is an enemy of communism." But one charge against the Republican candidate could not be so easily ignored. Murray Chotiner had relayed a warning to Nixon on August 24. Carl Greenburg, the L.A. *Examiner* political editor, had called Chotiner with what he considered reliable information: The Douglas people, "including Mrs. Douglas," were spreading by word of mouth the claim that Gerald L. K. Smith, the outspoken anti-Semite, was supporting Nixon, "and that you are a 'Fascist' in league with him."

The same scenario had developed a few weeks earlier in the governor's campaign, and Warren had solved the problem, Chotiner advised Nixon, by issuing "a blistering repudiation of Smith which received widespread publicity." Now Nixon should do the same. Then, if Smith responded by blasting Nixon, "it would be perfect from our standpoint." Chotiner added that delaying would be a mistake, for if the renunciation came late in the campaign, "it would appear that you were forced to make the statement."

Two days later a Nixon worker at his Los Angeles office sent Chotiner and Brennan a message informing them that the "whispering campaign" was gaining momentum and that the candidate ought to respond. No one knew for sure whether the Douglas campaign was behind it. No hard evidence had surfaced, and certainly the press had ignored the whispering, if in fact it was going on. Nixon had reported similar whisperings to Murray Chotiner long before Helen Douglas became the Democratic nominee.

There was, however, a certain disingenuousness to Nixon's objections. That Smith supported him was more than a vicious rumor. As far back as February, Smith had endorsed Nixon, telling a Christian Nationalist Crusade rally in California, "The man who uncovered Alger Hiss is in California to do the same housecleaning here. . . . Help Richard Nixon get rid of the Jew-Communists." Then, that summer, Smith publicly referred to "my friend Richard Nixon," denounced the "movie Jews" supporting Douglas, and advised that "Californians can do one thing very soon to further the ideals of Christian nationalism, and that is *not* to send to the Senate the wife of a Jew." Yet neither Nixon nor his top advisers had felt any urge to distance the candidate from G.L.K. Smith until now.

Further, the charges of anti-Semitism, although exaggerated, were founded on some reality, as indicated by the extraordinary interest Nixon aides (and the candidate himself) expressed in what might be called the Hesselberg question. Occasionally, in public appearances, Nixon himself would "slip" and refer to his opponent as Helen Hesselberg, before correcting himself. He also allowed Jack Tenney, who was very close to Smith, to stand in for him at some campaign rallies when he was called back to Washington. Tenney later referred to his "warm, cordial" relations with Nixon—despite his dislike for Murray Chotiner, "a Jewish attorney."

In any case, Smith was an easy target for scorn, and Nixon could solve multiple problems by attacking him. Thus the candidate issued a press release from Washington accusing his opponent of attempting to create the impression that he had accepted the support of Smith and his organization. "I want to make it clear," he announced, "that I do not want that support and that I repudiate it. . . . Any individual or organization which promotes dissension between racial or religious elements of our population has my unqualified disapproval." But he would not leave it at that. Instead, he tried to slip the shoe gently onto the other foot. "I am ONE candidate," he added, "who can state that I have never sought nor accepted the support of either a fascist or a communist organization."

CHAPTER NINE

A Stoolie for
J. Edgar Hoover

As Helen Douglas prepared to kick off her fall campaign, the Nixon team concluded research on the Democratic candidate's connection to Vito Marcantonio. Bernie Brennan had celebrated the Douglas-Marcantonio marriage in his August 29 statement, but now the time had come to put it in a printed form that could be widely distributed. Murray Chotiner did not find this unfair. Attacking a candidate's personal life or family—that was a "smear," he once said. "But it is not a smear, if you please, if you point out the record of your opponent."

Chotiner settled on the final form for a flyer: a fact-filled, legal-size sheet of solid type, unassuming but devastating, issued under the name of the Nixon for U.S. Senator Campaign Committee. Across the top, a bold heading would read, DOUGLAS-MARCANTONIO VOTING RECORD. While it "should not be expected" that any member of Congress would always cast a vote contrary to Vito Marcantonio's, the flyer explained, it was significant that Helen Douglas had voted with him such a "great number of times" and that the issues on which they always voted alike concerned "Un-American Activities and Internal Security."

Then came another bold heading—HERE IS THE RECORD!—followed by a straightforward, now somewhat familiar account of Douglas's votes "Against National Defense," against HUAC, and "Against Loyalty and Security Legislation," as well as a description of her "Communist-Line Foreign Policy Votes." In every case, Nixon had cast a vote opposite Douglas's. Finally, near the bottom, in larger type, the flyer asked, "Would California send Marcantonio to the United States Senate?" This went beyond simply exposing her record, for here the Republican was not simply linking Douglas to Marcantonio but equating the two. They were not merely two peas in a pod but essentially the same person. If you wouldn't dream of voting for Marcantonio, why would you even consider voting for Douglas?

This line of argument held great promise, but the occasionally puckish Chotiner wasn't taking any chances. At the Aldine printing plant in Los Angeles, after approving the final copy and layout of the flyer, he and his aides asked to see the choice of paper. The campaign had already widely used black and white, and blue and white, and, Chotiner later explained, "we wanted a different color." Chotiner would later offer two explanations for the pink paper. He told his son, with a grin, that just by luck that was the only color the printer had in stock. In the other version, he was shown several choices, among them pink, and "for some reason or other it just seemed to appeal to us for the moment." In any case he ordered an initial print run of fifty thousand copies of what would soon be known as the Pink Sheet.

Richard Nixon must have chuckled when he read the postcard that arrived at his congressional office in early September. Sent to a broad mailing list, it invited the recipient to the Alexandria Hotel in Los Angeles on September 6 to attend the kickoff of Helen Gahagan Douglas's Senate campaign. Would she open with what Chotiner called "a bang"?

In a half-hour radio speech, she again attempted to defend herself against charges of anti-Americanism while raising some positive issues to set a loftier tone for the campaign. Back in the spring, she had fantasized about attracting so many Republican votes that she might even carry the GOP primary. Now she had obviously abandoned the crossover notion. In asserting that California was a "liberal state" that wanted a "liberal voice" to speak for it in the Senate, Douglas took dead aim at the undecided Democrats who would swing a close election. Many or most of the undecideds were men, and in this opening address she made not a single reference to her sex or her support among women.

The success of the campaign, she predicted, "will depend upon our ability, yours and mine, to bring the facts to the voters of California." Casting herself as the underdog—making a virtue out of the undeniable—she observed that "funds will be limited" and "only a handful of newspapers in California will carry the facts about the Democratic program and the Democratic record." The mudslinging so far was surely only a sample of what awaited her, and Nixon—"beside whom Bob Taft is a flaming liberal"—would no doubt distort her record of "militant support" for President Truman. "But," she continued, "I have no doubt as to the outcome. The

facts are with us. The record is with us. The people are with us, even if big
money is not. The opposition cannot change the facts. It cannot erase the
record. Upon a Democratic victory in California and throughout the nation depends the future course of this nation—yes, upon our winning depends the future course of the world."

That should have got the listeners' attention. But instead of moving immediately to domestic issues, she dwelled on foreign affairs. Again she recalled Nixon's early stand on Korea, hinting that he had invited Soviet
aggression. Not until the second half of the speech did she attack her opponent's weakness, his domestic program, raising issues relating to jobs,
housing, small business, "a sound and prosperous farming economy," Social
Security, the development of natural resources, and equal opportunity.
"Richard Nixon has demonstrated no concern for the welfare of the people of America," she charged. Instead, he had voted with the "blind leaders"
of his party in opposing every social reform proposed by the Democrats.
Rather than sloganeering and slandering, "we must build economic conditions that will prevent communism from breeding."

The speech partly neutralized the Red-baiting, bought Douglas time to
make a positive case, and no doubt encouraged some in the audience to give
her a second look. Still, it seemed to fall short of offering those undecided
Democrats a clear incentive for putting their fears aside and following this
very assertive and very liberal woman. The next day the headline in the L.A.
Daily News, the major paper most sympathetic to the Democratic candidate, reduced her speech to one tired theme: REP. DOUGLAS BLASTS NIXON
OVER KOREA. An editorial cartoon in another newspaper showed the two
Senate candidates, dressed in children's clothes, teasing each other: "Dickie's
helping the Reds" and "Helen's helping the Reds." Looking on over the
horizon, Joe Stalin comments, "Keep It Up Kids. I'm Enjoying It."

Given her problems with conservative Democrats and male voters overall,
Helen Douglas might have awaited Eleanor Roosevelt's arrival in Los Angeles with some ambivalence. Instead, she felt it might turn the whole campaign around. Roosevelt was still widely admired and loved—and perhaps
most important, the press could not ignore her or fail to report at least some
of what she said. Douglas had wanted to schedule Roosevelt's campaign
swing closer to election day, but that was impossible because ER had to return to the United Nations for its fall session.

On September 10, Roosevelt arrived in Los Angeles for her whirlwind,
two-day tour. The following morning, she greeted interviewers and newsreel cameras at her son's home on North Bedford Drive in Beverly Hills.
Dressed in a gray jacket over a black blouse, Roosevelt—in what Westbrook

Pegler called her Empress Eleanor mode—spoke vigorously, gesturing or laughing often, declaring certain remarks "off the record" with the aplomb of an experienced media personality. She spoke affectionately but in generalities about her son and her friend Helen, who was there also; they deserved support because they were good Democrats, and that was enough. A few hours later, at Bixby Park in Long Beach, she addressed a record crowd of more than seven thousand. The Democratic Party, she said, offered the best answer to communism, providing a strong military *and* a strong economy, and she praised President Truman as "a very human person who occasionally makes mistakes."

It was at this rally that Douglas supporters first noticed Republicans passing out pink sheets of paper comparing her voting record with Vito Marcantonio's. The candidate laughed when she saw the flyer, thinking it ridiculous, absurd, ineffectual. Others immediately felt it was trouble. Among them was the young newspaperman Frank Mankiewicz—a nephew of Joseph L. Mankiewicz, as well as a candidate for an assembly seat in L.A. and a close Douglas associate. He believed she was one of those "somewhat isolated liberals" who would dismiss mudslinging and harsh editorials because nobody *she* knew would be fooled by it.

That evening, Roosevelt made a fifteen-minute television appearance in her son's behalf. Then, before a delighted, overflow throng of fifteen hundred—predominantly women—at the Biltmore, she again hailed Jimmy and Helen. The following morning she flew to San Francisco, dressed in the same gray suit but now wearing a blue straw hat. In the Tonga Room of the Fairmont Hotel, she told the crowd that she strongly supported Douglas because she "will work for the good of the people. . . . We need three kinds of leadership: military, economic and—the one in which we lag most—spiritual leadership."

Press coverage of the visit, as expected, was broad, if often shallow. Richard Nixon made no comment. Governor Warren planned to respond negatively but was talked out of it by an aide who argued that he could not criticize a "legend" and come out ahead. So Warren simply remarked, "You wouldn't expect a mother to be against her own son, would you? I don't like to argue with a mother about her boy."

The Los Angeles *Daily News* observed that at the Biltmore "the beautiful Mrs. Douglas" had charmed the buttons off the audience, and the women in the audience allowed that Mrs. Roosevelt "had a right nice hair-do, and all in all the Democrats here went for her in a big way." But Kyle Palmer, predictably, had another view. Political "geiger counters" detected little evidence of lasting impact from Roosevelt's visit, he wrote a few days later. ER was gracious but spoke with little "force or frankness." Palmer couldn't understand why she had come at all if she was going to speak so "pointlessly" about California issues.

A few days after returning to Hyde Park, the former first lady wrote Douglas a brief note describing an incident that must have given the candidate pause. An elderly woman in Alhambra had just informed ER that she had been walking on the street with a friend when they were stopped by another lady who wanted to know whom they were going to vote for. When they mentioned Douglas, the lady said, "You are both making a mistake. Helen Gahagan and Mr. Douglas are both communists and Mrs. Roosevelt is working for Helen Gahagan." In her note to Helen, ER added this commentary: "I thought you might like to know of this type of electioneering."

While Eleanor Roosevelt was in California, the Los Angeles City Council approved an ordinance requiring Communists and other subversives to register with local authorities or face jail. The measure passed 12–1. The lone dissenter, Edward Roybal, admitted he was signing his "political death warrant" but declared that the law left every citizen at the mercy of "any biased crackpot." Two weeks earlier the county supervisors had passed a similar measure. Local Communist Party leader Dorothy Healey immediately announced that no one she knew would comply with the county order.

Healey, who was being closely followed by the FBI, was among several CP organizers in Los Angeles who violently disagreed with the state party's decision not to support Helen Douglas. She blamed Nixon for inspiring the McCarran bill and felt he had to be prevented from doing further damage. But state CP chairman William Schneiderman, who was based in San Francisco, viewed Douglas as merely the lesser of two evils, adding that Communists could not back anyone who endorsed the Korean War. Douglas had been moving to the right since 1947, he charged, calling her one of the "chief liberal apologists for the reactionary policies of the Truman Administration."

Red Channels had been published in late June, but it took several weeks for the letter-writing campaigns it inspired to find the producers or sponsors of shows that featured suspected Communists. CBS officials assured protesters that "through control of programs on the air, we believe we have made Communist infiltration impossible." In reply, the creators of *Red Channels* printed in their newsletter the names of nine tainted performers—none very well known—who had recently appeared on CBS.

The television industry was only now beginning to boom. Such stars as Jack Benny who had made their name in other media made fun of television but knew it represented the future and signed up for their own shows that fall. Groucho Marx, who had just launched *You Bet Your Life,* said that TV stood for "Terrible Vaudeville." Most shows were still live, but Groucho's program was filmed, and the *Hollywood Reporter* called this "a preview of television's future"—the replaying of shows over years "for new audiences around the country at low cost." Color television seemed just around the corner. All of this represented a terrible threat to the film industry, for as Sam Goldwyn noted, Americans could now watch bad TV shows "for nothing," whereas they had to pay to see inferior movies.

"With television going into its third big year, come this Fall," Ed Sullivan wrote, "the entire industry is becoming increasingly aware of the necessity to plug up all Commie propaganda loopholes. Network and station heads, with a tremendous financial stake, want no part of Commies or pinkos. . . . For that reason, *Red Channels* . . . will be a reference book in preparing any program." A survey of major sponsors found that nearly nine of ten believed they must "concern themselves with artists' or writers' ideologies."

While protests and boycotts percolated, some of those exposed in *Red Channels* stepped forward to try to head off trouble. Usually, they were minor stars; the big names could afford to wait and see what developed. One of the first to attempt to clear his name was actor Roger De Koven, whose *Red Channels* listing had included only one infraction: cosponsoring the World Peace Conference at the Waldorf-Astoria Hotel in 1949. After he pleaded his case, his accusers revealed in *Counterattack* that he had impressed them "with his sincerity." He also signed a statement declaring that he had "absolutely no sympathy for the Communist movement," was opposed to the Soviet dictatorship, and had not known the Waldorf affair was organized by Communists. Many others then came to *Counterattack* to deny, explain, or recant in an attempt to gain clearance. Labor columnist Victor Riesel called it "the popular sport of political delousing."

The subterranean influence of *Red Channels* burst into the open in August 1950 after Young and Rubicam announced that its client General Foods had hired veteran movie actress Jean Muir, a *Red Channels* listee, to star in its *Aldrich Family* NBC television series. *Counterattack* immediately organized a protest, and General Foods was deluged with letters and phone calls. Some of the protesters were just average folks; others, such as Rabbi Benjamin Schultz, claimed to speak for large groups.

Muir vigorously denied any Communist connections. General Foods responded by firing her, but not because it agreed with the protests. Whether she was a Red or not, she had become controversial, the company's statement explained, and the "use of controversial personalities or the discussion of controversial subjects in our advertising may provoke unfavorable criticism and even antagonism among sizable groups of consumers." The company was so eager to cut its losses it agreed to pay the actress in full for the length of her eighteen-week contract. Muir spoke for many when she declared, "It seems unbelievable that an actress can have such a setback to her livelihood and career based on nothing more than unsubstantiated accusations made over the telephone and by telegraph." At the age of thirty-nine and barely at mid-career, Muir was understandably worried.

The American Civil Liberties Union came to her defense and promised to investigate the claim that a wider blacklist was already in effect in the industry. Others threatened to boycott General Foods if it did not rehire her. Max Lerner, the columnist, called the new blacklisters "the locust-plague of the democratic harvest." Commenting on the Muir case, *The Nation* decried a pattern of "such degrading foolishness" that Americans would one day recall the present year of "heresy hunting" with embarrassment. Rudy Vallee, a singer not known for his liberal views, defended Muir and promised to "horsewhip" anyone who accused *him* of any political misdeed. But these views were overwhelmed in many newspapers by supporters of the blacklist. "Guilt by association is an old and respected principle of jurisprudence," Westbrook Pegler wrote. "If you hang out in a low resort and are picked up as a low character, that is your fault."

After the Muir case, the blacklist took on a new gravity and momentum, with *Red Channels* still the catalyst. Gypsy Rose Lee, the famous stripper, had to block a drive to force ABC to drop her as an emcee of a new TV program. An executive at MGM suggested to songwriter Yip Harburg that he compose a letter to explain the twenty-two listings under his name in *Red Channels*. Harburg wrote a statement admitting his membership in several fronts but decried the notion of guilt by association and proudly attached copies of his songs "God's Country" and "Brother, Can You Spare a Dime?," explaining that they spoke for themselves "as well as for me."

Hazel Scott, noted pianist (and wife of Congressman Adam Clayton Powell, Jr.), voluntarily came before HUAC to protest her listing in *Red Channels*. She declared that most of the claimed affiliations were bogus and called on the television networks to stand up to "the bigots"—and for the moment she was left alone. Folksinger Josh White, on the other hand, chose the confessional route after losing many bookings. He told HUAC that Communists had played him "for a sucker" for years and he wanted his "sad experience to stand as a warning" to other artists. Chairman John Wood thanked him for coming and added, "I hope others similarly inspired will do the same." White soon found work again.

Another *Red Channels* listee, Ireene Wicker, the children's entertainer known as the Singing Story Lady, was not so fortunate. She had starred on television for Kellogg's for over a year, but now the cereal company canceled her contract. Earlier in the summer, after learning of her appearance in *Red Channels,* Wicker had visited the offices of *Counterattack* editor Ted Kirkpatrick. She challenged the one black mark against her: She had allegedly cosponsored the committee that nominated Benjamin Jefferson Davis, Jr., a black Communist, for the New York City Council in 1945. Wicker said she had never heard of Benjamin Davis and wasn't even in New York in 1945.

Kirkpatrick replied that his source, the *Daily Worker,* was definitive, and he would not "clear" her. Wicker's attorney, after scanning all thirty thousand names on Davis's nominating petitions for 1945 and failing to find Wicker's name, turned this evidence over to Kirkpatrick, who admitted his source was probably wrong. But it was too late. Kellogg's had already fired the singer and would not rehire her.

In his HUAC testimony, Josh White refuted Paul Robeson's famous assertion of the previous year that oppressed African-Americans should not fight for their country in any war against Russia, and he took his old singing partner to task for giving comfort to those who "despise America." White apparently had warned Robeson about his testimony in a friend's bathroom with the tap water running in case the house was bugged. "They've got me in a vise," he explained.

No one in America was in a bigger vise than Paul Robeson—but then he was a big man. The State Department revoked his passport in August, and NBC not only canceled his appearance on Eleanor Roosevelt's television show but also announced that he would never appear on the network so long as he retained his pro-Communist beliefs. The mayor of Boston banned the display of Robeson's portrait in a traveling exhibition of paintings of famous black Americans. Even Communist Party leaders in the United States urged him to cut down on his public speaking and concentrate on singing, believing he could do the cause more good in that manner, but he refused, despite his recently diminished income. He continued to tell his audiences that blacks did not take the Communist threat seriously. Ask them to identify the greatest menace, and they would answer, according to Robeson, "Jim-Crow justice! Mob rule! Segregation! Job Discrimination!"

What had finally moved the government to void his passport, however, was his assertion that summer that Negroes should fight for freedom at home, not in Korea. This merely confirmed the sentiment he had expressed in 1949—but this was another year. He drew strong support in the African-American community, but few public figures protested the State Department's action. Officials at Madison Square Garden refused to rent the arena to a political group planning a pro-Robeson rally. As Robeson sought legal redress, the State Department announced it would reconsider its travel ban only if he agreed in writing to make no political speeches while abroad.

In early September, Harry Warner called all his employees together at sound stage 21 on the Warner Bros. lot. He told them he favored revoking the citizenship of members of un-American organizations and shipping them back to "their hidden land or the country in whose hidden employ they are." If the studio workers allowed "communistic teachings" on the lot or in their films, they were "worse" than the Communists, he added. Warner, along with other studio bosses, also ordered employees to attend mass meetings and listen to a recording of General Eisenhower asking them to sign the Scroll of Freedom, which was being circulated nationally. Soon, fourteen thousand in Hollywood would sign, about 95 percent of those eligible.

As autumn approached, it became clear that a new HUAC investigation of the movie industry was in the offing. A third disillusioned Hollywood Communist, Leo Townsend (best known for cowriting *Night and Day*), had joined Sterling Hayden and Richard Collins in secretly offering to assist the FBI.

The fact that these three men were willing to name names in exchange for favorable treatment was still not public knowledge. Widely publicized, however, was the first break in the ranks of the Hollywood Ten. Edward Dmytryk, the director, was serving a sentence in federal prison in West Virginia when he announced that he was ready to answer the question put to him by HUAC in 1947. As he later put it, he wanted to escape not only from jail "but out of my real imprisonment, my associations." And so on September 9, Dmytryk signed an affidavit (sent to the U.S. attorney general) revealing that he had not been a member of the Communist Party at the time of the HUAC hearing and was not a Communist sympathizer today. He did not discuss his pre-1947 affiliations, when he did belong to the CP, and although he did not promise to cooperate with authorities, that step now seemed inevitable. (He was eager to work again in Hollywood.)

Sterling Hayden, meanwhile, had given a full statement to FBI officials in L.A. and agreed to name names whenever HUAC got around to reopening its Hollywood hearings, probably the following spring. Suddenly, the actor received a new seven-year contract from Paramount. In conversations with his therapist, he started referring to himself as "a stoolie for J. Edgar Hoover." He said his therapist didn't have "the foggiest notion of the contempt I have had for myself" since deciding to cooperate with the witch-hunters.

A more illustrious actor was also taking the first slow steps down the road to clearance. Edward G. Robinson hadn't been asked to make a film in Hollywood since *House of Strangers* in 1949. He was a strong liberal who had donated to all of Helen Douglas's campaigns and to the support of the Hollywood Ten, but he was hardly a Red. (He hadn't even backed Henry Wallace in '48.) Concerned that a blacklist existed and that he was on it, he gave his attorney, Mendel Silberberg—the Nixon fund-raiser—a copy of *Red Channels* and asked him to analyze it.

On September 5, Silberberg sent the actor a lengthy memo suggesting that he check his records to see whether his listings in *Red Channels* were correct and whether he had severed his connections with any of the groups. The attorney clearly wanted Robinson to come forward and come clean. The lawyer suggested that he draw up a factual statement "showing the innocent character of your connections."

Walter Wanger, the producer and another well-known liberal (and Douglas contributor), had already taken steps to shore up his patriotic credentials, volunteering to chair the Scroll of Freedom drive in Los Angeles. But that didn't satisfy the industry's right-wing watchdog group, the Motion Picture Alliance for the Preservation of American Ideals. Its president, John Wayne, praised him for taking on the task, but Wayne had one question: Now that he had seen the light, did Wanger want to "correct" his earlier statement that the Motion Picture Alliance had made unsupported charges of communism in the film industry? Wanger wrote back immediately, admitting that "time and history" had proved the correctness of the Alliance's charges. He even agreed to let the organization publish his mea culpa in the *Hollywood Reporter.*

For Charlie Chaplin, however, no such rapprochement appeared possible. His years of left-wing activities—and unwavering support for the Hollywood Ten—had finally caught up with him. (Richard Nixon had lamented that "the nickels and dimes of the good American moviegoers" were underwriting his activism.) Chaplin planned to return to his native England to shoot his new film, *Limelight,* but wanted assurances from the State Department that he would be allowed back into the United States. Columnist Louella Parsons happily reported that the State Department had advised Chaplin that if he left this country, "it is extremely doubtful if he will be allowed to re-enter."

Frequently a mouthpiece for the studio bosses, Parsons warned that it was time for actors listed in *Red Channels* to declare their opposition to the Communist Party, for if they did not, "they will be conspicuously absent from our motion picture screens. No producer is willing to sign any actor who is not one hundred percent American."

Leading producers and studio executives, including L. B. Mayer and C. B. DeMille, sponsored ads in the trades to announce that "from now on, let us make no mistake about it: The war is on, the chips are down. Those among us who defend Russia or Communism are enemies of freedom and traitors to the U.N. and the U.S." Even mythical Indian heroes came under suspicion. *Daily Variety* revealed that the Monogram studio and producer Walter Mirisch had shelved plans to make a movie about Hiawatha because the character was known for his "constant striving for peace among the warring New England Indians," and this "might be construed now as Communistic." A Monogram executive explained that producers were being "extremely cautious in preventing any subject matter to reach the screen which might possibly be interpreted as Communistic propaganda to even the slightest degree."

As Helen Douglas opened her campaign, Richard Nixon remained in Washington, giving the impression of attending to important duties while his opponent somehow found time to fly around California grubbing for votes. On September 8, Nixon wrote his constituents a letter mainly on the Korea situation, making full (and fully legal) use of his franking privileges.

Since the Korean conflict began, Nixon had remained relatively supportive of his commander in chief. But the fall campaign was at hand, and he had to find a way to break with the Democrats but not seem disloyal. So he now called for a "full scale mobilization" of our forces, denouncing the use of the term "police action" to obscure the fact that what was going on in Korea was a war. This statement achieved two political purposes: It proved Nixon was fully behind the fighting men, and it elevated the conflict to an even higher level of concern for voters.

He might have left it at that but instead observed that there was "much discussion everywhere as to how we got into our present predicament," thus signaling that the Republicans were about to make political capital out of the war. Giving careful examination to this question *now*, not after the soldiers came home, was important so as to "avoid a repetition of our past mistakes." And those mistakes—both diplomatic and military, including the failure of the Democrats to adopt the same hard-nosed strategy in Asia that they had adopted in postwar Europe—"cannot be denied." Furthermore, Secretary of State Acheson should be immediately replaced by someone who might earn the "faith and confidence" of the American people.

Even if the war started to go well, Nixon's carping on the causes of the conflict might resonate with many voters. And if the war dragged on, then he was poised to take full advantage of it.

In early September, President Truman approved a bold, desperate, perhaps even foolhardy plan by General MacArthur to save the fifty thousand U.S.

troops trapped behind the Pusan perimeters and turn the tide of the entire Korean War. Clearly, *something* had to be done, for both military and political purposes. U.S. casualties in Korea now exceeded twelve thousand, and with election day less than two months away the press and the public had grown restive (when they weren't being downright hostile to the war). A Gallup poll suggested that 57 percent of the respondents thought the United States was "actually now in World War III."

A *Time* correspondent had recently called it "an especially terrible war," "sickening," "ugly." While noting the appalling fighting conditions and the brutality of the enemy, the correspondent, John Osborne, also recorded with remarkable frankness the apparent slaughter of civilians by Americans: "the blotting out of villages where the enemy *may* be hiding; the shooting and shelling of refugees who *may* include North Koreans in the anonymous white clothing of the Korean countryside, or who *may* be screening an enemy march upon our positions."

Actually, the killing was far worse than Osborne knew, for he had access (and partial at that) only to what was occurring in South Korea. Over the past several weeks, General Curtis Le May's SAC bombers, with little fanfare, had dropped more than three thousand tons of bombs on North Korean targets—said to be "military" or "industrial" in nature but often the centers of large cities. As in World War II, "precision bombing" was a misnomer of profoundly tragic dimensions. Le May had also introduced a little-known weapon, napalm, a mixture of phosphorus-ignited acids that burned inside wounds for as long as fifteen days. Thousands of civilians had already perished in this limited war, and a U.S. military dispatch described a "wilderness of scorched earth" across parts of North Korea.

Al Jolson, visiting the troops in the south, asked one young American what he was fighting for. "My life," the soldier replied. Vito Marcantonio's office observed that even Walter Lippmann now felt that Korea was not a vital national interest. While the cause might be just, "we are not all-powerful," Edward R. Murrow observed. "We must accept the proposition that the *people* of Asia will decide their future. . . ."

Frustration reached such a level that several U.S. military leaders expressed openly what had long been whispered: America should wage and win a "preventive" nuclear war against the Soviet Union itself. On August 25, Navy Secretary Francis P. Matthews, a prominent Catholic layman, called for such a war, with the United States as "the first aggressors for peace." Hanson Baldwin of *The New York Times* called Matthews's statement a "trial balloon" and noted that Secretary of Defense Louis Johnson "has been selling the same doctrine of the preventive war in private conversations around Washington." Truman disavowed Matthews's views but allowed the secretary to stay on the job. Not so fortunate was Major General Orvil A. Anderson, commander of the Air War College, who was suspended on September 1 for teaching a course on preventive war and for saying in an interview, "Give me the order to do it and I can break up Russia's five A-bomb nests in a week. . . . And when I went up to Christ—I think I could explain to Him that I had saved civilization."

Truman was so concerned about this trend that he declared for the record, "We do not believe in aggressive or preventive war." But he knew that the talk would not cease until the United States somehow turned things around in Korea.

MacArthur, determined not only to avoid another Dunkirk but also to go on the offensive at last, had proposed a massive amphibious landing at Inchon, far across the southern peninsula from Pusan, to outflank the enemy. General Omar Bradley called it the most risky military assault he had ever discussed. Because of the high tides and the virtual absence of beaches, the landing craft would have only a few minutes in which to motor to shore and clear the sea wall. But to MacArthur, this was one of the virtues of his plan, for Inchon would be about the last place the enemy would expect such a landing. After much debate and some dissension, the Joint Chiefs of Staff and then Truman approved the landing, utilizing seventy thousand men and over two hundred ships, with September 15 as the target date.

Amazingly, the assault succeeded. The enemy, indeed, was caught by surprise. Inchon fell in a day, and as the Americans swept north and east, the North Koreans fell back from Pusan in full retreat. A rout, beyond all U.S. expectations, was on. Soon, after frightfully destructive U.S. shelling, the enemy abandoned Seoul and by the end of the month had recrossed the border, fleeing north. After three months of battle, Korea was once again divided at the 38th parallel, which the United States had established as its goal when it intervened in the conflict. "Well and nobly done," Truman cabled MacArthur. But the fighting and the bloodshed had just begun.

At the same time to the south, another Asian war wore on. Ten U.S. military advisers had just arrived in Vietnam, and plans called for the number to increase to sixty-five by the fall. Back in June, President Truman had ordered a dramatic increase in assistance to the French in Indochina. Soon the thirty-one-million-dollar U.S. military-aid program was surpassed only by the war effort in Korea. Tons of U.S. military equipment, including a few bombers and fighter planes, accompanied the first military advisers, and none too soon: After a year of preparation across the border in China, General Vo Nguyen Giap had launched the first assault on isolated French forts in the far north.

American advisers were alarmed, however, by the constraints the French put on their activities: They were restricted from dealing directly with the Vietnamese army and forbidden from supervising the use of U.S. equipment. The French obviously wanted to use the Vietnamese and their puppet leader, Bao Dai, to maintain colonial control over the country without U.S. political interference. The Americans were also kept away from Vietnamese civilians, and so information on the progress of the war came only from the French. The United States could not influence, or perhaps even understand, what was happening in the country. Observers could not fathom whether insurgent leader Ho Chi Minh was a tool of the Red Chinese or a native patriot.

At the same time, State Department officials warned that with its new commitment, U.S. "prestige" was now on the line in Vietnam. Allies in the region and around the globe were said to be monitoring America's resolve. A National Security Council report warned that if the French lost Indochina, nearby Thailand and Burma would fall, and the balance of power in the region "would then be in grave hazard." Dean Acheson affirmed that the United States "does not intend to permit further extension of Communist domination of Asia or in the southeast Asia area." Veteran diplomat George Kennan felt, however, that the West's position in Vietnam was hopeless and advocated a pullout, even if it meant Viet Minh or Communist Chinese domination of the country. He wrote Acheson:

> In Indo-China we are getting ourselves into the position of guaranteeing the French in an undertaking which neither they nor we, nor both of us together, can win. . . . We cannot honestly agree with them that there is any real hope of remaining successfully in Indo-China . . . it would be preferable to permit the turbulent political currents of that country to find their own level, unimpeded by foreign troops or pressures.

But Kennan's recommendation found few friends in the administration. The French had committed 140,000 troops to the area, and nearly 20,000 French soldiers had lost their lives there since 1945, more than 2,000 during the first six months of 1950. When the United States in 1950 finally established an embassy in Saigon, President Truman extended his condolences to the wives and families of the French casualties and vowed "to bring this war to a victorious conclusion and to pacify the area."

· · ·

Beyond the candidate's press releases from Washington, the Nixon campaign was seemingly quiet, perhaps to make the bang of his kickoff on September 18 deafening. The media was doing a pretty good job on Douglas anyway. A Hearst paper, for example, suggested that no matter how Douglas portrayed her record, voters who studied it carefully would find that she was "obviously . . . friendly and favorable to those who are plotting for the overthrow of the American way of life." Bald statements like this sounded better coming from third parties than from Nixon himself. But behind the scenes, sometimes in esoteric ways, Nixon staffers continued to lay the groundwork for the brutal battle to come.

Murray Chotiner, for example, directed a barrage of orders to publicity aide Charlie Bowen. Bowen was to "prepare a quote" for Nixon to use in a press release commending "Negro troops for their courageous actions in Korea." He was to release a story quoting a woman, preferably a Democrat, "pointing out that Douglas says one thing and votes another," particularly on un-American activities. And he was to prepare sample editorials that newspapers all over the state could publish as their own. With the Pink Sheet already a tremendous success, Chotiner ordered thousands of additional copies. "We are going to point up the record," he told a reporter, "so that no matter how good an actress Mrs. Douglas is, she is not going to be able to sustain her new role as a foe of the Communists." Douglas hadn't received so much praise for her acting in years.

A Republican official in L.A., Evelle Younger, wrote in a party bulletin that Helen Douglas "expects to devote her campaign to convincing the citizenry that, being a woman, she has the right to change her mind, and her record." That statement had also been used in a campaign press release, along with a reference to the "blushing complexion" of Democratic candidates. Dana Smith, the Nixon finance director, mailed fund-raisers a form letter, suggesting that they "bear down" if they want to "shove the 'Pink Lady' out of the political picture." A Committee of Ten Thousand, meanwhile, had been formed under Robert A. Millikan, the famed scientist and president of California Institute of Technology. *Ten Thousand* referred not to a dollar figure but to the number of relatively small donors the committee hoped to inspire.

Besides sending out sample editorials, Chotiner and Bowen distributed press releases that could be reprinted in their entirety as news articles, thus saving editors and reporters a lot of trouble. The body of each "article" was the same, but the opening paragraphs were slightly different for each paper so that the articles would appear to have been written by a staff reporter. A press release sent to the *L.A. Times,* for example, would be labeled "for the *Times* . . . lead not duplicated."

Efforts to organize front groups seemingly independent of the Nixon campaign intensified. Two such groups were especially important in this race. Democrats for Nixon, under George Creel, prepared to go public, having attracted a stellar list of supporters, including James "Linn" Beebe, the prominent L.A. attorney and civic leader, MGM art director Cedric Gibbons, and Los Angeles Jewish leader Rabbi Max John Merritt. Creel notified a friend that the state Democratic Party apparatus in the north was at present "doing nothing for Helen, and Sheridan Downey is on the ground, doing everything in his power for Nixon, but very secretly."

Women for Nixon launched its effort on September 19 with a series of luncheons and radio and TV broadcasts. Its director had already blamed Douglas for the "bitter bloody war in Korea" and referred to her voting record in Congress as "most pleasing to the Kremlin." Pat Nixon attended the luncheon in Los Angeles. Principal speaker was Mrs. Harry Goetz, a former Democratic leader in Kentucky. Women, Goetz said, "would naturally like to support a woman for public office, but when a woman does not measure up we must turn to a man, and Richard Nixon because of his demonstrated ability is the kind of a man we can support wholeheartedly."

To ensure this, the group would continue to distribute tens of thousands of plastic Nixon thimbles to women around the state, to "sew up" the election, as they put it. This was clearly an attempt to highlight what could be called the housewife versus professional woman split in the campaign, as if Pat Nixon were running against Helen Gahagan Douglas. Most voting-age women in the nation were homemakers and, if a recent Gallup poll could be believed, fairly happy about it (80 percent of them said they got "a lot" or a "fair amount" of pleasure and satisfaction out of housework). Many of them viewed Helen Douglas as an "uppity" woman, whereas Pat Nixon symbolized the stability of home and hearth most Americans craved after the trauma of World War II. Republican pamphlets had always played to this constituency, portraying women (inevitably suburban housewives) in supportive, even submissive roles on and off the campaign trail.

The Nixon women also planned to circulate a chain letter reporting that their candidate wanted to remove luxury taxes on cosmetics, baby oils, handbags, "and many other necessities [that] cost us 20% more than they should." Furthermore, because Nixon had no "slush fund," he had to depend solely on his congressional salary to provide for his wife and "two lovely little girls." He and Pat therefore understood "the problems confronting the American woman today in trying to maintain a comfortable home and rear her children to become worthy citizens." By implication, Helen Douglas did not.

It was clear that the female candidate in the California Senate race could not count on automatically gaining a majority of the "distaff vote." Women activists, in fact, would form the lifeblood of Nixon's grassroots campaign, and they were not exactly shrinking violets. One of his supporters in Beverly Hills wrote a letter to members of her women's club denouncing the Douglas "propaganda campaign" to stampede women into "blind allegiance to a member of their sex. . . . I think it is time to point out," she added, "that Helen Gahagan Douglas is neither truly representative of her sex nor her party."

Nixon himself would pay his female volunteers a kind of tribute. They were, he told Tom Dixon, the "great haters."

A Women for Nixon telecast featured the candidate with Hollywood figures Hedda Hopper, Irene Dunne, and Louise Beavers. But a radio broadcast was something else. Instead of opening with a statement identifying itself as a political commercial, it began with the sound of a rainstorm. Four women, waiting for a bus, had dashed under a doorway to escape the downpour. They were (according to the script) a "kindly old Negress" with two sons in Korea, "a foreigner" who had fled brutal conditions in Russia, "a cynic," and a woman who doubled as narrator of the program (Hedda Hopper).

The "venomously sarcastic" cynic supported Helen Douglas because the candidate opposed sending aid to countries to help fight communism. The woman played by Hedda Hopper explained that this was exactly why *she* was for Nixon. "Ah'm votin' foh him too," the Negress interjected. Hopper pointed out that Nixon fought to keep our atomic secrets whereas Douglas wanted to give them away. He was against "subversion and Communist plots" whereas Douglas was against investigations. In fact, many of Douglas's ideas were "Un-American." And Douglas was also against the small businessman.

CYNIC: "Say! I don't like the sound of that."

HEDDA: "If you stand too close to a red lamp, you're bound to get burned."

The cynic confessed that now Nixon had her vote. "I guess I've been listening to the wrong radio program," she added.

NEGRESS: "Yes, ma'am! You listen to de sweet-talk o' dat Douglas woman, it gonna lead you right into a trap."

With that, the storm ended, and the sun came out.

At this point, Hedda Hopper retreated to the role of narrator, asking listeners to join Women for Nixon. The foreigner gave out the main phone number for the campaign, and the Negress followed with a different number for "our group dat is workin' hard fuh to elect Mr. Nixon."

Of all the contrasts between Nixon and Douglas, none was more striking and more exploitable in 1950 than their family lives. Douglas's rich, famous Jewish husband was rarely around, at least one of her kids always seemed to be away at camp or across the country, and her posh home in the hills hardly reflected middle-class living. Richard Nixon, on the other hand, had it all, at least in terms of voter identification: a starter home in an all-American community; a pretty, Irish Protestant wife usually at his side when she wasn't cooking and sewing and looking after the house, and two cute little daughters close by.

The Nixon campaign tried to capitalize on this by featuring the candidate's family in much of its publicity material. The San Francisco office sent Adela Rogers St. Johns out to Honeysuckle Lane in Whittier to write a glowing tribute to the candidate's family, which it then circulated to newspapers to run as a guest feature. St. Johns qualified for this task on several scores. During the 1930s, she had been hailed by her employer, the Hearst Corporation, as the world's greatest "girl reporter" (she was then in her mid-thirties). Like many other members of her profession, she was hard drinking and tough talking and Irish to the core; she even covered prizefights. Later she wrote screenplays and religious novels, and her life was immortalized in the film *His Girl Friday,* starring Rosalind Russell.

While living on a ranch outside Whittier, she had encountered young Dick Nixon when he delivered groceries from his father's store. Usually a Democrat, Adela was turning Republican when she met Nixon again in 1950. She liked him so much she introduced him to her friends John Clements (Hearst's intelligence chief) and Howard Hughes—and told him he would one day be president of the United States.

Her lovely newspaper profile portrayed the Nixons as "sound, right, the very grassroots of the nation." It was all there: the five-room, one-story house, the Irish setter, the two adorable girls (one in cowboy boots, the other in a straw bonnet), the living room with green chintz curtains (sewn by the lady of the house), a dining alcove with potted begonias, the modern kitchen, and Pat, the perfect wife and housewife, in a print housedress, "a tall, slim young woman with a face full of character, and lovely red-gold hair." Dick was lucky he had met Pat because she had once taught economics and knew how to stretch a dollar.

Adela took time out from chatting with Pat Nixon to ask the candidate a few policy questions and then gushed, "To talk statesmanship with Nixon in his home, with his wife bringing you the best cup of coffee you ever tasted, all the kids in the block congregated in the Nixon back yard, his neighbor playing Mr. Belvedere, the folk who know all the facts about him coming to wish him luck, convinces you that America still produces the Uncommon man from the Common man—as long as she does that we know we're safe."

Nixon had always utilized Pat in his campaigns, and she had performed admirably in the role of candidate's wife: standing by his side or passing out literature or thimbles and chatting with well-wishers (but never speaking from the stage). She was, as one reporter put it, "quite an asset to Mr. Nixon." As necessary, she reassured Nixon advisers when events did not break their way. "Don't worry about Dick," she told Roy Day. "The tougher the going the better he gets." Nixon claimed that she had been one of the few who enthusiastically urged his run for the Senate, but friends suspected that she resented her role as candidate's wife and politics in general. She was game, however, even on the long campaign trips in the station wagon, which left her face a mask of weariness. She hated leaving her daughters with neighbors or housekeepers and worriedly phoned home several times a day.

On these trips, Pat could not wear clothes she liked but only what her husband wanted—the most conservative dresses and never, never slacks. (The candidate insisted that none of his female aides or campaign workers wear pants.) She once explained that a "wife's first duty is to help and en-courage her husband in the career he has chosen," but surely she sometimes doubted it. When Mary Ellen Leary interviewed her at the St. Francis Hotel in San Francisco she found the candidate's wife extremely "uneasy" about her role in the campaign. Adela St. Johns, who knew Pat as a charming, gay schoolteacher in the 1930s, later observed that she didn't have the "tem-perament" for political life; the "agony" she went through for her husband was simply heartbreaking.

Often on the campaign trail the candidate humiliated his wife in front of others. Adela's son Mac heard him snap "I'll go when I'm damned well ready" after she reminded him it was time to leave for the next stop. Wait-ing to go on the air at a radio station, he brusquely motioned her out of the studio. It was "like he was telling a dog to go outside," the wife of Nixon's radio announcer, Tom Dixon, recalled. Later Pat explained to the Dixons, "You know Richard doesn't like to have me in there. I don't know why but I make him nervous. He's such a great man." Tom Dixon had never seen any man cut off his wife in public "so curtly" without ever getting a retort or a dirty look in response. "I felt sorry for her," he added. "She was gracious and honorable but weak with him. His ego had to be toadied to. Why did she take it unless she wanted to see her man scale the ladder? She had a little of the martyr complex in her to take that with so little grumbling." Dixon added that he never saw the candidate touch his wife's hand. "She was farther away from him than I was, . . ." he said. "I never have seen quite as cold an arrangement."

As the campaign wore on, Pat Nixon's feelings about the savagery of her husband's attacks on his female opponent were unclear. Asked by a reporter what it was like to campaign against a woman, Pat replied, "She's a candidate for office. That's how we look at her. Not as a woman." Sometimes she seemed repelled by the general tone of the campaign and, particularly, by the tactics and manner of Murray Chotiner, whom she had never liked. On other occasions, when Douglas made personal attacks, Pat urged her husband to reply in kind. "How can you let them do that?" she challenged him. Sometimes she criticized his speeches or pronounced a campaign appearance "a disaster," but Chotiner, who desired no inside interference, isolated Dick from Pat as much as possible. "Murray got her to go away," one insider later explained.

Between Douglas's campaign kickoff and Nixon's promised launch, the McCarran bill finally came before the Senate. It promised to be an historic debate. Democrats in the Senate, many of them facing the voters that fall, scrambled to propose their own measure. The group, led by liberals Paul Douglas, Hubert Humphrey, and Herbert Lehman, was so desperate to appear tough on communism it drafted what one White House aide privately labeled "a concentration camp bill." It authorized the president to declare, under specific conditions or at his discretion, an "internal security emergency," during which the attorney general would be authorized to round up persons whom the president had "reason to believe" might engage in espionage, sabotage, or other acts of subversion. Even some of its sponsors recognized that it was, as Senator Lehman put it, "a very bad bill," but they advised Truman to embrace it as a possible way to beat McCarran.

In the Senate debate, the liberals argued that their preventive-detention measure was superior to one that simply called for registering Communists, for it would focus on acts, not just on agitation. Unlike the McCarran bill, it would avoid character assassination. "Defamation is really more injurious than detention," argued Paul Douglas, surely without conviction. Humphrey ridiculed the McCarran bill as a "hoax" and the "cream-puff special."

Now it was time for the Republicans (and conservative Democrats) to rail against an "unconstitutional" measure that would lead to "dictatorship."

But that didn't mean they could not live with it. For the Democrats had blundered badly. Rather than attempt to vote down the Democrats' substitute measure, the GOP brain trust (which included Congressman Nixon) decided to incorporate the detention-camp aspect into their own bill. And the Democrats, desperate for a get-tough measure they could take partial credit for, acceded.

On September 12, the Senate passed the McCarran bill with the detention-camp provision. Liberals like Humphrey, Paul Douglas, Warren Magnuson, and Wayne Morse all voted in favor of it, and only seven opposed it. Then the liberals had second thoughts and, bizarrely, urged Truman to veto the bill they had just endorsed. Hubert Humphrey congratulated Estes Kefauver on his nay vote and added, "I wish I could say the same for myself." That night he reportedly had trouble sleeping and called Paul Douglas, who was awake for the same reason, well after midnight. Connecticut senator William Benton, in the midst of a tough campaign against Prescott Bush, would later confess that his vote for the McCarran bill "troubled me more than any vote I made during my entire period in the Senate."

While Truman decided whether to make good on his threat to veto the measure, the White House was flooded with nine thousand letters on the issue. An elderly gentleman from Chicago wrote that "it should be made a national law that anybody that even thinks of Communism should be strung up by their neck until dead, or electrocuted." From a Realtor in Portland, Maine: "There are lots of little lights in windows along the shores of Maine, beaming out to sea from homes where there is a vacant chair; a chair where a young man used to sit a few weeks ago but who tonight is on the battle front in Korea. Yes, mothers of these boys are thinking of them tonight, and of you, Mr. President, afraid you might veto this bill; afraid you may have forgotten their boy."

Helen Douglas, on the other hand, wrote Truman to suggest that if he did veto the measure, he should appoint a presidential commission to recommend more effective actions than those prescribed by the present bill, which she depicted as "hasty, essentially emotional." Richard Nixon broke off campaigning in Sacramento and flew back to Washington, ready to cast his vote to override the expected veto of the bill he essentially fathered back in 1948.

President Truman, meanwhile, told his cabinet that he wanted to step up civil-defense measures, "but it has to be done in a way which will not too greatly alarm our civilian population." He asked Congress for nearly $140 million with which to prepare for atomic attack by constructing offices for some thirty-five thousand to forty thousand federal workers outside Washington. It was unclear whether this signaled the beginning of a gradual dispersal of the entire federal government—to offer the Russians a more difficult target—or was simply meant to provide standby facilities in the event of a hasty evacuation. In any case, the request was far from reassuring.

Other officials and some urban planners favored dispersal from *all* major cities, a kind of forced suburbanization. It was often stated that the Soviet bomb "doomed" the American city. Builders of suburban subdivisions and shopping malls, already riding a societal trend, gained impetus from such predictions. *Life* magazine published a plan by MIT mathematician Norbert Wiener (and others) calling for the construction of eight-lane "beltways" around cities to speed evacuation. Campsites would be built adjoining these new superhighways.

Behind the scenes, however, the United States pursued an aggressive new policy—yet another 1950 turning point. In August, as the war in Korea worsened, Truman asked AEC and military officials to consider a dramatic expansion in nuclear facilities. On September 6, they responded with a $1.4-billion plan for doubling the military's nuclear program. It called for a vast new network of atomic reactors and nuclear production, processing, and storage facilities, as well as the acquisition of "essentially all of the foreseeable world supply of uranium ore" outside the Soviet bloc. Five days later the Joint Chiefs of Staff set "production objectives" based largely on "anticipated development of new types of atomic weapons," including "atomic warheads for guided missiles."

It was becoming increasingly clear that the Republican strategy called for isolating Douglas from the political mainstream and from her own party by picturing her as a left-wing ideologue—and hinting that any woman running for office should be considered something of a freak. Treating Douglas as a radical could be done in a fairly harsh fashion; but the female question had to be handled more delicately. Nixon had so far done a fair job of keeping any sexist opinions to himself (or sharing them only with close friends). Now Kyle Palmer helped out in an *L.A. Times* column that earned wide attention.

Without even mentioning Douglas's gender, Palmer described her behavior in hard-to-miss stereotypes. She was "an emotional artist," a "good actress" and a "gifted mimic" who had been "emotionally attracted" to the left-wing doctrine of her day. "Her emotional reactions took her far afield. . . . Mrs. Douglas was influenced by a state of mind—by an emotional concept." There were "many instances of her emotional powers—and reactions." A good example was "the emotional reaction that caused her to weep" when her idol, Henry Wallace, was kicked off the Roosevelt ticket in 1944. Palmer also cited Senator Downey's claim back in May that Douglas lacked the "temperament and training" to be a U.S. senator. The lady was "a veritable political butterfly, flitting from flower to flower and from bower to bower while others—Nixon among the foremost—have pulled up the weeds." There was, Palmer concluded, "nothing superficial about [Nixon's] make-up and no emotional instability whatsoever."

To offset such an attack and minimize the defections from the party at the local level, Helen Douglas would have to import as many well-known national Democrats as possible. Eleanor Roosevelt was the first but, the candidate hoped, by no means the last would-be rescuer to come over the horizon. Douglas aides pressed the candidate's friends in Washington to record radio and TV spots for her, and many of them—including Vice President Alben Barkley, Senator Lyndon Johnson, and House Speaker Rayburn—obliged. But all of them put together still couldn't replace a personal blessing by the president. Douglas pulled out all stops to lobby Truman to come to California or at least to issue a strong endorsement from Washington. She spoke with him about it directly, and used friends as surrogates. Nothing worked. On September 11, responding to a Douglas telegram, Truman told her, "I hope everything is going well with you," but offered no help.

Three days later Douglas called the president's press officer, Charlie Ross, asking if she could use Truman's name on billboards as one of her endorsers. The following day, Truman decided that was fine, but he ruled out sending a specific letter of support. Eban Ayers, a Truman aide, recorded in his diary that the president at this point called Helen Douglas "one of the worst nuisances." A few days later she asked the president whether she could have her picture taken with him when he signed a water bill that benefited northern California. He declined.

Despite his mother's visit, Jimmy Roosevelt's campaign was dead in the water. The gubernatorial candidate called himself the champion of the "even break" and said that like his father he had dedicated his life "to the good cause of all our people." But his opponent was perhaps the most trusted public figure in the state, whereas he was one of the most distrusted. Roosevelt, with his pedigree, could not even charge the governor with shattering the unspoken limit of two gubernatorial terms. Finally, James Roosevelt was no FDR. He seemed to lack nearly all of his father's estimable qualities: the common touch, a sense of purpose, shrewd political judgment, a way with the press—a fine mane of hair to throw back, like a lion, when he laughed. The bottom line was that James Roosevelt was mediocre and either didn't

know it or chose to ignore it. He was also, according to one of his top political aides, "a consummate liar."

Jimmy Roosevelt had once been perfectly positioned, despite his faults,
to win elective office in California. This was just after World War II ended,
when he was still in his mid-thirties. He had served with valor during the
war, and if he had come back to California, quietly worked as a Democratic
wheelhorse, and a few years later run for, say, Congress, he might have
pitched his mediocrity on a safer plane or bought time in which to rise
above it. But this Roosevelt—tall, lean, and nearly bald—was overly ambi-
tious, particularly since he already had two political strikes against him: a divorce and a reputation as a playboy. If that wasn't enough, he publicly
encouraged General Eisenhower to replace Truman as the Democratic
nominee in 1948, an idea that went nowhere and earned him the lasting ire
of the president, party leaders, and such funders as Ed Pauley. "Old-line California Democrats," *Time* magazine commented in late 1949, "regard Jimmy
as something of a Typhoid Mary."

Then, to top it off, he decided to run for governor in 1950 instead of set-
tling for a seat in the state legislature (as his father had done before running
for governor of New York) or in the U.S. Congress. Now Jimmy Roosevelt
would pay for it with an almost certain landslide defeat. Democratic activists
had other places to direct their energy—toward Helen Douglas, who was
more likable and more competent than Roosevelt, or toward Pat Brown,
who was more electable.

Well, Roosevelt would go down fighting anyway. His only issue was that
Warren was too many things to too many people. He claimed—and this was
true enough—that Warren's programs were not as progressive as the GOP
claimed and Democrats presumed. Also, Warren had not anticipated California's massive postwar boom and had not spent enough money on
schools, housing, and highways. But this last assertion, again valid, held little
sway with the voters, who liked the fact that Warren had balanced seven
consecutive state budgets and recognized that the California boom was un-
precedented and the governor was playing catch-up about as well as one
could expect. Roosevelt, in other words, was doomed. He could not even
borrow a bit of Helen Douglas's personal popularity and attractiveness,
since the two were running wholly separate campaigns. Hecklers from the
Nixon campaign repeatedly asked Douglas whether she favored Roosevelt
for governor, knowing that if she said yes, Earl Warren would finally endorse
Nixon, but she had managed to keep her cool and resist the trap so far.

This Roosevelt's distance from the average voter became laughingly obvious on the very day he launched his election bid. His wife, Romelle, told
reporter Mary Ellen Leary that if she was "doing it over," she would buy

modern furniture for the couple's Beverly Hills home. "The 18th century things," she complained, "take too much dusting."

After weeks of buildup, Murray Chotiner launched Richard Nixon's Senate election campaign, as promised, at four successive rallies across California—a precursor of the hit-and-run political campaigns that emerged years later. The candidate, flown around by an old army buddy, James Udall, would deliver the same remarks at a breakfast meeting in San Diego, over lunch in L.A., at an afternoon rally in Fresno, and at a nighttime gala at the Scottish Rite Temple in San Francisco. It was a powerful speech, and crowds of people and a friendly press turned out in droves everywhere Nixon appeared. A radio hookup carried it across the state, accompanied by a mass mailing of Nixon literature from campaign headquarters. Compared with this, Helen Douglas's campaign opener was somnambulant.

"I believe that this election year is the most important in our nation's history," Nixon began. "The fate of our nation and our way of life will be determined by those who are elected this November." Listening at home, Douglas found Nixon's voice calm and reassuring. But if she expected him to moderate his attack and strike a statesmanlike stance now that he was appealing to all Californians, she was to be sadly disappointed. The San Francisco *News* would later refer to the speech as a "detonation." Nixon's address indeed reflected one of Murray Chotiner's cardinal rules: A candidate must be willing to put on "a fighting campaign" because the people "like a fighter."

From the tone and content of his remarks—which would serve, with variations, as his basic stump speech—one could surmise that Nixon had won the argument with some of his aides concerning the focus of the campaign. He barely mentioned domestic issues, concentrating instead on stopping communism, "the one issue which is more important than all the others combined." Voters had a clear choice on this issue because the record of his opponent "disqualifies her from representing the people of California in the United States Senate." After exploring that record—citing data lifted directly from the Pink Sheet—he declared that if Douglas had her way, "the Communist conspiracy in the United States would never have been exposed and instead of being a convicted perjurer, Alger Hiss would still be influencing the foreign policy of the United States." She opposed forcing Communists to register with the attorney general "at a time when millions of young Americans are being required to register for the draft to fight Communists abroad." And she had opposed aid to Taiwan. "All that we have to do," he explained, "is to take a look at the map and we can see that if Formosa [Taiwan] falls, the next frontier is the coast of California."

As the speech built, Nixon sharpened the innuendo. Douglas, he charged, did not vote as a Democrat but as "a member of a small clique" that joined Vito Marcantonio in voting against the interests of national security. He declared that "we cannot afford to take the risk of placing anyone in our top councils who has demonstrated . . . that they at the very least have a tendency toward weakening in the face of our enemy."

Finally, and perhaps most effectively, Nixon resorted to a simple rhetorical trick he would rely on for the rest of the campaign: claiming that unnamed advisers had urged him to avoid certain issues, but he was going to talk about them anyway. No matter that the "warning" from his aides might be apocryphal. Murray Chotiner believed that these avowals demonstrated to the voters that the candidate was "willing to meet" difficult issues.

Usually, the issue Nixon purportedly was told to ignore concerned the Hiss case or some other aspect of the Communist threat. But in his kickoff speech, the subject he claimed to have been advised to avoid was the gender of his opponent. "At the outset of this campaign," Nixon explained, "I am confronted with an unusual situation. My opponent is a woman." Some advisers had insisted that "because she is a woman I should raise no questions as to her qualifications for the position she seeks. They say to criticize a woman might cost the election." But after weighing the matter carefully, he had decided he could not go along with that because this woman was "asking the people of California to send her as their representative to the United States Senate, where she could make decisions affecting their very lives." And so he would eschew chivalry and question her credentials.

"I want my position to be crystal clear," Nixon explained. "There will be no name calling, no smears, no misrepresentation. *We* do not indulge in such tactics. But I do say here and now that to the extent that Mrs. Douglas does not reveal, or conceals, her record, I feel I have an obligation to expose that record to the voters of California." And then, rather threateningly—certainly from Douglas's standpoint—he warned, "This is *one* election where the candidate will not fail to meet the issues head on."

This Tricky Young Man

If not for a scheduling conflict, the fall campaign might have reached a climax almost before it began. The Business and Professional Women's Club had invited the two Senate candidates to debate "The Trend of Communism in the United States" at the Biltmore in Los Angeles on September 20, two days after Nixon's campaign kickoff. As the date approached, however, Douglas canceled her appearance, citing pressing business in Washington. Indeed, Congress had not yet adjourned, but when Nixon confirmed his decision to appear his supporters suggested that Douglas was running scared.

Considering her previous experience debating Nixon—when he produced the endorsement from the "other" Eleanor Roosevelt—this may have been at least partly true. But then James Roosevelt rode to the rescue. He offered to pinch-hit for Douglas, claiming that a "full discussion seems essential." Nixon responded coolly. Douglas should speak for herself, he declared, so that everyone in California would know exactly why she had "followed the Communist Party line so many times. Mr. Roosevelt has not been in the Congress to hear and observe Mrs. Douglas reveal her soft attitude on Communism." Confident in his skills as a debater, Nixon accepted Roosevelt as his opponent, however.

The evening, predictably, was a triumph for Nixon. Five hundred people turned out, mostly Nixon supporters, and they greeted with "gales of laughter" the announcement that Douglas could not appear, according to a press account. The Republican candidate's opening statement on the dangers of communism evoked such powerful applause that he was forced to call for quiet so the debate could proceed. Then, in the question-and-answer period, he showed off all his skills. Taking issue with the claim by Roosevelt that J. Edgar Hoover opposed the McCarran bill, he read a telegram from the FBI director. Hoover claimed that he had never publicly expressed an opinion on the measure. When Roosevelt asserted that Hoover's boss, the attorney general, *was* against the bill, Nixon quickly snapped, "Let's let Mr. Hoover speak for himself."

The following day the local newspapers gave the debate wide play, concentrating on Nixon's scintillating performance. A Hearst paper complained that Douglas had ducked more than one debate with Nixon and cited the comment of one observer, "That's a lady's privilege." The *Chicago Tribune* accused Douglas of failing to debate because she knew she could not refute Nixon's accusations, for she was a "consistent follower of the Communist party line." It was clear that Helen Douglas, three thousand miles away, had lost the campaign's first showdown.

On September 22, President Truman vetoed the McCarran bill, repeating in his five-thousand-word message many of the criticisms he had voiced in previous months. All of the federal intelligence agencies, including the FBI, agreed that the bill would weaken, not strengthen, the fight against communism. He likened the Communist-registration rule to requiring thieves to register with the local police. He said the so-called concentration-camp provision was probably unconstitutional, adding, "There is no more fundamental axiom of American freedom than the familiar statement: In a free country, we punish men for the crimes they commit, but never for the opinions they have."

Would Congress vote to override? Nixon, who had just returned to Washington, condemned the veto. Douglas predicted that the president's veto message would "go down in history as a truly great American statement. It should be studied by every American." Senator Hubert Humphrey, who had flip-flopped, endorsed the veto with one of his famous flights of rhetoric. The president, he declared, "has said to Hubert Humphrey, and I think he has said to other people, 'This is your chance to come clean.' This is your opportunity to vote your convictions. . . . I join the ranks of free men. I am going to rectify the miserable mistake I made [in voting for the bill]."

Truman had earnestly asked Congress to study "very carefully" his reasoning. The president's appeal "sounds like Communist propaganda," Congressman Rankin responded. He read off the names of Julius and Ethel Rosenberg and other accused atomic spies and commented that there was

"not a single Christian" among them. The House, with Nixon as floor manager, took less than an hour to override the veto, by a vote of 286–48. Now
it went to the Senate.

The Washington Post denounced the "stampede" on Capitol Hill. Truman
told Lyndon Johnson that the current session of Congress had hit "all-time
lows" in character assassination. The White House felt it had a glimmer of a
chance in the Senate, but the House had acted so hastily that most Americans still had not heard the president's explanation of his veto. To buy time
for media coverage, Truman ordered a filibuster, which began at six-thirty
that evening, led by Senator William Langer.

Eleven hours later Langer collapsed from exhaustion on the floor of the
Senate and was rushed to a hospital. Senator Humphrey took over, invoking
Jefferson, Voltaire, Milton, Plato, and Socrates. Some proponents of the bill
believed in Hitler's "big lie" technique, he warned, adding, "There are
would-be Hitlers in America, Mr. President." At nine-thirty in the morning,
Senator Knowland good-naturedly accused Senator Lehman, who was then
speaking, of repeating word for word one of his previous speeches on the
subject. Lehman said he would be glad to make it "again and again and
again" if it would change any minds. By eleven o'clock only six senators remained on the floor. A few hours later, when it became clear that Truman
had not swayed many votes, the filibuster ended, and the vote to override the
president was an embarrassing 57–10.

Two days later India Edwards sent Democratic Party boss William Boyle
the private comments of several prominent senators. Among those who
went against the president, Lyndon Johnson explained that he wished he
could have done otherwise; Scott Lucas of Illinois, who was embroiled in a
tough reelection fight, said he was sorry, "but he could take no other step";
and Senator Tydings of Maryland (who was in the same boat) agreed that
conditions were such in his state "that anything else would be impossible."

Having embarrassed both Jimmy Roosevelt and Harry Truman within
three days, Richard Nixon returned to the campaign trail with gusto. Visiting Alhambra and Monrovia, then Lodi and Stockton, and then Madera and
Merced counties, the candidate re-created his spring offensive, squeezing in
more than half a dozen appearances every day: motorcades, intimate luncheons, brief conferences with newspaper publishers, as well as the so-called
station stops. One line on Nixon's schedule simply read: "4:30 P.M. Arrive at
Merced. Meet townspeople." Everywhere he stopped, he hailed the passage
of the McCarran Act, claiming credit for writing it and guiding it through
Congress.

Then he returned by private plane to Los Angeles for a women's meeting, an American Legion luncheon, a speech to hundreds of Forest Lawn employees, and a USC football dinner. Wherever possible, a Democrat introduced him. Depending on the audience, speeches would be frankly political or "nonpartisan"; if the latter, Nixon talked about the Hiss case and other examples of Communist subversion without mentioning his opponent. Two days later he flew to Modesto, where he talked about farm policy (for a change), and then pushed on to San Francisco for an important meeting on campaign publicity with Chotiner, Harvey Hancock, Bill Arnold, and others. Along the way, he wooed and won the support of local doctors' groups; he opposed Truman's national health-insurance plan as socialistic while Douglas supported it.

In a rare, light moment in the campaign, Nixon and his entourage pulled into a town in their station wagon and noticed that the local committee had hired a small plane to tow a sign across the sky. Instead of reading NIXON, however, the sign read NOXIN.

At every campaign stop, the candidate stuck with some form of the basic stump speech, concentrating on the Red menace. He tied even tangential issues to this theme. Asked in Marysville to observe National Newspaper Week, he noted that Congress had written into its foreign aid program the requirement that no country would be permitted to receive funds unless it allowed the U.S. press to report freely within its borders, effectively denying all aid to Communist countries. Helen Douglas, he added, "was one of the leftwing clique" who voted against this provision. With the U.S. position improving in Korea, Nixon rarely failed to remind listeners that the Democrats still had to answer for inviting the conflict in the first place. He compared North Korea's crossing of the 38th parallel with Pearl Harbor—"both cleverly engineered sneak attacks for which we were almost totally unprepared."

Frequently, on the back of his prepared remarks, he scribbled notes to himself in pencil, key phrases to inspire an ad-lib. One page held the following thoughts: "Korea—why—*Soviet power* . . . Military *strength* . . . Foreign Policy—sane . . . Subversion—Hiss—atomic. . . . Moral, spiritual time to fight." Preparing for an appearance in the town of Alisal, he wrote on the back of a letter, "The problem: a) why Korea? b) why prices? c) why taxes? d) why draft? *THE COMMUNISTS.*" On top of another speech, he wrote this notation, apparently referring to criticism of the Pink Sheet: "Ask Douglas to name one vote which is wrong."

At nearly every appearance, Nixon tooks pains to introduce the gender issue, if only by repeatedly referring to his "female" or "woman" opponent. Often he feigned sympathy for her, remarking that rugged campaigning was hard on a woman. Sometimes before all-male or extremely friendly audiences, subtlety disappeared in crude remarks or sexual innuendo. Douglas, he said on more than one occasion, was "pink right down to her underwear." Or with a few words and raised eyebrows he would suggest that Douglas and Truman were in bed together—in more than the political sense. On these occasions, either the press was barred, or it could be counted on to sanitize the remarks.

By most measures, the Nixon campaign was going well. The crowds were generally enthusiastic, the press coverage positive. Nixon's face appeared on billboards—forty-four in San Francisco alone—nearly everywhere Helen Douglas looked. In one spot that lacked a billboard someone painted NIXON in huge white letters on a hillside. Money poured in to headquarters from near and far. Democrats for Nixon had emerged with full fanfare, and Mary Ellen Leary called this the "biggest campaign boost" he had received yet. In its opening statement, George Creel's group declared, "We California Democrats are Americans first of all. We cannot, we must not, weaken the national effort in this time of crisis by electing Mrs. Helen Douglas to the high office of U.S. Senator." Nixon, the Democrats said, had "never failed to put his country's needs above party partisanship," and they predicted that most party members would vote for a Republican senator in November.

If oil money from Democrats like Ed Pauley or Jack Elliott flowed to the group, it was kept hidden. Nixon, in any case, announced that he welcomed the support of Democrats "rallying in this mighty crusade" to protect Americans from communism. "I say that I am proud to join hands with you," he added, "so that we may march and fight together to reject those whose voting record or beliefs are contrary to the safety and well-being of this nation." The Nixon campaign made the most of the bipartisan support—and secretly subsidized it with cash outlays—without allowing it to detract from the central effort. "We never let the [Democrats'] committee think it was running the campaign" or feel it was "above and beyond the pale of the regular organization," Murray Chotiner later remarked.

Besides the Pink Sheet, Nixon headquarters mailed out in mass numbers another flyer aimed at voters of both parties. Also printed on pinkish paper, "Let's Look at the Record" provided a side-by-side comparison of how the two candidates had voted in Congress. Chotiner refused to rely on just a few basic pamphlets; he believed in distributing "as many different pieces as possible, in order to give something new and something different to the people." He was not, he cheerfully admitted, an issues man, but as he observed, "There is always a group of people in your campaign that want the facts . . . they say we just want this campaign on the facts," so issues-oriented material had to be produced. On the new flyer, therefore, issues beyond the Communist threat, for once, were included: labor (Nixon supported Taft-Hartley; Douglas opposed it); taxes and domestic spending (he wanted less of both; she was for more); small business (he favored cutting red tape; she was for further controls); and, of course, oil rights in the tidelands.

Nixon headquarters also sent a memo to local campaign chairmen, probably drafted by Murray Chotiner, announcing an "IMPORTANT STRATEGY." Helen Douglas was "trying to portray a new role as a foe of Communism. Do not let her get away with it! It is a phony act." Whenever they had the opportunity, the Nixonites were to point out that even after the United States went to war in Korea, Douglas cast votes in Congress "which prove her real philosophy." They should also emphasize her "astounding" 1946 assertion, "I think we all know that Communism is no real threat to the Democratic institutions of our country." Soon that quote—accurate if out of context—started appearing everywhere voters looked. It was the most significant statement of the 1950 campaign, four years after its appearance.

When Nixon filmed a twenty-second TV commercial, he barely had time to express one thought, but it was a zinger: "In applying for the job of U.S. Senator, I promise you California voters, my employers, to represent you and your interests in Washington and not the half-baked theories of left-wing intellectuals at pinko cocktail parties."

Behind the scenes, from his apartment at the Waldorf-Astoria in New York, Herbert Hoover lent a hand. When wealthy friends around the country asked how they could contribute to Nixon's campaign, the former president directed them to Bert Mattei, the oil-company executive in San Francisco. Nixon looked like a winner, *Oakland Tribune* publisher Joseph Knowland informed Hoover in September. "His opponent is a vote-getter, particularly among women," he reckoned, "but now that we are involved with Communists in Korea her attitude on that issue is certainly not helping her."

The character of the Nixon campaign in northern California differed somewhat from that in the south. Although under the command of Brennan and Chotiner, the northern managers often did things their own way, sustaining the California stereotype of the refined north versus the adolescent south. The chairman in San Francisco, forty-five-year-old attorney John Walton Dinkelspiel, and his publicity man, Harvey Hancock (who had worked for Pan Am), went along with the casual smearing of Douglas but discouraged dirty tricks and distributed the Pink Sheet only in limited quantities. Dinkelspiel didn't think that basing the campaign on the Douglas-Marcantonio link was "a proper approach."

On one of Nixon's visits to San Francisco, Dinkelspiel was shocked to witness a bit of Douglas trickery. As Nixon spoke in a plaza near Marina High School, some Douglas people started blaring noise from sound equipment nearby. The candidate stood with his hand up until the static ceased, then calmly announced that the incident showed why he believed so strongly in Americanism and the right of free speech. Fine, let's debate, he said, but at least he should have the right to speak. The crowd, of course, rallied even closer to his side after that.

On another occasion in the north, the candidate noticed that a young woman, cradling a baby with one hand and holding an anti-Nixon sign aloft with the other, seemed to follow him from one station stop to another. Everywhere she appeared, she earned the wrath of a crowd. Nixon, speaking through a loudspeaker, instructed Bill Arnold to "make sure this young lady has plenty of gas to get to the next stop because she is doing us more good than harm."

But perhaps the most memorable incident, in Arnold's opinion, occurred one evening at a hotel in Salinas. The candidate and his entourage arrived to discover that their reservations had been either lost or never made. While the weary men lounged in the lobby, a woman approached each of them individually and offered to share her room and her bed—for a price. Apparently she found no takers.

The California loyalty-oath debate seemed to have crested in August with the decision by the Board of Regents to dismiss thirty-one University of California faculty members (and dozens of other employees). But it was only beginning. Many of the dismissed teachers immediately took their cases to court. The university, meanwhile, began to pay the price of losing professors outraged by the oath.

Some UC professors resigned in protest, including psychologist Erik Erikson. The chairman of the Physics Department at Berkeley complained that "we cannot now induce a single first-class theoretical physicist to accept a position." Many professors planning to join the faculty now had second thoughts. Robert Penn Warren, the poet, then at the University of Minnesota, resisted an invitation to join the English Department at Berkeley (and manage Mark Twain's papers), citing his opposition to "political tests." As a compromise, President Sproul offered to grant him a hearing in advance, clearing him of any Communist connections and making the signing of an oath unnecessary, but still Warren balked. Atomic scientist Edward Teller, who had just agreed to join the Physics Department at UCLA in 1951, threatened to back out due to the oath. "No conceivable damage to the university at the hands of the hypothetical Communists among us," a college dean observed, "could have equaled the damage resulting from the unrest, ill-will and suspicion engendered by this series of events."

Governor Warren seemed to agree, as he announced that the oath unfairly singled out UC employees for suspicion. His solution? Rather than work to rescind the oath, he decided to make it fairer by requiring that *all* public employees in California (local, state, and federal) take it. "So long as we are in conflict with Soviet Russia, we are in imminent danger of sabotage," Warren explained, apparently afraid to act otherwise during an election year.

The state assembly hailed the governor's proposal and on September 25 passed the measure, which became known as the Levering bill (after Harold Levering, the assemblyman who drafted it). When it passed the state senate, Jack Tenney urged his colleagues to be the first to swear allegiance, and all but two obliged. A few days later a caretaker for a municipal theater in Carmel signed the oath despite being a confirmed Communist. He explained that he felt comfortable disavowing any intent to overthrow the government. America, he predicted, would "collapse from its own rottenness."

Earl Warren, while slow to burn, had what Earl "Squire" Behrens of the *San Francisco Chronicle* once called a "turkey neck." That is, when he did get mad, the governor's neck would turn a bright red. In his younger days, in fact, his nickname was Pink or Pinky—and not because of his politics. The governor approached the boiling point often in September, when he was under a withering attack from James Roosevelt. Warren might have accepted the criticism with his usual composure had it come from what he considered a worthy opponent, but he could not accept it from this mediocrity. Roosevelt, he pointed out in response, hadn't held a real job in his life—what did *he* know about providing jobs for workers? How could Jimmy Roosevelt criticize the governor's education policy when he had never entered a public school in his life "except to make a political speech"?

Despite his big lead, Warren took nothing for granted, flying around the state in a Beechcraft D-18, making three or four stops a day. His campaign slogan was "Re-Elect a Good Governor." The *Los Angeles Times,* far more conservative than Warren, nevertheless announced that Californians were "fortunate to be able to keep such a good man in office." The Hearst papers declared that the state must not be turned over to "untried theorists and political adventurers" (meaning both Roosevelt and Douglas).

Throughout Warren's long career, one of his most appealing and most unusual qualities was that he had avoided the taint of corruption, practically a first for a California governor. Still, when it came to election campaigns, like anyone else, he welcomed donations from huge companies and wealthy individuals, a custom that may have influenced his policies at least a little. However bipartisan his image, his money in 1950 was overwhelmingly Republican, from titans like Asa Call, Mortimer Fleishhacker, R. Stanley Dollar, Walt Disney, Walter Haas, Jr., Dean Witter, Major Charles Tilden, John J. Garland, Colbert Coldwell, W. W. Crocker, George Murphy, Charlie Blyth, and B. J. Feigenbaum—plus $1,000 from Alioto's Fish Grotto in San Francisco, $1,000 from the Truck Owners Association, $5,000 from Bechtel, and $10,000 from the California Motor Transport Association.

That Warren could inspire this support as well as that of very conservative newspapers—and a near majority of Democrats—testified to his shrewdness, decency, genuine optimism, and moderate outlook. "He is cautious and deliberate," the *Saturday Evening Post* explained during the campaign. "He knows how to straddle a fence when necessary, but he also has a knack for picking the right time to stick his neck out on important issues, and has frequently done so," most notably in his crusade for a state health-insurance program (recently killed by the medical lobby) and his June 1950 swipe at Joe McCarthy.

Born in Bakersfield in 1891, Warren attended law school at the University of California, served in World War I, then practiced law in Oakland. Starting in 1925, he made a national reputation as district attorney of Alameda County, exposing bootleg operations, insurance rackets, and official graft. He became a state Republican leader and was nominally in charge of the landmark GOP campaign against Upton Sinclair in 1934, when the district attorney joined in the Red-baiting of the Democratic candidate for governor. In 1938, he won both parties' nods for attorney general. Along with several positive initiatives, he made the tragic wartime decision to support strongly the confinement of Japanese Americans in internment camps.

In 1942, Warren ran for governor, his campaign managed by Clem Whitaker and Leone Baxter, and easily defeated incumbent Culbert Olson. The bearish, friendly-faced Warren, although an old warhorse in politics, seemed like a breath of fresh air. Voters also seemed to feel that their big state needed a large-size man to run it. Four years later, after navigating a zigzag philosophical course to even greater popularity, he captured both major parties' primaries. (One of his opponents, Robert Kenny, commented on Warren's penchant for using photos of his six children in campaign material: "Is this an election or a fertility contest?") Somehow Warren managed to reduce taxes while increasing medical, unemployment, and old-age benefits, earning Democratic support despite attacking the New Deal as impractical and bureaucratic. He also knew who his friends were. When Senator Hiram Johnson died, Warren appointed as his successor William Knowland, son of *Oakland Tribune* publisher Joseph Knowland, one of the governor's longtime patrons.

In 1948, Warren won the GOP vice presidential slot, the perfect choice to balance a ticket headed by New York governor Dewey. In that election, Warren made one mistake that might haunt a run for the top spot some day—failing to deliver California's electoral votes to Dewey. So when he announced for a third term in 1950, he clearly needed a smashing victory if he was to regain momentum for a presidential race in '52. Now, by all accounts, he was about to get it.

Early in 1950, Edmund G. "Pat" Brown, the San Francisco DA, recognized that to win his second attempt for state attorney general, he would have to keep his distance from Jimmy Roosevelt, a certain loser, and Helen Douglas, an underdog. They were politically to his left, as well. Brown knew he had a fighting chance this time. Earl Warren despised his own party's candidate, Edward Shattuck, one of the governor's longtime critics, and practically anointed Brown.

Brown decided to concentrate most of his media buys on TV, not the radio, so he could highlight his photogenic family: his wife, Bernice; his three daughters; and his twelve-year-old son, Jerry. Now, in the closing weeks of the campaign, he got an idea for sewing up the election. He told Governor Warren that he wanted to run a series of ads calling for ticket splitters to elect both of them. Multimillionaire industrialist Norton Simon had agreed to submit ten thousand dollars in cash for this purpose. Warren replied that he wouldn't publicly praise this effort but promised not to repudiate it either.

Richard Nixon was pretty much on the same wavelength. Seeking to tap Brown's strength among Catholic Democrats, he told the Democrat in a private meeting, "I'll help you if you help me. We won't come out for each other but we'll do something together."

September 28 would be a productive day for the Nixon campaign. Democrats for Nixon went public: Manchester Boddy told a group of publishers that he personally favored the GOP candidate, and the candidate himself met privately with Sheridan Downey in Los Angeles. The same day, also in L.A., Nixon received an indirect endorsement from a newly prominent Republican—Senator Joseph McCarthy.

The senator from Wisconsin had come to California ostensibly to speak at a Biltmore dinner sponsored by a group of Republican women, not to back Nixon. And indeed, he would not mention any candidates by name. But this was clearly a partisan visit, and it put Nixon in a bit of a bind. His opponent suspected that he welcomed—had even solicited—the visit, but this may not have been the case. Nixon had made political hay ridiculing Douglas's need to import outsiders who knew little about California issues. And Joe McCarthy was not just an outsider. He was also controversial, an extremist, even a fanatic, who arrived in California at precisely the moment Nixon was moving to the center to secure Democratic support. Nixon's brand of judicious anticommunism was going over well in the state; the taint of McCarthyism might hurt him. And so, when McCarthy appeared at the Biltmore before a packed and cheering crowd of nearly one thousand, Nixon was nowhere in sight.

McCarthy gave the crowd what it wanted: a lusty denunciation of Acheson, Lattimore, and the Communist menace in all its forms. He also met with reporters eager to profile him on this visit to California, only his second since he became infamous. Kyle Palmer found him more charming, soft-spoken, and handsome than expected, and all of these qualities, the reporter predicted, would "bring him far, perhaps very far, in politics." McCarthy did not comment on the California Senate race, but with Palmer's considerable help he emerged on the page as reasonable and decent; like William Jennings Bryan, he was simply a "silver-tongued young man from the farm belt." The senator raised many of Nixon's key issues—Taiwan, the McCarran Act ("causes poison to be labeled poison"), the lack of preparedness that led to the Korean War. And so without risking a public embrace of McCarthy, Nixon benefited from his presence after all.

Despite the latest boost, Nixon felt doubts, even worry. Perhaps his campaign had peaked too early, with his ripping September 18 opening or even further back, in June. He dictated a scathing letter to his handlers, explaining that after one week on the road he had "run across several weaknesses" in their effort that "must be worked on" as soon as possible. He feared that the campaign was "not going as well as it was during the primaries" and was convinced that "unless we face up to the realities right now, we are in for a licking in November."

The candidate described a disastrous day in the Stockton area. At a breakfast with businessmen, tables were set for 125 but only 38 people attended, an attendance he attributed to "no advance sale of tickets." At a luncheon meeting for women, 110 were expected but less than 50 showed up ("No telephone calls have been made"). An evening meeting was canceled altogether because a local organizer had "failed to notify the Lodi people in time." In addition, no one had arranged for a newspaper interview or photographs. "I did that myself after I got there," Nixon complained.

"Several conclusions can be drawn from the foregoing," he fumed. Two of the local chairmen are "not fit—are completely incompetent." Local fund-raising was going poorly, so the state party was about to take over in that region and tie his campaign to those of other GOP candidates. He also was upset that "rules" for his appearances that he had previously circulated were disregarded during the first week, so he restated some of them. "I again wish to emphasize," he added, "that if meetings cannot be reasonably successful they should not be held at all." Most alarmingly, his San Francisco headquarters appeared to be doing a bad job of "coordination," and he suggested hiring a new staffer. One important figure in the San Francisco office, he charged, was "incompetent and a liability to our campaign."

The memo brought results. Bernie Brennan called old Nixon hand Roy Day and told him that the candidate needed his help. He asked Day to travel with Nixon for the rest of the campaign, keeping in touch with local organizers and making sure the events went smoothly—starting and ending on time, with no hecklers in the front rows. Day had some vacation time coming at his printing office, so he was able to accept the challenge. A savvy operator, Roy Day was the perfect choice for this task. "I like to win and play hard to win," he once explained, describing his political activities. "You have to carry the fight all the way, never get on the defensive."

The Nixon team, meanwhile, had pulled off quite a coup in the religious field. If their man was to win, he would have to convert tens of thousands of blue-collar Democrats, most of whom were Catholic and favored Helen Douglas's embrace of New Deal and Fair Deal social policies. Then, on September 25, Pope Pius XII, denouncing "cowardly and uncertain church leaders," had called on the Catholic clergy to attack courageously both "the iniquity of Communism and the abuses of capitalism" and "remain faithful to the social doctrine of the Church." The most powerful Catholic in California, however, was rigidly anti-Communist. Not surprisingly, J. Francis McIntyre, archbishop of Los Angeles, secretly agreed to help Richard Nixon. He sent all parish priests in the archdiocese a letter ordering that each of their weekly sermons in October be devoted to the evils of communism, particularly the Communist infiltration of government. An outline of such themes also included a list of candidates, including Nixon, favored by the archbishop.

Perhaps even more could be done in this area, Murray Chotiner advised his candidate. Reverend John Cronin, the well-known Red hunter, FBI informant, and mentor of both Nixon and Senator McCarthy, had sent along several campaign tips from his office in Washington. Among them was the suggestion that the candidate "talk directly but privately with Archbishop McIntyre . . . he may have useful suggestions how to get further support."

While all this was going on, Bernie Brennan kept the Nixon fund-raising machinery running smoothly at the state and national levels. Anti-Douglas Democrats such as Ed Pauley and Jack Elliott contacted friends in the oil business elsewhere, but the Nixon operatives were also not shy about soliciting donations in other states. The wealthy comprised one group of outsiders whose involvement they craved, especially since their identities could be kept secret.

In early October, Brennan mailed letters to a number of wealthy businessmen beyond California. Typical was a brilliantly persuasive letter to Houston magnate J. H. Parten. "I am writing you regarding an outstanding young man," Brennan began, "a public servant with the fire, honesty, good judgment and Americanism which has made our country great. . . . I'm sure that you are familiar with the issues—Nixon, the American, versus Helen Gahagan Douglas." She had the financial backing of "the Hollywood left-wing crowd, plus that of most of the similar elements nationwide, with all the money her campaign needs." Nixon, on the other hand, was "so far short of money to conduct the campaign *successfully* that it is a reflection on our Americanism." And this reflected poorly on all Americans, for the "Nixon campaign" was not only "statewide, but nationwide. . . . It will be another death-knell to the country you and I grew up in, if Nixon is not elected to the United States Senate in November, 1950."

To make sure Parten understood that this crusade was a matter of profits as well as ideology, Brennan highlighted in capital letters the following request: "NOTE NIXON'S AFFIRMATIVE VOTE ON THE VERY IMPORTANT TIDELANDS ISSUE versus his opponent's negative vote on the same issue." Nixon, he observed, "needs the financial support of men and women who believe in this great land of ours; people who believe in free enterprise. . . . You have a great stake in this wonderful land of ours," Brennan concluded, "and it is my hope that you will protect what's left of it, with a substantial contribution to the Richard Nixon Campaign."

. . .

Brennan's claim that Nixon was short of cash and Douglas flush with it could not have been more misleading. The Democrat's lack of money, in fact, had reached such a critical point that she was forced to fire off telegrams to key supporters, inviting them to an emergency dinner at her house on September 26. "I have run into a frightening crisis," she confessed. "I need your help, your advice, your support." Her campaign was so short of cash it had to hold off printing brochures and buying radio and television time—six weeks before election day. When one Douglas fan asked head-quarters for a campaign button, Ruth Lybeck informed him that none had been produced "because of a shortage of funds." She added, "This is really a 'shoe-string' campaign." The Douglas press office fired off only a fraction of the releases pouring forth from Charlie Bowen's operation. One columnist observed in early October that Douglas "has practically no organization in-sofar as press relations are concerned," perhaps because 90 percent of the newspapers were against her, whereas "Nixon is in there pitching all the time," his supporters "armed with press releases to meet almost any subject."

Douglas had counted on major contributions from labor groups, but money was slow to arrive. A leader of the CIO Central Council in Los An-geles explained that Nixon's smears were having an affect within Douglas's labor stronghold. Even some CIO leaders were "asking questions," he re-vealed, despite being Red-baited themselves.

The candidate's declaration of emergency worked, however. Labor re-sponded. Roy Reuther personally assured Douglas of a large donation, adding that the CIO PAC would "fully mobilize our efforts to the West Coast." (A $2,000 donation soon arrived.) Douglas received gifts of $1,000 to $3,000 from labor unions and PACs representing the International As-sociation of Machinists, the United Textile Workers, and the Communica-tions Workers, among others. "Yes, I think that most liberals, but I think particularly the men I knew, would be inclined to melt before Helen's en-thusiasm," one of her chief labor organizers later commented. Referring to one specific group, he added, "When Helen wanted something out of those men in the Amalgamated Clothing Workers, she got it." A handful of wealthy individuals also contributed, including advertising legend Albert Lasker ($1,000), California attorney John Packard ($3,500), James Warburg ($1,000), Madeline Kirschner ($5,000), and Helen's brother Walter Gaha-gan ($2,000).

After attending a successful party that targeted wealthy Democrats in New York, Douglas and aide Mercedes "Merci" Davidson counted the checks on the flight back to Washington. "We should do this every night!" Douglas exclaimed.

Fund-raisers also targeted Hollywood, but this effort had to be carried out quietly. Douglas did not want to appear reliant on celebrities and millionaires, especially since Nixon and his allies were using her Hollywood past and skills as an actress against her. Some of her potential funders, in addition, had appeared in *Red Channels* and other listings of fellow travelers. Certainly her Hollywood friends could have staged a gala fund-raiser, but that was out of the question. Donations had to be solicited via phone calls and letters, mainly by Allen Rivkin and Paul Ziffren and, to a lesser extent, by screenwriters Philip Dunne, Michael Blankfort, and Norman Panama. A Douglas crony at Universal Pictures approached William Goetz, a producer at the studio and a liberal Democrat (as well as a son-in-law of Louis B. Mayer), reminding him that he had given the candidate one thousand dollars for the primary run and should now contribute another two hundred to support his "investment." Goetz replied, "No, let's send Helen five hundred dollars."

In early October, Douglas made another emergency plea, sending telegrams to friends and supporters in the movie biz who had contributed earlier but had failed to come through for the finals. This list included Dinah Shore, Harpo Marx, writer Richard Brooks, Joseph Cotten, Hal Wallis, Otto Preminger, Burt Lancaster, John Huston, producer Ray Stark, and Vincente Minnelli. She was "deeply distressed" that she had to do this, but "all the props I must have to win"—TV, radio, billboards—were expensive and heavily utilized by her opponent. "You can do more than send me your own check," she implored. "You can ask your friends, you can talk it up and the only gratitude I can offer you is to serve in the Senate as you would want me to." Contributions soon arrived, but most were rather small, considering Hollywood salaries. The directors William Wyler and Charles Vidor each gave $500; director Mark Robson and screenwriter Sidney Sheldon, $250; Eddie Cantor and George Jessel, $200; Gene Kelly, Billy Wilder, Stanley Kramer, and screenwriter Robert Riskin, $100.

Ronald Reagan, a strong backer of Douglas in previous campaigns, this time donated just fifty dollars, earlier in the race. Why he seemed to shy away was something of a mystery. As president of the Screen Actors Guild, he was as politically active as ever. And while his film career had stalled at a middling level, he was still making plenty of money as one of the busiest second-echelon stars. "My screen career is in good shape," he told Hedda Hopper. *Storm Warning,* in which he took on the Ku Klux Klan, was about to come out. His next film, he told Hopper, was *Bedtime for Bonzo,* "in which I'll try to steal scenes from a chimpanzee."

When Philip Dunne notified Douglas of William Wyler's donation, he noted that the director wanted to make sure she had opposed the McCarren bill. Dunne offered to drive up to Santa Barbara and try to get some more money out of people he knew there. "You are wonderful," he added, "and we are going to win." Robert Ardrey, another screenwriter, sent a check for $150, congratulating her for "not ducking for the showers in this fateful year."

One thing was certain: Helen Douglas would not be blinded by overconfidence now. Replying to Philip Dunne's sunny prediction, she observed, "The next five weeks will be strenuous ones. There is so much to be done in so short a time." Thanking Sidney Sheldon for his contribution, she explained that the campaign was "increasing in intensity. It's going to take a lot of work," but she felt "we will win."

Her financial crisis had receded for the moment, but that was only half the problem. Douglas still hadn't quite found her footing in the campaign. When she returned again to California in late September, she started stumping the state, playing catch-up. "I don't think she knew what fatigue was," a labor organizer later remarked. When reporters asked how she did it, the candidate revealed that she had an unusual ability to "catnap" in a car while hurtling between events, and besides, she gushed, "I have a clear conscience, so I sleep well at night." She had also mastered the art of yanking a dress out of her suitcase and changing in a rest room or in the backseat of a car in under a minute—and coming out looking like a million dollars.

On television and before a live audience her face became so animated that one didn't notice the lines of age. Douglas, a reporter revealed, favored suits made for her by a Hollywood tailor, wore pumps for fancy occasions but flat shoes, as recommended by Eleanor Roosevelt, on all other occasions, and because of the pace of the campaign kept her nails short and her hair simply coiffed. Sometimes she wore on her suit jacket a gold donkey clip with a diamond in its tail, a gift from an admirer. Another reporter noticed that she brought along on her travels a flame-colored camel hair coat "to cheer her when she is tired. She likes color." Because she normally did not wear a hat she "need never worry . . . that female listeners are wondering whether or not it is a John-Frederics," a local columnist observed. "Nobody will ever come up to her after a speech and murmur: 'My dear, I couldn't take my eyes off that stunning hat.' "

Her speaking style—orating for thirty minutes when ten minutes would have done—meant she could make fewer appearances in an average day than her opponent. Frank Mankiewicz, the assembly candidate, made joint appearances with her in L.A., sometimes driving her around in his car. Her speeches were more like lectures, he observed, and sometimes did not move her audience. She was also less vibrant now than during the primary race, as if she were only just realizing what she was up against. Mankiewicz could sympathize, for his opponent, Harold Levering, accused him of harboring far-left views and the *Los Angeles Times* called him socialistic, and he expected to lose in this Republican district that included Pacific Palisades and Brentwood. But Levering, at least, was running a low-key campaign. Mankiewicz called his opponent "an amiable do-badder" and tried to enjoy himself. Douglas, he noted, didn't seem to be having any fun on the campaign trail, a situation that can be fatal for a candidate.

Even more troubling, a consistent, positive approach had eluded her so far. Often she spent most of her time replying to Nixon's taunts, walking directly into the trap Chotiner and the candidate had set for her. Her staffers spent an inordinate amount of time, for example, responding to the Pink Sheet. They compiled a massive manuscript (known as the Blue Book because of the color of its cover) that contrasted her voting record with that of her opponent in excruciating detail. The Pink Sheet could be reproduced in the hundreds of thousands, easily distributed and quickly read. The Blue Book was so cumbersome and so costly to produce it could be sent to only a few of Douglas's allies and members of the press (who took little notice of it).

At other times, she responded to the bait by going on the attack herself, sometimes in an unseemly or utterly unconvincing manner. It was as if she felt this was required as a holding action while awaiting a defining moment when the media or the public would signal that they had heard enough of the smears and wanted—no, demanded—a debate on the real issues. But that moment had not yet come, and it was becoming obvious it would not come.

And so Douglas told a crowd in Santa Rosa that Nixon's January vote on Korea was "an invitation to the Politburo to have North Korea strike against South Korea." In a statewide radio speech, she charged the Republicans with the "high crime" of "sabotaging the American program of resistance to Communist aggression." Referring to the GOP triumph at the polls in 1946, she called the conservatives elected that year—Nixon and George Smathers and Joe McCarthy, among others—"unscrupulous young men . . . a new group of political opportunists." This was standard campaign oratory, but Douglas went on to refer to them as a "backwash of young men in dark shirts," and to highlight the apparent analogy to European fascism, she added, "These young men are on the march again."

Every time she vowed to stay on the high road, Douglas suffered another attack on her patriotism and felt she had to respond. When a reporter in Santa Rosa asked how she felt about the perception among voters that her husband was a Communist or pro-Communist, she dignified the question with a passionate response. "This makes my blood boil," she said. "It makes me feel like getting up and walking out of this house and giving up politics." Instead of leaving it at that, she rambled on, noting that Melvyn had sacrificed one and a half million dollars in Hollywood salary to join the U.S. Army in World War II because he hated every kind of totalitarianism.

Douglas was also torn by conflicting advice from advisers. Some urged her to stick to her own themes and issues and ignore her opponent. Others felt that if she let the lies remain uncorrected they would appear credible. An adviser urged Douglas's manager, Harold Tipton, to "wrap the flag around her." She should "lay off" labor groups and speak before businessmen and veterans organizations, eschew factual detail and concentrate instead on "keeping America strong." She should use the words *America* and *Americanism* over and over again, as Nixon did. "This will probably be hard for her to do because she is used to campaigning on the issues," he admitted, but that is "the big issue today." At the minimum, every Douglas headquarters "should be decorated extensively with American flags."

Trying another approach, the Douglas campaign produced an eight-page comic book that showed a group of average voters—mainly war veterans—debating the veracity of various Nixon smears. On the last page, the Nixon boosters tossed their bumper stickers into the gutter, where they were seen crumpled, spelling out NIX ON NIXON.

Uncertain of how best to proceed, Douglas once again turned to friends in the East for help. An aide wired Mary McLeod Bethune: "Much Negro support faltering due to vicious Redbaiting tactics." Bethune, the famous African-American educator and political figure, agreed to come to California. So did Vice President Barkley, Averell Harriman, and Attorney General McGrath. Douglas's friend India Edwards wrote the national party chairman, "Now that the fighting in Korea is less hot, couldn't the President make a campaign trip? I can think of nothing that would help our candidates more." She suggested that Truman head for California, stopping in nine other states on the way out and eight on the way back.

Douglas virtually begged Harold Ickes to come to California, sending him letters on three consecutive days. As a close friend of the late Hiram Johnson, Ickes carried considerable weight in the state. But he still refused to travel west, explaining that among other things he couldn't come to California without being expected to say a kind word for Jimmy Roosevelt, which he refused to consider. Douglas tried again, explaining that the "red hysteria" had become so great the Democrats "were threatened with the loss of the state." But Ickes, despite proclaiming his platonic "love" for Helen, would not budge, although he agreed to record radio and TV commercials for her and sent her a personal donation of $250 as well. He also wrote an appeal for funds that was published in the *New Republic,* hailing her courage: "If she were a man I would say 'guts.' "

Ickes's radio speech served her well, injecting a bit of badly needed humor into her campaign:

> Fate had something to do with the christening of Congressman Nixon. His first name is Richard. Richard so easily becomes the diminutive "Dick" between friends and all of us feel friendly to Dick Nixon, although we do not like a house "dick" who goes about looking under beds for communists. We do not care for a dick who listens to anonymous gossip and points an accusing finger at citizens, some of them bad, but many of them good, without giving them a chance to confront their accuser. . . . If you want a dick, by all means vote for Dick Nixon. But if you want a statesman to do a Senator's job, which is what you ought to want, vote for Mrs. Douglas. She is appealing to you on her record. She is not trying to scare a vote out of you.

Douglas had tried everything else to make Nixon's smears appear ridiculous. Perhaps making fun of his name might work. On September 26, Douglas headquarters sent a press release to the *Independent Review,* the pro-Democratic weekly in L.A., referring to Nixon as "this tricky young man" who wants to "save you from the communist menace." Lampooning the candidate's "deceptiveness," it revived the nickname Tricky Dick that the *Independent Review* had coined in the spring (but it had never really caught on). "Tricky Dick is pretty good at the hidden ball play," the publicist observed, "but this time he certainly fumbled the pigskin."

Three days later *Independent Review* publisher Dan Green, apparently after consulting the Douglas release, wrote a front-page editorial, "The BIG LIE in California," which exposed "Tricky Dick Nixon" as the latest exponent of a technique used by Hitler and Stalin. The citizens of California, Green predicted, would soon send "little Tricky Dick Nixon" into "the gutters of political oblivion."

Harold Ickes picked up on the nickname in a five-minute television spot for Douglas. He contrasted Douglas's record on issues vital to California—power and water, farming and inflation—with that of "super sleuth . . .

headline-hunting . . . Tricky Dick Nixon." When the interests of Californians needed attention, where was Tricky Dick? "Under the bed looking for
a Red," Ickes explained. What California needed was "the intelligence, industry, integrity, and courage of Helen Gahagan Douglas."

Ickes declared that Douglas would be elected in November. With help
arriving in the form of famous visitors from the East and an influx of campaign funds—and the United States near victory in Korea—that seemed, at
long last, a reasonable possibility. "I am swinging into active campaigning
throughout the state," Douglas wrote Drew Pearson, another friend who
would soon be coming to California, "and despite the ever-present lack of
sufficient money we are in good shape."

Hope for a personal blessing from the president, however, was waning.
Jimmy Roosevelt had written Truman, shamelessly pleading with him to
come to California. He and Douglas were "badly outdone" in financial resources for advertising, and he predicted that in the last ten days of the campaign the opposition "will use every dirty trick" that had already proved
successful in other states. A whispering campaign to the effect that Truman
was not coming because he actually favored the Republican candidates was
causing damage. Because Roosevelt knew that Truman disliked him, he emphasized the importance of a Douglas victory. Having recently debated
Nixon, he could testify that the Republican candidate was "a smooth and
capable person" who in the U.S. Senate would prove to be "a thorn in the
side of the Democratic Party." But if Truman came to California in early
November, even briefly, it would "completely knock the opposition over"
and "rally the Democrats—and we have a winning majority of them." Since
the change in fortunes in Korea, the president's approval ratings had shot up.

On October 10, Truman informed Roosevelt that he would soon be flying to the Pacific to meet with General MacArthur, and when that trip was
over, "it would not, of course, be possible for me to return" to the West
Coast.

Hollywood Dramatics

"The national Democratic high command has begun its California vote putsch," Earl Behrens observed in the *San Francisco Chronicle* on October 7. The White House was "rushing its loudest voices and its key Cabinet orators into the state." Another San Francisco paper said the same thing more colorfully: "An impressive galaxy of Democratic knights in shining armor is heading to California to rescue a damsel in distress. . . . Maybe before the campaign is over, Head Knight Harry will come charging in on a white helicopter, too." The press apparently believed that the influx of outside support for Douglas could be neutralized or even turned against her if voters were warned about it in advance.

In an indignant column titled "The March of the Brass Hats," Kyle Palmer encouraged readers to wonder why "this horde of strange politicians" was descending on them and meddling in their affairs. After listing the expected arrivals, starting with Vice President Barkley, he observed that there was "not a man among them qualified to instruct the voters of this State on any of the issues awaiting action." And even if *that* didn't bother the reader, consider that "taxpayers are getting a sizable nick in the pocketbook" from the cross-country travel. He pointed out that Barkley knew nothing about California issues and ideologically was about as distant from Douglas as possible. And with the veep around, the Democrats had better lay in a good supply of bourbon.

Alben Barkley would arrive in Los Angeles on the morning of October 9. Perhaps not coincidentally, another famous outsider, this one sympathetic to Nixon, came to San Diego the very same day: Joe McCarthy was back in California less than two weeks after appearing in Los Angeles.

Obviously, the state was important for McCarthy. In recent months, he had received two thousand requests for speeches (more than all other senators combined) but could accept only a tiny fraction of them—including two in southern California within twelve days. This reflected a national GOP decision to continue to press the Red issue despite the mixed response it evoked. "Only by 'mucking' can we win," one GOP leader explained, referring to McCarthy, "and only a 'mucker' can muck." Another party leader observed, "The public may agree with the intellectuals that McCarthy has never proved a single one of his charges. But I'm sure the public is still saying, 'There must be something to this.' " So McCarthy was scheduled to visit fifteen states. His prime target remained archenemy Millard Tydings in Maryland. He also went back to Illinois to help Dirksen.

Before a crowd of eighteen hundred enthusiasts at San Diego's Russ Auditorium and a regional radio audience, McCarthy endorsed Richard Nixon, citing the congressman's success in bringing down Alger Hiss and producing other HUAC victories. The only way to get rid of "Red Dean Acheson," the senator added, was to elect Republicans and kick the "Commiecrats" out of Washington. "The chips are down," he warned, "between the American people and the administration Commiecrat Party of betrayal." He concluded his performance by asking, "Now I want to ask a question. How is Nixon doing?"

Oddly, the senator's speech was reported only in San Diego. None of the newspapers in nearby Los Angeles or in any other city even revealed that McCarthy had come to California. His support for Nixon carried considerable political baggage; Helen Douglas had referred to him as "the discredited Senator McCarthy." The visit also compromised the GOP's attacks on meddlesome outsiders. But thanks to the press blackout, the impact of McCarthy's visit was limited to where it might do the most good—in San Diego, the state's most conservative major city.

Douglas charged that Nixon had invited McCarthy to California and then tried to hush up the visit. Nixon replied that keeping any McCarthy speech secret was impossible, and in any case "we have invited no outsiders to appear on my behalf."

Vice President Barkley's visit, on the other hand, would be widely covered by the media, although rarely with the sort of slant Helen Douglas desired. On arrival in L.A., Barkley faced loaded questions from the press. He had called Douglas's help in Congress "invaluable" to the White House. How, then, would he explain her hundreds of votes in common with Marcantonio? Barkley, trying to put a positive spin on the question, said he was sure "she voted her conscientious convictions" and that Marcantonio had not influenced her at all.

His speech at the Olympic Auditorium, before four thousand Democrats, was carried over statewide radio. The rally, organized by MGM's Dore Schary, opened with Keenan Wynn introducing Dinah Shore, who introduced Helen Douglas and other candidates. Then Schary welcomed Barkley. The high point, rhetorically, came when the vice president, after praising Margaret Chase Smith's courageous attack on McCarthyism, gushed, "The U.S. Senate, that dignified body, can well stand another shock of brains and beauty!" He added that "if we have bad government, either moral or economical or political . . . the housewife, the mother, is the first to realize that fact . . . the women feel it before the men feel it. I think all men will acknowledge that fact." It was under the leadership of a great Democrat, Woodrow Wilson, that women finally gained the right to vote. But if there was anyone in California who had the feeling that "it was all right to allow women to vote but not elevate them to high office—please dissipate that notion and know that we welcome good women . . . who understand the problems that beset every household, which are discussed around every fireside and at every social gathering."

Some in the Douglas camp were privately appalled by Barkley's conduct before and after his major speech. Alvin Meyers, treasurer of the campaign, thought the vice president did little more than sit in his hotel "drinking bourbon and branch." Barkley spoke ineffectually at a fund-raising cocktail party. (He also sabotaged Jimmy Roosevelt when he told reporters that he would not say anything bad about Earl Warren because he heard he was a great governor.) Newspapers, meanwhile, focused on his off-the-cuff reference to Douglas's voting her "conscientious convictions" in siding with Marcantonio. Many commentators pointed out that this statement, intended as a testimonial, merely confirmed a negative. And if those votes really expressed firm "convictions," how could her views have changed since? Didn't this prove that her newfound opposition to communism was pure flimflam?

"They may be Mrs. Douglas's conscientious beliefs," Nixon fired back, "but they are definitely not mine." Nor, he added, were they the conscientious beliefs of Alben Barkley, the majority of Republicans *and* Democrats in Congress, and most voters in California. An editorial cartoon pictured a huge hammer and sickle labeled "Douglas's Vote Against Un-American Activities Committee," the notation "Just her conscientious convictions— Barkley," and the caption "Let Your Conscience Be Your Guide."

The uproar over the Barkley remark inspired a nervous White House to ask Douglas's office for *her* analysis of the voting link to Marcantonio. Ken Hechler, the Truman aide, privately referred to Barkley's statement as "very unfortunate. . . . No doubt the question was a Nixon-planted one."

Much the same scenario—a potentially helpful visit from a Democratic leader sabotaged by the other side—played out a week later, when Attorney General McGrath arrived. After the Barkley experience, the Douglas forces worried about any statement that could be misconstrued, especially since McGrath was intimately involved with internal-security matters. When Douglas campaign manager Harold Tipton sent McGrath the schedule, he enclosed several clippings, showing how far the press "will go in misinterpreting and misrepresenting."

McGrath's visit, on October 15, marked a high point for the Douglas campaign. Earlier that day, Douglas had hosted a highly successful tea at her home for India Edwards. She had also learned that President Truman would be stopping in San Francisco on his way back from Wake Island and would deliver an important speech the following evening at the Opera House. Although billed as a nonpartisan affair, the White House invited Douglas to attend. Happily, she canceled all her appearances on October 16 to be there.

Before doing that, she attended a gala dinner in McGrath's honor at the Beverly Hills Hotel, the first of several campaign appearances for the visitor. Douglas wore her signature elegant black dress with a double strand of pearls and corsage. ("Mrs. Douglas comes on well-gowned and well-groomed," a reporter observed.) Also attending was Sam Yorty, whose race for Douglas's seat in the House was going well; assembly candidate Frank Mankiewicz; and a number of Hollywood celebrities. Seated next to Douglas, McGrath told reporters that no intelligent person possibly could believe that she was a Communist. He endorsed her votes against HUAC because the FBI "has the matter under satisfactory control." He also called the new McCarran laws useless because in many respects they could not be enforced. Then he made another one of those comments that left the Nixon strategists just enough ammunition to burn down the fort. "Alger Hiss," McGrath said, "would have been prosecuted in any event by the Department of Justice." The attorney general's office, not Nixon or HUAC, had brought the Hiss case to the fore.

It didn't take long for a reaction to materialize. While Nixon readied his own response, Murray Chotiner exploited an accident of good timing: Ralph de Toledano, co-author of the bestselling book on the Hiss case, *The Seeds of Treason,* had just arrived to cover the campaign for *Newsweek.* De Toledano had been pleading with his editors for weeks to let him come to

California, to no avail. Knowing this, Nixon had arranged an invitation for his friend to reenact the Hiss case before the prestigious Commonwealth Club in San Francisco. With this inducement, *Newsweek* relented. "Nixon set it up because he knew I could help his campaign," de Toledano later disclosed. "It wasn't because he loved me."

After speaking in San Francisco, de Toledano took the *California Zephyr,* the overnight train to Los Angeles. At noon, the thirty-four-year-old reporter walked into Nixon headquarters. He had met Murray Chotiner once before, in New York, and considered him soft-spoken and easygoing. Now Chotiner grabbed him and showed him McGrath's remarks on the Hiss case. "We want you to answer this for us!" the campaign manager demanded.

"But I'm only a journalist," de Toledano protested. "I can't get publicly involved in a political fight."

"But you've written a book!" Chotiner reminded him. Then he brought out a typewriter, and de Toledano quickly banged out his response to Mc-Grath, which Nixon's publicity office released, along with the author's phone number at his hotel.

McGrath's assertion that the Justice Department would have prosecuted Hiss without any help from HUAC "surprises me," de Toledano wrote. Mc-Grath was "setting the record on its ear," so it was time to produce the facts. In de Toledano's telling, the Hiss investigation was "colder than a mackerel" until HUAC called Whittaker Chambers as a witness. Even then, the Justice Department did nothing until Dick Nixon called for further hearings. Still Justice balked, and Truman called the case a "red herring." Only after Nixon produced the Pumpkin Papers, causing a public outcry, did the department take action. "I want to make it clear again that I am not intruding in a political fight but merely attempting to set the record straight," the reporter concluded. "Mr. McGrath was speaking as a political partisan, not as the Attorney General when he made his statement. I'm speaking as a newspaperman."

The following day, October 18, the *L.A. Times* reprinted the statement in its entirety, along with an additional de Toledano quote: "Without Rep. Nixon and HUAC there would have been no Hiss case." The newspaper noted that it was good fortune that de Toledano was in town to take apart McGrath "verse by verse." The attorney general's "political mission" on behalf of Douglas had exploded in her face.

Nixon, in a statewide radio address, cited de Toledano's expert attack and denounced McGrath's "frantic effort" to help Douglas. If McGrath would stay in Washington and devote himself to his duties instead of playing party politics, "the security of our country would receive the protection it really needs." Douglas was so isolated in California that "the principal support now being given her candidacy comes from outside the state," he added.

Another leading Democrat from the East also came to California, but with much less fanfare and on unknown business. Congressman John F. Kennedy made no public appearances or statements concerning the Senate race, but he privately favored Nixon. Still, he could not openly embrace any Republican.

Nixon, too, was receiving visitors from the East. At the Ambassador Hotel in L.A., he privately met with Leo Casey and David Charney, who represented a major New York public relations firm. Leo Casey, a veteran of several GOP campaigns, including Wendell Willkie's run for president, had been instructed by his superiors to found an Independent Voters Committee for Nixon. It would focus on gaining votes by emphasizing the candidate's role in nailing Alger Hiss. Why was he doing this? Casey had been told that his firm, Allied Syndicates Incorporated, was donating its services in the hope that Nixon would "open some doors" to future business in California.

Eventually, however, Casey learned that he was actually servicing "the China account": The firm had been retained by the Bank of China, which was aligned with the Nationalists, at sixty thousand dollars a year to short-circuit any Washington move to recognize Mao's regime. Naturally, the China Lobby wished to elect Richard Nixon. While acknowledging his firm's work for the Bank of China, David Charney would later claim that Casey was actually paid by the Nixon campaign.

In any event, a few days after the meeting at the Ambassador, Nixon made a statewide radio broadcast forcefully renewing his promise to "free China" and return Chiang Kai-shek to power on the mainland. Leo Casey, meanwhile, set up shop at the Beverly Hills Hotel, organizing campaign activities under the Independent Voters banner.

The conflict in Korea, for so long a liability for the Democrats, now rebounded somewhat in their favor. America was riding high again. "Throughout the history of mankind," Senator Lyndon Johnson declared, "there has never before been such a prompt and forceful answer to the challenge of armed aggression. When the Communist armies crossed the thirty-eighth parallel, they were not merely on the road to Seoul or Pusan. They were marching down a road of conquest that led to St. Louis and Washington—and your home town. We have thrown the Communists off that road." Reversing a previous opinion, Americans now told pollsters, by a wide margin, that it was not a mistake to defend Korea.

But an unsettling new phase of the war had arrived. General MacArthur, with the support of his president, had not halted his army's advance at the 38th parallel but in early October had surged ahead, his objective the complete "destruction of the North Korean Armed Forces" (according to instructions from the Joint Chiefs). Rather than calling for a cease-fire or for a surrender on specific terms, the United States called for unconditional surrender. No longer did we merely seek a return to the prewar status quo, a divided Korea; now we sought the "liberation" of the entire nation. U.S. aircraft and artillery pounded enemy positions and populated cities with deadly abandon. Many North Korean civilians, their villages a wasteland, retreated to caves. "I regard all of Korea open for military operations," MacArthur declared, although Truman asked him to refrain from crossing the Chinese and Soviet borders and to remain wary of Chinese or Soviet entry into the conflict.

As early as September 1, *The New York Times* had reported that the Chinese had shifted troops to the border area, enabling them "to intervene militarily in Korea if they wish." China was uncomfortable with the prospect of a massive army led by Douglas MacArthur (one of Chiang Kai-shek's strongest advocates) at its doorstep. But there were economic concerns as well: A giant power plant on the Yalu River, at the border, supplied badly needed electricity for projects in Manchuria. Chou En-lai, China's foreign minister, warned that his country would send troops into battle if MacArthur carried the fight deep into North Korea. U.S. experts, including Dean Acheson, felt he was bluffing and that the Chinese knew the North Koreans were doomed. At a cabinet meeting, Acheson outlined a vision of a postwar Korea, no longer divided, that would serve as a shining example of how "Western Democracy" could rescue and revive the underprivileged nations of the world.

At this moment, Truman had suddenly decided to fly halfway around the world to confer with MacArthur on Wake Island. The president despised and distrusted MacArthur but had never met him and explained to the press that now was the time to get to know his commanding general and learn first-hand what he thought about future operations involving not only Korea but Japan, China, and Vietnam. The press was skeptical of this explanation, noting Truman's obvious desire to bask in military glory three weeks before election day. Senator Harold Stassen called the trip a "sinful political escapade."

In truth, Truman's journey was largely motivated by election-year politics. Because of that, Acheson and others disapproved, claiming it would only stroke MacArthur's already gargantuan ego, but Truman was all too aware of this himself. Flying across the Pacific, he wrote that he had to "talk to God's right-hand man tomorrow."

The conference on October 15 was seriously uneventful. MacArthur reported that the war would end by Thanksgiving and that most of the U.S. troops would withdraw by Christmas. Truman expressed some concern about Chinese intervention, but the general assured him this would not occur. Both men admitted they were puzzled by France's inability to neutralize Ho Chi Minh in Indochina. Truman, now in an exuberant mood, asked MacArthur if he had ever thought about running for president; the general replied that the president should keep his eye on Eisenhower instead. "Eisenhower doesn't know the first thing about politics," Truman replied with a chuckle. The two men spoke for less than two hours and then flew their separate ways with almost absurd haste. Nothing of consequence was decided except that they liked each other more than they had supposed, which perhaps was no small thing. Heading back to the States, Truman called the meeting an overwhelming success.

The next day, however, U.S. intelligence received the first unconfirmed reports of small numbers of Chinese troops crossing the Yalu River into North Korea. Still, MacArthur's forces continued their relentless drive north, closing to within miles of the Yalu. Weeks earlier, when several U.S. military leaders openly advocated a "preventive" war against the Soviets or the Chinese, Truman had rejected the idea. But as I. F. Stone would soon observe, "so long as MacArthur remained Supreme Commander in Tokyo, the power to precipitate 'preventive war' remained in hands which might be disposed to it." Truman, he added, could not decide whether he wanted to continue a dangerous war or risk a negotiated peace, but "MacArthur wanted war. Indecision made Truman at best an irresolute superior, at worst a passive collaborator in MacArthurism. . . . To leave MacArthur in command was bad. To be unsure of whether one really wanted the war to end was worse."

On his way back to Washington, Truman stopped off in San Francisco as planned. After a night at the Fairmont Hotel, he took his customary early-morning walk, up and down the hills in the rain and fog, swinging his cane, waving to passengers on cable cars, and offering a hearty half salute to a pair of female marines on Leavenworth Street. Then he got a shave, haircut, and manicure at the hotel barber shop (after waiting his turn with other customers).

If Helen Douglas had ever hoped that leading national Democrats could save her campaign, she must have harbored serious doubts by mid-October. Yet she welcomed President Truman's brief stay in the state as yet another opportunity to staunch the Democratic defections to Nixon and thereby turn the tide in the race. Surely the Nixon team could not toy with the president as easily as it had discredited Barkley, McGrath, and Eleanor Roosevelt.

Truman's twenty-eight-minute speech at the Opera House (where the United Nations was born) was carried by radio networks throughout the country and telecast live throughout California, a first for a presidential address. It was also sent by shortwave radio around the world, even across the Iron Curtain. Earl Warren, his wife, and four of his six children occupied a center box. Down below, in the third row, sat James Roosevelt, Helen Douglas (in another black dress), and Senator Knowland. Wearing a blue suit, bathed in the TV lights, and appearing tiny on the massive stage, Truman described his talks with MacArthur and hailed progress in the war in Korea.

Immediately afterward Truman left San Francisco—without offering a word in support of the Democratic candidates in California. Still, *The Christian Science Monitor* reported that his very presence there had "contributed to the running strength" of the Democrats. "For Republicans," the reporter observed, "there was nothing much to do but watch the show and wonder whether or not the linking of General Douglas MacArthur in the public mind with President Truman will in some measure weaken GOP strength on a state level."

According to Drew Pearson, the White House was split over Truman's plans for campaigning. Democratic chairman, Bill Boyle, and others urged the president to crisscross the country during the last ten days before election day, for "confidential and alarming" reports indicated that the party would lose in such key states as New York, Illinois, Ohio, and California if it didn't get out the vote. According to Pearson, the GOP's Red-baiting tactics had produced apathy among voters, and so any "excitement" produced by the president might boost the turnout and swing badly needed votes in his party's favor. Other top advisers had thrown cold water on this idea, but not for the reason made public—that Truman had to focus on urgent problems. Instead, one of the president's aides told Pearson, "If the boss goes out and does his best and we still lose seats in Congress, he won't be the champ any more. That would hurt in 1952."

Harry Truman may have left California, but Ralph de Toledano was just getting started. After authoring his attack on Attorney General McGrath, he returned to his hotel, exhausted. At eight o'clock that evening he was resting in bed when the phone rang. It was his friend Morrie Ryskind, who had penned some of the Marx Brothers' best movies and written the political play *Louisiana Purchase* with Irving Berlin. "You've got to come out to Irene Dunne's," Ryskind said, referring to the well-known actress. "A lot of people are here—some for Helen Douglas, but you can convince them otherwise."

De Toledano got dressed, drove out to the house in Bel Air, and knocked on the door. As he stepped inside, he collapsed on the floor from exhaustion. Recovering, he recognized Adolphe Menjou, Ward Bond, and other right-wing movie stars. The party, he learned, had been arranged primarily to win over a prominent pro-Douglas Catholic priest and a woman active in religious affairs. By the end of the night, the woman had made the switch, and the priest had declared himself neutral. To celebrate, some of Ryskind's movie friends took de Toledano to lunch the following day.

The reporter had known Nixon since 1948. At first, he had received little newsworthy information from him. Nixon later told him he wanted to wait until he had learned more about de Toledano's political views and whether he could be trusted. Once he passed the test, he became (as he later put it) Nixon's "eyes and ears" in New York. This intimate relationship did not concern *Newsweek* when it assigned de Toledano to the California campaign. The magazine was Republican in outlook, and its editor figured the journalist would get some inside tips from his friends in the Nixon camp.

So on his second day in California, de Toledano went out on the stump with Richard Nixon in the station wagon. The candidate stopped by three newspaper offices, met with plant workers in Lynwood, made a station stop in Bellflower, spoke at Bixby Park (joined by Pat Nixon), and visited with paraplegics at a veterans hospital in Long Beach. That evening he gave a major speech at the VFW hall in Compton and then drove to San Bernardino. Everywhere they went, Nixon got his greatest applause when he called for the dismissal of Dean Acheson. De Toledano still admired Nixon but now discovered that the candidate was an awkward, somewhat "weird" fellow, startlingly self-centered—"an introvert in an extrovert profession," he later said. Yet Nixon's personal appeal and popularity remained strong.

At several stops, Nixon told his audience, "Ralph de Toledano of *Newsweek* is covering me—Ralph, come up here and say a few words about the Hiss case." The reporter didn't mind doing the candidate's bidding behind the scenes, but not before the public; he thought it would reflect badly on *Newsweek* and his editors might protest. He asked his friend to stop introducing him at the rallies, but Nixon kept doing it.

Day two of the trip focused on special interest groups as the candidate met with Democrats for Nixon, Doctors for Nixon, and black and Chicano supporters. Referring to the problem of campaigning against a woman, Nixon told de Toledano that "if she was a man, I could hit as hard as I want, but with her I have to be careful."

At some point, de Toledano visited Murray Chotiner in his room at the California Hotel in San Bernardino and found him meeting with Adela Rogers St. Johns, who was arguing that the campaign should not put out a new flyer reminiscent of the Pink Sheet (which she had worked on). She had just deleted several scurrilous passages from the proposed copy, which surprised de Toledano, for at the age of fifty-six she still had a reputation as a hard-boiled "newspaper gal." When she left, Chotiner took off his jacket, rolled up his shirtsleeves, and said to de Toledano, "Okay, let's get to work— help me write this," and Ralph consented. The flyer ended up as fiery as Chotiner had envisioned.

After two days with Nixon, de Toledano traveled with Helen Douglas, whom he had never previously met. He realized that Douglas knew where his sympathies lay—his attack on McGrath had just been printed—and she made little effort to ingratiate herself with him, which surprised the reporter. In fact, she spoke rather sharply to him as a United Auto Workers official drove them around in a car, Douglas in the backseat, de Toledano in the front. He was also startled to learn that Douglas did not always maintain a glamorous façade in her dress or makeup. And as she relaxed in the backseat, she seemed unaware that when the reporter turned around, he could look up her dress.

One thing Douglas said to him was "Do you want a good story? Joe McCarthy is going up and down the state campaigning secretly for Nixon, but the Republican press is so ashamed of McCarthy they don't publish a word about it." When he asked how anyone could campaign secretly, she replied, "You just check and you'll see I'm right."

He decided she would surely lose the election after they pulled up at a factory gate for a rally and found only a few workers, mainly women (which caused Douglas to chew out her local organizers). At another appearance, the reporter got a tip that some of the people in wheelchairs sitting behind her had supposedly been paid by her campaign to take part in the rally. De Toledano had the good fortune, however, of leaving the Douglas campaign before disaster nearly struck. Douglas had left San Francisco in her famous helicopter for a tour of the Central Valley. Heavy rain and fog forced the pilot to land near Highway 50 in the area of Altamont Pass. The candidate, intent on keeping a date in Modesto, reached the highway, stuck out her thumb, and hitched a ride with a couple from Waterford.

De Toledano's article for *Newsweek* would take the Nixon line from beginning to end. It presented the wheelchairs-for-hire story ("there was a feeling she was playing with people's sympathies") and noted that many voters resented her "Hollywood dramatics." Still, he concluded that in California "anything can happen, and usually does." The vote might hinge on personalities, not issues, and two weeks before the election many Californians "have not yet made up their minds."

"Just finished marking my absentee ballot," actor-hoofer George Murphy notified Richard Nixon. "Hope I may have the honor of being the first to vote for the new Senator from California." Hollywood split over the Senate race pretty much along traditional party and ideological lines. Nixon, however, did attract a few members of that new breed of fiercely anti-Communist Democrat. For several longtime Democrats in the industry, the polarizing 1950 race—much like the 1932 presidential campaign—clarified their true beliefs and the political party most likely to reflect them in the future. One of these individuals, apparently, was Ronald Reagan.

A staunch Democrat, Reagan flirted with leftish groups during the mid-1940s and landed on one of Myron Fagan's blacklists. He was so far left that Douglas organizers would not let him officially take part in her maiden run for Congress in 1944; he was "too hot to handle," as one of them put it. (The writer Howard Fast later claimed that Reagan "desperately" wanted to join the Communist Party.) When the Red scare came to Hollywood, FBI agents showed him how he had been manipulated by front groups, and he agreed to act as a confidential informant on SAG activities, with the ID number of T-10. He also campaigned against Communist-inspired labor actions within SAG and appeared as a friendly witness before HUAC.

Reagan appeared obsessed with politics. Because of his passion and his speaking ability, his glad-handing and his garrulousness, friends suggested he run for public office one day. Some Democrats, in fact, had hoped Reagan, not Helen Douglas, would run for the Senate in 1950, believing he was more electable. In a guest column he wrote for right-wing labor reporter Victor Riesel in 1950, he declared, "We've gotten rid of the Communist conspirators in Hollywood," adding that any former Communist should be willing to stand up, admit he was wrong, "and give all the information he has to the government agencies who are combatting the Red plotters."

In the fall of 1950, Douglas organizers counted on Reagan for further fund-raising support—he had just sent $50—but he never delivered. On October 23, Douglas sent him a brief note thanking him for his "help and support," but it was quite cool, as she addressed him not as Ron or Ronnie but as Ronald Reagan. The next day, Reagan's new film, the very minor *Louisa,* opened, with the actor winning praise from *The New York Times* for his "amusingly befuddled" performance.

By then, if not earlier, his support for Douglas had wavered. For almost a year he had been dating the politically conservative actress Nancy Davis, whose career finally seemed to be on the rise after a well-received role (as a pregnant housewife) in *The Next Voice You Hear.* Nancy often socialized with comedienne Zasu Pitts, who was a friend of J. Edgar Hoover and a Nixon activist. Earlier that year, Zasu had phoned Hedda Hopper to report that in the mid-1930s, Helen and Melvyn Douglas had helped organize a farmers' union in South Carolina that was later revealed to be a Communist front and had also contributed one thousand dollars to assist farm strikers in Salinas. Later in the campaign she publicly smeared Douglas so savagely that the candidate considered suing her for slander. Nancy Davis at some point took Reagan to a meeting where he heard Pitts rail against Douglas and her pro-Communist record.

Reagan was close to another Nixon activist, actor Dick Powell. In previous years, when Reagan and then wife Jane Wyman had dinner with Powell and his spouse, June Allyson, the two men often argued politics. In fact, arguing drew the men together, especially since Wyman abhorred all political talk. June Allyson would later explain, "I do not know whether it was Richard [Dick Powell] or Nancy and her staunchly Republican family who finally switched Ronnie. I only know that Richard, chortling with glee, took full credit for it."

Now, one late night, actor Robert Cummings, who had vaguely Republican sympathies, received a telephone call from Reagan. The two had acted together in *King's Row* in 1942 and remained good friends. When Reagan was still a New Dealer, the two actors had taken opposing stands on many issues, but Cummings considered Reagan one of the most honorable men in town and had joked that he should consider running for president of the United States. Cummings, on the other hand, had tried to steer clear of political controversy. Hedda Hopper reported on October 1, 1950, that Cummings had been duped by an unnamed film director into speaking at a school for the underprivileged. Later he learned that it was a "Red front," and he vowed never to do anything like that again.

Cummings would later recall the late-night phone conversation with Ronald Reagan this way:

"I'm trying to help a senator get elected," Reagan said, "and we're giving a party for him tomorrow night. Can you come?"

"You know I'm not political, Ronnie."

"Couldn't you just come and be there anyway?"

"Who is the senator?"

"His name is Richard Nixon."

"But isn't he a Republican?"

"I've switched," Reagan explained. "I sat down and made a list of the people I know, and the most admired people I know are Republicans."

. . .

After several weeks of infighting, the dispute over the proposed Screen Directors Guild loyalty oath, the first in Hollywood, finally came to a head. Guild president Joseph L. Mankiewicz questioned the morality and legality of the oath and disputed his board's poll of membership, conducted by open ballot. Accepting an award from B'nai B'rith for his film against racism, *No Way Out,* Mankiewicz excoriated the witch-hunt and called American liberals the "new minority . . . being slandered, libeled, persecuted and threatened with extinction." Privately, he believed that Cecil B. DeMille wanted to become (as he later put it) "Commissar of Loyalty for the whole industry."

DeMille, the sixty-nine-year-old director who first promoted the oath, was only getting started. He privately screened several of Mankiewicz's films, looking for Communist propaganda. His chief ally, Albert S. Rogell, vice president of the guild, openly accused *Daily Variety* of being "un-American" and harboring left-wing attitudes because it had published one of Mankiewicz's antioath statements. On the other hand, he added, the *Hollywood Reporter* was "patriotic" for ignoring Mankiewicz. *Variety* responded, "The absurdity that the suppression of news is patriotic speaks for itself." According to the trade papers, an industry-wide loyalty oath was now in the works. "I'm all for this," Louella Parsons told her radio audience, "because Hollywood can very well be an example to the rest of the country."

On October 8, Mankiewicz (covering his bases) served as director of an American Legion pageant at the Hollywood Bowl. The following night, at a heated SDG board meeting, he continued to rail against the oath, particularly the requirement that the guild send producers a list of all directors who failed to sign it. He proposed a full meeting of the membership to discuss it and said he would refuse to sign the oath in protest. This would put 1950's Oscar-winning director—whose *All About Eve* was about to premiere in New York City—on his own guild's blacklist.

DeMille and one of his key supporters, Frank Capra, disputed the use of the word *blacklist,* pointing out that producers could still hire anyone they wished. "This guy's un-American *but* you can hire him—that's a blacklist!" Mankiewicz replied. John Ford, who couldn't decide what he thought about all this, remarked, "I will not stand for any blacklist, but why shouldn't a man stand up and be counted?"

"Because," Mankiewicz answered, "nobody appointed DeMille to do the counting." When the SDG president added that "Russia is the only place I

know where the populace is not entitled to a secret ballot," DeMille answered, "Well, maybe we need more of that here."

Two days later DeMille called for a secret meeting of guild members
known to oppose Mankiewicz on this issue. They decided to launch an un-
precedented movement to recall their president. This group of sixteen—
which included Frank Capra, Leo McCarey, and Andrew Stone but mainly
included directors of the second rank—would try to pull it off before
Mankiewicz had a chance to stop them. To accomplish the recall would require the support of 60 percent of the guild's membership, or 167 votes.

The following day, Vernon Keays, the guild's executive secretary (and De-
Mille's former assistant director), mobilized the entire SDG staff to prepare
slips of paper carrying the simple message "This is a ballot to recall Joe
Mankiewicz. Sign here . . . [ ] Yes." There was no explanation of why
Mankiewicz should be ousted, no opportunity to vote no—and once again
the balloting would be open, not secret. Then the secretaries addressed the
ballots, carefully avoiding several dozen members close to Mankiewicz who
might tip him off. The membership list was locked in the office vault to prevent Mankiewicz partisans from obtaining it. Finally, the ballots were
shipped to DeMille's office at Paramount and given to messengers on mo-
torcycles, who hand-delivered them well into the night.

Despite the precautions, Mankiewicz learned of the recall movement
sometime that evening, when his brother Herman, the screenwriter,
reached him by telephone while he was screening a film in the projection
room at Twentieth Century–Fox. "What do you have in common with
President Andrew Johnson?" Herman asked.

"Oh, come on," Joe replied.

"You're being impeached, my boy!"

On Friday, October 13, the SDG board brought additional pressure on
Mankiewicz by taking out ads in the trades announcing with pride the pro-
oath membership vote in August, but without mentioning the open ballot.
Leo McCarey and George Marshall had each put up five thousand dollars
of their own funds to finance the ads.

That night, Mankiewicz called a meeting of likely supporters in the
backroom of Chasen's restaurant. The group included Billy Wilder, Elia
Kazan, John Huston, William Wyler, and King Vidor, among others.
Mankiewicz's attorney, Martin Gang, predicted that if the recall succeeded,
the director's film career would probably be over. Gang proposed two actions: a petition calling for a general meeting of the SDG membership and
a legal injunction nullifying the result of the recall vote.

The injunction was actually the easy part; it needed only one director to
sponsor it, and John Huston quickly signed on. But the petition required

twenty-five names, so the antioath faction spent the rest of the evening hunting all over town for signatures. Some guild members indicated they would sign, then backed off; agents warned second-tier directors that if they endorsed the petition, they would enrage DeMille, who would find a way to punish them. (Among those who did sign were Nicholas Ray, Richard Brooks, George Seaton, Mark Robson, Robert Wise, Fred Zinnemann, and Joseph Losey.) Finally, after two in the morning, a limousine was dispatched to Walter Reisch's home to secure signature number twenty-five.

There was one more thing, Gang explained: For their document to have effect, they had to be members in good standing of the guild, and they could qualify *only if they signed the oath*. The petitioners would have to swallow their pride.

But the intrigue was only beginning. The next morning, Robert Aldrich went to the SDG office, which was always open on Saturdays, to file the petition and secure a full list of guild members but found it inexplicably closed.

On Monday several members of the SDG board, including Frank Capra, fired off a telegram to the guild's members finally explaining the case against Mankiewicz. Among the allegations: Mankiewicz was trying to overturn the board's "legal and orderly" decision on the oath; he was making "untrue and incendiary" allusions to a "blacklist"; he was using the office of the president in a dictatorial manner. Still, the board had no choice but to accept the Mankiewicz petition and schedule a general meeting, which was called for the following Sunday evening at the Beverly Hills Hotel—and quickly became the most eagerly awaited political gathering in the history of Hollywood.

The anti-DeMille faction was clearly growing. Most of the directors, no matter where they stood on the loyalty oath, recognized that the original vote was rigged. Robert Wise raised more than eleven hundred dollars to fight for Mankiewicz's survival. DeMille, now on the defensive, privately proposed a compromise: He would drop the recall motion if Mankiewicz would perform "an act of contrition" and suggested that the SDG president write up something and give it to Louella Parsons, "who can read this to the American people . . . that you are sorry for what you have done."

"Oh, hell," Mankiewicz reportedly replied, "you can stuff your act of contrition." Frank Capra, now disgusted with DeMille and the whole affair, resigned from the SDG board. The October 22 meeting would clearly be one of those rare Hollywood blockbusters that lived up to its billing.

But how would anticommunism in the arts play in Peoria? While appearing at a Conference to Combat Communism in Peoria, Illinois, Vince Hartnett, chief detective for the *Red Channels* gang, learned that a theater there would soon present a road-company version of Arthur Miller's *Death of a Salesman*. Miller had made the *Red Channels* dishonor roll, with eighteen citations no less, and the show's producer, Kermit Bloomgarden, and star, Albert Dekker, were also (according to Hartnett) suspected pinks. On top of that, the theme of Miller's play was far from commendable. "You in the audience," Hartnett said, "hold the purse strings for most entertainers." Referring to the *Death of a Salesman* booking, he asked, "Why should you support such a performance?" He had somehow deduced that exactly 7½ percent of the play's gross would go to Communist organizations.

The American Legion and the Peoria Chamber of Commerce promptly asked the local sponsors to cancel the performances and pleaded with playgoers to boycott the show if it went on as scheduled. And indeed, when the sponsors refused to buckle, few Peorians bought tickets. This response was widely publicized, carrying another chilling message to all producers of plays and motion pictures.

The radio and television industry, which had felt the freeze earlier, starting with the Jean Muir case, now faced another public controversy. CBS, which telecast *The Goldbergs,* and the program's sponsor, General Foods, had received letters calling for the removal of costar Philip Loeb, who had earned seventeen citations in *Red Channels*. In dismissing Muir a few weeks earlier, General Foods had announced a policy of dissociating itself from "controversial" performers, and thanks to the protests Loeb now fit the bill. But *The Goldbergs* was a very popular show, and network president Frank Stanton and the show's producer-star, Gertrude Berg, supported Loeb wholeheartedly. For the time being he remained on the air, but with a sword over his head while the network, the sponsor, and Berg met frequently to discuss his fate.

At one meeting, the president of General Foods bluntly asked Loeb when he was going to clear himself and remove the stigma attached to the show. Loeb knew he was doomed when he heard that. Still, he rejected a suggestion that he make a Voice of America broadcast, feeling that this would lend credence to the notion that he had something to prove—something to repent for.

Loeb's future remained unresolved, but a turning point had been reached in the radio and TV industry. Broadcast executives and sponsors recognized that they would face a continuing pattern of revelation, protest, and dismissal if they didn't take the bull by the horns. The problem: Their artists were being exposed by outsiders long after being hired. But what if the networks and the sponsors screened their performers and writers before they were attached to new programs, before their presence caused any controversy?

Industry executives loathed the *Red Channels* detectives for causing them so much grief. But now they recognized how the same Red hunters, and others like them, could prove useful: They could be hired to condemn or clear potential employees in advance, not after the cat was out of the bag. That way the industry could establish for the first time not only a true blacklist of untouchables but also a "white list" of the politically clean. These listings, black and white, could be institutionalized—privately, secretly. There would be no public protest, no exposés in the press, for there would be no one to expose or protest; the tainted would have already been kept off mike or off camera. And none of those barred could protest either, because they would not know (and certainly could not prove) why they had been passed over for a role or an assignment. That was the beauty of it.

CBS took the political screening a step further, instituting a loyalty oath for each of its twenty-five hundred employees. When the Authors League of America questioned this decision, a CBS spokesman replied that the system's rise or fall would depend on "how intelligently and how fairly" it was administered, "and this obviously cannot be proved or disproved in advance." One CBS employee promptly refused to sign the oath and was dismissed. Others resigned. Tony Kraber, a CBS producer listed in *Red Channels,* informed the network of his past activities. In response, a top executive told him, "The network is bigger than any of us," and asked him to quit. When Kraber pointed out that he had signed the loyalty oath, the executive replied, "Oh, that. . . . That doesn't mean a thing."

One *Red Channels* listee certain to be banned from CBS sooner or later decided to enjoy his surprising success selling records while he could. Pete Seeger's folk group, the Weavers, had the number-one hit in the country, a lovely version of Leadbelly's "Good Night, Irene." Recently, they had also done well with Woody Guthrie's "So Long (It's Been Good to Know You)." Seeger wondered how long the blacklisters would allow even the most apolitical Weavers' song to be played on the radio. Members of the group had records of radicalism well-known to FBI agents and HUAC investigators. Seeger himself had garnered thirteen citations in *Red Channels,* including a notation for attending a recent May Day rally.

Another left-wing folksinger had already drawn the agents' attention. Woody Guthrie's name was missing from *Red Channels,* but his ties to the Communist Party—among other things, he once wrote a column for the *Daily Worker*—were obvious. In June 1950, an FBI informant in Los Angeles had placed Guthrie in something called the Factionalist Sabotage Group, made up of ex-Communists and veterans of the Abraham Lincoln Brigade. J. Edgar Hoover believed that left-wingers with military experience were forming underground groups to prepare for guerrilla action in the event that the Soviet Union and the United States came to blows. So Washington headquarters advised the L.A. office to make sure Guthrie and other members of the Factionalist Sabotage Group were "closely followed."

Now the FBI learned that Guthrie was no longer in Los Angeles. He was, the agents confidently reported, living in El Paso, Texas, with his wife, Mary. But the folksinger was in fact no longer married to Mary and had not lived in El Paso for ten years. His health faltering from the onset of Huntington's disease, he had moved with his second wife, Marjorie, and his kids to Coney Island.

On October 16, Ed Sullivan, in his syndicated column, reported that "California bookies" rated the Nixon-Douglas race "a toss-up," but the first opinion poll released to the public suggested otherwise. Mervin Field, the local Gallup, had been surveying voters since 1945, and his first poll on the Senate race showed Nixon leading, 39 to 27 percent—but with an amazing 34 percent undecided. "At this stage of the campaign," he observed, "the undecided voters definitely hold the balance of power." The other key finding was that while Nixon was trouncing Douglas among registered Republicans by a four-to-one margin, her edge among Democrats was not quite three to two. But Field still gave her a good chance for victory because of two factors: the wide Democratic edge in registration and the great many Democrats who had not yet made up their minds. Both candidates, he noted, would be spending the balance of the campaign courting those voters.

The Field poll—as well as a report that Corbett's, the state's leading betting parlor, had set the "smart money" odds favoring Nixon at two to one—did not alarm the Douglas camp; it merely confirmed what the Democrats already sensed. While grassroots efforts proceeded at a feverish clip, Douglas continued to lobby outsiders to help save her candidacy.

As election day neared, that support came not so much from personal appearances as from testimonials via radio and television. Lyndon Johnson called her "a great person, possessed of a great mind and a great character," adding that "as a Texan I want to tell you that I know greatness when I see it." His fellow Texan, Sam Rayburn, extolled her "splendid Americanism" and said he had known thousands of representatives but did not know of one "who would make a better Senator than she." Congressman Mike Mansfield of Montana, who served with Douglas on the Foreign Affairs Committee, called her a "real asset" to that panel and to the entire country. Senator John

Sparkman of Alabama considered her "one of the best Democrats ever to serve" in the House and said she had the "respect and confidence" of her colleagues across the country. And so on. Many of the TV spots were quite primitive, with a recorded voice playing while photographs—not film—of the speaker and Congresswoman Douglas appeared on the screen.

Supporters from outside the state continued to arrive. When Drew Pearson came to California for some speaking engagements, he predicted that Douglas would stage a come-from-behind victory, for Red-baiting would boomerang before November. Pearson also did some poking around, and on his Sunday-night radio program he revealed that Nixon "has been appealing to Texas oil men to contribute to his race for the Senate. As a result all kinds of money has been pouring into California for Nixon's campaign." Then, in his syndicated column, he denounced the "vicious election campaign" in California, in which "powerful forces, including the big ranchers, the utilities, and oilmen" had "combined to wage one of the most skillful and cut-throat campaigns" he had ever witnessed. "There is nothing too vicious for the opposition to say against Mrs. Douglas." Pearson cited, in particular, the Pink Sheet, "one of the most skillful pieces of propaganda I have seen in the current election." Voters should be grateful for Nixon's persistence in the Hiss case, but his Red-scare antics in the current campaign would not "help him with the fair-minded American electorate in the long run."

Mary McLeod Bethune, spectacularly white haired, came to speak for Douglas before large crowds in both the north and the south, mainly in black churches. Her endorsement, however, was more than offset by an editorial in the *Los Angeles Sentinel,* one of the largest black-owned newspapers in the state (circulation, twenty-five thousand). Back in May, it had backed Douglas, citing her record on fair employment and anti–poll tax and antilynching bills and her vocal "public stands" against racial discrimination. The *Sentinel* had long praised her service to her constituents, although it had favored black candidates who ran against her for Congress.

Now the *Sentinel* fully repudiated its support and endorsed her opponent. "We are amazed at her weak-kneed stand on the issue of Communism," the editorial announced, citing a number of votes recorded on the Pink Sheet. It dismissed her domestic record (which it had previously lauded) in two sentences: "Of course, she favors civil rights legislation. At election time . . . what politician doesn't?" While affirming that America's "so-called democratic system needs overhauling," the editors nevertheless found that "the future of American Negroes is inexorably related to the future of America itself." They must support the candidate most likely to help the country combat communism, and that candidate was Richard Nixon.

Douglas recovered from the shock somewhat with the support of the largest black paper in the north, the Bay area's *Sun Reporter,* which noted that she had been present at the birth of every major civil rights action, including the hiring of a "colored secretary," an act that "set official Washington agog for months. Now there are a number of non-white Congressional secretaries." She also received the endorsement of black labor leader A. Philip Randolph. Douglas's outside support no doubt helped, but it possibly carried less weight in the African-American community than did the local pro-Nixon celebrities, like actress Louise Beavers and former All-American football star Kenny Washington.

Still, Nixon strategists knew that victory probably would not rise or fall on his "colored" and "Mexican" votes (as they were often referred to), and so they acted accordingly, planning few major events in minority neighborhoods. Adela Rogers St. Johns felt this was a mistake. On October 5, she called Nixon secretary Dorothy Cox and gave her an earful. She reported that one of Chotiner's aides had allegedly told a Nixon worker, referring to Negroes, "You know what we do with them where I come from—put 'em in a truck and dump them in the river," or words to that effect. The Nixon worker was so outraged he refused to do any more campaigning in downtown Los Angeles. St. Johns also revealed that actor Leo Carillo, whom she had recruited to work for Nixon in Mexican districts, had not yet been put to use. She herself had volunteered to speak to "low-income groups," but no one had taken her up on the offer. She had tried to pass these complaints along to Murray Chotiner and Bernie Brennan, but for some reason they would not return her calls, so she asked Dorothy Cox to get word to Nixon directly; she was certain that he didn't know about any of it.

Four days later Cox sent Nixon a memo covering this conversation and suggesting that he mollify St. Johns. St. Johns was popular with Democrats, and Cox added she was on the "frumpish" side, which would be an "asset" among those who complained that Republicans had to be rich and well-dressed.

While Nixon may not have been aware of racism at his headquarters, many observers noticed he was uncomfortable around blacks. On one occasion, he and St. Johns attended a rally in an Oakland gym and were surprised to encounter a largely African-American audience. "He saw it," she recalled later, "and cursed like a pirate." Others observed that Nixon was growing increasingly uneasy in any urban setting. "He was comfortable in the crossroads, the one-signal towns, the Whittiers," Dick St. Johns, Adela's son, recalled. "Those were his folks." Los Angeles and San Francisco, he added, "scared the shit out of him."

As the election neared its climax, Nixon, like Douglas, increasingly turned to the radio. He recorded a half-hour speech on the Hiss case while continuing his spot announcements and Monday-night statewide broadcasts. And his use of television helped usher in what one observer described as "some of the biggest changes in the history of American electioneering" and another called "a media revolution."

America was still getting used to politicking by television; the medium had been lightly used in the '48 elections, when only about half a million Americans owned TV sets. To many voters, television advertising seemed shallow, vulgar, and loud, and was not to be trusted. *Variety* referred to Senator William Benton of Connecticut "haranguing" voters with groundbreaking TV spots during his 1950 campaign for reelection. A popular comic strip showed a candidate challenging his opponent to a radio debate, adding "Or I'll wrestle him on television!"

But 1950 would be the turning point in the marriage of television and politics. In a story headlined HUCKSTERS TAKE OVER GOP CAMPAIGN, a New York newspaper revealed that "the politicians are beginning to apply all the smart advertising techniques used . . . to merchandise autos, bath salts, and lawn mowers." Across the country, dozens of candidates for the Senate used TV in important if often unimaginative ways. Appropriately, it was Senator Benton, a famous adman (cofounder of Benton and Bowles), who pointed the way. Most candidates simply used the TV screen as a billboard, with one simple photo and a soundtrack. But Benton, who produced his own spots, used multiple images in what he called "quickie one-minute films," inventing small-screen political grammar to "project" himself "as a person." It was customary, he said, for candidates to use handbills, newspaper ads, and radio, but television was potentially a "far more effective method of political communications—second only to a face-to-face meeting."

Earlier in the year, Benton had urged President Truman to push the party in the direction of television. Truman, in turn, told him to go out and shake hands with twenty-five thousand voters. Now Benton collected his innovative TV spots and took them to the White House to show the president.

Jimmy Roosevelt's campaign manager had revealed that the only thing about TV that prevented him from relying on it extensively was "its prohibitive expense." That didn't stop Richard Nixon. In the space of two weeks, the Nixon team placed thirty-three television spots on three stations in San Francisco. One wag attributed this saturation to the fact that only Republicans in San Francisco could afford TV sets.

Nixon also filmed six two-minute spots on the theme "On Guard for America." After an orchestral fanfare, a marginally famous local or national figure, such as radio announcer Harry Von Zell, would often introduce Nixon as "my candidate." Then Nixon would simply speak into the camera for a minute or two. Usually, he would blast Helen Douglas as a coddler of Communists. "If you want Communism pampered and helped," he said, "then I am the man to beat." Or he would call for supporting our boys in Korea by going to war with the enemy within the United States. "I see no sense in fighting Communism everywhere else in the world and playing footsie with it at home," he observed.

In one spot, he denounced those who refused to sign loyalty oaths. "From a 'parlor pink' comes a smell of 'red herring,' " he explained. "I have no tolerance for them, pink or red. The time for sentimentality, hypocritical cant and soft-hitting has passed; the time for action is here." As November neared, Nixon announcer Tom Dixon watched the candidate "ingeniously" weave Helen Douglas and Alger Hiss together in almost every statement.

Nixon also started borrowing a bit more glamour, inviting author Kathleen Norris and such Hollywood figures as Harold Lloyd to appear with him on the radio. Lloyd said this was one of the few times he had ever endorsed a candidate; he did so now because it was vital to promote a "defender of American liberties." Norris explained that no thinking person could compare the records of the two candidates without "a sense of amazement, and possibly shock, and even more a feeling of indignation that so flagrant a disregard of America's interests has been allowed to go on in the Douglas and Marcantonio camp as long as it has." Actor George Murphy made several appearances for Nixon, telling audiences that among other shortcomings, Helen Douglas had never been a good actress.

A major advantage the Nixon campaign had over the scattered Douglas effort was its ability to transform a routine statement or event into a long-running story, thanks to a cooperative press. In early October, for example, Herman Perry notified Bernard Brennan of a nineteen-year-old soldier in Korea who had supposedly asked his mother back in Los Angeles to draw fifty dollars from his savings account and donate it to Nixon. "We believe that any newspaper would be glad to make a headline story of the request of this veteran," Perry wrote. A week later the story appeared in newspapers all over the state. Murray Chotiner had laid it all out in a press release, complete with a photo of the marine's mom presenting the check to Nixon. Her son, she said, had helped drive the Communists out of Seoul, losing several buddies in the process, and he indicated that he wanted Nixon to win so that "his country would remain as he has always known it."

Nixon told her, "When you write to him next, please tell him how grateful I and all those at home who are fighting Communist aggression are. Tell him too, please, that the spirit of his contribution is characteristic of so many others we are receiving." Indeed, the campaign was so flush Nixon was able to funnel several thousand dollars to Republican candidates for Congress, earning gratitude that could be exploited in the future. One Nixon fundraiser passed out one-hundred-dollar bills for petty cash expenses as if there were money to burn.

As expected, every major newspaper in the state (with the exception of the neutral *Fresno* and *Sacramento Bees* and the L.A. *Daily News*) reaffirmed support for Nixon in vivid editorials. All emphasized the primacy of the Communist issue. Some painted Douglas as a fellow traveler while others repudiated that idea but noted that she had *voted* Red. Even the moderate San Francisco *News* had to admit that Douglas "lacks important qualifications that are essential to the responsibilities of the office"—although it failed to disclose what those qualifications were, accusing her only of "pussyfooting" and "weak-kneed opposition" to radicalism. Like many other papers, it hailed Nixon's record as a Red hunter while stressing that he was no Joe McCarthy, for he left "smear tactics to others. He is no witch-hunter."

Two weeks from election day, however, the Nixon camp vowed to take his "rocking, socking" campaign tactics to a lower level. The candidate himself provided perhaps the most insidious smear of the campaign so far. Nixon declared that as a result of the U.S. failure to aid "Free China," that great nation was "engulfed by Communism." That, in turn, had led to Communist aggression in Korea. With "regret," Nixon reported that months ago Helen Douglas was one of six who sponsored what he termed a "get out of China" resolution, a call for the withdrawal of U.S. forces. This was typical mudslinging for the campaign, but the Republican candidate took it a step further, reporting the "findings" of Congressman Walter Judd, who had traced the genesis of that resolution directly to Joseph Stalin.

"This action by Mrs. Douglas," Nixon explained, "has been established to have come just two weeks after [U.S. Communist Party leader] William Z. Foster transmitted his instructions from the Kremlin to the Communist national committee." He said that "this demand found its way into the Congress," but he did not explain exactly how that happened or how Douglas was involved.

Then, in a dramatic statewide radio speech from Bakersfield on October 23, Nixon cited five misstatements of fact made by his opponent and then added:

> Up to this time I have deliberately disregarded the smear tactics being used by my opponent in the hope she would recognize that such tactics were failing and that she like myself had a responsibility to meet the issues squarely in open public debate. Only two weeks remain now until election day. She still persists in the same tactics. . . . Therefore, tonight and from now until November 7, I am going to take the gloves off and lay the situation between myself and my opponent squarely on the line.

Nixon claimed that his campaign was "based solely on the record." Douglas had not named one instance "in which her record has been misrepresented. If there is a smear involved, let it be remembered that the record *itself* is doing the smearing. And Mrs. Douglas made the record. I didn't."

Douglas supporters could only listen with amazement to Nixon's claim that only now was he taking his gloves off. Herm Perry told Bernard Brennan how pleased he was that Nixon "at last has commenced to slug it out with Helen." Her smear campaign, he revealed, was "holding many wavering Democrats in line," and the huge undecided vote "can yet upset the whole apple cart," a possibility that explained why the Nixon campaign had decided to mount a late offensive.

But there may have been another reason. The women Nixon most resented "were those gifted at attack," Fawn Brodie later observed in her character study. Nixon, she added, "found the open political attacks of the political woman matched against him intolerable."

Kyle Palmer, ever loyal, mimicked the new Nixon line. "There have been more appeals to prejudice, suspicion, class hatred, individual bias and group intolerance in the current election campaign than at any time during the last two decades," he wrote, placing responsibility directly at the door of Helen Douglas and James Roosevelt. Each, he wrote, "has reveled in a demagogic spree calculated to inflame and mislead the electorate." Because of that, the election was still up for grabs.

Nixonites also went after Douglas for her unfortunate reference to the "dark shirts" now on the march in California. A war veteran admitted that Nixon had worn such a shirt, part of his uniform when he served with millions of other young men "who wore the dark shirts of the Navy, Marine Corps, and the Army, fighting the fascist dictators of the world."

A flood of new anti-Douglas material emerged. Her supporters charged that postmasters around the state were sticking Nixon's unaddressed campaign material into all post office boxes. A four-page leaflet, printed in pink on white with HOW WOULD *YOU* HAVE VOTED? on the front, compared "Congressman Nixon vs. Two Left-wingers," Douglas and Marcantonio. A new flyer carried much the same message but on a single sheet, in the manner of the Pink Sheet. This one, however, was printed on blue paper—reportedly at the insistence of Nixon, who felt one pink sheet was enough.

Herb Klein, who served as a publicist for the candidate, believed that one was more than enough. Klein had just moved to Washington for his paper, *The San Diego Union,* and although he still admired Nixon, he felt lucky to have escaped California just as the Pink Sheet, which he considered a "smearing distortion," appeared. "I was glad I had no part in the idea," he later recalled, "and was in Washington as a newsman during the worst of the battle."

The Douglas campaign, which may have been on the verge of finding its feet, was thrown into chaos by the latest Nixon attacks. Nixon would refer to this as keeping Douglas "pinned to her extremist record." Pinned is exactly how the candidate and her supporters felt. They had reached a point of near paralysis and powerlessness; so much dirt was flying at them from so many directions that they felt almost like throwing up their hands and surrendering. Douglas tried to stick to the issues "with Gahagan stubbornness" but confessed that she felt constantly "off-balance" and, worse than that, "ashamed and debased," as if she were "standing in the path of tanks."

What one Douglas supporter called "the vilest of graffiti" appeared on fences and walls. A United Nations official was shocked that the "whispering campaign" against the Democratic candidate and her husband reached even the sleepy town of Carmel. Ellie Heller, the party's California committeewoman, recalled that Douglas "never could draw a breath once it got going, to really map out any sort of a campaign. . . . Her problem was she just *had* to answer everything he said. And she got really more and more upset by his attacks. . . . And every time she'd speak, she'd have to go after the last statement. That doesn't get you very far. You're on the defensive the whole time." A top Douglas adviser recognized that it was "a *masterful* hatchet job. I hate to use the word, but it was!" At the same time, Douglas was running out of money, and Ed Pauley, the Democratic oilman, refused to contribute despite pressure from Washington.

A Douglas campaign worker reported witnessing Nixon, on the stump, greeting a woman carrying a baby with the words "If you vote for Douglas we will still be at war in Asia when he's old enough to fight."

Evie Chavoor came to realize that it was much harder to prove you weren't a Communist than it was to prove you were an American by simply waving the flag. Because of her office duties, Chavoor rang far fewer doorbells in 1950 than she had in previous races. But the few times she ventured out, many people slammed the door in her face "abruptly and with a kind of a mean snarl about communists, or words to that effect." One day on her way to Douglas headquarters in downtown L.A., she came upon a group of Women for Nixon, who had been deployed at every street corner over several blocks near major department stores. They wore Nixon banners across their chests and passed out Nixon thimbles and literature to many of the female shoppers. When one of the Nixon women made a snide remark questioning Douglas's patriotism, Chavoor slapped her—"a terrible thing to do," she admitted—and then "ran like hell."

San Diego organizer Helen Lustig also had what she called "personal confrontations" with Nixonites, "some of them ugly . . . frightening incidents." On several occasions while driving her car, which had a small Douglas billboard attached to its roof, she was forced to the side of the road by other automobiles. Other times "there were epithets, usually on the theme of her [Douglas] being a communist or a fellow-traveler, that sort of thing." Douglas claimed that even children threw rocks at her car. When a woman told Robert Clifton, husband of Democratic activist Susie Clifton, that Helen Douglas was a Communist, he replied, "She's no Communist—I named my daughter after her."

One young Democrat got punched out by a local postmaster, a former boxer, for objecting to an anti-Douglas slur. A cut lip required two stitches. The victim's chivalrous attempt to defend Helen Douglas was rewarded a few days later when she gave him a kiss. With that, two other Douglas admirers walked up to her and said, "Hey, how about me?"

Douglas, meanwhile, warned the media that the Nixon campaign was about to release a picture of her with Paul Robeson. "It was taken at a time when everyone was appearing at benefits," she explained. "I think that kind of thing is shocking. But that is what we are up against."

The increasingly savage Senate campaign even affected children. "Mummy, mummy—they are saying terrible things about you!" Mary Helen Douglas complained after listening to a searing radio assault on her mother. Mary Helen had survived the teasing that accompanied the campaign by concentrating on her studies and an upcoming singing role in a school production of *H.M.S. Pinafore.* Her friend Diane Baker (later a prominent actress) was taunted by classmates who knew the girl was friendly with the Douglases. Sharon Lybeck, eleven-year-old daughter of Ed and Ruth Lybeck, was tormented in a different way—that is, by the atmosphere of suspicion that surrounded her family. Her parents, who feared that their phones were tapped and their mail opened, also thought that Nixonites were following Sharon around, perhaps in the belief that she was carrying messages from Douglas headquarters (where she often visited her mother) to secret supporters or funders.

Another child upset by the campaign was the eight-year-old daughter of Jean Sieroty, wife of a department-store owner who one day hosted Douglas at her home on Rexford Drive in Beverly Hills. While Douglas met with Sieroty's friends and neighbors, including Mrs. Edward G. Robinson, local Republicans marched outside carrying signs suggesting that Communists were not welcome in Beverly Hills. In the middle of the event, Sieroty was summoned to the telephone; her daughter, who had been visiting a friend in the neighborhood, was on the line and very confused. She had come home but turned back when she came upon the anti-Douglas protesters. "Mother," she explained, "you always told me never to cross a picket line!"

The attacks had grown so persistent, ugly, and damaging that someone in the Douglas camp—the candidate herself or an adviser—finally decided that Melvyn Douglas, whose show had just closed in Toronto, must be enlisted to defend his wife by defending himself. Also, it was time to put to rest the rumors of marital discord. This was a risky proposition, of course. Although a longtime resident of Los Angeles, Mel had been on the road all year and might appear like just another outsider. Nor would his views appear objective: His endorsement could be likened to Eleanor Roosevelt's support for her son. And although he was a much-admired movie star, he carried the weight of his own political associations, as well as a religious affiliation unpopular with many.

Mel had remained beyond the fray so far. At times, he seemed to express guilt for this, but in October he assured his wife, "After all, it's your job and you do it very well." Then, on October 18, he spoke out for the first time in the campaign. That evening he released a public statement that was powerful and moving but also, in a way, pathetic. For the dignified actor felt he had no choice but to explicitly declare, "I am not now, nor have I ever been, a Communist or a fellow-traveler."

His wife, he explained, could speak very well for herself on matters of policy and her qualifications for office, "but I am informed that certain devious persons are attempting to defeat her by taking advantage of my absence from the state to spread malicious rumors to the effect that I am, or have been, a Communist or fellow-traveler. . . . Whoever makes such a statement is an unmitigated liar and whoever believes it is either painfully inept or woefully misinformed. The record speaks for itself." He then recited that record, always contrasting his stance—supporting the Marshall

Plan and U.S. intervention in Korea, and opposing Henry Wallace's run for president—with that of Communists and fellow travelers. And, of course, he highlighted his army service before concluding:

> I repeat that anyone who calls me a Communist or fellow-traveler is either a fool or a deliberate liar. In either case the fear of a libel suit deters him from making his accusations in public and he resorts to whispered insinuations. He is a political disease. As the husband of Helen Gahagan Douglas, and as an individual citizen, I endorse my wife's candidacy whole-heartedly and I trust that the voters of California will not be deluded by a troop of delinquents whose campaign tactics consist of dirty words and stink bombs.

It was hard to tell whether the "he" the actor referred to was specifically or by inference Richard Nixon. In any event, the statement received almost no play in the newspapers. Melvyn Douglas would have to go on the radio if he wanted to reach a wide audience.

Ten days before the election, Richard Nixon spent a wild day up north, dashing from Chinatown in San Francisco to a rally in the small town of Colfax, on to a mine shaft in the Mother Lode, then back to San Francisco (after a rainstorm forced his plane down in Concord). Frazzled by his travels, the candidate grew angry with the persistent questioning of a female reporter from a national magazine and afterward joked, "I think if there was a way of doing it, I'd have thrown her off the plane," while airborne.

Also accompanying the candidate was Mary Ellen Leary, the state's top female political reporter, who provided for her San Francisco paper just about the only balanced coverage of the campaign. She felt Nixon was a shifty character but admitted that turnout and response were quite positive everywhere. She observed, however, that the candidate appeared tired and seemed to have lost weight during what she described as a "man-killer" campaign. After a luncheon in Auburn, Leary overheard a woman whispering to Nixon, "I'll pray for you." Two other ladies said, "We hope to vote for you for president some day."

Red Sails in the Sunset

As election day approached, the Douglas campaign sensed that Nixon, in his latest attacks, had overplayed his hand, and the long-awaited backlash was about to begin. Evie Chavoor, thanking Douglas's younger sister, Lilli, for a three-hundred-dollar contribution, told her they were "picking up ground and despite the stinking lying newspapers, I feel that we are going to come out on the long end of this deal." The latest campaign tactics had "reached a new low. All this against your sister, who is, in my mind, the nearest thing to a saint that a human being can possibly be." Helen's friend Paul Taylor advised the candidate that now was the time to quit trying to enumerate her "entire good program" and concentrate on "a few points."

As the campaign entered its final two weeks, both candidates sought further public and monetary support from Hollywood. For Douglas, the donations were far more important than anything the celebrities might say. Still, the money came in slowly. She did not throw another emergency bash; the September affair had netted less than five thousand dollars from Hollywood, with only 24 of the 126 invitees attending. Late donations arrived through various channels—two hundred dollars from actor Robert Ryan, twenty-five dollars from screenwriter I.A.L. Diamond, and ten dollars from producer Jennings Lang—but few offered to write speeches or scripts, appear on radio or TV, or take part in a rally or forum. In vivid contrast to previous campaigns, there was not a single star-studded Democratic gala.

A United Press correspondent found activists in both parties complaining that "movie folk are scared of politics this year . . . the luminaries pulled the covers over their convictions and went into hiding." Democrats were afraid to express political views unpopular with the studio bosses; Republicans were said to be shy after having backed a loser, Tom Dewey, in 1948. But the liberals had a special worry. One Democratic organizer lamented that as a result of the HUAC hearings, "the studios frown on their players being politically active. . . . Some who used to be politically active got sidetracked into left front organizations. Now they're afraid to stick their necks out." Apparently, everyone agreed that in a divisive political era, with the movie industry in a box office slump, every Hollywood actor, director, and writer had to worry about what moviegoers might think "if they admit what side of the ballot they put their X on."

Two who did record radio spots for Douglas were Myrna Loy and Eddie Cantor. Loy put a feminist twist on hers. "We Californians know what it is to have a do-nothing man representing us in the U.S. Senate," she said. "We want no more of it. Helen Douglas's record . . . proves that she is a do-something woman!"

Humphrey Bogart went on CBS radio to boost Douglas but spent most of his airtime defending an actor's right to enter the electoral arena. "A movie star," he began, "pays a tremendous income tax. Mine, I don't even look at the check. I just put my hand over it and sign it. It'd buy an airplane, I'll tell you that. So . . . I've got a right to say what's done with my money." This hardly seemed destined to win votes for Douglas among the blue-collar Democrats and independents she desperately needed to attract. More appealing was Bogart's crack that "there are some Republicans who feel that a movie star should not have the right to engage in politics—if he is a Democrat." As for losing fans by standing up for Douglas: "I think there are a few diehards in the backwoods of, shall we say, Pasadena or Santa Barbara, who might not see my pictures because I'm a Democrat . . . but I think they forget very quickly, actually, as soon as the election is over. . . ."

Surprisingly, the Republican candidate drew the more creative support from the movie industry. Several studios collaborated on a Nixon newsreel: It was written at MGM and shot at Republic Pictures by a well-known director from Columbia (Edward Buzzell, who made the Marx Brothers films Go West and At the Circus). The head of the Fox West Coast chain of theaters then made one hundred copies of it to be distributed to movie houses. Morrie Ryskind wrote campaign material; so did James McGuinness, a key Nixon recruiter. Campaign notations on key Nixon supporters include the names of big shots Cecil B. DeMille, Howard Hughes, Herbert Yates (owner of Republic Pictures), Harry Cohn (founder of Columbia Pictures), Frank Freeman (Paramount boss who contributed $450), Louis B. Mayer (who contributed $750), and Mayer's longtime secretary, Ida Koverman, as well as the names of actors Ward Bond, George Murphy, Randolph Scott (Helen Gahagan's costar in *She*), Anne Baxter, and Forrest Tucker.

Some of them had opened a Nixon office on North Rodeo Drive in Beverly Hills and raised money to sponsor radio programs and newspaper ads. "Right now Nixon is losing!" the group warned in fund-raising letters. This celebrity roster included long-established Nixon supporters John Wayne and Charles Brackett as well as new blood: actor Edward Arnold and actresses Jeanette MacDonald, Rosalind Russell, and Ann Sothern. With ample resources, they staged lavish public events, for example, rallies in Bakersfield (featuring Guy Madison and Richard Arlen) and Santa Monica (with Hoagy Carmichael and Charles Coburn) that featured free food and other refreshments.

The group also presented a major radio soap opera, dramatizing the Victor Lasky–Ralph de Toledano book, *Seeds of Treason*. It began, "From start to finish the Alger Hiss story is a 'Who-dun-it' astutely plotted, incredibly acted, a terrifying criminal melodrama. It is the sort of story that would thrill Sherlock Holmes or Chesterton because it involves the subtlest of all investigations, an inquiry into conscience, the almost medical problem of tracking down a virus of the mind." Narrator Dick Powell described a "bizarre cast of characters," starting with Chambers and Hiss but also including Richard Nixon, "the law-maker, who doggedly moved through the persistent vapors of deceit. . . ."

The celebrity effort climaxed with a Cavalcade for Nixon, a torchlight march and raucous, well-attended program at the Hollywood American Legion Stadium, hosted again by Dick Powell, with Hedda Hopper, actor Dennis Morgan, and Nixon's influential Whittier College football coach, Wallace "Chief" Newman, among the stars. A pregnant June Allyson testified about her fears for her child's future should Helen Douglas be elected.

Several hundred movie directors convened in the Crystal Room of the Beverly Hills Hotel on the evening of October 22 for an emergency meeting of the Screen Directors Guild. It would be "the most tumultuous evening" in the history of Hollywood, according to one participant. The showdown over a loyalty oath—and an attempt by C. B. DeMille to remove Joseph Mankiewicz as president of the organization—had finally arrived. Mankiewicz would later call it "the most dramatic evening in my life."

The Mankiewicz faction, led by John Huston, George Stevens, and William Wyler, had carefully drawn up its strategy. "Gentlemen, the fat is on the fire," Huston declared. He had scribbled on scraps of paper disjointed notes representing views he hoped to express: "hypocritical flag wavers . . . unappointed arbiters of loyalty. . . . They have employed the very same tactics of those who they profess to have rallied against. . . . Now is the time, they say, to stand up and be counted. . . . They want to count me, do they? Well, I am not having any of their numbers. . . ."

Mankiewicz had come to the hotel with Elia Kazan, who had just finished shooting *A Streetcar Named Desire,* but as their car pulled up outside Kazan announced that he could not attend the meeting with the SDG president: DeMille knew of Kazan's past Communist Party membership and would use it (and anything else) against Mankiewicz.

Shaken, Mankiewicz opened the meeting with a low-key recital of the facts in dispute, ending his remarks with an attack on the "Politburo quality" of the move to recall him from office, which won wide applause. He was careful, however, not to single out any of his tormentors. Then DeMille took the stage, opening, appropriately enough, with a theatrical reference: "I have come before you neither to praise Caesar nor to bury him." He declared, "No one has accused Mr. Mankiewicz of being a Communist," but he insisted that the SDG president should be removed from office for attempting to thwart the will of the majority.

DeMille, however, would not leave it at that. Instead, he veered into an assault on many of Mankiewicz's key supporters, reciting a list of Communist front groups they had once been associated with. He adopted the classic Red-baiting technique of claiming to make "no accusations against anybody" while suggesting that if Mankiewicz stayed in office his left-wing backers would completely take over the guild.

This provoked a torrential response. "I resent paper-hat patriots who stand up and holler, 'I am an American,' and contend that no one else is," said Don Hartman (who had written many of Bing Crosby and Bob Hope's *Road* pictures). He added that the need for such a stance was "a very sad commentary on our times" and likened it to the case of "decent people" feeling compelled "to sign a paper saying, 'I am not a burglar' " just because a neighbor's house has been broken into. John Huston bitterly pointed out to DeMille that many of Mankiewicz's supposedly un-American admirers were World War II veterans who "were in uniform when you were wrapping yourself in the flag." But the dignified and highly respected George Stevens delivered the coup de grâce, reading from a report of his personal investigation of the recall movement. "It was rigged," he announced, "and it was organized, and it was supposed to work . . . Mr. Mankiewicz would have been out. . . . He would just have been smeared and out . . . quick, overnight, or in thirty-six hours, if you please. . . ."

Now on the run, Leo McCarey, one of DeMille's allies, explained, "Everybody was moving pretty fast, and it was a fire, and maybe we used the wrong nozzle." The always witty Mankiewicz commented, "But I am the only one that got wet." Still, DeMille held firm and continued to refer to several directors' susceptibility to communism. Adopting a Yiddish accent, he read off the names of "Mr. Villy Vyler . . . Mr. Fleddie Zinnemann . . ."

This was too much for Wyler. "I am sick and tired of having people question my loyalty to my country," he protested. "The next time I hear somebody do it, I am going to kick hell out of him. I don't care how old he is or how big." Fritz Lang added, "Mr. DeMille, do you know this is the first time since I'm in America that I'm afraid because I have an accent?"

Then, to wild applause, someone called for kicking DeMille off the board of directors. Some started hissing or heckling the man who practically invented Hollywood, and the imperial DeMille suddenly looked flustered. This spectacle left Mankiewicz with a sense of sadness.

After several hours, Mankiewicz still felt uncertain of his support—until master director John Ford, hardly known for his Communist leanings, took a stand. Mankiewicz believed that only Stevens and Ford could "swing" the audience, and he was worried about Ford. He had watched him throughout the meeting, sitting on the floor, smoking a pipe (and sometimes, in agitation, chewing on his handkerchief). Finally, after midnight, he saw Ford raise his hand, and he thought to himself, *This is it!* And when Ford opened by recalling how far back he went with DeMille and how much he respected him, Mankiewicz figured, *I'm sunk.*

But then Ford, addressing DeMille, added, "I admire you—but I don't like you, and I don't like a thing you stand for." He explained that he was "sick and tired and ashamed of the whole goddamned thing." The notion of "the two blackest Republicans I know, Joseph Mankiewicz and C. B. DeMille" slugging it out over communism was "getting laughable to me." He had helped found the guild "to protect ourselves against producers. . . . Now somebody wants to . . . give out to producers what looks to me like a blacklist."

Ford closed by calling for the resignation of the entire board. "Let's turn the guild over to the Polack [Mankiewicz] and go home," he pleaded. "Tomorrow, let's go back and make movies." Amid thunderous applause, Mankiewicz sighed with relief. The meeting adjourned at two-twenty in the morning with DeMille trudging from the hall disgraced but still defiant. "It's terrifying," Hedda Hopper would write, "when a man like DeMille is let down by a group of young whippersnappers."

The issue appeared settled. Almost lost in the fireworks and then the preternatural calm that followed was the fact that the SDG loyalty oath, promoted by the now deposed board, remained in place, and no one, including

Joe Mankiewicz, seemed to be in a big hurry to dismantle it. On October 27, just five days after his triumph over DeMille, Mankiewicz wrote an open letter to the guild members, published in the trade papers, calling on them to sign the oath—as he had now done—setting aside "whatever reservations you may have concerning any aspect of the oath or its method of adoption." Why? He explained that "a wicked and widespread misconception" continued to exist "both within our industry and without. A misconception that continues to villify and smear both our persons and our Guild. It is essential that you help to remove that misconception."

It was true that this was a request, not a demand, and that the nonsigners would not necessarily be placed on a blacklist. Also, many agreed with Mankiewicz that the oath was meaningless, since any red-blooded Communist could hold his nose and sign it. Still, many sensed that the battle-scarred Mankiewicz had abandoned his principled opposition to all such oaths. *Variety* reported that an industry-wide oath would soon be adopted, also "voluntary" in nature. The Mankiewicz victory had thwarted only the very worst excesses of Red hunting in Hollywood; the overall pattern remained. Joseph Losey would later comment that if "the loyalty oath hadn't gone through the guild, history might have been slightly different, because it started the ball rolling."

On October 27, Edward G. Robinson, one of Helen Douglas's principal supporters in Hollywood, appeared before investigators from the House Un-American Activities Committee in Washington. On the advice of attorney Mendel Silberberg, he finally had decided to combat, rather than ignore, the inferences in *Red Channels* and elsewhere that he was a Red sympathizer. In doing so, he became perhaps the first top-rank Hollywood celebrity to provide those who would no doubt follow with a textbook example of how to gain "clearance" and resume a lucrative career in motion pictures, but at some cost. It was debasement with dignity, but debasement nonetheless.

Robinson had followed a two-track strategy, ridiculing the *Red Channels* witch-hunters while privately acknowledging that the evidence they presented needed to be taken seriously and refuted, with the aim of earning an apology (or at least forgiveness). *Red Channels,* he announced, had introduced "a new self-constituted court of political inquisition alien to our American traditions. . . . Even the tyranny of the Star Chamber proceedings allowed the prisoner to be heard before he was put on the rack." To clear the air, he released a statement denying membership in some of the organizations *Red Channels* had placed him in and explaining that he had belonged to other pro-Soviet groups only while Russia was our wartime ally. "I wish to avow absolutely and unequivocably," he declared, "that I am not now nor have I ever been either a member of the Communist Party or a Communist sympathizer. . . ."

Yet Robinson and his attorneys recognized that he would have to go further than that to purify himself. The actor had then asked screenwriter (and conservative activist) James McGuinness for help, and McGuinness had suggested he go straight to HUAC. Robinson's friend Morris Ernst, the famed ACLU leader, personally informed J. Edgar Hoover that the actor would be "happy" to turn over documents about his past associations and was quite eager to answer any and all questions. Some of Robinson's advisers suggested, further, that the award-winning actor meet personally with his attackers and plead for clearance—and they scheduled meetings with representatives of the American Legion and *Counterattack* for just that purpose. Robinson even offered to hand over to the two groups personal records, letters, and financial statements.

This rubbed Morris Ernst the wrong way. He sent Robinson a confidential letter on October 24—the actor was staying at the Gotham Hotel in New York—telling him in the strongest terms that his record was fine and there was no reason why he should appease anyone. He was outraged that Robinson was not only willing to meet with the *Counterattack* crew but would do so, like a supplicant, in its humble office on West Forty-second Street.

Robinson's meeting with the *Counterattack* editors went ahead as planned the following day, but at a neutral site. Still, Ernst told Robinson on October 26 that he should not expect an apology. Why not? Gaining clearance, Ernst argued, did not solely depend on persuading them "that you are completely O.K." but rested far more on the "fact that if they clear you they will be deluged by two dozen other people who should be cleared and if *Counterattack* clears all of them, *Counterattack* will be out of business."

Nevertheless, Ernst gave his blessing to the actor's planned testimony before HUAC the following day and to a meeting with an American Legion commission that had compiled a dossier on him. He urged Robinson to present material that was factual and "agreeable to your own conscience," while at the same time giving the "self-appointed appraisers of human beings that element of victory and success which they want and which they are in a position to get as a condition of aiding what might be called the 'clearing of Eddie Robinson.' I refer to some formula indicating that you were at times unwittingly used, as were many eminent upholders of democracy, by communist groups. . . ."

At the same time, Ernst and others advised Robinson to pursue a more positive approach, such as volunteering to speak over the Voice of America and visiting U.S. soldiers in Korea, actions that would speak louder than words. To that end, Robinson played the part of the Soviet leader V. M. Molotov in a Voice of America drama and spoke directly to listeners in his family's country of origin, Romania, denouncing their "tragic enslavement . . . by a foreign power which broke so many beautiful promises." He also notified the secretary of the treasury that he was available to sell war bonds if the Korean situation worsened. Even with all that, Robinson could not rest easy, Ernst warned. He suggested that the actor appoint an attorney to handle this "full time job for a long period of time."

Edward G. Robinson's October 27 HUAC appearance was a low-key affair. The actor presented a paper that explained each of his nine *Red Channels* listings in numbing detail; he discussed his bountiful charitable and political contributions since 1939 (down to the last dime), attempting to show that his donations to Communist fronts were "microscopically small" in comparison; and he submitted letters he had written to officers of some of those groups. Once again, under oath, he declared that he was neither a Communist nor a fellow traveler but rather "a patriotic American citizen."

Then came the question perhaps uppermost in the investigators' minds. "Do you know any Communists?" they asked. It was time to name names, if he knew any. Robinson seemed willing but unable. "No," he answered, "I don't know of any Communists among my friends or acquaintances." The investigators tossed off one name after another—Paul Robeson, Dorothy Parker, playwright-screenwriter Donald Ogden Stewart, and on and on— and Robinson kept replying that he had no idea whether they were or were not Communists. It was impossible to tell whether he was testifying truthfully or acting dumb. But he did give the committee two things it wanted: He set an example of volunteerism for other troubled celebrities who might have fewer principles and/or more names to offer, and he did not refuse to answer, or even object to, questions about the political activities of his colleagues.

With that, the committee thanked him for his time, and HUAC investigator Louis Russell told the press the actor had acquitted himself quite well—a kind of clearance. While in Washington, Robinson also met briefly with J. Edgar Hoover and afterward forwarded to him a copy of his sworn statement to HUAC for his files, "so that I may be subject to prosecution by the FBI if I am untruthful." He also volunteered to confront anyone who accused him of subversive tendencies. Then he turned himself over to the director completely: "I would also be pleased to submit myself for your examination or cross-examination with regard to any and all of my prior activities and expose to you all of my life and my files in connection with any investigation you may see fit to make. I am fully aware of your preeminent sense of fairness and justice and do not hesitate to make the above mentioned offer. . . ."

Daily Variety had recently reported that "it has become apparent that a probe is on in Hollywood" with personnel being asked "pointed questions" about their past associations. Now it hailed Edward G. Robinson's appearance before HUAC. His eagerly cooperative nature planted a new approach in the minds of HUAC staffers. Rather than portray the next Hollywood hearing as a prosecution, they could make it seem as though they were doing the suspects a favor—by giving them a chance (as one publication put it) to "explain away" the "smears."

Hollywood may have let Helen Douglas down, but Washington continued to send help her way. The visit of Averell Harriman—described by the L.A. *Daily News* as "perhaps the party's Number 2 factotum"—could provide a turning point, coming as it did in late October, just as the undecideds usually make up their mind. For that reason, Douglas asked friends in Washington, such as Arthur Schlesinger, Jr., to work closely with Harriman on his speech, making sure it bolstered her foreign policy credentials.

When Harriman arrived in Los Angeles, Douglas's secretary, Juanita Terry, went to his room at the Biltmore Hotel and typed the speech for him, transferring it from note cards. Harriman told the press that he had never campaigned for a candidate before, but Helen Douglas was badly needed in the U.S. Senate. He condemned Nixon's "witch-hunt." Harriman was not speaking for Truman, but "the President approves of my being here," he added. (He also gave Douglas a personal donation of five hundred dollars.)

Harriman's appearance was promoted as a major event. George Jessel would emcee, aided by Will Rogers, Jr., and there would be musical entertainment. Paul Ziffren had rented the Biltmore Theater, adjoining the hotel, which seated eighteen hundred. Tickets were priced at one dollar, but to guarantee an overflow crowd, Ziffren distributed fifteen thousand free tickets to Democratic groups. Confident of a high turnout, he arranged to have the program piped into several public rooms at the hotel, including the grand ballroom. Alas, the big night arrived, and Ziffren noted to his chagrin that the theater was not quite sold out and therefore the rooms meant to handle the overflow were embarrassingly empty.

Although its impact was limited, Harriman's speech was quite strong. The former ambassador drew on his days in Moscow—even quoting Stalin—to offer a firsthand account of why Helen Douglas understood communism better than her opponent did. Douglas, whom he had met during his many years dealing with the House Foreign Affairs Committee, knew that the "right way to fight communism is to eliminate the source of the disease," what Stalin himself had once referred to (in Harriman's presence) as "the quagmires of capitalism."

With the Harriman visit a fizzle, the Douglas team again turned frantically to Harry Truman. California's senior Democrat, Sheridan Downey, was speaking for Nixon on radio spots every day. It now appeared certain that only the president, whose popularity in the polls was still improving, could save Helen Douglas.

This was underscored by a new Mervin Field survey, which found the gap between the two candidates narrowing, from twelve percentage points in the previous poll to ten in the present one (at 49 percent to 39 percent). But the bad news for Douglas was that the number of undecideds had plummeted from 34 percent to just 12 percent. Apparently, in the two weeks since the first poll, Douglas had picked up a majority of the undecided, but only by a slim margin, not the strong swing she needed to overcome Nixon's early lead. So now her only hope rested on getting many of the conservative Democrats—and other party members reluctant to vote for any woman—to return to the fold. The new poll found that registered Republicans backed Nixon by 85 percent to 7 percent, whereas Democrats favored Douglas by only 52 percent to 33 percent. Yet Field declared that "the contest is still close and anything can yet happen . . . any noticeable change in voter sentiment could alter considerably the line-up of the votes as it appears today."

If Truman couldn't come to California, would he at least issue a statement strongly endorsing Douglas? Her supporters pointed out that she had stuck her neck out for him in supporting his veto of the McCarran Act. On October 27, Truman aide Ken Hechler told another top aide, George Elsey, that the chief issue the Republicans were raising against Democrats around the country was "softness toward Communism" and suggested that a "devastating answer" to these charges from the president could lift the party's chances in several key states, including California. The reports from California were not good, Hechler told a student at Princeton, because "a lot of the red mud which Nixon is throwing around seems to be sticking out there. In other areas, the outlook is good."

Truman told his staffers that looking back thirty years he could not recall an election season so dominated by "low" tactics. He decided to deliver a major radio or television address on November 4, the Saturday before election day, calling for support for Democratic candidates.

. . .

On the morning of November 1, a day of record-breaking heat in Washington, Harry Truman learned that thousands of Chinese soldiers appeared to have entered the conflict in Korea. He returned, troubled, to his temporary living quarters at Blair House (the White House was under repair) for lunch and a brief nap. As usual, two Secret Service agents kept watch downstairs, with uniformed White House policemen posted out front.

Blair House, unlike the White House, stood just off the sidewalk on Pennsylvania Avenue. Suddenly, two young men in dark suits and hats burst past the guard booths. One fired a German-made Walther P-38, striking the right leg of the officer guarding the front door. The other, armed with a Luger, shot point-blank and mortally wounded another guard and put three shots into a third officer. A fourth policeman and the Secret Service agents fired back; twenty-seven bullets in all flew within two minutes. The attackers, fanatic Puerto Rican nationalists, never made it to the front door. When the shooting was over, one of them was dead, the other seriously wounded, and the president, still upstairs, was safe.

Ambulances arrived, crowds gathered, traffic came to a standstill. Police soon learned that the attackers, Oscar Collazo and Griselio Torresola of New York, supported independence for Puerto Rico and had attacked the symbol of U.S. control, the president, in the hopes of inspiring a revolt on the island.

A few minutes after the dead and injured were taken away, Truman came downstairs. He was scheduled to attend the unveiling of a statue at Arlington National Cemetery that afternoon, and off he went with no change in plans, in part to dispel rumors that he had been assassinated. At the cemetery, he chided reporters for having missed "a lot of excitement" at Blair House a little earlier in the day. That evening, Arthur Krock completed a column for *The New York Times* that began, "The thin and flimsy veil which separates public order from anarchy was suddenly thrust aside in a violent instant today, a grim reminder of the perils which envelop those in high office, especially when passions are blazing throughout the nation and the world and war is still taking its toll of deranged minds."

The following day, after months of soft-pedaling, Truman finally spoke publicly in Helen Douglas's behalf. This occurred, however, only after a late-October visit to the White House by Senator Sheridan Downey, who afterward revealed that Truman had asked him to reverse course and endorse Douglas at the eleventh hour. Downey refused the request. "I am strictly neutral," he announced, a gross fabrication.

Then, during a November 2 press conference, Truman abruptly volunteered the observation that "there has been a lot of misrepresentation of Mrs. Douglas in the press in California. Whenever they mention her—although they boycott her most of the time—they mention her in an unfavorable manner. They have got out rumors now that she is not wholeheartedly in favor of the foreign policy that is being pursued by the President of the United States." On the contrary, he stated, Douglas was a strong ally on the House Foreign Affairs Committee and was "wholeheartedly in accord" with his policies, "which is more than can be said for most California papers," he added, evoking much laughter.

The Truman statement got very little attention in the very newspapers he ridiculed. The *Los Angeles Times,* for example, buried his comment in a short item on page 19. Several Douglas supporters sent telegrams to the president, calling his attention to the continuing press "boycott" and urging him to repeat his comments in his campaign speech on November 4, which would be carried throughout the nation. Harold Tipton called the White House for permission to use Truman's press-conference remark in any way Douglas saw fit. The White House approved—but had Truman acted too late to do Douglas much good?

At the same time, perhaps pointedly, he had said nothing on behalf of James Roosevelt. This did not escape Jimmy's mother, and for several hours she seriously considered resigning her post at the United Nations in protest.

On November 4, the president left Washington for St. Louis to deliver his promised last-minute appeal for Democratic votes. It reached tens of millions over the radio and a much smaller number via television. Periodically, the Kiel Auditorium speech was interrupted (probably on cue) by shouts of "Give 'em hell, Harry," from someone in the audience, whom the president would answer with "I'm going to!" or "All right, I'm doing it!" Truman called for "truth" as an antidote to the Republicans' "awful mudslinging campaign." GOP candidates, he explained, were ashamed of their record, and so they had to resort to scaring the voters. "They have lost all proportion," he added, "all sense of restraint, all sense of patriotic decency." Rank-and-file Republicans, he said, must be ashamed of these tactics, "and I believe they will repudiate them at the polls."

When the McCarran Act passed Congress over President Truman's veto on September 23, it served notice that Communist organizations and Communist front groups had exactly thirty days in which to step forward and register with the U.S. attorney general. Finally, a way had been found to flush the Communists and fellow travelers out of hiding. But when the offices of the Department of Justice in Washington closed for the day on October 23, not a single group or individual had registered or expressed interest in registering, and it was now up to the attorney general to find the Reds, go after them, and punish them—if he could.

With November 7 fast approaching and the polls in his favor, Richard Nixon and his advisers decided on a two-track strategy to prevent a last-minute swing to Douglas. On one level, Nixon himself would pull back; on another, his forces would pull out all the stops.

Late in the campaign, Nixon had punched out his attacks against the Pink Lady more vigorously than ever, which had obviously helped him stay out in front. But with only a few days left, the Republican candidate apparently believed he would lose only if the long-dreaded boomerang effect finally appeared. To prevent it, he started toning down some of his allegations and on October 30 delivered a radio address that actually concentrated on domestic issues.

The draft of one major Nixon speech from this period noted Douglas's "association with Communist sympathizers," which was edited to refer vaguely to her soft "attitude on Communism." In this draft, the candidate was to point out the absurdity of his opponent's claim that the poor were most susceptible to communism, because men like Alger Hiss "and the other traitors to Democracy were, like Mrs. Douglas, raised in wealth." In the final version, the reference to Douglas was deleted. Another speech was screened for libel by a Republican attorney. At the lawyer's insistence, Nixon cut references to Democratic visitors as "political itinerants" and "a covey of migrants," although he was allowed to retain the reference to "carpetbaggers."

Murray Chotiner printed ten thousand postcards with a personal message from Nixon thanking his supporters for their "wonderful friendship and confidence." He promised to continue his rigorous campaign schedule and suggested they do the same because of the large undecided vote. Then he added, "Pay no attention to last-minute smears. They are designed to throw our campaign into confusion. We will match the opposition's fantasy with plain truth."

Bernard Brennan, meanwhile, urged Kyle Palmer and other friends to alert Republicans to the dangers of overconfidence, lest they be in for the same kind of shock Tom Dewey endured in 1948. Palmer obliged with a column warning of a "photo finish" attributable to Douglas's "emotionalism," which never failed to stimulate her audiences. Privately, however, Brennan felt the race was over, telling William Knowland that they had a chance for a "telling victory for Dick. . . ."

A columnist for *The Cincinnati Enquirer* wrote Nixon to wish him "the best of luck against 'That Woman.' Even her looks do not influence us!"

But beneath the candidate's more reserved public statements was a second track to Nixon's closing strategy: Partisan activity at the grassroots level and in the press had brought new elements of distortion and trickery to an already dirty campaign. If Nixon himself was taking a somewhat higher road, others plugging his candidacy were under no such constraint.

George Creel of Democrats for Nixon charged that Douglas had not repudiated her support for Red front groups, adding that she "remains deaf and blind to the redemptive possibilities of recantation." Another leader of the group, Oliver Carlson, a well-known California writer and former aide to Governor Olson, produced what he called "proof beyond a doubt" that Douglas had given "aid and comfort" to the Communists. (This was simply a new list of her political associations.) The group also mailed a leaflet to thousands of Democrats. On its cover in large letters was the question, IS HELEN DOUGLAS A DEMOCRAT?, and the answer, THE RECORD SAYS NO.

From Washington, the head of Californians for Nixon in that city solicited absentee votes by sending out copies of the Pink Sheet. He reported to Nixon that he had given Fulton Lewis a copy and that the right-wing radio commentator subsequently gave Nixon "a plug." That plug was so slanderous that the radio network offered a Douglas supporter an opportunity to respond.

New radio and TV spots pounded out fear slogans: "Old Glory Forever—Red Glory Never," "If you want to work for Uncle Sam instead of slave for Uncle Joe, vote for Dick Nixon!," "Be an American, vote for Nixon," and "Don't vote the Red ticket, vote the red, white and blue ticket!" A GOP bulletin predicted that the tune Californians would be humming on election day was "Red Sails in the Sunset." Some of Nixon's strongest grassroots support came from the right-wing women's group Pro America.

A writer for *People's World* crashed a tea for Nixon at a Telegraph Hill mansion in San Francisco, at which Adela Rogers St. Johns "had the tired, middle-class audience baying for Douglas's blood." Among the questions raised about Douglas was: If she was such a hot actress, why had she made only one movie?

A rash of ever cruder material appeared, none of it officially emanating from Nixon's headquarters but all of it supporting his candidacy. One cartoon pictured Henry Wallace courting Helen Douglas while Joe Stalin (as the man in the moon) smiled down on them. Another depicted Douglas in a toilet that was about to be flushed; the caption read, "Good-bye Cruel World!" A cartoon in a San Francisco paper showed Douglas on a footstool, her skirt hiked up and her underwear showing as she reached for jars labeled "Red Apples," "Red Peppers," and "Red Herrings." Small weekly newspapers printed ads contrasting the names of local men killed or wounded in Korea with evidence of a Douglas-Marcantonio axis; the ads asked, "What are we fighting for in Korea when we have this representing us in the United States Congress?"

Outside many of the 350 Catholic churches in southern California the Pink Sheet was openly distributed to those attending mass, while inside, on bulletin boards, church officials posted sample ballots with Nixon's name checked off. As they had been doing since the beginning of October, under orders from Archbishop McIntyre, many of the priests spoke about the evils of communism and the need to elect the strongest anti-Red candidates. Without mentioning names, they made their preference in the Senate contest clear by speaking favorably of "the man" in the race. In Burbank, a priest warned against voting for "the woman" who voted with Marcantonio. In Alhambra, a priest stated that Catholics were not going to send a Communist to Washington and should remember who went after Alger Hiss. Some priests ordered pro-Douglas Catholics to quit distributing their campaign literature outside the church. A priest at St. Joseph's Church in Los Angeles went out front to order one of his parishioners to stop handing out Douglas leaflets. "You attend to your duties inside," she replied, "and I'll attend to mine outside." In a letter to Nixon, one of his Catholic supporters described the final Sunday in glowing terms:

> The clergy of the Catholic Church . . . pointed out in very clear words who in California were known by their record as being sympathetic toward these Reds. The name of Helen Gahagan Douglas was mentioned as the one to defeat. They went still further by warning that it was folly to stick to the party just because one had always voted that way. This was mentioned by the pastors at the suggestion of Archbishop McIntyre. As a result of this you polled a heavy Catholic vote. . . .

A Douglas backer, meanwhile, wrote a letter to a church official: "California is not France, and Archbishop McIntyre is not Richelieu." Paul Ziffren arranged for Douglas to speak at a dinner honoring a prominent church leader in Los Angeles, but remained wary of her tendency to say too much. "Tell them that you pray for the boys in Korea every night," he instructed, "and then sit down."

Nixon had also won the strong support of Jewish leader Rabbi Max John Merritt in Los Angeles as well as that of a number of Quakers, who announced that his militant foreign policy views met with their approval "As

Quakers we are pacifists," they explained, "but not pacifist to the extent of being pushed around." Nixon leaflets even fluttered down from the sky, dropped by helicopters and bearing the message "Every Communist Who Goes to the Polls Will Vote Against Nixon and for Mrs. Douglas—Which Way Will YOU Vote?" But when garment workers supporting Douglas put out a flyer answering the Pink Sheet and exposing her opponent's record, Nixonites kidnapped most of the copies and, according to Roy Day, "threw them out in the Pacific Ocean."

Dirty tricks proliferated, some conceived and carried out by the Nixon campaign, others conducted by unidentified freelancers. Some voters in all-white Republican strongholds received postcards from a mythical Communist League of Negro Women urging them to "Vote for Helen for Senator—We Are with Her 100%." Thousands of Californians received phone calls from unidentified people asking, "Did you know that Helen Douglas is married to a man whose real name is Hesselberg?" Democratic campaign offices received pro-Nixon postcards addressed to Helen Hesselberg Douglas.

These smears became so prevalent that the Anti-Defamation League of B'nai B'rith investigated. Although it failed to trace them directly to Nixon, his campaign aides worried about the taint of anti-Semitism, which one described as "a very difficult problem to solve." Nixonites kept their distance from Gerald L. K. Smith, who had returned to Los Angeles for a pair of shows at the Embassy Auditorium. Fortunately for Nixon, Smith billed the appearances specifically as "Stop Roosevelt" rallies, with Douglas barely mentioned ("Helen Gahagan Douglas, Alger Hiss's pet"). Smith seemed most concerned with what he called the Roosevelt "Jewish family tree" and their "glorification of sex perversion."

A campaign trick used in 1946 to defeat Jerry Voorhis was revived throughout southern California and in some parts of the north. Phone banks of Nixon supporters started calling registered voters—half a million of them, according to one count—asking whether they were aware that Helen Douglas "is a Communist" and then hanging up. Douglas supporters who received such calls were shocked and enraged, but the calls only confirmed what her aides, recalling the '46 race, expected all along. One mused, "We couldn't get a bank of telephones and say, 'That's not true.' "

A Methodist minister in Los Angeles finally took his phone off the hook after receiving calls for hours from people labeling him a Communist for backing Douglas. Eventually, he traced the calls to members of a Bible group at a nearby church who, he said, "felt compelled to stand up for God and Tricky Dick."

Another last-minute gimmick from the Voorhis campaign resurfaced. Nixon headquarters distributed thousands of sheets titled WIN WITH NIXON.

The flyer explained that anyone who answered the phone on November 6 or 7 with the words "Vote for Nixon" may be "the lucky winner of a valuable prize"—a toaster, an electric clock, a Silex coffeemaker, a set of salt and pepper shakers, a candy or butter dish. A final meeting in South Central L.A. hosted by black actress Louise Beavers and football star Kenny Washington promised door prizes for those who attended.

Over KNX radio, elderly L.A. civic leader Joseph Scott addressed what he called a "campaign undercurrent"—the message that Helen Gahagan Douglas had been attacked because she was a woman. Scott worried that "this little lady" may feel incensed if she hears his claim that Nixon "is to be congratulated upon the way he has conducted this campaign with the utmost chivalry." The simple truth was that in "these perilous days we need a man representing this great state who has been tried and tested in the years he has been in Congress already."

Newspapers continued to go after Douglas with a vengeance. Even the Communist *People's World* denounced the Democratic candidate's "frantic efforts" to "prove she is a better anti-Communist" than Nixon and disputed linking her with Marcantonio. "Unfortunately, the charge is not basically true," the editors complained, noting that unlike Marcantonio she had "voted to support every Administration war measure."

A columnist for a Pasadena paper quipped that Douglas favored labor all right—"slave labor." Kyle Palmer urged readers to "vote American," describing Douglas as a "rainbow chaser" and a "bubble blower." In its penultimate editorial on the Senate race, the *Los Angeles Times* reaffirmed its passionate support for Nixon. But in doing so, it committed a faux pas, a typographical error all too inevitable, given the tone of the campaign:

> His opponent is the glamorous actress, Rep. Helen Gahagan Douglas, who, though a Communist, voted the Communist Party line in Congress innumerable times. . . .

The following day the *Times* explained exactly what had happened, for "the purpose of preventing an injustice to a political candidate and in the interests of fair play." The editorial had meant to acknowledge that Mrs. Douglas was *not* a Communist, and the mistake had been caught just as the presses printing the first edition had started to roll. No papers left the printing plant "except a few bound for out of town." Supposedly, no copies reached the street, and nearly thirteen thousand tainted issues were burned in the newspaper's incinerator. The editors hastened to remind readers, however, that while they never believed, or in any manner intended to imply, that Douglas herself was a Communist, she had, it must not be forgotten, "voted often with the Communist-line Rep. Marcantonio of New York."

Four days before election day, Hearst's *Los Angeles Examiner* topped its rival with its Nixon endorsement. It appeared under an enormous half-page editorial cartoon depicting Congressman Nixon, biceps bulging, shirt-sleeves rolled up, ready for action, with a shotgun ("Military Preparedness") in one hand and a net ("Communist Control") in the other, standing in front of a brick wall ("National Security"), guarding the American farms and factories behind it. Running from him, scared out of their wits, were rodents of varying sizes, labeled "Appeaser," "Propagandist," "Soviet Sympa-thizer," "Professional Pacifist," and the like. But it was the heading that gave the cartoon a real kick: ROUGH ON RATS! it read.

The same day another Hearst paper ran perhaps the most misleading headline of the entire campaign: DOUGLAS OUTSPENDS NIXON BY BIG SUM. It seems that in their latest financial reports to the state, Douglas had listed con-tributions of $42,757, whereas Nixon claimed to have received $4,209. A Fresno labor paper suggested that the actual figure for Nixon was $4.2 mil-lion—an exaggeration but surely closer to the mark than the official figure.

"This is the final week of a bitterly fought campaign," Douglas wrote to a contributor from New York, "and we must be victorious." There was reason for hope after all. The chain of *Bees,* expected to offer a lukewarm endorse-ment of Nixon, instead professed neutrality. The *Independent Review* claimed that its political "barometer" now found Douglas ahead in the race by a 57 to 43 percent margin. Although Manchester Boddy did not declare for a candidate himself, his *Daily News* finally endorsed Douglas. This might have happened anyway, but Paul Ziffren guaranteed it by offering to raise money to pay off Boddy's campaign debt. (Ziffren later said he was "ashamed" of what he did and claimed that he "never did tell Helen Douglas about it.") In *The Nation,* Carey McWilliams, while criticizing the content of both candidates' messages to the voters, predicted a Douglas victory.

Harold Tipton told a *New York Times* reporter that his campaign strategy was working. From the outset, he explained, the plan was to "needle" the other side into overreacting by claiming that Nixon had voted against aid to Korea and other U.S. allies. "They fell for it," Tipton boasted, flooding the state with "phony voting records. But our theory," he added, "was that he couldn't keep up the red smear indefinitely." This theory was obviously tot-tering, but Tipton still professed confidence in an election-eve "boomerang."

But with only days remaining until November 7, Helen Douglas finally grew discouraged. Referring to the new torrent of abusive campaign at-tacks, she told one audience, martyrlike, "I welcome the mud, and the sticks, and the stones!" Bodyguards began traveling with the candidate after she was splattered with red ink at a campaign stop and rocks were tossed at her car. She wondered whether this was merely an election campaign—or a war. She was moved to silence in Visalia after she delivered a ringing defense of her record and a farmworker approached her and said in gratitude, "They haven't made you afraid. . . ."

Feeling she had little to lose, she flailed at her opponent with abandon. "I accuse my opponent and his spokesmen, including Senator William Knowland, of trying to steal this election by drugging the voters with political poison concocted of misrepresentation and false charges," she told a statewide radio audience. "I accuse those newspapers dominated by the *Los Angeles Times* and *Oakland Tribune* axis of aiding and abetting them. I accuse those newspapers of denying their readers the facts and of twisting and distorting the news." In a draft of the same speech, she raised questions about who had paid for the hundreds of new Nixon billboards (when she could afford, she said, only forty-four), but this reference was deleted from the final copy.

At a noontime rally at Berkeley's Sather Gate, she told a thousand students that Nixon "doesn't dare discuss his record. Instead he wages a campaign of character assassination unsurpassed by Hitler's followers or in the Communist countries." On another occasion, she referred to this as "communism, Nixonism, nazism." For the first time, she referred to her opponent from the podium as Tricky Dick. If she had lost hope, audiences never knew it. Douglas motored, flew, or helicoptered all over the state in a frenzied drive, finally skirting the small towns and concentrating on the big cities. She was in Los Angeles one day, San Francisco the next, and San Diego the day after (and then back to L.A.). On their last helicopter flight, her pilot, a Republican, told her she had finally converted him. She would get at least one crossover vote.

By now, it was apparent that there would be no full-fledged Nixon-Douglas debate. Kyle Palmer, referring to Nixon on the stump as "a killer type," claimed that a Douglas aide told him that Douglas would "never make the mistake of debating with that buzz saw." Douglas must have been tempted to seek a debate, to refute Nixon's charge that she was afraid to meet him or just to go for broke no matter what humiliation awaited her. Still, when the League of Women Voters attempted to set up a debate at Beverly Hills High School a week before the election, Douglas agreed to speak only after Nixon sent his regrets, citing a prior commitment.

But as one Nixonite involved in the episode later confessed, that excuse was a deliberate lie. The night of the event, Nixon and his advisers left an out-of-town campaign appearance early and rushed back to Los Angeles. Roy Day and his candidate went to the Beverly Hills Hotel to hide out for a while, with their car waiting outside. Murray Chotiner, meanwhile, rushed to the high school to find out what Douglas was saying.

A comically awkward scene ensued at the hotel's check-in desk. Day handled the arrangements, paying in advance for a room on a top floor, for they would have to leave hurriedly when Chotiner gave them the signal. But Day worried what the hotel managers would think of two men renting a room for just an hour. "It looked a little suspicious," he later confessed. So he suggested that Nixon visit the magazine stand in the lobby until Day had the room key and they were ready to go upstairs. Day also didn't want anyone to identify Nixon and then report the next day that the Republican candidate had been waiting at the hotel to spring a trap for his opponent.

Up in the room, a few minutes passed, and still no word came from Chotiner. Nixon started pacing the floor. "We ought to get the word," he said, "we ought to get the word, Roy. It's time." Finally, the call came, and the two men roared downstairs, jumped into their car, and headed to the meeting. Chotiner met them outside the school and briefed Nixon on what Douglas had said so far. Striding down the aisle, carrying a briefcase, Nixon naturally caused a stir as Douglas tried to continue to speak over the clapping and foot stomping from the Republicans in the audience. He went backstage, introduced himself to the organizer of the event, who said she was delighted that he had made it and ushered him onstage.

Sitting behind Douglas, he signaled boredom and impatience, crossing and recrossing his legs and consulting his watch. This drew titters and guffaws from the audience. "It was really funny to see Helen Gahagan Douglas, an experienced actress and a very fine actress," Roy Day recollected. "Her shoulders just absolutely slumped. She answered one question and ducked out, explaining that she had to get to another meeting. She just absolutely tore out of there. That is where Nixon tore her to shreds. He really let her have it." Day added, "That was one of the most interesting incidents that I've ever been involved in, in politics; it was really a lot of fun."

Another observer remembered that in his remarks after Douglas left, Nixon again referred to his opponent as Mrs. Hesselberg. This deeply offended the many Democrats in the audience, some of whom were Jewish and knew an anti-Semitic appeal when they heard it. Booing broke out, but most of the Democrats kept quiet until the event ended. Then, according to Douglas backer Jean Sieroty, Republicans and Democrats nearly came to blows. After nearly two months of charges, countercharges, and resentments on both sides, the 1950 Senate contest had come to a full boil.

The Final Straw

If Helen Douglas had any chance for victory, it evaporated on November 3 as a result of another inspired Nixon stratagem. The decision to send campaign field director Joe Holt and his Young Republicans to shadow Douglas's press conferences—heckling here, asking provocative questions there—finally paid off. In San Diego the weekend before the election, a tired, beaten-down Douglas finally took the bait. Asked once again by a Nixon plant whether she supported James Roosevelt in his race against Governor Warren, Douglas made her intentions clear. "I hope and pray he will be the next governor," she said of her fellow Democrat, "and he will be if Democrats vote the Democratic ticket." Kyle Palmer later referred to this as "tricking her into the declaration."

Excitedly, Joe Holt called Murray Chotiner in Los Angeles. Chotiner had Douglas's remarks typed up and quickly got a copy to William Mailliard, Warren's secretary, who was about to fly with the governor on a campaign trip to San Francisco. Chotiner, with the help of Kyle Palmer, sent word to friendly reporters, suggesting they demand a response the following day from Warren, who had steadfastly refused to endorse Nixon. As recently as October 27, the governor had ruled out any endorsements, explaining, "We are all running independent campaigns. I've never believed in package deals." Privately, Warren continued to find Nixon's style and tactics repugnant, particularly since he considered Helen Douglas a decent woman. He told his press aide Pop Small that Nixon was "not content with defeating an opponent . . . he wants to destroy."

The following day, Warren did not wait for the inevitable questions about Douglas's remarks. Because he wanted either to put the matter quickly to rest or to punish Douglas for her last-minute change of heart, he issued a written statement from Sacramento that was carried in every daily newspaper in the state. The message was "very cautious," as Mailliard later described it—a masterpiece of understatement. "As always," Warren explained, "I have kept my campaign independent from other campaigns. The newspaper reports from San Diego that Mrs. Douglas has said she hopes and prays Mr. Roosevelt will be the next governor of California does not change my position. In view of her statement, however, I might ask her how she expects I will vote when I mark my ballot for U.S. Senator next Tuesday?"

Just in case some voters didn't understand what Warren meant—and to finally and firmly link Nixon to the popular, moderate governor—Bernard Brennan immediately issued his own statement, also carried widely by the newspapers. "I am sure whether Mrs. Douglas chooses to answer Governor Warren's illuminating question or doesn't," he stated, "every voter in California who reads his statement will realize that Earl Warren intends to mark his ballot for Dick Nixon on election day." And let there be no doubt, he added: Dick Nixon, like the vast majority of other Californians, Republicans and Democrats, would happily mark *his* ballot for Earl Warren.

It was election eve, but all anyone in California wanted to talk or write about were the dire reports from across the Pacific. On its front page, the *Los Angeles Times* carried the headline CRY OF "VOTE TUESDAY" GOES UP ACROSS STATE, but it was overwhelmed by the huge banner head, M'ARTHUR IN THREAT TO STRIKE AT REDS IN CHINA.

Despite hints of massive Chinese intervention, General MacArthur had carried the conflict ever closer to the Yalu River and Korea's northern border. Then, around November 1, the CIA reported to Washington that Chinese troops, ten thousand or twenty thousand strong, may have crossed the Yalu and joined the fighting. Similar unconfirmed reports from other sources persisted in the following days, with estimates of Chinese troop strength as high as seventy-five thousand. MacArthur reported that even if this was true, it would not affect his final offensive, a claim that seemed absurd. Truman, in any case, gave MacArthur permission to continue his assault and even bomb the bridges across the Yalu. *The New York Times* commented, however, that "cheerful reports that the war was virtually over" had now been "squelched."

Then, on the morning of November 6, the day before the midterm elections in the United States, General MacArthur issued a special communiqué accusing the Chinese Communists of committing "one of the most offensive acts of international lawlessness on historic record" by intervening in the war from their "privileged sanctuary" across the border. MacArthur's office now admitted that China could immediately send three hundred thousand troops into Korea, vastly outnumbering its opponents. Already an untold number of Chinese troops had swept across the Manchurian border. Even though the United States was not officially at war with China, there could be no escaping the fact that Chinese Communist troops were firing on, and likely killing, American soldiers. MacArthur sought permission from Truman to strike back.

If Helen Douglas wasn't already facing a crushing defeat, she was certainly staring at one now. Democratic candidates elsewhere in the country found themselves in a similar position. Any candidate would have had difficulty passing up a chance to make political capital out of the breathtaking and (from the Democrats' perspective) ill-timed news, and Richard Nixon seized the opportunity eagerly. He called the Chinese attack "the direct result of our State Department's policy of appeasing Communists in China" and said that voters must therefore elect a new, "independent Congress" that would take a firm stand in dealing with Communist aggression wherever it arose.

He also raised to fever pitch an issue that had emerged two days earlier, when the first rumors of the Chinese entry surfaced. Asked recently by an editor whether he favored admitting Red China to the United Nations, Nixon had thundered, "No," while Douglas, uncertain of what was happening in Korea, had hedged. Now Nixon charged that Douglas's refusal to reveal "whether she supports the government of Red China or whether she opposes it" was "reason enough for her overwhelming defeat at the polls." As far as he was concerned, "this is the final straw . . . doesn't she care whether American lives are being snuffed out by a ruthless aggressor? I knew that my opponent was committed to the appeasement policy of the State Department toward Communism in the Far East, but I never dreamed that she would stick to it even after we were attacked."

There was no way for Douglas to respond effectively to this latest charge, or to the shocking events in the Far East, before the polls opened. Recognizing this, she didn't really try.

CAMPAIGN STEAMS TO A CLIMAX, the San Francisco Chronicle declared. The San Francisco News predicted a record turnout of voters, in excess of five million. Kyle Palmer endorsed a call for all Californians to fly the U.S. flag on election day, "marking it as a day of great import in the life of the nation." Boxing champ Joe Louis appeared at a Nixon rally in L.A. Original Nixon promoter Herman Perry predicted a comfortable win but complained about Earl Warren's belated "confession" that he would vote for Nixon. "Unless a man is a crook," Perry told Nixon, "he is entitled to the *united support* of the party he represents."

Murray Chotiner had arranged what he called a "traditional Nixon close" to "keep our crowd pepped up." Nixon and a caravan of cars visited each of his Los Angeles–area headquarters on November 6. The candidate also attended a luncheon gala at the Biltmore sponsored by Democrats for Nixon, where he warned that only his opponent's last-minute "campaign of falsehood" could threaten his victory. This tactic, he said, "will have some effect on our vote, since there is not time for the truth to catch up with the lies."

That evening, Nixon appeared on television with his wife and daughters, and at eight forty-five he delivered his last radio speech. Introducing the candidate, Tom Dixon called this the climax to a crusade "the likes of which California has never seen before." Nixon opened by reminding listeners that when he kicked off his campaign in September he had asserted that combating communism was more important than all other issues combined. Events, he said, had certainly borne this out. He hit hard at Douglas for following the "Owen Lattimore" line in the Far East and then landed one of the lowest blows of the entire campaign: "Right at this moment, as I speak to you, the lives of American boys are being snuffed out by the ruthless aggression of Chinese Communist forces in North Korea. . . . It seems incredible that a candidate for the highest legislative body in the land . . . would ask you for your votes tomorrow while flatly refusing to tell you which side she is on in this conflict."

On that appropriate note, the Nixon campaign ended. Pat Nixon and the two girls went home, and the candidate, still keyed up and more worried about the balloting the next day than he should have been, went with some of his top aides (Chotiner, Day, Adela Rogers St. Johns, and her son Mac) to the home of Kenny Washington in South L.A., where he drank beer and banged out some tunes on the piano, propelled by nervous energy.

Like her opponent, Helen Douglas finished the campaign close to home, and with the same headlong rush she had maintained for weeks. At her final major appearance on November 6, a huge noontime labor rally, she fired away at Nixon for the last time, urging her supporters to "get out like Paul Revere and bring out the votes!" In a preelection press release, she averred that she was "confident that the people of California will show with their votes their disgust at the campaign tactics of my opponent and send me to the United States Senate."

Douglas's managers, fighting the odds, had funneled a high proportion of their remaining resources into full-page newspaper ads. One declared that NO SMOKE SCREEN CAN HIDE WHAT HONEST, RESPONSIBLE AMERICANS SAY! and went on to quote twenty-five leading Democrats, including Eleanor Roosevelt, Sam Rayburn, and Will Rogers, Jr. Another listed thirteen issues on which the two candidates differed, including Social Security and fair-labor laws.

Nigel Bruce, the portly actor who appeared with Douglas in *She,* was presently living in Pacific Palisades and sent regrets that he could not vote for her because he was a British citizen. From New York, Lorena Hickok wired, "I shall be thinking about you tomorrow. . . ." This spoke for Douglas's many fans around the country, many of them women. But her strongest backer remained her husband, and he reemerged on election eve with perhaps the most moving statement of her entire campaign.

Just moments before Richard Nixon delivered his final radio address, Melvyn Douglas, introduced by Humphrey Bogart, appeared on a rival network. His remarks had been recorded in Cincinnati a few days earlier. In October, in his first statement of the campaign, he had focused on refuting the smears directed at him during the campaign, explaining that Helen was eminently capable of speaking for herself. Now he stood up squarely for his spouse, despite feeling that Nixon probably would have contempt for his remarks because they came from an actor. "I had not intended to make a campaign speech for my wife," he began. "But I am angry." He continued:

In California a Congressman named Nixon is pursuing the same course being used by the Republicans throughout the country. And what is this course? Let us be frank about it. . . . It is a course based on the refuge of all reactionaries—do nothing and attack your opponent as radical or subversive. Men and women in Government who have sound policies, based upon their respect for and responsibility to their constituents, are always attacked. They strive for the best interests of human beings. . . . It is easier—as a matter of fact it is the easiest thing in the world—to call people of good-will dirty names—to call them Communists.

Well, I resent this with all my heart and all my soul. . . . In my book, doing something to alleviate the shameful lacks in our society is the best possible way of fighting the Communists. That is what I believe, and that is what my wife believes. For years we have worked side by side, honestly, frankly, and openly, on the side of human decency—honestly, frankly, and openly, against dictatorship, against Fascism, against Communism. . . .

I also understand that my wife is being criticized because of her career in the theatre. It is true. My wife was an actress. I am an actor. I will not speak of myself, but I will tell you my wife was an extremely good actress, and made a very fine living at it. I will tell you that while she was an actress, she raised two children, and while she was an actress and raised two children, she read the newspapers and listened to the radio, and her heart bled—and she decided to do something about it. She knew and I knew the kind of criticism we'd have from the Nixons, the Tafts and the McCarthys. She knew and I knew that she'd be attacked as just-an-actress. It's pretty funny, ladies and gentlemen. Anybody who's ever been in show business will tell you what courage and fortitude, what disappointment and perseverance, go into the life of an actor. But she knew and I knew that the voters of this country would judge her on her merits, on her accomplishments, on her reputation as a human being. They judged her three times and three times they sent her to Congress. They judged her and they nominated her for the United States Senate. I'm very proud of that.

Nobody discounts the real menace of Communism, both in the world and in the nation—but the McCarthys and the Nixons are taking advantage of this menace in their frantic, grasping thirst for political power. I don't think the people of the State of California, or the people of America, like this kind of thing. And the only way to show it is on November 7th when, in the voting booth, you can vote against what is the most un-American of all un-American activities—false witness against thy neighbor—libel and slander against good and honest public servants.

And so, with no modesty whatever, I ask you to vote for my wife, Helen Gahagan Douglas, for the United States Senate. I have known her a long time. I have loved her a long time. What is strongest and best in Helen is what is strongest and best in America. All her life she's lived by one thing alone—her love for her fellow man. I know of no better quality in a wife. I know of no better quality in a senator.

Even a phenomenal number of last-minute television commercials were unlikely to propel James Roosevelt to within hailing distance of Earl Warren. And Helen Douglas, who still believed she had some chance, had done something that roiled a number of Roosevelt people, including her friend Susie Clifton. At a joint appearance for the two candidates in Los Angeles the day before the election, Douglas approached an attractive black woman on Roosevelt's staff and reportedly said in so many words, "You know Jimmy will lose, so will you consider joining my staff when I enter the Senate?"

In the final days of the campaign, Earl Warren proved he was not above Red-baiting, even with an election in the bag. At a labor rally in San Francisco, he recalled James Roosevelt's being paid twenty-five thousand dollars after the war to represent "a group of leftwingers in Southern California," referring to a Hollywood organization that included Dalton Trumbo as well as Ronald Reagan. Warren vowed that *he* would "never play 'footsie' with Communists or their fellow travelers."

.   .   .

On election eve, Harry Truman returned, as usual, to Missouri to vote. Still certain of a Democratic triumph despite the dire news from Korea, he announced that he would fly back to Washington and spend election night on the presidential yacht, *Williamsburg*. He would retire early, he said, and monitor the returns at daybreak.

Republican leaders also expressed confidence. Guy Gabrielson, the national chairman, suggested that the Chinese intervention in Korea raised the specter of "a ghastly third world war" and predicted that the American people would elect Republicans as a check on the Democrats' appeasement policies. Former president Hoover, from his apartment in New York, wrote to a Republican friend in New Mexico, "Tomorrow is the election. On one side is decency and hope for America; on the other is demagoguery, corruption and buying of the electorate wholesale. This election will be a test. Like you I have but little hope."

Election-day. TV FINDS POLITICAL POT O'GOLD, *Daily Variety* gushed that morning, explaining that seven stations in Los Angeles had raked in $107,000 from candidates that fall. An L.A. newspaper predicted unprecedented broadcast coverage of the election results, with television for the first time offering "sharp competition to radio in a battle for attention." One local station would attempt to switch to five remote feeds.

Richard and Pat Nixon planned to vote the minute the polls opened, at seven o'clock, at the American Legion Hall on East Mayer Road in Whittier, but the baby-sitter was late, and they arrived a half hour behind schedule, smiling at the photographers. The *Los Angeles Times* had given Nixon a ringing send-off that morning with an editorial calling for his election, which "will be a portent understood in Moscow as well as Washington." But the *Times,* reflecting Nixon's fear, worried about the turnout, which had reached 80 percent in 1948 but would surely fall in this off-year election.

Anxious, Nixon took his family for a picnic at the beach, but poor weather drove them indoors, to a nearly empty movie theater near Long Beach. On the way home, he saw Douglas sound trucks still cruising the streets in West L.A. and feared a humiliating upset. After dinner, dressed in a medium-gray double-breasted suit, he went to his Garland Building headquarters, where his aides and hundreds of other organizers and well-wishers had gathered.

Soon it became apparent that the turnout was fine, and he was smiling and making the OK sign with his thumb and forefinger for photographers. More than seven in ten registered Californians had trooped to the polls, and that ended the suspense. Nixon was holding his own or trouncing Douglas almost everywhere—northern, central, and southern California. The only question was how great a victory margin he would run up. A final Field poll, which predicted an overall three-to-two Nixon edge, was proving remarkably accurate. He took all but 9 of 320 precincts in Orange County. He carried his congressional district by better than two to one whereas Douglas struggled to hold her home territory (despite her five-to-one edge among African-American voters in South Central). Nixon's projected margin of victory in Los Angeles County—where nearly half of all ballots in the state were cast—was three hundred thousand votes.

Douglas certainly was not helped by the top of the ticket. Jimmy Roosevelt was losing every county and trailing by two to one overall, but Pat Brown survived the Republican onslaught and won the attorney general race by a narrow margin. The GOP seemed to be doing well in other states as well.

Richard Nixon, his family, and his advisers breathed an enormous sigh of relief and then celebrated well into the night. Dick and Pat visited one victory party after another. Every home or restaurant that had a piano found Nixon at the keyboard, banging out "Happy Days Are Here Again." He was thirty-seven years old, about to become the second youngest U.S. senator, and he knew that most of his political career, blessed so far, stretched before him.

Helen Douglas had not shared Nixon's dark mood that day. Knowing that she had campaigned tirelessly against difficult odds, she was almost serene as she relaxed at home. "Melvyn's speech last night was magnificent," a telegram from Democratic activist Stanley Mosk affirmed. Her two main organizers in San Diego, Ben Lindsley and Helen Lustig, told her, also via telegram, "Helen, dear, we think you are the greatest gal we have ever known." The candidate may have laughed, however, when she received a telegram from another supporter predicting her victory by two hundred thousand votes, which would mean "the Vice Presidential nomination in '56."

While Douglas awaited the returns, a woman named Frances Fisher, who lived on South Western Avenue in Los Angeles, sat down and typed out a letter to tell her that she hoped and prayed Douglas would be elected, but win or lose she had her admiration. The woman had Douglas posters displayed all over the outside of her house, "even though it is a dilapidated looking place, with no lawn cut or anything else, which the landlord neglects." Fisher asked the candidate, when she became senator, to "please remember all the things you promised. Take your market basket to the Senate again and show what an increase in living is doing to the people." She had one more request. Her son, at nineteen, was serving in the army in a perilous time. "The glorious youth of this nation is always being sacrificed and why, why?" she wondered. "Please do something about war, can't we really have a better world for all without you being called a Communist and me too, I guess?" Then, in closing, she added, "I also am an admirer of Mr. Douglas as an actor, he is as capable an actor as you are a Career Woman."

That evening, with the polls nearly closed, Helen Douglas chatted with her former campaign manager, Ed Lybeck. "I'm going to lose, aren't I?" she asked. Lybeck, of course, had predicted this all along. "Yes, honey," he replied, "but not as bad as Roosevelt."

The scene at Douglas campaign offices around the state was not a pretty one. Many of her supporters, female and male (but mainly female), had remained convinced of victory right to the bitter end and so felt crushed by defeat, especially since it was overwhelming. At San Francisco headquarters, one Douglas supporter observed "strong young men" weeping for hours "as the truth became apparent."

Wearing a dark, satiny, slightly V-necked dress (a staple of this campaign), with a corsage pinned above her left breast and a triple strand of pearls, Douglas visited her headquarters in downtown Los Angeles. Her hair, often blown around by the elements during the campaign, was now attractively arranged, and the candidate appeared almost radiant. She took phone calls from friends but spent most of her time consoling staffers and volunteers, who alternated between anger and grief. Juanita Terry told her that she felt this was the end of the world, but Douglas kept smiling. Alone among them, she carried herself with an air of both resignation and accomplishment, an almost supernatural dignity. Friends and advisers could not decide whether this was just one more acting role for Helen Douglas, perhaps her greatest performance ever. "I think inside," one later commented, "she was deeply hurt."

Following the script of primary night, she asked Paul Ziffren to drive her home. She had chosen to get up at six the following morning and fly to San Francisco to meet with supporters. As she dropped off to sleep, almost numb, she wondered how she would feel in the morning, whether the magnitude of the defeat and the way her opponent and his advisers had achieved it would embitter, even devastate her. She had seen this happen to others who had suffered similar setbacks and had taken the political rejection personally, as if their entire lives, their intrinsic worth, had been judged severely and found wanting. She was determined that Nixon (as she later put it) would not "have the final victory of destroying me along with my political career."

The next morning, as it turned out, she felt "free, uninjured, whole. Nixon had his victory but I had mine. There wasn't any part of me that was twisted. I wasn't a soul in torment who would brood about Richard Nixon for years to come. He hadn't touched me."

Across the country, some of Helen Douglas's ideological foes awoke on the morning after the election still feeling the effects of a drunken celebration. A reporter named Ed Nellor had invited famous Red hunters to his suburban Virginia home to toast an expected Republican landslide. Richard Nixon, of course, could not attend, but Senator Joseph McCarthy did make it. Late that night, as fate would have it, Nellor's septic tank backed up, but according to one source, this did not stop a sloshed Joe McCarthy and others from taking off their shoes to wade contentedly in the waste.

On November 7, while voters trooped to the polls at home, U.S. B-29s carried out a saturation bombing raid on the North Korean outpost of Sinŭiju on the Yalu River, using incendiaries that burned down 90 percent of the city and killed thousands of civilians. "Tokyo headquarters, with or without connivance by Washington," I. F. Stone soon wrote, "deliberately took action which might have provoked a third world war. . . . The mass bombing raid on Sinŭiju was the beginning of a race between peace and provocation. A terrible retribution threatened the peoples of the Western world who so feebly permitted such acts to be done in their name."

The full dimension of Helen Douglas's defeat was not clear until the final returns came in the next day. The Democratic candidate had lost every county except four small ones (Contra Costa, Solano, Lassen, and Shasta) and every assembly district in L.A. except those dominated by minorities or Jewish Democrats. Only in Sacramento County did she run nearly even with her opponent in a metropolitan area. Nixon had won by a 59 to 40 percent margin, gaining a slightly higher percentage of the vote in the south (61 percent) than in the north (57 percent). He won by nearly two-to-one margins in Santa Cruz, Santa Barbara, Marin, and Riverside counties. Since Republicans made up only 37 percent of the registered voters, he obviously owed his victory to massive Democratic defections.

Bone weary, Helen Douglas kept her promise to fly to San Francisco and thank Harold Tipton, Ellie Heller, and other supporters for their hard work. After a postmortem with the candidate, a hulking labor leader from the United Steelworkers burst into tears as soon as he got out the door. "My God, this whole thing, this whole defeat," he told another Douglas fan, "was because the church ordered the people to talk about not wanting a Communist in the Congress!"

Completing a brief but "most depressing" analysis of the vote, Ruth Lybeck informed Douglas that at least "the minorities were true blues" and quoted another woman as saying that she hoped "the Negro people will never have to ask Nixon for anything!" Lybeck seemed most struck by the strong vote for Nixon in the subdivisions in Burbank, Van Nuys, and Lakewood. "They voted more conservatively," she added, "than the Real Estate men that hold the mortgage. . . . The new homeowners, those who for the first time in their lives have something to call their own . . . looked into their new TV screens, were convinced by what the Republicans had to say, and went out and voted themselves back into mother-in-law's apartment. . . . Honestly, it's enough to make a person go crazy."

Jimmy Roosevelt, meanwhile, had lost by the greatest margin of any Democratic candidate in state history: more than 1.1 million votes. Pat Hillings swamped Stephen Zetterberg in the race for Nixon's seat in Congress and at twenty-seven would become the youngest member of the House. Frank Mankiewicz was trounced in his L.A. assembly race, but a few other Democrats, besides Pat Brown, fared well. Sam Yorty, the Democratic assemblyman, narrowly won Douglas's congressional seat. Congressman Chet Holifield was reelected. Among the ballot measures, legalized gambling lost by a three-to-one margin, but a measure to permit the blind to practice chiropractic won by four hundred thousand votes.

Nationally, Republicans picked up five seats in the Senate and twenty-eight in the House, a strong showing if somewhat under par for a midterm election with a Democrat in the White House. The Democratic edge would narrow to 49–47 in the Senate and 234–199 in the House, and that meant, as *U.S. News & World Report* pointed out, that the new Congress "will be run by a coalition of conservatives—Southern Democrats and Northern Republicans."

The GOP had won most of the key Senate races in which candidates, like Nixon, had campaigned primarily on anticommunism. In the four big contests, Dirksen defeated Lucas in Illinois, Butler topped Tydings in Maryland, Taft beat Ferguson in Ohio, and Bennett ousted Thomas in Utah. How positive a role Joseph McCarthy played overall was unclear since several candidates he actively promoted, such as Prescott Bush, lost. *U.S. News* reported that the biggest surprise of the election was the degree to which McCarthy's charges "had taken root and grown into votes." Radio commentator Elmer Davis called the election a "triumph of McCarthy's tactics."

Harold Ickes bemoaned the "widespread hysteria" that induced Americans to vote "not as sentient and reasonable human beings, but as white rabbits."

Senator-elect Dirksen called for a new investigation of Joe McCarthy's charges and sent a letter to Sheridan Downey, thanking the Democrat for "making possible a great VR-Day . . . Victory for Republicanism."

President Truman announced that he felt about equally gratified and disappointed, but his wife had rarely seen him so discouraged. (His aide George Elsey would later reflect that he saw Truman "drink to excess" only one time and "that was the night of the mid-term elections in November, 1950.") He felt his failure to confront McCarthyism actively had cost his party, and him, dearly. India Edwards advised him that Republicans had taken unfair advantage of the confusion and the uneasiness caused by fears of communism and said, "I do not think we did a very good job of overcoming them." But she also boldly pointed out that the party's leaders do not "take the woman's viewpoint into consideration enough," and that as vice chairman of the DNC she did not have a voice in making policy and was "nothing but an empty title." She said she would refuse to serve as a figurehead again.

BIG GOP VICTORY the headline in the *San Francisco Chronicle* boomed. "It's Warren and Nixon by a Mile." Then, in smaller type, the ironic news: "Marcantonio Is Out in NY." It was true: He had lost in a landslide.

The San Francisco *News* said Nixon had received his "most effective boost" from the Democrats for Nixon. The candidate attributed his victory mainly to voter disgust with Truman's Far East policy and fears about "internal security" and called it "a mandate to make changes in the State Department." He claimed that he received 750,000 Democratic votes, attributing the number at least in part to his deliberately avoiding a debate on Joe McCarthy.

The senator-elect received hundreds of congratulatory telegrams: from Herbert Hoover (calling his victory "the greatest good that can come to our country"); from Sheridan Downey and Manchester Boddy; from contributors Justin Dart, Joe Di Giorgio, Jim Kemper, and Walter Haas; from Hollywood celebrities James Stewart, Ginger Rogers, Louis B. Mayer, Harry and Jack Warner, and Morrie Ryskind ("Sorry not to be with you but we're up at Las Vegas spending some of that money the new Congress will save us"). From New York, Ralph de Toledano exclaimed, "Hallelujah, Senator. White House next stop."

Five fans from Los Angeles wired, "Bravos for returning Helen to her job of housewife and mother." To encourage that transition, several Nixonites wrote President Truman, urging him not to appoint Douglas to any federal position, noting that she had been rejected by many members of his own party. One woman from L.A. suggested to the president that Douglas "be retired to political oblivion and to her own profession, the stage. I respectfully urge you to accept the wishes of Californians."

When the wife of L.A.'s Mr. Big, Asa Call, learned that one of Nixon's funds ended the campaign five thousand dollars in debt, she promptly took out her checkbook and settled the account.

Helen Douglas received at least one thousand messages of thanks and commiseration. Her brother and sister-in-law wrote from New York, "California's loss will be our gain. Get a good rest and remember mother's philosophy, everything happens for the best." Others disagreed strenuously. Average citizens expressed affection, hurt, and loss, with many using the word *tragedy*. Typical of the feelings expressed was the sentiment, "We, the working people, have lost our most precious jewel."

Political friends—Abe Fortas, Jacob Javits, Averell Harriman, and Lorena Hickok among others—searched for explanations for Douglas's first political setback or urged her to fight on. "I wish there were something I might do," Lyndon Johnson offered. Hubert Humphrey said he heard the results with a "heavy heart" and chided the voters of California for making "a serious error in judgment." Claude Pepper said she should recognize that her "political star has only paused on its rise, it has not stopped." Historian Arthur Schlesinger, Jr., told Douglas how "deeply depressing" he considered her defeat in "an unusually unfair and dirty campaign," but he doubted that the American people "will continue to be taken in by these methods for very long" and thought that Republicans, intoxicated by their victory, would engage in excesses that would ensure a liberal victory in 1952.

"It is discouraging to women everywhere," advised Mary Norton, who was stepping down from Congress after decades of service. She lamented that, incredibly, the new Congress would include fewer women than the paltry nine that had been serving there. Carey McWilliams told her to take satisfaction from "knowing that you lost—momentarily—out of loyalty to democratic principles, while your opponent won—temporarily—by betraying those principles." Writing in the *New Republic,* Harold Ickes asserted that Nixon had demonstrated "how low a man can sink when his ambitions outrun his scruples. Few would care to live with Mr. Nixon's conscience."

California Democrats, as usual, were left to point fingers and argue among themselves about how to avoid another disaster like this one, in which their two most prominent figures were defeated in the same year.

Ruth Lybeck, however, believed that top Democrats conspired to make sure that only the moderate Pat Brown would succeed and then planned to rebuild the party around him. She told Douglas they were led by Bill Malone in the north and Ed Pauley in the south, two men who feared the Democrats would lose the White House in 1952 and thus believed "there are only two years left to increase their personal fortunes."

Helen Douglas never did congratulate Richard Nixon on his victory (a snub he resented decades later). But six days after the election, she told one of her top labor organizers that "there was nothing that we did or did not do that would have made any difference in the result." Prices were high, voters questioned Truman's foreign policy, and a war was on. "We lost in California," she explained insightfully, "because the opposition was able to split the labor vote and the women's vote." In another explanation, however, she blamed "rampant McCarthyism."

John Anson Ford, the Los Angeles County supervisor, told Douglas that she owed her defeat to Nixon's skill as a speaker and the "almost complete abandonment by the daily press of skilled objective reporting." The screenwriter Philip Dunne informed her that she was beaten by "an irresistible combination of lies, public hysteria and a new low in yellow journalism throughout the state. . . . It is just one of those times when democracy, in its fear and anger, turns and rends itself." Harold Ickes attributed the loss to two factors: Nixon's use of the Red scare and the weak candidacy of Jimmy Roosevelt. Alvin Meyers, Douglas's campaign treasurer, observed that the bulk of her money came from labor, "but they didn't vote for her." He also mentioned "a strong feeling" that she was "dumped by the Administration." How else to explain Truman's friends' donating so heavily to the Nixon campaign?

But one state Democratic leader later reduced the defeat to the bare bones. Rollin McNitt, who had backed Boddy and never warmed up to Douglas in the finals, said, "Frankly it was the Pink Sheet that the Nixon people put out that defeated her. . . . It was," he added, "just enough."

Speaking to a group of students at Harvard three days after the election, Congressman John F. Kennedy remarked that he was "personally very happy" that Nixon had defeated Helen Douglas. He reportedly explained that Douglas was "not the sort of person I like working with on committees," but he did not make clear whether this was because of her manner, her politics, or her gender. On November 14, Kennedy wrote his friend Paul "Red" Fay, "I was glad to . . . see Nixon win by a big vote," and he predicted that the winner would go far in national GOP politics, for he was "an outstanding guy."

·   ·   ·

Near the end of November, more than a quarter of a million Chinese troops mounted a desperate counterattack in Korea, and General MacArthur's forces started to retreat. Now Truman's decision to allow MacArthur to cross the 38th parallel did not seem so wise. The president rose to the occasion. "This is the worst situation we have had yet," he told his staff. "We'll just have to meet it as we've met all the rest. . . ." MacArthur called for blockading and bombing mainland China, but one thing was clear: He would not bring the boys home by Christmas, as he had promised.

On November 30, the president told reporters that using the atomic bomb in Korea was under "active consideration." He added, "It is one of our weapons." When the remark triggered alarm around the world, the White House issued a clarifying statement, revealing that Truman had merely meant that because it possessed the weapon, the U.S. always had the option of using it. Still, a crisis atmosphere continued. Three days later some of the president's top civilian and military advisers finally proposed that Truman consider relieving MacArthur of his duties. For the first time, Dean Acheson observed later, "someone had expressed what everyone thought—that the Emperor had no clothes on."

Shortly after election day back in Washington, Richard Nixon attended one of columnist Joseph Alsop's famous Sunday-night suppers. Averell Harriman walked in, noted Nixon's presence, and loudly announced, "I will not break bread with that man." A few minutes later, Harriman left.

On December 4, 1950, Nixon took the oath of office and became the ranking member of his Senate class, giving him first crack at committee assignments. He received this boost in seniority thanks to Sheridan Downey, who in offering to take an early retirement paved the way for Governor Warren to appoint Nixon to serve out the remainder of Downey's term. Douglas backers cried quid pro quo when Nixon revealed that he would support the appointment of two federal judges Downey had favored. (One of them was William Byrne, the man Douglas refused to approve despite President Truman's urgings.) Drew Pearson suggested that Nixon would ask for a spot on the Judiciary Committee, "a strategic spot to block federal control of tidelands oil," and pointed out that Downey was indebted to such oilmen as Ed Pauley (and might have retired early for that reason).

At a press conference announcing Nixon's appointment, Warren suggested, rather pompously, that the new senator would probably call him almost every day seeking advice. Nixon interjected, "Or vice versa," causing the governor's face to turn pink. The new senator decided to hire a new secretary, named Rose Mary Woods. Downey, meanwhile, became a well-paid lobbyist for the Los Angeles Harbor Commission to fight for tidelands control.

Three days after Nixon took office, the court of appeals in New York affirmed Alger Hiss's conviction. Only a long-shot appeal to the Supreme Court stood between Hiss and imprisonment the following spring.

A few days later, Senator Nixon attended a Christmas party in the ballroom of the Sulgrave Club in Washington. Among the guests were two men with a burning hatred for each other: Joe McCarthy and Drew Pearson. After months of wrangling, McCarthy had privately threatened to "kill" or at least "maim" the columnist for gathering information on an alleged homosexual on his staff. By chance or morbid design, the antagonists happened to be seated at the same table, and before long they were heckling each other. McCarthy abruptly reached across, cuffed the smaller, older Pearson by the back of the neck, and demanded that he step outside and "settle this." Congressman Charles Bennett, attempting to mediate, got pushed to the floor. Pearson, a professed pacifist, walked away, but McCarthy set off after him.

He overtook the columnist in the cloakroom. When Pearson reached into his jacket for his claim check, McCarthy feared (he later claimed) that he was reaching for a weapon, and so he grabbed the writer's arms and kneed him twice in the groin. Doubling over in pain, Pearson asked, "When are they going to put you in the booby hatch?" This inspired the senator to smack him a few times in the face, knocking him to the floor.

At this moment, Senator Nixon arrived on the scene. "This one's for you, Dick!" McCarthy said, about to hit Pearson again. But Nixon shouted, "Let a Quaker stop this fight," and then, "Let's go, Joe." As Pearson staggered away, Nixon walked McCarthy outside, found his car, and got him to drive home. McCarthy promptly called reporters to brag that he had kicked Drew Pearson "in the nuts." Pearson responded by asserting that McCarthy's punching ability equaled his "senatorial behavior." Twenty senators reportedly called McCarthy's office to congratulate him, but Richard Nixon refused to comment, except to decry "such foolishness" with a war going on. Privately, he claimed that McCarthy might have killed the columnist if he hadn't intervened. A few days later, on the floor of the Senate, McCarthy villified Drew Pearson as a "Moscow-directed character assassin" and the "sugar-coated voice of Russia."

A report from a research institute at Stanford released shortly after the election confirmed the obvious: California newspapers had slanted news coverage strongly toward Nixon. Of the major papers, only Scripps-Howard's San Francisco *News* and McClatchy's *Sacramento Bee* provided relatively balanced coverage. The *Los Angeles Times* and Hearst's *L.A. Examiner* were particularly biased. Carl Greenburg, political editor of the *Examiner*, was proud of this finding. He brought the survey to Nixon's attention, boasting of his paper's "rating," and explaining that it "indicates quite graphically what our performance was during the campaign." Nixon thanked him and observed that he could not imagine "how the *Examiner* could have done a better job than it did."

A later survey of press coverage of the 1950 race found that the *L.A. Times* did not publish a single photograph of Helen Douglas during the campaign.

Helen Douglas informed a friend in Washington in December that she was thinking of embarking on a lecture tour around the country. "The job facing us as Democrats and liberals," she explained, "is tremendous if we are to win in '52." Philip Dunne had suggested that she consider doing radio commentary. "It would be one way of keeping your name before the public," he explained, "while at the same time putting your talent and experience to the service of the nation and fanning a perpetual fire under our two awful senators. . . . Liberals sometimes do their most effective work while out of office."

Richard Nixon's effort to drive Helen Douglas out of public life did not end, as one might have expected, with his smashing victory in November. Privately, Nixon worried over rumors that his opponent would resurface as a top-level Truman appointee to the United Nations. In early January 1951, Nixon's friend Hedda Hopper asked him what she could do "to kill Helen Gahagan's chances at the U.N." The new senator from California replied that he hadn't been able to confirm the rumors but added, "Just as soon as I do, I am inclined to think that we might be able to stir up a little potent opposition."

Epilogue

When the new Senate convened in January 1951, Joseph McCarthy appointed Richard Nixon to a HUAC-like investigations subcommittee. The California senator took the place of Margaret Chase Smith, who had dared criticize McCarthy in her "Declaration of Conscience" the previous June. But Nixon was already looking beyond the Senate, embarking on a series of speeches in twenty-two states with an eye toward making "a few friends" around the country who might help him in a national race.

This was only one part of the grand strategy, and by no means the most fateful part. About a week after Nixon defeated Helen Douglas, his finance chief, Dana Smith, started calling major donors. He wanted them to contribute to a secret fund to make Nixon impregnable in California and, at the same time, a viable candidate for higher office. Money soon arrived from longtime supporters, including Harry Haldeman, Jack Garland, Herbert Hoover, Jr., and various oil magnates, and was quickly spent. The slush fund was of a rather modest size—less than twenty thousand dollars the first year—but critical to Nixon's national strategy. Soon it would also produce the first Nixon scandal.

In the Senate, Nixon made his strongest impression as an outspoken supporter of MacArthur when the general was relieved of command in Korea by President Truman in April 1951. The senator said that "only the Communists and stooges for the Communists" were happy about the president's decision. He introduced a measure to override Truman's authority and restore MacArthur to power, claiming that the general was a victim of "one of the most vicious smear campaigns in history." Echoing the views of MacArthur that helped get him fired, Nixon called for complete military victory in Korea and advocated bombing Red China.

Others went even further. Complaining that Korea had become "a meat grinder of American manhood," Congressman Albert Gore, Sr., of Tennessee advised Truman to use the atomic bomb to "dehumanize a belt" across the peninsula, creating a deadly neutral zone. Any Communist soldiers who entered the area would face "certain death or slow deformity," he explained, but this would be "morally justifiable under the circumstances."

The Korean stalemate continued, however, until July 1953, when an agreement partitioned the peninsula into two antagonistic states, just as in June 1950. In the interim, some thirty-five thousand Americans and at least three million Koreans had died.

In 1952, Nixon unexpectedly emerged as Dwight D. Eisenhower's running mate, just two years after the two men met at Bohemian Grove. Television, which began to play a key role in political campaigns in 1950, now took center stage as more than one third of all households had TV sets. The campaign had hardly begun when Nixon's secret slush fund was made public, and the candidate was forced to make a national television appeal to save his spot on the ticket, the so-called Checkers speech. It would be mocked by his enemies for years, but the gambit worked. Nixon cleverly took the decision out of Eisenhower's hands by asking viewers to send their opinions to the Republican National Committee. This informal poll strongly backed Nixon, and Ike had no choice but to keep the senator on the ticket as the GOP mudslinger. Nixon labeled Ike's opponent an appeaser who "got his Ph.D. from Dean Acheson's College of Cowardly Communist Containment" and charged that "nothing would please the Kremlin more" than an Adlai Stevenson victory. Stevenson responded by calling Nixon "the white collar McCarthy."

Although Helen Douglas remained silent, the 1950 Senate race played a small role in the '52 campaign. The perception that Nixon had manhandled her was widespread (and highlighted by the media), although Tricky Dick was not yet a household name. Many liberals still carried a torch for Douglas and later claimed that they campaigned all the harder for Stevenson to exact revenge against Nixon for defeating her. But they failed, and Eisenhower won easily. Like Nixon and others in 1950, many Republicans ran and won solely on anticommunism, allowing the GOP to pick up twenty-two seats in the House and seize control of the Senate.

· · ·

Senator McCarthy, meanwhile, raged and blustered and generally intimidated Truman during the final years of his presidency and Eisenhower during the first year of his term. He railed against Red influence at the Voice of America and the United Nations and within the U.S. Army. Finally, in 1954, after the Wisconsin senator had accused Eisenhower and General George C. Marshall of treason and had thoroughly abused his senatorial powers in countless ways, his colleagues drew the line. He could not survive both the Army-McCarthy hearings and Edward R. Murrow's searing *See It Now* documentary series, and the U.S. Senate voted to censure him. Richard Nixon belatedly turned on his old friend, aiding the investigations that brought him down. Still, Ed Murrow advised caution, pointing out that McCarthy did not create, but only exploited, a "situation of fear." Cassius was right, Murrow added; "the fault, dear Brutus, is not in our stars, but in ourselves."

Indeed, ridding America of McCarthy was far easier than ridding it of McCarthyism. All the elements of inquisition and thought control that came to the fore in 1950—from loyalty oaths on campus to blacklisting in the entertainment industry—flourished for years. A librarian in Oklahoma, for example, was fired for subscribing to the *New Republic, The Nation,* and *Negro Digest.* As HUAC investigators promised (following Edward G. Robinson's testimony), a second round of hearings on communism in Hollywood took place in March 1951, and they made the 1947 probe "look like a college musical," as one writer commented. This time, ex-Communists, such as actors Larry Parks and Sterling Hayden, were all too willing to turn on their old friends, and a blacklist was solidly enshrined. Seventy-two "friendly" witnesses, including Elia Kazan and Lee J. Cobb, would name names before the blacklist faded at the end of the decade.

The scenario was similar in radio and television as the influence of *Red Channels* endured. In 1951, Dave Garroway's TV program and the Ohio State Fair canceled bookings of the Weavers, one of the most popular recording groups, following protests against the political associations of Pete Seeger and other members of the group. One estimate placed the number of blacklisted performers at fifteen hundred in 1954. The writer Dashiell Hammett went to jail, and his Sam Spade and *Thin Man* dramatizations were banned from TV and radio. Others fared even worse, suffering fatal seizures or committing suicide after being exposed as "Reds."

Despite her defeat in the Senate race, Helen Douglas had a bright future in politics. She had just turned fifty and was qualified for any number of federal appointments while awaiting another run for office. Longtime supporters implored her to lay the groundwork for a return to Congress in '52. Others lobbied President Truman to appoint her to a top post at the United

Nations or in the Interior Department. But Truman considered her political dynamite, and India Edwards reportedly commented that she could not
be appointed dogcatcher. Because of that and her own inclinations, Douglas
decided to put public life behind her. She felt guilty for not having spent
enough time with her children as they grew up and believed her marriage
needed repair work, too. A close friend explained that the 1950 defeat "was
very bad psychologically," and "Melvyn wanted her to concentrate on the.
family." So in 1951 the couple sold their home on Senalda Road and rented
an apartment in Manhattan, where Melvyn was about to open in a new
play. The family was under one roof again.

Still, Melvyn continued to appear in out-of-town productions, and for
much of the rest of the decade he was away from home a lot. Helen, meanwhile, struggled to return to former careers. She played the lead onstage in
a political comedy, *First Lady,* and sang several recitals at Carnegie Hall,
among other venues. Reviewers were not particularly kind, and Douglas
moved on to the lecture circuit, at least partly to pay off her campaign debts.
She also joined many activist groups, particularly in the field of disarma-
ment, and campaigned for Adlai Stevenson in 1956.

Only then, six years after her defeat, did she attack Nixon personally, and
only after being asked by a reporter whether her opponent had ever directly
accused her of being a Communist. Douglas admitted that he had never
used the word but had designed his whole campaign to "create the impression that I was a communist or at least 'communistic,' " and she suggested
the reporter dig up a copy of the Pink Sheet. Later that fall she drafted some
reflections on the 1950 race but did not circulate them widely:

- My impression of Dick Nixon as an opponent is that of a candidate who
  was smart and adaptable, who did not discuss issues but campaigned on
  character assassination.
- What I remember: the fear in one's own people. I was followed by hate.
- There have been campaigns where my opponents sought, as Mr. Nixon
  did, to avoid the issues, because discussion of issues might lead to defeat.
  But no one had ever done it so slickly and so professionally before. And he
  was clever. I would be the first to say it. . . . And he can think on his feet.
- I couldn't believe people would believe what Nixon and his supporters
  were saying about me. It was so low . . . diabolical. . . . That's the reason
  why the campaign waged in 1950 is not dead today.
- People may say: "You yourself call Nixon very clever, Mrs. Douglas.
  Don't you think he's clever enough to *change?*" I'd say that was a possibility. There is nothing in his record to indicate he has strong convictions
  about anything except success.

With that, Douglas put Nixon aside forever—she hoped. From her apartment in Manhattan, she turned away requests for interviews, believing any comments from her would sound like "sour grapes."

In 1956, on a visit to California—and looking ahead to a presidential race—Senator John F. Kennedy admitted to Paul Ziffren, now one of the state's Democratic leaders, that he had supported Nixon in the 1950 race. He apparently wanted to "come clean" and "clear the decks," according to Ziffren's wife, Mickey.

In 1960, Helen Douglas went to Wisconsin to campaign in the presidential primary in behalf of Hubert Humphrey (who had stumped for her in 1950). He was facing John F. Kennedy. That fall, Kennedy's opponent was Richard Nixon, and Douglas felt compelled to endorse the Democrat. Kennedy now admitted that he had supported Nixon against Douglas, calling it "the biggest damnfool mistake I ever made."

During a lecture at Boston's Jordan Hall, Douglas was splattered with eggs thrown from the balcony. She stood her ground, as she had during the hay-and-seltzer assault at USC in 1950, and continued her remarks, ridiculing the idea of a "new Nixon." Republicans, perhaps even Nixon himself, would "dearly like to forget" the old Nixon, "the *real* Nixon," she added.

In 1963, a few days after Kennedy's assassination, Lyndon Johnson told some friends of Douglas's that he wouldn't be president if it hadn't been for the 1950 Senate race in California. Everyone had advised LBJ not to take the second spot on the ticket in 1960, but he felt he simply had to keep Nixon out of the White House. "I figured that because of the way he behaved toward Helen Douglas in 1950 he should not be president," he asserted.

It was a good story, anyway. Douglas herself never believed it, but no one can doubt that memories of the 1950 race played at least a small part in Johnson's surprising decision to accept the vice presidential nod—and thus contributed to Nixon's defeat in his first run for president. Douglas was "a fine person," he later told a friend, and Nixon "destroyed her."

Nixon, in fact, recognized that the 1950 race was an albatross, or a cross, he had to bear. Through such sympathetic authors as Ralph de Toledano and Earl Mazo, he disseminated his version of the campaign—namely, that he had only responded to Douglas's "smears" and did nothing more than take Manchester Boddy's attacks and embellish them. Murray Chotiner said, "We only stated the facts," and repeated that the Nixon team had never accused Douglas of "sympathizing" or "being in league with" the Communists. But Nixon himself said little about the 1950 race and left it out of his book *Six Crises.*

In 1958, however, he allegedly told a British publisher that he was "sorry" about some of the tactics he used in the Senate race. "I was a very young man," he explained. When these private remarks were leaked to the press, he denied them, and soon he was circulating a defense brief. It explained that any impression that Douglas was pro-Communist was "justified by her own record" and claimed that the color of the Pink Sheet was apt because she was indeed "soft on communism." It also asserted that as "a birthright Quaker," Nixon was "constitutionally incapable of bigotry."

After losing to Kennedy in 1960, Nixon thanked Norman Chandler of the *Los Angeles Times* for his paper's steadfast support over the years. "I have often said to friends that I would never have gone to Washington in the first place had it not been for the *Times,*" he explained. But two years later, when he failed in a foolhardy race for governor of California against Pat Brown, he included the *Times* in his complaints about unfair press coverage. At this, Chandler confided to a friend that Nixon "must have temporarily gone off his rocker."

In any case, it looked as if Helen Douglas would never have to answer any more questions about her former rival. One of her old supporters, Harpo Marx, sent her a note, "We finally buried the bum for good." Nixon proclaimed that he had held his last press conference.

But he arose from the ashes and won the presidency in 1968, this time without much opposition from Helen Douglas. The reason? She was such a strong foe of the Vietnam War that she had broken with her close friend Lyndon Johnson and refused to campaign for Hubert Humphrey until the final days of the campaign.

Two years later she took to the stump in Vermont, where she and Melvyn had their summer home, in behalf of a Democrat running for the U.S. Senate. A reporter noted that, white-haired and nearing seventy, she seemed to have lost none of her passion for causes, nor her theatrical style of speaking. Douglas explained that she rarely discussed the 1950 race because she found it "so sad when candidates lose an election and can do nothing but talk about it." But she was willing to denounce the present policies of her former opponent. "Nixon has lied to the people about the [Vietnam] war," she said, "and that's why there is such great despair around the country."

By then, the strain in the Douglases' home life had eased. Melvyn traveled less often and had enjoyed a strong comeback since appearing in such movies as *Hud*. Mary Helen served in the Peace Corps, and Peter became a social worker and therapist. Helen continued working with antinuclear groups, such as the National Committee for a Sane Nuclear Policy (SANE) and the Women's International League for Peace and Freedom, and collaborated on a book about her mentor Eleanor Roosevelt. The first actor to star in politics, she was skeptical of the growing legion of entertainers running for office. "She never liked to be compared to anybody like Ronald Reagan or George Murphy," a friend reported.

In the spring of 1972, Douglas was diagnosed with breast cancer and underwent surgery. That fall she felt strong enough to campaign for antiwar candidate George McGovern in his race against Richard Nixon. The present administration, she said, was "the greatest snow job in history," and as a result, America was afflicted with a "moral sickness." Nixon would not discuss issues but rather "tricks his opponents into defending their stands," such as claiming McGovern was "soft on Communism"—the same charge used against her in 1950. A friend told Douglas that the only honest thing about the '72 campaign was the slogan, "Nixon—Now More Than Ever!"

Nixon triumphed again that November. Herbert Parmet, another Nixon biographer, later pointed out that he had replayed his 1950 strategy, splitting the Democrats and siphoning off "the discontented and disillusioned." Yet this time he planted the seeds of his own destruction. The following year, as the Watergate scandal deepened, reporters often came to Douglas, expecting her to gloat, but at first she withheld comment. She had regained national prominence for another reason: the growth of the women's movement. *Ms.* put her on its cover, and women's political groups sought her out for conferences and fund-raising appeals. (Interest was so intense she complained of "being called a cult.")

Douglas declared that women had made little political progress since 1950 and still did not "participate in any meaningful way in the formulation of national policies." She advised that the only way for women to develop "female clout" was for them to study the issues and band together according to common interests. "I'm all for Women's Liberation," she added, "but I know that the first step toward liberation for any group is to use the power in hand. . . . There are more women in this country than there are men. . . . Women themselves fail women. Women don't support women."

A reporter sat with the Douglases at their Vermont home while they watched John Dean's testimony before the Senate Watergate Committee. The couple had followed the unfolding controversy closely, and Helen explained that she wasn't surprised by any of it. She didn't "feel the need for vindication—and satisfaction is totally out of place." But when she finally publicly called for Nixon's impeachment, she was not alone. Phillip Burton, the California congressman who led the charge for impeachment proceedings, revealed that he had taken a private oath after Nixon's victory in 1950 "to work to see the day that man would be retired from public life."

Several months later, in August 1974, Nixon resigned his office and returned to California. Earl Warren, his reluctant supporter in 1950, commented, " 'Tricky' is perhaps the most despicable president this nation has ever had. He was a cheat, a liar, and a crook." Again reporters badgered Helen Douglas for comment. She generally refused, tired of her and Nixon being linked like "Siamese twins all these years."

Two years later cancer recurred, now in her left lung, and her schedule slowed, but she continued to gain new honors, including an award from the Academy of Science Fiction, Fantasy, and Horror Films for her role in *She*. She also worked on her autobiography.

During this period, Jerry Voorhis, also a Nixon victim, told her that whatever happened next, "you have indeed blessed this world, this nation . . . just by being your exemplary self and being with us through all these years." Helen Gahagan Douglas died on June 28, 1980, and her ashes were buried outside her Vermont home. Her husband died the following year.

A chapter on the 1950 race in Douglas's autobiography, *A Full Life*, published posthumously, closed with this sentence: "There's not much to say about the 1950 campaign except that a man ran for Senate who wanted to get there, and didn't care how."

Blacklisting on a broad scale would never return, but under President Nixon, the FBI, the CIA, and local police engaged in an elaborate program of domestic spying and dirty tricks that targeted leftists, black militants, antiwar protesters, and troublesome journalists. The blacklist was succeeded by a White House "enemies list."

Twenty years after McCarthyism peaked, two writers under siege in 1950 took conflicting stands on whether it might return. Howard Fast said he didn't think that "kind of terror . . . will ever occur again," but Arthur Miller observed that "the principle of a secret government, so to speak, has not been discarded. . . . There's no question in my mind that it could happen again. But it won't be the same. It never is."

At the University of California today, any professor who accepts full- or part-time employment still must sign the state's loyalty oath, now known as the Oath of Allegiance.

Over the years, a number of prominent novelists have satirized Nixon's life and his early campaigns, but the man himself rarely looked back and almost never discussed the 1950 race. Perhaps this was because of the nastiness of the campaign or, more likely, its gender edge.

On a rare occasion, he informed columnist Stewart Alsop that he "never said or implied that Helen Douglas was a Communist," and in any case, one had to remember the atmosphere of that year. In 1968, he again blamed Sheridan Downey and Manchester Boddy for starting the smears against Douglas. "I had been presented with a great deal of ammunition . . . and I did not hesitate to use some of it," he told a San Francisco newspaper. "Some I did not use, I ignored it, because I felt it was unfair." He also claimed that his campaign staff knew nothing about the Hesselberg innuendos and the anonymous phone calls. If that did occur, he explained, "it was done by some of our opponents . . . pretending it was us to create an issue." The only reason the 1950 race remained notorious was because Douglas and her backers were "infuriated" that he had won by such a "handsome majority."

Robert Finch later revealed that in private conversations about the 1950 race, Nixon invariably emphasized how grueling it was—traveling up and down California in the prefreeway era. But Nixon hadn't forgotten a thing; he could still name all his local campaign chairmen.

In the years after he resigned from the presidency—and after President Gerald Ford's pardoning of any crimes he had, or may have, committed while in office—Nixon struggled for respect and rehabilitation as an elder statesman, particularly in the field of foreign affairs, and largely succeeded. Although he gave several lengthy interviews covering his political career, he still rarely mentioned the 1950 race. In his memoirs, *RN* and *In the Arena*, the Senate race accounted for only a handful of pages. He again thanked the Democrats for calling his attention to the Douglas-Marcantonio link. He complained that his own campaign was plagued by hecklers and noted that Douglas had called him a "peewee," "pipsqueak," and Tricky Dick. In return, he had merely "kept her pinned to her extremist record." Douglas lost simply because "she was not a mainstream Democrat."

In 1992, when Bill Clinton became a leading contender for the presidency, Nixon warned that Hillary Rodham Clinton could sabotage her husband's chances because "if the wife comes through as being too strong and too intelligent, it makes the husband look like a wimp." Many voters, he noted, agreed with Cardinal Richelieu's epigram "Intelligence in a woman is unbecoming." Privately, he referred to Hillary Clinton as "what we used to call a *red-hot*," a "real lefty like Eleanor Roosevelt"—or, he might have added, like Helen Gahagan Douglas.

As Helen Douglas observed near the end of her life, women made few advances in electoral politics for decades following her 1950 setback. Women made up more than 50 percent of the electorate but voted less often than men and rarely held male incumbents accountable on women's issues. In the 1980s, they finally made their mark, reaching a peak in 1992, the so-called Year of the Woman. Eleven women won Senate nominations that year, and California elected its first two female senators, both Democrats. The number of congresswomen nearly doubled, to forty-seven. A 1996 study found, however, that the proportion of women serving in Congress—a little over 10 percent—was actually below the world average for national assemblies. In the national elections that fall, women made few gains, with representation leveling off at ten senators, forty-eight members of Congress—and just two state governors.

When Richard Nixon passed away in April 1994, a writer for *The Wall Street Journal* claimed that the original enemies list was drawn up by journalists, and Nixon was on it—because of (among other reasons) "kicking the sand in the liberal establishment" by beating Helen Gahagan Douglas in 1950. Nixon revisionism was rampant. The media he despised engaged in "a group conspiracy to grant him absolution" following his death, a *New York Times* columnist charged.

A few months later the publication of H. R. Haldeman's diaries, filled with Nixon's rants against Jews, cast a darker shadow over the "Hesselberg" aspect of the 1950 campaign. Haldeman also quoted Nixon denouncing H. G. Wells's notion that the solution to all problems is universal education—"a terrible idea, especially for women." But the Nixon revival continued, with the arrival of a U.S. postage stamp, Hollywood and television movies, and a Broadway play. At no time since Watergate had the "idea" of Nixon been "more potent," a leading political writer observed. Nixon had gone from outcast to elder statesman to icon. At his presidential library in Yorba Linda one could purchase coffee mugs, T-shirts, and watches bearing the famous photograph of Nixon shaking hands with Elvis Presley, and a TV movie about that meeting would soon follow. Contenders for the GOP presidential nomination, most of whom, like Bob Dole, had old ties to Nixon, competed for the label of the candidate he would have endorsed had he lived. Mocking this effort, Roger Stone, Nixon's confidant in his final years, wore a button declaring, DYING IS NO EXCUSE: NIXON IN '96. Another longtime Republican activist, John Sears, commented, "It's like Elvis. Nixon isn't dead either."

It was, an op-ed headline announced, SPRINGTIME FOR NIXON.

Bibliography

BOOKS

This is a list of books cited in the Notes. It omits many books used for general reference and background only. It also does not include newspaper and magazine articles, which are described in full in the Notes.

Allyson, June, with Frances Spatz Leighton. *June Allyson.* New York: G. P. Putnam's Sons, 1982.

Ambrose, Stephen E. *Nixon: The Education of a Politician, 1913–1962.* New York: Simon and Schuster, 1987.

Arnold, James R. *The First Domino: Eisenhower, the Military, and America's Intervention in Vietnam.* New York: William Morrow, 1991.

Arnold, William A. *Back When It All Began: The Early Nixon Years.* New York: Vantage Press, 1975.

Bontecou, Eleanor. *The Federal Loyalty-Security Program.* Ithaca, N.Y.: Cornell University Press, 1953.

Boyer, Paul S. *By the Bomb's Early Light: American Thought and Culture at the Dawn of the Atomic Age.* New York: Pantheon, 1985.

Brodie, Fawn M. *Richard Nixon: The Shaping of His Character.* New York: W. W. Norton, 1981.

Bullock, Paul. *Jerry Voorhis: The Idealist as Politician.* New York: Vantage Press, 1978.

Cannon, Lou. *Reagan.* New York: G. P. Putnam's Sons, 1982.

Caughey, John. *Report on Blacklisting.* New York: Fund for the Republic, 1956.

Caute, David. *The Great Fear: The Anti-Communist Purge Under Truman and Eisenhower.* New York: Simon and Schuster, 1978.

Ceplair, Larry, and Steven Englund. *The Inquisition in Hollywood: Politics in the Film Community, 1930–1960.* Garden City, N.Y.: Anchor Press, Doubleday, 1980.

Clifford, Clark. *Counsel to the President.* New York: Random House, 1991.

Cole, Lester. *Hollywood Red: The Autobiography of Lester Cole.* Palo Alto, Calif.: Ramparts Press, 1981.

Cook, Bruce. *Dalton Trumbo.* New York: Charles Scribner's Sons, 1977.

Costello, William. *The Facts About Nixon: An Unauthorized Biography.* New York: Viking Press, 1960.

Counterattack. *Red Channels: The Report of Communist Influence in Radio and Television.* New York: Counterattack, American Business Consultants, Inc., 1950.

Crouch, Winston, and Dean E. McHenry, *California Government.* Berkeley: University of California Press, 1949.

Cumings, Bruce. *The Origins of the Korean War.* Princeton, N.J.: Princeton University Press, 1981.

David, Lester. *The Lonely Lady of San Clemente: The Story of Pat Nixon.* New York: Crowell, 1978.

de Toledano, Ralph. *One Man Alone: Richard Nixon.* New York: Funk and Wagnalls, 1969.

Donovan, Robert J. *Tumultuous Years: The Presidency of Harry S Truman, 1949–1953.* New York: W. W. Norton, 1982.

Douglas, Helen Gahagan. *A Full Life.* Garden City, N.Y.: Doubleday, 1982.

Duberman, Martin B. *Paul Robeson.* New York: Alfred A. Knopf, 1989.

Edwards, Anne. *Early Reagan.* New York: William Morrow, 1987.

Eisenhower, Julie Nixon. *Pat Nixon: The Untold Story.* New York: Simon and Schuster, 1986.

Engler, Robert. *The Politics of Oil.* Chicago: University of Chicago Press, 1961.

Gardner, David P. *The California Oath Controversy.* Berkeley: University of California Press, 1967.

Geist, Kenneth L. *Pictures Will Talk: The Life and Films of Joseph L. Mankiewicz.* New York: Charles Scribner's Sons, 1978.

Goodman, Walter. *The Committee: The Extraordinary Career of the House Committee of Un-American Activities.* New York: Farrar, Straus and Giroux, 1968.

Gottlieb, Bob, and Irene Wolt. *Thinking Big: The Story of the* Los Angeles Times, *Its Publishers, and Their Influence on Southern California.* New York: G. P. Putnam's Sons, 1977.

Griffith, Robert, and Athan G. Theoharis, eds. *The Specter: Original Essays on the Cold War and the Origins of McCarthyism*. New York: New Viewpoints Press, 1974.

Gunther, John. *Inside U.S.A.* New York: Harper Brothers, 1947.

Halberstam, David. *The Powers That Be*. New York: Alfred A. Knopf, 1979.

Hayden, Sterling. *Wanderer*. New York: Alfred A. Knopf, 1963.

Hellman, Lillian. *Scoundrel Time*. Boston: Little, Brown, 1976.

Henderson, Lloyd Ray. "Earl Warren and California Politics." Ph.D. dissertation, University of California–Berkeley, 1965.

Herken, Gregg. *The Winning Weapon: The Atomic Bomb in the Cold War, 1945–1950*. New York: Alfred A. Knopf, 1980.

Kahn, Gordon. *Hollywood on Trial: The Story of the Ten Who Were Indicted*. New York: Boni and Gaer, 1948.

Kanfer, Stefan. *A Journal of the Plague Years*. New York: Atheneum, 1973.

Katcher, Leo. *Earl Warren: A Political Biography*. New York: McGraw-Hill, 1967.

Klein, Herbert G. *Making It Perfectly Clear*. Garden City, N.Y.: Doubleday, 1980.

Lash, Joseph. *A World of Love: Eleanor Roosevelt and Her Friends, 1943–1962*. Garden City, N.Y.: Doubleday, 1984.

Lifton, Robert Jay, and Greg Mitchell. *Hiroshima in America: Fifty Years of Denial*. New York: Grosset/Putnam, G. P. Putnam's Sons, 1995.

McClelland, Doug. *Hollywood on Reagan: Friends and Enemies Discuss Our President, the Actor*. Winchester, Mass.: Faber and Faber, 1983.

McCullough, David. *Truman*. New York: Simon and Schuster, 1992.

McWilliams, Carey. *Southern California: An Island on the Land*. New York: Duell, Sloan, and Pearce, 1946.

———. *California: The Great Exception*. New York: Current Books, 1949.

———. *Witch Hunt: The Revival of Heresy*. Boston: Little, Brown, 1950.

———. *The Education of Carey McWilliams*. New York: Simon and Schuster, 1979.

Mankiewicz, Frank. *Perfectly Clear: Nixon from Whittier to Watergate*. New York: Quadrangle Books, 1973.

Matthews, Christopher. *Kennedy and Nixon: The Rivalry That Shaped Postwar America*. New York: Simon and Schuster, 1996.

Mazo, Earl. *Richard Nixon: A Political and Personal Portrait*. New York: Harper & Row, 1959.

Melder, Keith. *Hail to the Candidate: Presidential Campaigns from Banners to Broadcasts.* Washington, D.C.: Smithsonian Institution Press, 1992.

Mitchell, Greg. *The Campaign of the Century: Upton Sinclair's Race for Governor of California and the Birth of Media Politics.* New York: Random House, 1992.

Morris, Roger. *Richard Milhous Nixon: The Rise of an American Politician.* New York: Henry Holt, 1990.

Murrow, Edward R. *In Search of Light: The Broadcasts of Edward R. Murrow, 1938–1961.* New York: Alfred A. Knopf, 1967.

Navasky, Victor. *Naming Names.* New York: Viking Press, 1980.

Nixon, Richard M. *RN: The Memoirs of Richard Nixon.* New York: Grosset and Dunlap, 1978.

―――. *In the Arena: A Memoir of Defeat, Victory, and Renewal.* New York: Simon and Schuster, 1990.

O'Neill, Tip, with William Novak. *Man of the House: The Life and Political Memoirs of Speaker Tip O'Neill.* New York: Random House, 1987.

Oshinsky, David M. *A Conspiracy So Immense: The World of Joe McCarthy.* New York: Free Press, 1983.

Parmet, Herbert S. *Richard Nixon and His America.* Boston: Little, Brown, 1990.

Pearson, Drew. *Diaries, 1949–1959.* Edited by Tyler Abell. New York: Holt, Rinehart and Winston, 1974.

Pepper, Claude, with Hays Gorey. *Pepper: Eyewitness to a Century.* San Diego, Calif.: Harcourt Brace Jovanovich, 1987.

Pilat, Oliver. *Pegler: Angry Man of the Press.* Boston: Beacon Press, 1963.

Radosh, Ronald, and Joyce Milton. *The Rosenberg File: A Search for the Truth.* New York: Holt, Rinehart and Winston, 1983.

Rhodes, Richard. *Dark Sun: The Making of the Hydrogen Bomb.* New York: Simon and Schuster, 1995.

Robins, Natalie S. *Alien Ink: The FBI's War on Freedom of Expression.* New York: William Morrow, 1992.

Schneir, Walter and Miriam. *Invitation to an Inquest.* Garden City, N.Y.: Doubleday, 1965.

Schrecker, Ellen W. *No Ivory Tower: McCarthyism and the Universities.* New York: Oxford University Press, 1986.

Schwartz, Nancy Lynn. *The Hollywood Writers' Wars.* New York: Alfred A. Knopf, 1982.

Scobie, Ingrid Winther. *Center Stage: Helen Gahagan Douglas, a Life.* New York: Oxford University Press, 1992.

Spalding, Henry D. *The Nixon Nobody Knows.* Middle Village, N.Y.: Jonathan David, 1972.

Starr, Kevin. *Material Dreams: Southern California Through the 1920s.* New York: Oxford University Press, 1990.

Stewart, George Rippey, in collaboration with other professors at the University of California. *Year of the Oath: The Fight for Academic Freedom at the University of California.* 1950; reprint, New York: Da Capo Press, 1971.

Stone, I. F. *The Hidden History of the Korean War, 1950–1951.* New York: Monthly Review Press, 1952.

———. *The Truman Era.* New York: Monthly Review Press, 1953.

Theoharis, Athan G. *Seeds of Repression: Harry S. Truman and the Origins of McCarthyism.* Chicago: Quadrangle Books, 1971.

Toland, John. *In Mortal Combat, Korea, 1950–1953.* New York: William Morrow, 1991.

Truman, Harry S. *Memoirs.* Vol. 2, *Years of Trial and Hope.* Garden City, N.Y.: Doubleday, 1955–56.

———. *Public Papers of the Presidents of the United States, 1950.* Washington, D.C.: U.S. Government Printing Office, 1965.

———. *Off the Record: The Private Papers of Harry S Truman.* Edited by Robert H. Ferrell. New York: Harper & Row, 1980.

Waldie, D. J. *Holy Land: A Suburban Memoir.* New York: W. W. Norton, 1996.

Warren, Earl. *The Memoirs of Earl Warren.* Garden City, N.Y.: Doubleday, 1977.

Weinstein, Allen. *Perjury: The Hiss-Chambers Case.* New York: Alfred A. Knopf, 1978.

Wicker, Tom. *One of Us: Richard Nixon and the American Dream.* New York: Random House, 1991.

Wills, Garry. *Nixon Agonistes: The Crisis of the Self-Made Man.* New York: New American Library, 1970.

Witt, Linda, et al. *Running as a Woman: Gender and Power in American Politics.* New York: Free Press, 1994.

AUTHOR'S INTERVIEWS

Diane Baker, Leone Baxter, Edmund G. "Pat" Brown, Kenneth Chotiner, Florence "Susie" Clifton, Robert Clifton, Alan Cranston, Ed Cray, Robert Dallek, Mercedes Davidson Eichholz, Ralph de Toledano, Mary Helen Douglas, Philip Dunne, McIntyre Faries, Robert Finch, Ray Haight, Jr., Sharon Lybeck Hartmann, Augustus Hawkins, Patrick J. Hillings, Mary Ellen Leary, Dean McHenry, Frank Mankiewicz, Joseph L. Mankiewicz, Sam Marx, Wendell Miller, Allen Rivkin, Jean Sieroty, Elizabeth Snyder, Dick Tuck, Jerry Voorhis, Billy Wilder, Sam Yorty, Mickey Ziffren, and others.

ORAL HISTORIES

Bancroft Library, University of California, Berkeley
Most of these oral histories are shared with University Research Library, UCLA.

Helen Gahagan Douglas Component of the California Women Political Leaders Oral History Project: Juanita Terry Barbee, Margery Cahn, Evelyn Chavoor, Bert Coffey, Alis de Sola, Helen Gahagan Douglas, Tilford Dudley, India Edwards, Arthur Goldschmidt, Elizabeth Wickenden Goldschmidt, Leo Goodman, Kenneth Hardings, Charles A. Hogan, Chet Holifield, Byron F. Lindsley, Helen Lustig, William Malone, Alvin Meyers, Philip J. Noel-Baker, Walter Pick, Frank Rogers.

Richard M. Nixon in the Warren Era, Earl Warren Oral History Project: Roy Crocker, Roy Day, John Walton Dinkelspiel, Frank Jorgensen.

Earl Warren Oral History Project: Edmund G. Brown, Asa Call, Oliver Carter, Florence "Susie" Clifton, McIntyre Faries, Patrick J. Hillings, Robert Kenny, Roger Kent, William Knowland, Rollin McNitt, William S. Mailliard, George Outland, James Roosevelt, Earl Warren.

Other oral histories: Jean Fuller, Elisabeth Gatov, Victor Hansen, Elinor Heller, Pat Hitt, Clark Kerr, Goodwin Knight, Mary Ellen Leary, John Francis Neylan, Julia Porter, Elizabeth Snyder, Robert Gordon Sproul, Paul Taylor, Jack Tenney, Earl Warren, Roz Wyman, Sam Yorty.

Columbia University Oral History Collection

Oral histories: Prescott Bush, Goodwin Knight, Adela Rogers St. Johns.

Lyndon Johnson Library, Austin, Texas

Oral histories: Edmund G. Brown, Helen Gahagan Douglas, India Edwards, Elizabeth Wickenden Goldschmidt, D. B. Hardeman, Bryce Harlow, George Reedy.

Los Angeles Times Archives, Los Angeles, California

Oral history: Kyle Palmer.

Harry S Truman Presidential Library, Independence, Missouri

Oral histories: Alben Barkley, Oliver Carter, India Edwards, Harold McGrath, Earl Warren.

University Research Library, University of California, Los Angeles

Oral histories: Dick Darling, Dorothy Healey, Patrick J. Hillings, Carey McWilliams, Paul Ziffren.

ARCHIVES

Carl Albert Congressional Research and Studies Center, University of Oklahoma, Norman

Papers: Helen Gahagan Douglas.

Bancroft Library, University of California, Berkeley

Papers: Edmund G. Brown; Edmond Coblentz; Roy Day, including oral history; Sheridan Downey; William Randolph Hearst; William Knowland; Mary Ellen Leary; John Francis Neylan; Robert Gordon Sproul; Thomas M. Storke; Paul Taylor.

California State Archives, Sacramento

Papers: Earl Warren.

Cinema-Television Library, University of Southern California, Los Angeles

Papers: Hal Humphrey; Louella Parsons; Edward G. Robinson.

Margaret Herrick Library, Academy of Motion Picture Arts and Sciences, Beverly Hills, California

Papers: Hedda Hopper; John Huston; Louella Parsons; George Stevens, including Joseph L. Mankiewicz oral history.

Clippings files: Blacklisting; Communism; Helen Gahagan Douglas; Myron Fagan; Sterling Hayden; Hollywood Ten; HUAC; Ronald Reagan; Edward G. Robinson; Paul Ziffren.

Herbert Hoover Presidential Library, Ames, Iowa

Papers: Herbert Hoover; Westbrook Pegler, columns.

Lyndon Johnson Library, Austin, Texas

Papers: Lyndon B. Johnson Prepresidential; Drew Pearson.

Los Angeles Times Archives, Los Angeles, California

Various papers related to the newspaper and its campaign coverage.

National Archives and Records Administration, Laguna Niguel, California

Papers: Richard M. Nixon Prepresidential, including series 435, papers on the 1950 campaign.

New York Public Library, New York

Papers: Vito Marcantonio.

Richard M. Nixon Presidential Library and Birthplace, Yorba Linda, California

Papers: Aylett Cotton; Richard M. Nixon Prepresidential, including PPS 3, papers on the 1950 race; Herman Perry.

Franklin D. Roosevelt Presidential Library, Hyde Park, New York

Papers: Eleanor Roosevelt; James Roosevelt.

Harry S Truman Presidential Library, Independence, Missouri

Papers: Dean Acheson; Eban Ayers; Oscar Chapman; Matthew Connelly; Democratic National Committee; India Edwards; George Elsey; Kenneth Hechler; J. Howard McGrath; National Security Council; Westbrook Pegler, columns; Stephen J. Spingarn; Harry S Truman, including official files, personal files, and president's secretary's files.

University Research Library, University of California, Los Angeles

Papers: American Civil Liberties Union; California Republican Assembly; Robert Craig; Augustus Hawkins; Dorothy Healey; Ed and Ruth Lybeck; Carey McWilliams.

Notes

Full citations for all books mentioned in the Notes appear in the Bibliography, beginning on page 263. Full citations for all abbreviations that include the letters *OH* appear under Oral Histories, beginning on page 268. Full citations for all other abbreviations appear under Archives, beginning on page 269.

NARA	National Archives and Records Administration, Richard M. Nixon Prepresidential Papers
NYPL	New York Public Library
RMN	Richard Nixon Presidential Library
URL	University Research Library, UCLA
URL-OH	University Research Library, UCLA, oral histories

CHAPTER ONE: TRICKS, DECEPTIONS, AND WONDROUS VISIONS

3   KFI loyalty oath: *The Nation,* July 1, 1950.

3   " 'dopesters' went 'stir-crazy' ": *Hollywood Reporter,* June 6, 1950.

3   Garbo to Douglas: Telegram, June 6, 1950, CA.

4   "the fundamental ability": Downey radio address, May 1950, RMN-Aylett Cotton Papers.

4   "a self-seeking . . . old girl": Harry Crowe to Downey, BAN, Downey Papers.

4   "decidedly pink": *San Jose News,* June 2, 1950.

4   Pegler on Douglas's deficiencies: King Features column, May 29, 1950.

4   Palmer on Boddy and Douglas: *L.A. Times,* May 18, 1950.

4   "subversive clique," "communist sympathies": L.A. *Daily News,* May 11, 1950.

4   "The Pink Lady": L.A. *Daily News,* May 18, 1950, and other occasions.

4   "I know I am going to win": Douglas to India Edwards, April 11, 1950, CA.

4   "With whom they can't make deals": Ingrid Winther Scobie, *Center Stage.*

4   IF A BODY: *L.A. Times,* March 31, 1950.

4   New York newspaper on Douglas: New York *Daily News,* June 4, 1950.

5   Another writer's observations: *L.A. Mirror,* May 22, 1950.

5   "But mother!": Ibid.

5   Douglas's visit to Santa Clara: *Mountain View Daily Register,* April 7, 1950.

5   Douglas to San Diego organizer: BAN-OH, Helen Lustig.

5   NEVER UNDERESTIMATE: San Francisco *News,* June 1, 1950.

5   "Money alone": Douglas radio script, June 1, 1950, CA.

5   68,500 leaflets: Nixon Whittier headquarters, report on work from March 27 to June 6, 1950, RMN.

6   Nixon passed photo to Chotiner: Nixon to Chotiner, March 23, 1950, NARA.

6   "viciously false circular": L.A. *Daily News,* June 5, 1950.

6   WARNING TO ALL DEMOCRATS: Ibid.

6–7   "forget blind partisan politics": Nixon press release, June 6, 1950, NARA.

7   "socialistic program": Nixon speech, Modesto, March 24, 1950,
    RMN.
7   Truman complaint about "fuss": letter to Clyde A. Lewis, quoted
    in Carey McWilliams, *Witch Hunt.*
8   McCarthy's Wheeling speech: David M. Oshinsky, *A Conspiracy
    So Immense,* and others.
8   Nixon speech before Congress: January 26, 1950.
8   Truman on McCarthy: Oshinsky.
8   "egg-sucking phony liberals," "Communist queers": Ibid.
9   "You will be in an untenable position": Earl Mazo, *Richard
    Nixon.*
9   Mosinee takeover: Oshinsky.
9–10   "give him the courage": Fawn M. Brodie, *Richard Nixon.*
10   Smith opposition to McCarthy and response: Oshinsky.
10   The section on California is largely based on John Gunther, *In-
    side U.S.A.;* Carey McWilliams, *Southern California* and *Califor-
    nia: The Great Exception;* Roger Morris, *Richard Milhous Nixon;*
    Garry Wills, *Nixon Agonistes;* and Kevin Starr, *Material Dreams.*
11   Lakewood as the world's largest subdivision: Joan Didion, "Trou-
    ble in Lakewood," *The New Yorker,* July 26, 1993, and D. J. Waldie,
    Holy Land.
12   Wills's observations: Wills.
13   "There is only one way": Nixon kickoff speech, November 3,
    1949, RMN.
13   "I welcome Mrs. Douglas": *L.A. Times,* June 6, 1950.
13   "a colorful . . . candidate": San Francisco *News,* February 11,
    1950.
14   "There's no use trying": BAN-OH, John Walton Dinkelspiel.
14   Nixon on castrating Douglas: William Arnold, *Back When It All
    Began.*
14   Nixon would later admit: Richard Nixon, *RN.*
14–15   Douglas with bus driver: Scobie.
15   Ziffren drove Douglas home: Ibid.
15   "Whittier's . . . gift to the Republican party": L.A. *Daily News,*
    n.d.
15   UC Berkeley student: Letter from Dick Miller to Douglas, April
    20, 1950, CA.
16   Douglas's reply to Miller: April 26, 1950, ibid.

CHAPTER TWO: THE GAL FROM CAL

17   "We are proud": Edwards to Douglas, June 7, 1950, CA.
17   Douglas to Truman: June 7, 1950, HST-PF.
17   Truman's reply to Douglas: June 8, 1950, ibid.
17   Douglas told a Chicago friend: Douglas to Bea, June 26,
    1950, CA.

18   The section on Douglas's background is drawn primarily from Helen Gahagan Douglas, *A Full Life;* Ingrid Winther Scobie, *Center Stage;* BAN-OH, Helen Gahagan Douglas, Evelyn Chavoor, and others; author's interviews with Mary Helen Douglas, Sharon Lybeck Hartmann, and Florence and Robert Clifton; Roger Morris, *Richard Milhous Nixon* and other biographies of Nixon; and *Ms.,* October 1973.

19   "must have seemed": Carey McWilliams, *Frontier* magazine, June 1, 1950.

19   "a force of nature": Alis de Sola, "Helen Gahagan As I Knew Her," CA, box 203.

23   Roosevelt told her: letter, November 27, 1944, CA.

23   letters from Melvyn to Helen Douglas: Scobie.

23   "In the northwest corner": Douglas article, URL, Ed and Ruth Lybeck Papers.

23–24   "If I Were a Negro": *Negro Digest,* August 1945.

24   "not only on her part": Douglas speech, February 20, 1950, CA.

24   "attentive male colleagues": Scobie.

24   "still knocks them dead": "The Gal from Cal," *Liberty,* circa 1945.

25   "Congresswomen's ideas": Ibid.

25   "aura of glamour," "was on stage": BAN-OH, Margery Cahn.

25   "had been an actress": Ibid., Chavoor.

25   "Helen . . . in the smoke-filled rooms": Morris.

25   "brains, wit and courage,": *Atlanta Journal,* July 11, 1948.

25   Douglas as "idealistic harasser": Scobie.

25   Holifield's observation: BAN-OH, Chet Holifield.

25   "a little bit of flattery": *Ms.,* October 1973.

25–26   "could not have gotten a bill passed": Scobie.

26   Lybeck on hiring a Negro: Ed Lybeck to Douglas, November 1948, URL, Lybeck Papers.

26   "warming one's hands": Morris.

26   Melvyn Douglas's postwar comments: United Press, November 20, 1948.

27   "keeping you in the House": Ed Lybeck to Douglas, July 22, 1949, URL, Lybeck Papers.

28   Pegler on Downey: King Features column, May 29, 1950.

28   Edwards on Douglas as Senate candidate: BAN-OH, India Edwards.

28   An African-American leader and another activist on Douglas as Senate candidate: Scobie.

28   longtime supporter's view of Douglas: BAN-OH, Alvin Meyers.

28   Lybeck on Douglas as Senate candidate: Memo from Ed Lybeck to Douglas, "Present Situation in 14th Congressional District," URL, Lybeck Papers.

29 Chavoor on Douglas: Chavoor to Ruth Lybeck, April 1, 1949, ibid.

29 veterans' magazine on Nixon and Douglas: Scobie.

29 "Dear Richard": Douglas to Nixon, June 4, 1949, RMN.

29 "just going, hell-bent": Morris.

30 "raise $300,000": Robert Engler, *The Politics of Oil.*

30 Douglas on Elliott: Douglas, *A Full Life,* and BAN-OH, Douglas; author's interview with Mickey Ziffren.

31 Tipton's comments to Mitchell: Scobie.

31 Coffin: October 4, 1949, syndicated column.

31 San Diego newspaper on Douglas's appearance: *San Diego Broom,* n.d.

31 "There were a lot of people": BAN-OH, Chavoor.

31 Eleanor Roosevelt: Syndicated column, February 27, 1950.

32 "black lace negligee": Ed Lybeck to Chavoor, March 30, 1949, URL, Lybeck Papers.

32 "Oil money came in here": BAN-OH, Meyers.

32 "a scolding woman": Morris.

32 speechwriter on Downey's retirement: Ibid.

33 San Diego organizer on Douglas's energy: BAN-OH, Byron F. Lindsley.

33 thank-you for party: Letter from Douglas to Roosevelt, March 10, 1950, FDR.

33 "I would have been a traitor": BAN-OH, Elinor Heller.

33 "If I had my choice": Scobie.

33 "You throw me into a pond": BAN-OH, Helen Lustig.

34 "so much to give": Ibid.

34 "And she would stand there": Ibid., Chavoor.

34 "The only one I knew": BAN-OH, Heller.

34 Tipton on Douglas: Scobie.

34 Douglas scolding Chavoor: Ibid.

34 BUSY PATHS CONVERGE: *New York Post,* March 24, 1950.

34 "What's the latest": Letter from Sifton to Douglas, April 25, 1950, CA.

34 "rugged business": Douglas to Sidney Wilkinson, May 5, 1950, ibid.

34–35 letters from Melvyn to Helen Douglas: Scobie.

35 Behrens on Douglas's helicopter: *San Francisco Chronicle,* May 9, 1950.

35 the Helencopter: Author's interview with Dick Tuck.

36 "Even in towns": San Francisco *News,* May 24, 1950.

36 "like Heaven's own gift": Washington, D.C., *Daily News,* May 15, 1950.

36 Douglas on USC incident: USC *Daily Trojan,* May 17, 1950.

36–37 "She wasn't even pledged": Associated Press, May 17, 1950.

37 USC president on USC incident: USC *Daily Trojan,* May 17, 1950.

37 history professor on USC incident: Douglas, *A Full Life.*

37 "If someone threw paint": Fawn M. Brodie, *Richard Nixon,* and Morris.

37 Douglas to editor of *Daily Trojan:* Telegram, circa May 18, 1950, CA.

37 conflicting accounts of Press Club incident: Scobie; Richard Nixon, *In the Arena;* Douglas, *A Full Life;* and others.

37 "Mrs. Douglas now wishes": Chotiner to campaign committee, NARA.

37 Douglas on her chances: Douglas, *A Full Life.*

CHAPTER THREE: PRESIDENTIAL TIMBER

38 "a very strong fondness": Letter from Truman to James Roosevelt, November 4, 1947, HST-PSF.

38 "I wanted the hardest": David McCullough, *Truman.*

38 Nixon's meeting with Pauley: Roger Morris, *Richard Milhous Nixon.*

39 "Searching my memory": Chotiner to Roy Day, June 2, 1950, BAN, Roy Day Papers.

39 The account of Nixon's background is drawn primarily from Richard Nixon, *RN* and *In the Arena;* Morris; Stephen E. Ambrose, *Nixon;* Fawn M. Brodie, *Richard Nixon;* Tom Wicker, *One of Us;* Herbert S. Parmet, *Richard Nixon and His America;* William A. Arnold, *Back When It All Began;* Ralph de Toledano, *One Man Alone;* and others.

40 Harlow on Nixon's childhood: John Osborne, "White House Watch," *New Republic,* May 13, 1978.

40–41 "What starts the process": Kenneth W. Clawson, "A Loyalist's Memoir," *The Washington Post,* August 9, 1979.

43 "Why are you doing this?": Morris.

43 Nixon to Voorhis aide: Brodie.

45 "too slow a road," "a vocal but ineffective minority": Morris.

45–46 "I will say": Nixon to Brennan, March 14, 1949, RMN.

46 Call on fund-raising: BAN-OH, Asa Call.

46 "a bit of a boy debater": Author's interview with McIntyre Faries.

46 Nixon and Jorgensen on train to L.A. and Jorgensen on Chotiner: BAN-OH, Frank Jorgensen.

46 Background of Chotiner: Morris; Brodie; and "Nixon's Man to See," *The Nation,* July 2, 1955.

47 Julie Nixon on Chotiner: Julie Nixon Eisenhower, *Pat Nixon.*

47 St. Johns on Chotiner: St. Johns to Nixon, 1960, NARA.

47 Wills on the Nixon–Chotiner link: Garry Wills, *Nixon Agonistes.*

47 Nixon–Palmer lunch at the Biltmore: Nixon, *In the Arena.*

47 "Presidential timber": W. V. Offut to Nixon, February 20, 1950, RMN.

48 Finch on Nixon and Douglas: Author's interview with Robert Finch.

48 Haldeman et al.: Clancy Sigal, "the Boys of Watergate," *The New York Times,* November 27, 1993.

48 Chotiner to Hillings: Letter, November 8, 1949, RMN.

49 Faries to potential contributor: Morris, and author's interview with Faries.

49 Nixon's announcement of his candidacy: RMN.

49 "we must . . . remind ourselves": Nixon to Chotiner, October 7, 1949, RMN.

49–50 Nixon's scribbled notes: April 1950, ibid.

50 "great American past-time": Nixon to Chotiner, March 6, 1950, ibid.

50 Brennan on Nixon's qualities: Nixon press release, November 17, 1979, ibid.

50 Lewis on Nixon: Broadcast, October 3, 1949, ibid.

50 "This conspiracy": Nixon speech before Congress, January 26, 1950.

50 Stone on crackdown on Communists: Syndicated column, January 31, 1950.

51 "The car will stop," "meet the people": Letter from Chotiner to Jack Polzin, March 22, 1950, NARA.

51 "One human interest story": Letter from Nixon to Chotiner, April 4, 1950, RMN.

52 reprints of Nixon's speech on Hiss: Nixon Whittier headquarters, report on work from March 27 to June 6, 1950, RMN.

52 copies of HUAC pamphlet: Cox to Donald Clark, March 1, 1959, and Nixon to A. C. Mattei, March 3, 1950, ibid.

52 Nixon's notes for station stops: NARA.

52 use of confidential data: Nixon to Ruth Arnold, December 12, 1949, RMN.

52 Leary on Nixon's demeanor: San Francisco *News,* February 1, 1950.

52–53 Nixon to Chotiner and Hancock: Memo, April 8, 1950, RMN.

53 Nixon to Arnold: Memo, May 1, 1950, ibid.

53 bagman story: Morris, and Brodie.

53 "a new champion has arisen": *Argonaut,* March 31, 1950.

53 survey of media coverage: "Newspaper Support, Editorial Support and Comment etc.," NARA.

54 man in Pasadena: April 29, 1950, RMN.

54 Dixon's introduction of Nixon: May 22, 1950, RMN.

CHAPTER FOUR: JUDAS GOATS AND RED PEPPER

55 Nixon and Douglas attacks: *L.A. Herald-Express* and *L.A. Examiner,* June 8, 1950.

55 "Big political guns": United Press, June 7, 1950.

55 "two divergent . . . approaches": *Christian Science Monitor,* June 7, 1950.

56 "fireworks": Jim Bassett, *L.A. Mirror,* June 9, 1950.

56 "could serve no purpose": *L.A. Times,* January 29, 1950.

56 Hearst papers on Nixon: *L.A. Herald-Express,* June 9, 1950.

56 Douglas in the fight of her life: Jacobs, *New Leader,* June 17, 1950.

56 "little Nixie": L.A. *Independent Review,* June 16, 1950.

56 Douglas's vow to herself: Helen Gahagan Douglas, *A Full Life.*

56–57 Cranston on Douglas: Author's interview with Alan Cranston.

57 the lot of the California Democrats: San Francisco *News,* June 7, 1950.

57 Yorty on Douglas: Author's interview with Sam Yorty.

57 Pepper to Douglas: Telegram, June 7, 1950, CA, box 213.

57 Douglas's reply to Pepper: June 26, 1950, ibid.

57 "How'd you do it?": Christopher Matthews, *Kennedy and Nixon.*

58 Howard Hughes at RKO: *Hollywood Reporter,* June 8, 1950.

58–59 Tenney charges and reactions: L.A. *Daily News,* June 9, 1949.

59 "complete delousing": *L.A. Times,* May 16 and 17, 1950.

59 Trumbo and Lawson sentenced: *L.A. Times, The Washington Post,* and *Hollywood Reporter,* June 10, 1950.

60 "Before the Ten": Robert Kenny in Bruce Cook, *Dalton Trumbo.*

60 Background on the Hollywood Ten is based largely on Stefan Kanfer, *A Journal of the Plague Years;* Victor Navasky, *Naming Names;* Larry Ceplair and Steven Englund, *The Inquisition in Hollywood;* and David Caute, *The Great Fear.*

61 "what was done to the Ten": Carey McWilliams, *Witch Hunt.*

61–62 Douglas on the Hollywood hearings: Press release, November 24, 1947, CA, box 203, and letter from Douglas to Clyde Giles, ibid., box 204.

62 Rankin on additional Hollywood suspects: Kanfer.

62 Schary on firings of five of the Ten: Kanfer, and Ceplair and Englund.

62 Hellman on studio bosses: Kanfer.

63 "It's automatic": Ibid.

63 Trumbo on Pegler: Ibid.

64 "confidential" Santa Barbara retreat: Brennan to Herman Perry, June 5, 1950, RMN.

64 "let's get rid of the . . . vermin": Clive Shaffer to Nixon, June 8, 1950, NARA.

64 The account of the Santa Barbara meeting is based largely on BAN-OH, Frank Jorgensen; Roger Morris, *Richard Milhous*

Nixon; and Murray Chotiner, "Fundamentals of Campaign Organization," NARA.

64 "too much emphasis": Jorgensen to Nixon, March 17, 1950, ibid.

64–65 "outside so-called . . . circles": Nixon to Brennan, March 3, 1950, RMN.

65 new recruits had "pledged their support": Nixon to Brennan, March 3, 1950, RMN.

65 Jeffery suggestion: Jeffery to Arnold, May 3, 1950, NARA.

65 Arnold passed Jeffery memo to Nixon: Circa May 1950, ibid.

65–66 "if you do not deflate": Garry Wills, *Nixon Agonistes.*

66 Bush on women: CU-OH, Prescott Bush.

66 "Women have no business": Arthur Crowell to Nixon, October 24, 1949, RMN.

66 "Now we have a woman": BAN-OH, Jorgensen.

66 "a total scorn," "extra appendage": Fawn M. Brodie, *Richard Nixon.*

66 "I knew that": Richard Nixon, *RN.*

67 "Suggestions for renaming": Typed note attached to Douglas campaign leaflet, NARA.

67 Douglas on congresswomen: "Women's Status in a Changing World," speech delivered February 20, 1950, CA, box 181.

67–68 Much of the section on women in U.S. politics is based on Linda Witt, Karen Paget, Glenna Matthews, *Running as a Woman;* Ingrid Winther Scobie, *Center Stage;* Keith Melder, *Hail to the Candidate;* and BAN-OH, India Edwards, among others.

68 Pegler on Smith: King Features column, June 17, 1950.

68 "War to women": Douglas speech, February 20, 1950, CA, box 181.

68 "Government is only housekeeping": Douglas statement to Japanese women, n.d., circa 1948, at CA.

68 one columnist on female legislators: Robert Taylor, *Pittsburgh Press,* n.d., CA, box 73.

69 Edwards on politicians outside Washington: HST-OH, India Edwards.

69 the first loyalty of women activists: Associated Press, June 26, 1948.

69 "Where the average . . . Congressman": Ed Lybeck to Douglas, June 1946, URL, Lybeck Papers.

69–70 Sacramento newspaper on a female senator: *Sacramento Union,* November 1, 1949.

70 Smith on female legislators: Scobie.

70 Douglas address: Speech, February 20, 1950.

70 old friend on Douglas's energy: Alis de Sola, "Helen Gahagan As I Knew Her," CA, box 203.

70–71 LBJ to Douglas: June 16, 1950, LBJ-PP.

71 Douglas's reply to LBJ: June 29, 1950, ibid.

71   Reedy on LBJ: LBJ-OH, George Reedy.

71   Douglas-LBJ relationship: Author's interviews with Mercedes Davidson Eichholz, Mary Helen Douglas, and Robert Dallek; LBJ-OH, Helen Gahagan Douglas.

71   LBJ made passes: Author's interview with Mercedes Davidson Eichholz.

71   "Just saw the latest report": Douglas to LBJ, October 6, 1948, LBJ-PP.

71   LBJ's reply to Douglas: October 19, 1948, ibid.

71   LBJ as an SOB: Walter Pick to Ed Lybeck, March 16, 1949, URL, Lybeck Papers.

71   "an emotional girl": LBJ-OH, Elizabeth Wickenden Goldschmidt.

72   Edwards on Truman: HST-OH, Edwards.

72   Miller to Edwards on Truman's view of women in politics: August 17, 1950, HST, India Edwards Papers.

72   Truman to Miller: August 12, 1950, ibid.

72   complication reported by oil executive: A. B. Connelly to Truman, August 9, 1950, HST-OF.

73   Cohn on Truman's endorsement of Douglas: Cohn to A. B. Connelly, October 12, 1950, HST-OF.

73   Oppenheimer under renewed scrutiny: Tom Wicker, *One of Us*.

73–74 The background on Greenglass and the Rosenbergs is based on Ronald Radosh and Joyce Milton, *The Rosenberg File;* Walter and Miriam Schneir, *Invitation to an Inquest;* and *The New York Times,* June 16, 1950.

74   Nixon responds: United Press, July 12, 1950.

CHAPTER FIVE: WAR FEVER

75   The section on Truman and Korea is based primarily on David McCullough, *Truman;* Robert J. Donovan, *Tumultuous Years;* Harry S Truman, *Off the Record; The New York Times,* June 26–30, 1950; I. F. Stone, *The Hidden History of the Korean War;* and Bruce Cumings, *The Origins of the Korean War.*

77   Hearst's order to his editors: Hearst to Edmond Coblentz, June 27, 1950, BAN, Coblentz Papers.

78   "to feel out the opposition": *The New York Times,* June 27, 1950.

78   "We've got the rattlesnake": *New York Herald Tribune,* July 1, 1950.

78   "a marked buildup": Baldwin, *The New York Times,* June 28, 1950.

78   "We have drawn a line": Edward R. Murrow, *In Search of Light.*

79   "It happens that I am a Quaker": Roger Morris, *Richard Milhous Nixon.*

79–80 San Mateo friend reminded Douglas: David Freidenrich to Douglas, June 27, 1950, CA.

80   "My Irish always works overtime": Douglas to Eleanor Roosevelt, May 14, 1941, CA.

80   a "bombshell will be dropped": Sullivan, New York *Daily News,*
      June 21, 1950.

80–81 Background on *Red Channels* is based on David Caute, *The Great
      Fear;* Stefan Kanfer, *A Journal of the Plague Years;* John Caughey,
      Report on Blacklisting; and Counterattack, *Red Channels.*

82   "Every man's past": Kanfer.

82–83 Gridiron Club incident: David M. Oshinsky, *A Conspiracy So Im-
      mense.*

83   Gallup poll: May 21 and July 7, 1950.

84   Background on the Dies Committee: Oshinsky.

84   Hoover's count of Communists: Morris.

84   Background on the loyalty oath is based on Caute; Donovan; and
      McCullough.

85   loyalty issue "manufactured": Clark Clifford, *Counsel to the Presi-
      dent.*

85–86 "few observers have been willing": Carey McWilliams, *Witch Hunt.*

86   professional wrestlers and amateur archers: Caute.

86   suicide of Matthiessen: Natalie S. Robins, *Alien Ink.*

86   ACLU's opposition to communism: ACLU board meeting, June
      26, 1950, URL, American Civil Liberties Union Papers.

86   a "symptom of insecurity": McWilliams, *Witch Hunt.*

86   "the war situation makes it difficult": Oshinsky.

87   "In none of her characterizations": Palmer, *L.A. Times,* July 30,
      1950.

87   Background on Palmer is based primarily on David Halberstam,
      The Powers That Be; Mitchell, *The Campaign of the Century;* and
      Morris.

87   "They got into trouble": LAT-OH, Kyle Palmer.

88   "from time to time": Palmer, *L.A. Times,* May 9, 1950.

88   "Try and get him": LAT-OH, Palmer.

88   "a delightful woman": Ibid.

88   Palmer accused Nixon's opponent: Palmer, *L.A. Times,* July 30,
      1950.

88–89 Nixon to Palmer: Note, August 7, 1950, RMN.

89   San Diego businessman: Nixon to W. W. Stephens, July 14, 1950,
      NARA.

CHAPTER SIX: PHOTOSTATS WILL BE PREPARED

90   supporter from Los Angeles: Geneva Lynch to Nixon, August 11,
      1950, RMN.

91   woman from Iowa: Letter from A. Claire Dewey to the Repub-
      lican National Committee, July 29, 1950, forwarded to Bill
      Arnold the same day, RMN.

91   Nixon secretary's reply to Iowa woman: Letter to A. Claire
      Dewey, August 16, 1950, RMN.

91 reporter from the *Sacramento Union:* Letter to Nixon, July 11, 1950, RMN.

91 Nixon's reply to *Sacramento Union* reporter: July 13, 1950, RMN.

91 Collins to Nixon: July 11, 1950, RMN.

91 Nixon's reply to Collins: July 17, 1950, RMN.

91 request for a "complete report" on the Douglases: Nixon to Nelson Dilworth, August 1, 1950, RMN.

91 "family origin": Dilworth to Nixon, August 1, 1950, ibid.

91 Nixon to Arnold: Note, ibid.

92 Douglas to Truman: August 1, 1950, HST-OF.

92 Douglas and Truman on appointment of judge: URL-OH, Paul Ziffren.

92–93 Pepper to Douglas: July 27, 1950, CA, box 213.

93 Mundt to Nixon: May 8, 1950, RMN.

93 "What to Do . . . After Atomic Bomb Attack": Los Angeles Health Department.

93 "Old Man Atom": Stefan Kanfer, *A Journal of the Plague Years.*

94 NBC-radio dramas on the bomb: *Daily Variety,* June 23, 1950.

94 Sinclair on nuclear attack: Letter to *Saturday Review,* July 22, 1950.

94 Le May and atomic bombs: Richard Rhodes, *Dark Sun.*

94 attempt to invent a thermonuclear or hydrogen bomb: Rhodes, and Paul S. Boyer, *By the Bomb's Early Light.*

95 Douglas's reply to letter from constituent: March 31, 1950, CA.

95 Mumford on the arms race: Boyer.

95 Peale on "not talking": Ibid.

95 Boyer's reflection: Ibid.

96 Nixon to key businessmen: Letter, July 17, 1950, NARA.

96 "as long as possible": Mattei to Nixon, July 11, 1950, NARA.

96 Kemper expressed interest in Nixon: Telegram from Bill Arnold to Nixon, July 20, 1950, RMN.

96 Eisenhower at Bohemian Grove: Stephen E. Ambrose, *Nixon.*

97 Ike was in "enemy territory": Roger Morris, *Richard Milhous Nixon.*

97 "personality and personal mystique," "had a long way to go": Richard Nixon, *RN.*

97 "practically all the big men": BAN-OH, McIntyre Faries.

97 Nixon's backers: Morris; author's interview with McIntyre Faries; BAN-OH, Roy Day, John Walton Dinkelspiel, and Frank Jorgensen; and financial documents, NARA.

98 two separate bank accounts: Meeting of Nixon campaign staffers, July 21, 1950, RMN, Herman Perry Papers.

98 solicitation aimed at outsiders: Letter from Smith, n.d., RMN.

99–100 Accounts of Kennedy's visit to Nixon's office vary. See Ambrose; William A. Arnold, *Back When It All Began;* Morris, and other biographies of Nixon; and Richard Nixon, *RN.*

100 "Isn't this something?": Author's interview with Patrick J. Hillings, and Christopher Matthews, *Kennedy and Nixon*.

100 Robert F. Kennedy contribution to Nixon campaign: Records, NARA.

100 O'Neill on Joseph P. Kennedy: Tip O'Neill with William Novak, *Man of the House*.

100 Hickok on Baruch: Hickok to Douglas, April 18, 1950, CA.

100 Douglas's reply to Hickok: May 3, 1950, ibid.

101 "Our man Friday": Author's interview with Faries.

101 Ziffren background: URL-OH, Ziffren.

101 Rivkin background: Author's interview with Allen Rivkin.

101 "You're a cinch": Rivkin to Douglas, June 7, 1950, CA.

101 contributors to Douglas's campaign: Various documents, ibid., box 1, additional.

102 Peck turned Douglas down cold: Lists, CA.

102 screenwriter's offer to help Douglas: Scobie.

102 Jarrico wrote speech for Douglas: Ibid.

102 "saving a headline": Sheila Graham column, March 18, 1950.

102 "Nothing is further from the truth": Telegram from Melvyn Douglas, Sheila Graham column, March 20, 1950.

102 "what's at stake": Douglas to Remsen Bird, July 18, 1950, CA, box 65.

102 "It is sure to be": Scobie.

CHAPTER SEVEN: TELL NICKY TO GET ON THIS THING

103 incident at the Young Democrats convention: L.A. *Daily News* and *San Francisco Chronicle*, July 24, 1950.

103 L.A. attorney's advice to Douglas: Irving Hill to Ruth Lybeck, June 13, 1950, CA.

103–4 "Those persons who opposed public development": Ibid.

104 plans for a booklet on Douglas: Lonigan to Nixon, August 17, 1950, RMN.

104 Lonigan's files on Douglas: Ibid.

105 memo from Lonigan to Nixon: July 25, 1950, ibid.

105 later memo from Lonigan to Nixon: September 3, 1950, RMN.

105 Lonigan to managing editor of *Tablet:* Lonigan files, n.d., RMN.

105 *Tablet* managing editor's reply to Lonigan: Ibid.

105 Lovelace to Lonigan: August 19, 1950, RMN.

105 Nixon and Marcantonio in New York: Author's interview with Ralph de Toledano.

106 Nixon told Jorgensen: BAN-OH, Frank Jorgensen.

106 "Tell Nicky": Earl Mazo, *Richard Nixon*.

106 "that bitch": Herbert G. Klein, *Making It Perfectly Clear*.

106 Marcantonio to Boddy: Note, August 5, 1950, RMN, Herman Perry Papers.

106   Nixon on Marcantonio's letter to Boddy: Note from Nixon, n.d., ibid.

106   Nixon to Palmer: August 7, 1950, ibid.

106   "softly suffused with pink": Hearst to Edmond Coblentz, June 23, 1940, BAN, Coblentz Papers.

107   "He couldn't stand ladies": Roger Morris, *Richard Milhous Nixon.*

107–8   Leary on Douglas and Nixon and as a newspaperwoman: Author's interview with Mary Ellen Leary.

108   Chotiner's "special bulletin": July 20, 1950, RMN.

108   "Nixon knew what he wanted to say": Morris.

108   Dixon on Chotiner: Fawn M. Brodie: *Richard Nixon.*

108   "you can either be the candidate or the manager": Henry D. Spalding, *The Nixon Nobody Knows,* and Mazo.

108   twenty-eight observations: Perry to Nixon, July 12, 1950, RMN, Perry Papers.

109   "As a result of the Korean situation": Memo from Spingarn to Truman, July 20, 1950, HST, Stephen J. Spingarn Papers.

109–10   Pegler's escalating attacks: King Features columns, June 29 and 30, and July 15, 18, 25, and 28, 1950.

110   "police state methods": Spingarn memo, July 21, 1950, HST, George Elsey papers.

110   Spingarn and others met with Truman: Memo for the File on Internal Security, July 22, 1950, HST, Spingarn Papers.

111   "only a minor difference": *The New York Times,* June 30, 1950.

111   Danbury incident: Larry Ceplair and Steven Englund, *The Inquisition in Hollywood,* and Lester Cole, *Hollywood Red.*

111   an "amazing disproportion of Jewish talent": B'nai B'rith *Messenger,* October 13, 1950.

111   "we use steam": Carey McWilliams, *Witch Hunt.*

111   watching friends "succumb": Ceplair and Englund.

112   Red hunter Fagan: Pamphlets, 1949–50, MH, Myron Fagan file.

112–13   Collins as first to crack and his comments: John Caughey, *Report on Blacklisting,* and Victor Navasky, *Naming Names.*

113   Hayden as second to crack: Sterling Hayden, *Wanderer;* Caughey; and Navasky.

113   "in a moment of emotional disturbance": Letter from Gang to Hoover, July 31, 1950, in Caughey.

114   Hoover's reply to Gang: Ibid.

114   Kahn's leaving the country: Ceplair and Englund.

114   Material on the Rosenbergs' arrest is based on *The New York Times,* July 16, 1950, and other press clippings and on Ronald Radosh and Joyce Milton, *The Rosenberg File.*

116   Material on Pegler's troubles is based on Oliver Pilat, *Pegler.*

116   letter from Birkhead to McGrath: Reported in the *New York Post,* August 14, 1950.

116 *New York Post* on Birkhead: August 18, 1950.

117 broadcasts from Tokyo: Edward R. Murrow, *In Search of Light.*

117 Le May's atomic task force: Richard Rhodes, *Dark Sun.*

117 "Generalissimo Stalin can kick us": Baldwin, *The New York Times,* July 19, 1950.

117–18 The background on NSC-68 is based on Gregg Herkin, *The Winning Weapon,* and Robert J. Donovan, *Tumultuous Years.*

118 mid-July Cabinet meeting: July 14, 1950, HST, Matthew Connelly Papers.

118 review of Truman's performance: *The New York Times,* July 21, 1950.

119 incoming White House mail: Analysis of August 9 and analysis by Ken Hechler, HST, Hechler Papers.

119 "What this means": *The Washington Post,* July 20, 1950.

119 "The normal process of civilian life": Krock, *The New York Times,* July 20, 1950.

119 "Of course, you like Helen": BAN-OH, Tilford Dudley.

119 Douglas's performance at Long Beach: BAN-OH, Evelyn Chavoor.

120 Douglas's Long Beach speech: August 18, 1950, CA.

120 "One of Nixon's top organizers": Notes from Jack Drown, n.d., RMN.

121 The account of the violent debate over Tydings's report on McCarthy is based on David M. Oshinsky, *A Conspiracy So Immense,* and on *The New York Times,* July 21 and 22, 1950.

121 Childs on McCarthy: Childs, *The Washington Post,* July 25, 1950.

CHAPTER EIGHT: RUNNING FOR THE CYCLONE CELLARS

122 campaign strategy: Murray Chotiner, "Fundamentals of Campaign Organization," NARA.

122 a "simultaneous opening": Chotiner to Charlie Bowen, August 28, 1950, ibid.

122 Nixon in "outlying" areas: John Francis Neylan to Nixon, June 9, 1950, and Nixon's reply to Neylan, July 18, 1950, BAN, Neylan Papers.

123 "We didn't have to recruit him": BAN-OH, Frank Jorgensen.

123 Creel paid by Nixon committee: Roger Morris, *Richard Milhous Nixon.*

123 big ads made voters "think": Chotiner, "Fundamentals," NARA.

123 "kind of lean your way": Ibid.

123 boast of "a deal": Brennan to Charlie Bowen, August 23, 1950, NARA.

123–24 ad man to assistant to president of Union Oil: Robinson to Haynes Finnell, August 11, 1950, RMN.

124 "The billboards we have used": Chotiner, "Fundamentals," NARA.

124 internal survey of Nixon supporters: NARA.

124 late August Nixon finance committee meeting: Memo from Dana Smith to finance committee, September 8, 1950, RMN.

124 Call, "the man who called more shots," and Silberberg on Nixon finance committee: BAN-OH, McIntyre Faries.

125 Douglas was a "smarter woman": Author's interview with Faries.

125 follow-up: Memo to Nixon finance committee members, from Dana Smith, September 8, 1950, RMN.

125 citations from *People's World* and index file. Girvin to Bill Arnold, September 20, 1950, RMN.

125 Lonigan's proposed booklet: Lonigan files, RMN.

126 "you can take any vote": Chotiner, "Fundamentals," NARA.

126 Nixon conversation with Kempton: David Remnick, "Prince of the City," *The New Yorker,* March 1, 1993.

127 McCarthy helped Butler oppose Tydings: David M. Oshinsky, *A Conspiracy So Immense.*

128 Bush on McCarthy: CU, Prescott Bush.

128 tip from Truman aide: Ken Hechler memo to Philip Dreyer of the Democratic National Committee, September 3, 1950, HST, Hechler Papers.

128 "romantic news": *San Francisco Chronicle,* August 24, 1950.

128 Ziffren hit up Hollywood clients: URL-OH, Paul Ziffren.

129 Douglas "did have loyal people": BAN-OH, Elinor Heller.

129 "He insists that I come out": Letter from Roosevelt to Anna Boettiger, August 21, 1950, in Joseph Lash, *A World of Love.*

129–30 Rayburn's instructions to Douglas: Helen Gahagan Douglas, *A Full Life;* LBJ-OH, Helen Gahagan Douglas.

130 "His is the most devious face": Morris, and other books.

130 Douglas-Lybeck conversation on Mundt-Nixon: BAN-OH, Evelyn Chavoor.

130 Douglas-Holifield conversation on Mundt-Nixon: Douglas, *A Full Life,* and BAN-OH, Chavoor.

130 Douglas and others at lunch with McCormack: Douglas, *A Full Life,* and LBJ-OH, Douglas.

131 Hearst columnist on Mundt-Nixon vote: Brown, *L.A. Examiner,* September 4, 1950.

131 Background on the Screen Directors Guild controversy is based on Kenneth L. Geist, *Pictures Will Talk; Daily Variety,* August 25, 1950; and MH, George Stevens Papers.

132 *The New York Times* on SDG loyalty-oath issue: August 27, 1950.

132 "overwhelming victory": *Daily Variety,* August 28, 1950.

132 "I won't pull in my horns": *Daily Variety,* August 31, 1950.

133 Background on the University of California loyalty-oath issue is based primarily on David P. Gardner, *The California Oath Contro-*

versy; Carey McWilliams, *Witch Hunt;* and BAN, Carey McWilliams's oral history, in Robert Gordon Sproul Papers.

133 "a tragedy if . . . teachers left": USC *Daily Californian,* April 14, 1950.

135 "It was hard for me to align him": Morris.

135 campaign director's statement on Douglas: Nixon press release, August 29, 1950, NARA.

136 "red-hot broadside": *L.A. Times,* August 30, 1950.

136 San Francisco newspaper on Brennan: *Call,* September 4, 1950.

136 Plan to distribute *Seeds of Treason* condensation.: Brennan to Perry, August 29, 1950, RMN.

136 Chotiner notified Brennan: September 1, 1950, RMN, Herman Perry Papers.

136 Nixon's scribbled notes: RMN.

137 letter from St. Johns to Nixon: August 22, 1950, ibid.

137 Nixon's reply to St. Johns: August 30, 1950, ibid.

137 Nixon to Arnold (twice): September 2, 1950, ibid.

137 Nixon on publicizing Douglas's vote on McCarran: Chotiner to Bowen, September 5, 1950, NARA.

137 one-page statements: RMN.

138 the magic number 354: Bulletin, Republican Central Committee of Los Angeles, September 15, 1950.

138 "We have not put a statistician to work": Douglas press release, September 1, 1950, CA.

138 Chotiner to Nixon on Greenburg: August 24, 1950, NARA.

138 Chotiner to Nixon on Warren's solution to problem: August 24, 1950, NARA.

138 L.A. Nixon worker on "whispering campaign": H. Allen Smith to Chotiner and Brennan, August 26, 1950, RMN.

139 "The man who uncovered Alger Hiss": Morris.

139 Smith on Nixon during summer of 1950: Ibid.

139 Tenney on Nixon and Chotiner: BAN-OH, Jack Tenney.

139 "I want to make it clear": Nixon press release, September 6, 1950.

CHAPTER NINE: A STOOLIE FOR J. EDGAR HOOVER

140 "But it is not a smear": Murray Chotiner, "Fundamentals of Campaign Organization," NARA.

141 Chotiner at the print shop: Ibid.

141 postcard sent to Nixon's congressional office: RMN.

141 Douglas kickoff speech: L.A. *Daily News,* September 7, 1950.

142 Roosevelt's visit to L.A.: *L.A. Times* and *San Francisco Chronicle,* September 12, 1950, and San Francisco *Call,* September 13, 1950.

143 Douglas supporters notice Pink Sheet: Helen Gahagan Douglas, *A Full Life.*

143   Warren talked out of criticizing Roosevelt: BAN-OH, William
       S. Mailliard.

143   "You wouldn't expect a mother": San Francisco *News,* Septem-
       ber 12, 1950.

143   Palmer's view of Roosevelt: Palmer, *L.A. Times,* September 10
       and 17, 1950.

144   Roosevelt to Douglas: Note, September 16, 1950, CA, box 216.

144   Roybal's "Political death warrant": *L.A. Times,* September 15,
       1950.

144   Healey on Douglas: URL-OH, Dorothy Healey.

144   CBS officials assured protesters: Stefan Kanfer, *A Journal of the
       Plague Years.*

145   "With television going into its big third year": John Caughey,
       Report on Blacklisting.

145   De Koven's attempt to clear his name: Ibid.

145   Muir affair: Caughey; Kanfer, *A Journal of the Plague Years;* and
       The New York Times, August 29 and 30, 1950.

146   Vallee defended Muir: *Daily Variety,* September 20, 1950.

146   "Guilt by association": Pegler, King Features column, September
       15, 1950.

146   Gypsy Rose Lee: Kanfer; *L.A. Times,* September 12, 1950; and
       The New York Times, September 13, 1950.

146   Yip Harburg: Victor Navasky, *Naming Names.*

146   Scott before HUAC: *Daily Variety,* September 18, 1950; David
       Caute, *The Great Fear;* and Kanfer.

146   White before HUAC: *Billboard,* September 9, 1950; Caute; and
       Kanfer.

146–47 Wicker and Kirkpatrick: Caute, and Kanfer.

147   White and Robeson: Martin Duberman, *Paul Robeson.*

148   Dymytrk signed affidavit: Ceplair and Englund, *The Inquisition in
       Hollywood,* and *L.A. Times,* September 11, 1950.

148   Hayden and his therapist: Sterling Hayden, *Wanderer.*

148–49 Robinson and Silberberg: Memo from Silberberg to Robinson,
       September 5, 1950, CT, Edward G. Robinson Papers.

149   Wanger and Wayne: *Daily Variety,* September 8, 1950.

149   "the nickels and dimes of . . . moviegoers": United Press, April
       6, 1950.

149   Parsons on Chaplin: Radio transcript, June 18, 1950, CT, Louella
       Parsons Papers.

149   "They will be": Ibid, October 8, 1950.

149   "from now on": *Time,* September 11, 1950.

150   plans for Hiawatha movie shelved: *Daily Variety,* September 8,
       1950.

150   Nixon on Korea: Letter to constituents, September 8, 1950,
       RMN.

151   "the blotting out of villages": Osborne, *Time,* August 21, 1950.

151   Le May's bombers in North Korea: Richard Rhodes, *Dark Sun.*

151   "My life": Hedda Hopper, syndicated column, September 30, 1950.

151   Marcantonio on Lippmann: Press release, September 14, 1950, NYPL, Vito Marcantonio Papers.

151   "we are not all-powerful": Edward R. Murrow, *In Search of Light.*

151   Matthews on a preventive war: David M. Oshinsky, *A Conspiracy So Immense.*

151–52 Baldwin on Matthews: Baldwin, *The New York Times,* September 1, 1950.

152   Anderson's statement: *The New York Times,* September 2, 1950.

152   Truman's statement: Ibid.

152   The background on Vietnam is based on Robert J. Donovan, *Tumultuous Years,* and James R. Arnold, *The First Domino.*

153   Kennan wrote Acheson: Arnold, *The First Domino.*

154   Hearst newspaper on Douglas: *Los Angeles Herald-Express,* September 11, 1950.

154   Chotiner to Bowen: September 5, 11, and 13, 1950, NARA.

154   Douglas "expects to devote her campaign": Younger, bulletin, Republican Central Committee of Los Angeles, September 15, 1950.

154   Democratic candidates' "blushing complexion": Bulletin, Republican Central Committee of Los Angeles, July 17, 1950.

154   "shove the 'Pink Lady' out": Form letter from Smith to fundraisers, circa September 1950, RMN, Herman Perry Papers.

155   "for the *Times*": Nixon press release, NARA.

155   Democrats were "doing nothing for Helen": Creel to Thomas M. Storke, September 21, 1950, BAN, Storke Papers.

155   Women for Nixon on Douglas: *L.A. Times,* September 21, 1950.

155   Mrs. Harry Goetz on Nixon and Douglas: Nixon press release, September 20, 1950, and *L.A. Times,* September 21, 1950.

155   planned chain letter: Nixon L.A. headquarters, n.d., NARA.

156   Beverly Hills Nixon supporter: Letter from Mary Hogan to "Fellow Clubwomen," n.d., CA, box 204.

156   women as "great haters": Roger Morris, *Richard Milhous Nixon.*

156   Nixon radio broadcast: MH, Hedda Hopper Papers.

157   St. Johns on Nixon: St. Johns, "Meet the Nixons," distributed by Nixon San Francisco headquarters, NARA.

157   The description of Pat Nixon as candidate's wife is based on Morris, and Fawn M. Brodie, *Richard Nixon.*

158   Leary's interview of Pat Nixon: Author's interview with Mary Ellen Leary.

158   St. Johns on Pat Nixon: CU, Adela Rogers St. Johns.

158–59 Mac St. Johns on Pat and Richard Nixon: Morris.

158   "like he was telling a dog": Ibid.

158–59 other comments by Dixon: Morris, and Brodie.

159   "She's a candidate for office": San Francisco *News,* October 9, 1950.

159   "How can you let them do that?": Morris.

159   "Murray got her to go away": Ibid.

159   The section on the McCarran bill is based on Griffith and Theoharis, eds., *The Specter,* and on various press clippings.

160   "it should be made a national law," "There are lots of little lights": HST-OF.

160   Douglas to Truman: Letter, September 20, 1950, HST.

160   Truman on civil-defense measures: Cabinet meeting, July 11, 1950, HST, Matthew Connelly Papers; White House press release, August 30, 1950, HST, Stephen J. Spingarn Papers.

161   AEC on expanded nuclear facilities: Memo from James S. Lay, Jr., to Truman, October 2, 1950, HST-PSF.

161   Joint Chiefs of Staff "production objectives": Ibid.

161–62 Palmer on Douglas: Palmer, *L.A. Times,* September 10, 1950.

162   Truman to Douglas: Letter, September 11, 1950, CA.

162   "one of the worst nuisances": HST, Ayers's diary, in Ayers Papers.

162   Background on James Roosevelt is based on BAN-OH, Florence "Susie" Clifton and James Roosevelt; author's interview with Susie Clifton; *Saturday Evening Post,* October 7, 1950; and *Fortnight,* November 11, 1949.

163   "a consummate liar": Author's interview with Susie Clifton.

163   "Old-line California Democrats": *Time,* January 28, 1949.

164   "The 18th century things": San Francisco *News,* August 30, 1950.

164   Nixon's kickoff speech: San Francisco *Call* and *L.A. Times,* September 20, 1950.

164   "a fighting campaign": Chotiner, "Fundamentals," NARA.

CHAPTER TEN: THIS TRICKY YOUNG MAN

166–67 Nixon-Roosevelt debate: *L.A. Times,* September 20, 1950, and United Press, September 21, 1950.

166   why Douglas "followed the Communist Party line": Nixon press release, September 19, 1950, NARA.

167   *Chicago Tribune* on Nixon-Roosevelt debate: Ingrid Winther Scobie, *Center Stage.*

167   Background on Truman and the McCarran bill is based on a memo from Stephen J. Spingarn, September 2, 1950, in HST, Kenneth Hechler Papers. Truman's veto message is in HST.

167   Douglas on Truman's veto message: Douglas press release, September 22, 1950, CA, box 96.

167   Humphrey on Truman's veto message: *Newsweek,* September 25, 1950, and David Caute, *The Great Fear.*

167   Rankin on Truman's veto message: *Congressional Record,* September 22, 1950.

168   the "stampede" on Capitol Hill: *The Washington Post,* September 23, 1950.

168   Truman to Johnson: September 22, 1950, HST-PSF.

168   account of the filibuster: *Washington News* wire service, September 23, 1950.

168   Edwards to Boyle: September 25, 1950, HST, India Edwards Papers.

168–69   Nixon's campaign schedule: Itineraries, NARA.

169   NOXIN: William A. Arnold: *Back When It All Began.*

169   Nixon in Marysville: Nixon press release, L.A. headquarters, October 2, 1950, NARA.

169   comparison of North Korea with Pearl Harbor: Nixon press release, San Francisco headquarters, September 28, 1950, ibid.

169   Nixon's scribbled notes: Various documents, RMN and NARA.

170   "pink . . . to her underwear": First reported by John Dodds, an editor at William Morrow.

170   Truman and Douglas in bed together: David Halberstam, *The Powers That Be.*

170   "We California Democrats": *L.A. Times,* September 29, 1950.

170   Nixon welcomed the Democrats' support: Statement, n.d., NARA.

170   Chotiner on the Democrats: Murray Chotiner, "Fundamentals of Campaign Organization," ibid.

170–71   Chotiner on pamphlets: Ibid.

171   memo on IMPORTANT STRATEGY: BAN, Roy Day papers.

171   Nixon TV commercial: RMN.

171   "His opponent . . .": Knowland to Hoover, September 27, 1950, HH, Hoover Papers.

172   "a proper approach": BAN-OH, John Walton Dinkelspiel.

172   Douglas trickery in San Francisco: Ibid.

172   "make sure this young lady has . . . gas": Arnold, *Back When It All Began.*

172   woman in Salinas hotel lobby: Ibid.

172   Warren on UC loyalty oath: Memos from Sproul, June 6, and October 16, 1950, BAN, Robert Gordon Sproul Papers.

173   Teller on UC loyalty oath: Memos from Sproul, September 12, October 30, and November 22, 1950, ibid.

173   Carmel caretaker on loyalty oath: *The New York Times,* October 9, 1950.

173   The background on Warren is based on Leo Katcher, *Earl Warren;* Warren, *The Memoirs of Earl Warren; Saturday Evening Post,* October 7, 1950; and BAN-OH, Earl Warren.

174   contributors to Warren's campaign: Lists, CSA.

175   Warren on Brown's run for state attorney general: BAN-OH, Edmund G. Brown.

175   Simon agreed to fund Brown-Warren ads: Ibid.

175   "I'll help you": Ibid.

176   McCarthy's visit to California: *L.A. Times,* September 29, 1950, and Douglas broadcast, KECA radio, October 2, 1950.

176   Nixon's scathing letter: Stenographer's notes, September 1950, transcribed July 6, 1996, RMN.

177   Day joined Nixon campaign: BAN, Roy Day Papers.

177–78   McIntyre to parish priests: Morris, *Richard Milhous Nixon.*

178   Cronin's campaign tips: Chotiner to Nixon, October 20, 1950, NARA.

178   Brennan to Parten: October 3, 1950, HST, Oscar Chapman Papers.

179   Douglas's emergency dinner: Helen Gahagan Douglas, *A Full Life,* and Roger Morris, *Richard Milhous Nixon.*

179   columnist on Douglas's and Nixon's organizations: (Santa Clara) *Mountain View Daily Register,* October 2, 1950.

179   Reuther's assurance of a donation: October 12, 1950, CA.

179   "I think that most liberals": BAN-OH, Tilford Dudley.

179   wealthy individuals contributed to Douglas campaign: Records, CA.

180   "let's send Helen $500": William Gordon to Douglas, October 10, 1950, CA, box 1, additional.

180   Douglas's emergency plea: Telegram from Douglas to Dudley Nichols, October 9, 1950, ibid.

180   Reagan's donation: Douglas, *A Full Life,* and fund-raising lists, CA.

181   "You are wonderful": Dunne to Douglas, n.d., CA.

181   "Robert Ardrey contributes $150": Ardrey to Douglas, n.d., CA.

181   "The next five weeks": Douglas to Dunne, October 3, 1950, CA.

181   the campaign "was increasing in intensity": Douglas to Sheldon, n.d., CA.

181   "I don't think she knew": BAN-OH, Kenneth Hardings.

181–82   Mankiewicz: Author's interview.

182   "an invitation to the Politburo": Santa Rosa *Press-Democrat,* October 8, 1950.

182   charged of "high crime": Douglas broadcast, ABC radio, October 9, 1950, CA.

182   "unscrupulous young men," a "backwash of young men": Douglas broadcast, KMPC radio, October 9, 1950, CA.

183   "This makes my blood boil": Santa Rosa *Press-Democrat,* October 8, 1950.

183   "wrap the flag around her": David Freidenrich to Tipton, September 15, 1950, CA.

183   eight-page comic book: *Right! For United States Senator,* CA.

183   "Much Negro support faltering": Telegram from Douglas head-
       quarters to Bethune, September 28, 1950, CA.

183   "the fighting . . . is less hot": Edwards to William Boyle, October
       3, 1950, HST, Edwards Papers.

183   Douglas begged Ickes: Ickes to Douglas, September 20, 1950, and
       Douglas to Ickes, September 22, 1950, CA, box 212.

184   "Fate had something to do with the christening": Ickes radio
       speech, CA, box 204.

184   "this tricky young man": Douglas press release, Special to *Inde-
       pendent Review,* September 26, 1950, CA.

184   "The BIG LIE in California": Editorial, *Independent Review,* Sep-
       tember 29, 1950.

184   Ickes television spot: CA, ibid., box 203.

185   "I am swinging into . . . campaigning": Douglas to Pearson, Oc-
       tober 2, 1950, CA.

185   James Roosevelt to Truman: September 28, 1950, HST-PF.

185   Truman's reply to Roosevelt: October 10, 1950, ibid.

CHAPTER ELEVEN: HOLLYWOOD DRAMATICS

186   "An impressive galaxy": San Francisco *News,* October 7, 1950.

186   "The March of the Brass Hats": Palmer, *L.A. Times,* October 8,
       1950.

187   "Only by 'mucking' ": David M. Oshinsky, *A Conspiracy So Im-
       mense.*

187   "The public may agree": Ibid.

187   McCarthy's visit to California: San Francisco *Chronicle,* October
       29, 1950; USC *Daily Californian,* October 31, 1950; William
       Costello, *The Facts About Nixon;* Joseph C. Houghteling of Gilroy,
       California, dispatch to Paul Taylor, n.d., BAN, Paul Taylor Papers.

187   "we have invited no outsiders": Nixon speech, Santa Rosa, circa
       October 15, 1950, RMN, speech file.

187   Barkley's visit to California: *L.A. Times,* October 10, 1950; *Inde-
       pendent Review,* October 13, 1950; and San Francisco *Call,* Octo-
       ber 16, 1950.

188   "drinking bourbon and branch": BAN-OH, Alvin Meyers.

188   "Douglas's Vote Against Un-American Activities Committee":
       L.A. Times, October 11, 1950.

189   "very unfortunate": Hechler to Ted Tannenwald, October 13,
       1950, HST, Kenneth Hechler Papers.

189   the press "misinterpreting and misrepresenting": Tipton to Mc-
       Grath, October 13, 1950, HST, J. Howard McGrath Papers.

189   McGrath's visit to California: *L.A. Times,* October 17 and 18,
       1950.

189   De Toledano's visit to California: Author's interview with Ralph de Toledano.

190   De Toledano's written statement: October 17, 1950, NARA.

190   Nixon's statewide radio address: Nixon press release, L.A. headquarters, October 18, 1950, NARA.

191   JFK arrives: Roger Morris, *Richard Milhous Nixon.*

191   Casey and Charney's visit to California: Roger Morris, *Richard Milhous Nixon,* and Ralph de Toledano, *One Man Alone.*

191   "Throughout the history of mankind": Johnson speech, "America's Answer to Aggression," October 24, 1950, HST-PF.

192   Truman to "talk to God's right-hand man": David McCullough, *Truman.*

193   The account of Truman's visit to Wake Island is based on Robert J. Donovan, *Tumultuous Years,* and McCullough.

193   Stone's observations: I. F. Stone, *The Hidden History of the Korean War.*

193   Truman's stay in San Francisco: *The New York Times,* October 17, 1950; *San Francisco Chronicle* and San Francisco *News,* October 18, 1950.

194   Pearson on Truman's plans for campaigning: Syndicated column, circa October 10, 1950.

194   De Toledano in California: Author's interview with de Toledano, and de Toledano, *One Man Alone.*

196   Douglas hitchhiked to Modesto: Associated Press, October 23, 1950, and L.A. *Daily News,* October 25, 1950.

196   the *Newsweek* story: De Toledano, *Newsweek,* October 30, 1950.

197   "Just finished marking": Telegram from Murphy to Nixon, November 1, 1950, NARA.

197   "too hot to handle": Author's interview with "Susie" Clifton.

197   Fast on Reagan: Natalie S. Robins, *Alien Ink.*

197   "We've gotten rid of the . . . conspirators": Anne Edwards, *Early Reagan.*

197   Douglas to Reagan: Note, October 23, 1950, CA.

198   Davis–Pitts relationship: Edwards.

198   "I do not know": June Allyson with Frances Spatz Leighton, *June Allyson.*

198   Cummings duped into speaking: Hopper column, October 1, 1950.

198   Reagan-Cummings conversation: Morris, and Doug McClelland, *Hollywood on Reagan.*

199   Mankiewicz on American liberals: Kenneth L. Geist, *Pictures Will Talk.*

199   Rogell on *Daily Variety* and the *Hollywood Reporter* and *Variety*'s response: *Daily Variety,* September 26, 1950.

199   "I'm all for this": Parsons broadcast, September 17, 1950, CT, Louella Parsons Papers.

199–200 Mankiewicz-Ford conversation: MH, Joseph L. Mankiewicz oral history, in George Stevens Papers.

200 DeMille's call for a secret SDG meeting: Geist.

200 Keays mobilized the SDG staff: MH, Stevens Papers.

200 conversation between Joseph and Herman Mankiewicz: Mankiewicz oral history, ibid.

200 meeting at Chasen's restaurant: Geist.

201 telegram from SDG members: MH, Stevens Papers.

201 DeMille's proposed compromise: Mankiewicz oral history, ibid.

202 *Death of a Salesman* in Peoria: Stefan Kanfer, *A Journal of the Plague Years,* and *Daily Variety,* October 23, 1950.

202 the Loeb-*Goldbergs* controversy: Kanfer, and John Caughey, *Report on Blacklisting.*

203 the CBS loyalty oath: Kanfer.

203–4 Guthrie and the FBI: Daniel Wolfe, *Musician,* September 1990.

204 Field poll: October 12, 1950.

204–5 testimonials of Johnson, Rayburn, Mansfield, and Sparkman: CA.

205 *L.A. Sentinel* on Douglas and Nixon: *L.A. Sentinel,* May 11, August 31, and October 5, 1950, and Nixon press release, October 6, 1950, NARA.

206 *Sun Reporter* endorsement of Douglas: n.d.

206 Randolph's endorsement: Randolph to Douglas, October 27, 1950, CA.

206 St. Johns on "colored" and "Mexican" votes and Cox's response: Memo from Cox to Nixon, October 9, 1950, NARA, box 667, and Morris.

206 "He . . . cursed like a pirate": Morris.

206 "He was comfortable": Ibid.

207 *Variety* on Benton's TV ads: October 26, 1950.

207 television's "prohibitive expense": *L.A. Star,* May 10, 1950.

208 Nixon TV spots: Scripts, NARA.

208 Lloyd and Norris on Nixon: Nixon press releases, L.A. headquarters, October 16 and 20, 1950, NARA.

208 "We believe that any newspaper": Perry to Brennan, October 3, 1950, RMN, Herman Perry Papers.

209 "When you write to him next": Nixon press release, October 13, 1950, NARA.

209 one-hundred-dollar bills for petty cash: Morris.

209 the most insidious smear of the campaign: Nixon press releases, L.A. headquarters, October 11 and 16, 1950, NARA.

210 "Up to this time": Nixon press release, L.A. headquarters, October 24, 1950, ibid.

210 Perry to Brennan: October 24, 1950, RMN, Perry Papers.

210 Brodie's observation: Fawn M. Brodie, *Richard Nixon.*

210 Palmer mimicked: *L.A. Times,* October 1950.

210   war veteran on Nixon's shirt: Louis Greenbaum in Nixon press release, L.A. headquarters, October 16, 1950, NARA.

211   Klein on the Pink Sheet: Herbert G. Klein, *Making It Perfectly Clear.*

211   "pinned to her extremist record": Richard M. Nixon, *RN.*

211   "with Gahagan stubbornness": Morris.

211   "the vilest of graffitti": Ibid.

211   "never could draw a breath": BAN-OH, Elinor Heller.

211   "a *masterful* hatchet job": BAN-OH, Helen Lustig.

211   Pauley's refusal to contribute to Douglas's campaign: *L.A. Times,* October 17, 1950.

211   "If you vote for Douglas": Douglas, *A Full Life.*

211–12   Chavoor on ringing doorbells and Women for Nixon: BAN-OH, Evelyn Chavoor.

212   "personal confrontations": BAN-OH, Lustig.

212   "She's no Communist": Author's interview with Robert Clifton.

212   young Democrat got punched and kissed: BAN-OH, Bert Coffey.

212   Douglas and Robeson photo: *New York Herald Tribune,* October 22, 1950.

212   the campaign's effects on children: Author's interviews with Mary Helen Douglas, Diane Baker, and Sharon Lybeck Hartmann.

213   another child upset by the campaign: Author's interview with Jean Sieroty.

213   "After all, it's your job": Ingrid Winther Scobie, *Center Stage.*

213   "I am not now": Statement of Melvyn Douglas, October 18, 1950, CA, box 194.

214   "if there was a way of doing it": BAN-OH, Roy Day.

214   Leary on Nixon: Author's interview with Mary Ellen Leary.

CHAPTER TWELVE: RED SAILS IN THE SUNSET

215   "picking up ground": Chavoor to Lilli Webster, October 24, 1950, CA.

215   Taylor's advice: Taylor to Douglas, n.d., BAN, Paul Taylor Papers.

215   late donations to Douglas campaign: CA.

215   "movie folk are scared": L.A. *Daily News,* November 2, 1950.

216   "the studios frown": Ibid.

216   "A movie star": *Daily Variety,* November 6, 1950.

216   notations on key Nixon supporters: NARA.

217   "Right now Nixon is losing!": Independent Voters to "George," October 16, 1950, CA, box 204.

217   "From start to finish": Radio broadcast transcript, November 1, 1950, RMN.

217   "the most tumultuous evening": Kenneth L. Geist, *Pictures Will Talk.*

217   "the most dramatic evening": Ibid.

218   "hypocritical flag wavers": Huston's notes, MH, John Huston Pa-
       pers, Screen Directors Guild file.

218   Kazan's arrival at meeting with Mankiewicz: Geist.

218   The account of the SDG meeting is based on MH, Joseph L.
       Mankiewicz oral history, in George Stevens Papers; *Variety*, Oc-
       tober 24 and 25, 1950; and *The New York Times*, October 29, 1950.

219   "It's terrifying": Hopper syndicated column, October 27, 1950.

220   Mankiewicz's open letter: October 27, 1950.

220   "a new self-constituted court," "I wish to avow": Robinson state-
       ment, September 29, 1950, CT, Edward G. Robinson Papers.

221   Robinson would be "happy": Letter from Ernst to Hoover, Oc-
       tober 24, 1950, ibid.

221   Ernst on Robinson's record.: Ernst to Robinson, October 24,
       1950, ibid.

221   Gaining clearance: Ernst to Robinson, October 26, 1950, ibid.

222   Robinson to secretary of treasury: November 3, 1950, ibid.

222   this "full time job": Ernst to Robinson, October 26, 1950, ibid.

222   Robinson's HUAC appearance: Transcript of hearings, October
       27, 1950, ibid.

223   "it has become apparent" and *Daily Variety* hailed Robinson's
       HUAC appearance: *Daily Variety*, November 8 and December
       22, 1950.

223   Schlesinger should work with Harriman: Schlesinger to Ken
       Hechler, November 1, 1950, HST, Hechler Papers.

223   Terry typed Harriman's speech: BAN-OH, Juanita Terry Barbee.

223   Harriman's visit to L.A.: *L.A. Times*, October 31, 1950; Douglas
       to Harriman, November 3, 1950, CA; and URL-OH, Paul
       Ziffren.

224   Field survey: October 30, 1950.

224   Hechler to Elsey: October 27, 1950, HST, Elsey Papers.

224   "a lot of the red mud": Hechler to Pete Spruance, October 31,
       1950, HST, Hechler Papers.

225   The account of the assassination attempt is based on David Mc-
       Cullough, *Truman*.

225   "The thin and flimsy veil": Krock, *The New York Times*, Novem-
       ber 2, 1950.

225   Downey's visit to the White House: *L.A. Times*, October 27, 1950.

226   "there has been . . . misrepresentation": *L.A. Times* and United
       Press, November 3, 1950.

226   Douglas supporters sent telegrams: For example, telegram from
       John Valentine to Truman, November 1, 1950, and telegram from
       Sharpless Walker to Truman, November 3, 1950, HST.

226   Tipton called the White House: November 2, 1950, HST-OF.

226   Eleanor Roosevelt considers resigning: Joseph Lash, *A World of
       Love*.

227 drafts of Nixon's speeches from late in the campaign: NARA.

227 "wonderful friendship," "Pay no attention": Nixon campaign postcards, RMN.

227 "photo finish": Palmer, *L.A. Times,* October 29, 1950.

227 Brennan to Knowland: November 3, 1950, BAN, Knowland Papers.

228 "the best of luck": James H. Ratliff to Nixon, October 26, 1950, RMN.

228 "remains deaf and blind": Creel, Democrats for Nixon, press release, October 29, 1950, NARA.

228 "proof beyond a doubt": Carlson, Nixon press release, October 29, 1950, NARA.

228 D.C. head of Californians for Nixon solicited votes: Herbert C. Parker to Nixon, October 30, 1950, RMN.

228 fear slogans for radio and television: Transcripts, ibid.

228 Californians would hum "Red Sails . . .": Bulletin, Republican Central Committee of California, September 15, 1950.

228 "the tired, middle-class audience": *People's World,* October 31, 1950.

228 Wallace-Douglas-Stalin cartoon: Roger Morris, *Richard Milhous Nixon.*

229 Catholic churches in southern California: Memo from Zita Remley, n.d., CA, box 203, and Helen Gahagan Douglas, *A Full Life.*

229 "The clergy of the Catholic Church": Mildred Hunt to Nixon, November 1950, RMN.

229 "California is not France": Douglas, *A Full Life.*

229 "Tell them you pray": Author's interview with Mickey Ziffren.

229–30 "As Quakers we are pacifists": Nixon press release, October 1950, NARA.

230 "threw them out": BAN-OH, Roy Day.

230 proliferation of dirty tricks: Douglas, *A Full Life;* Morris; BAN-OH, Day, and other oral histories.

230 "Stop Roosevelt" rallies: Flyers, November 1 and 2, 1950.

230 "a very difficult problem": John Walton Dinkelspiel, OH.

230 Nixon supporters called registered voters: Morris.

230 "We couldn't get a bank of telephones": BAN-OH, Helen Lustig.

230 minister took his phone off the hook: Author's interview with Wendell Miller.

230 WIN WITH NIXON: Morris.

231 "this little lady": Scott, radio speech typescript, KNX, November 2, 1950, NARA.

231 Communist newspaper denounced Douglas: *People's World,* November 2, 1950.

231 "His opponent is the glamorous actress": Editorial, *L.A. Times,* October 31, 1950.

231 for "the purpose of preventing an injustice": Editorial, *L.A. Times,* November 1, 1950.

232 "This is the final week": Douglas to Shepard Traybe, October 31, 1950, CA.

232 Ziffren offered to pay Boddy's debt: URL-OH, Paul Ziffren.

232 McWilliams predicted a Douglas victory: McWilliams, *The Nation,* November 4, 1950.

232 Tipton claimed his strategy was working: *The New York Times,* October 31, 1950.

232 Douglas grew discouraged: Douglas radio speech, October 30, 1950, CA-HGD; USC *Daily Californian,* November 2, 1950; *San Diego Union,* November 4, 1950; and Douglas, *A Full Life.*

233 draft of Douglas's October 30 radio speech: October 23, 1950, CA.

233 Douglas's last helicopter flight: Douglas, *A Full Life.*

233 The account of the Beverly Hills High School debate is based on BAN-OH, Roy Day, and Herbert G. Klein, *Making It Perfectly Clear.*

234 another observer of the debate: Author's interview with Jean Sieroty.

CHAPTER THIRTEEN: THE FINAL STRAW

235 Douglas on Roosevelt versus Warren: Helen Gahagan Douglas, *A Full Life;* BAN-OH, William S. Mailliard; LAT-OH, Kyle Palmer; and *L.A. Times,* November 5, 1950.

235 Warren to Small on Nixon: Roger Morris, *Richard Milhous Nixon.*

236 "As always, I have kept my campaign": Ibid.

237 Nixon on the Chinese attack: *L.A. Times,* November 4, 1950.

237 Nixon on Douglas's position on China: Nixon press release, November 4, 1950, NARA.

238 Perry's complaint about Warren: Perry to Nixon and Bernard Brennan, November 6, 1950, RMN, Herman Perry Papers.

238 Chotiner's "traditional Nixon close": Chotiner to H. Allen Smith, October 31, 1950, RMN.

239 Bruce's regrets: Bruce to Douglas, November 4, 1950, CA.

239 "I shall be thinking about you tomorrow": Telegram from Hickok to Douglas, November 6, 1950, ibid.

239 "I had not intended": Melvyn Douglas radio speech, November 6, 1950, ibid., box 204.

240 "You know Jimmy will lose": BAN-OH, Florence "Susie" Clifton, and author's interview with Clifton.

240   Warren's Red-baiting of Roosevelt: Reported in various San Francisco newspapers, November 3, 1950.

241   "Tomorrow is the election": Hoover to Albert Simms, November 6, 1950, HH, postpresidential papers.

241   Nixon on election day: Morris; Henry D. Spalding, *The Nixon Nobody Knows;* and *L.A. Times,* November 8, 1950.

242   "Melvyn's speech last night": Telegram from Mosk to Douglas, n.d., CA.

242   "Helen, dear": Telegram, November 7, 1950, CA.

242   Fisher to Douglas: Letter, November 7, 1950, CA, box 1, additional.

243   Douglas-Lybeck conversation: Author's interview with Sharon Lybeck Hartmann.

243   Douglas campaign headquarters: BAN-OH, Juanita Terry Barbee.

244   "free, uninjured, whole": Douglas, *A Full Life.*

244   Nellor celebration: Morris.

244   "Tokyo headquarters": I. F. Stone, *The Hidden History of the Korean War.*

244–45   "My God, this whole thing": BAN-OH, Leo Goodman.

245   Lybeck analysis of the election: Letter to Douglas, November 14, 1950, CA.

245   *U.S. News & World Report:* November 17, 1950.

246   "widespread hysteria": Ickes, *New Republic,* November 20, 1950.

246   Elsey quote: Robert J. Donovan, *The Tumultuous Years.*

246   "I do not think we did a very good job": Edwards to Truman, n.d., HST, Edwards Papers.

246   telegrams to Nixon: NARA.

247   wife of Call on Nixon's debt: David Halberstam, *The Powers That Be.*

247   messages of thanks and commiseration: CA, box 213.

247   "how low a man can sink": Ickes, *New Republic,* November 20, 1950.

248   "there are only two years left": Lybeck analysis of the election, CA.

248   Ford told Douglas: Letter to Douglas, November 13, 1950, CA.

248   Dunne informed her: Letter to Douglas, November 8, 1950, CA.

248   Ickes attributed the loss to two factors: Ickes, *New Republic,* November 20, 1950.

248   Meyers's observations on Douglas's loss: BAN-OH, Alvin Meyers.

248   "Frankly it was the Pink Sheet": BAN-OH, Rollin McNitt.

248   Kennedy on Nixon and Douglas: Morris, and Christopher Matthews, *Kennedy and Nixon.*

249   Truman on Korea: David McCullough, *Truman,* and Robert J. Donovan, *Tumultuous Years.*

249   "I will not break bread": Morris.

249 Pearson suggested: Syndicated column, December 4, 1950.

250 Similar accounts of the McCarthy-Pearson fight are recorded in Morris; David M. Oshinsky, *A Conspiracy So Immense;* and Ralph de Toledano, *One Man Alone.*

250 Stanford research institute report: Stanford University press release, January 26, 1951.

251 Greenburg to Nixon: January 26, 1951, NARA.

251 Nixon's reply to Greenburg: February 19, 1951, NARA.

251 Douglas lecture tour: Douglas letter to Robert Nathan, December 7, 1950, CA.

251 Dunne had suggested: Letter to Douglas, November 8, 1950, CA.

251 "to kill Helen Gahagan's chances": Hopper to Nixon, January 4, 1951, MH, Hedda Hopper Papers.

251 "Just as soon as I do": Nixon to Hopper, January 20, 1951, ibid.

Index

Greg Mitchell's previous book on California politics, *The Campaign of the Century: Upton Sinclair's Race for Governor of California and the Birth of Media Politics,* won the Goldsmith Book Prize from Harvard University in 1993. It was also a finalist for the *Los Angeles Times* Book Award. He later served as consultant on the documentary *We Have a Plan,* largely based on his book, which was an episode in the acclaimed PBS *Great Depression* series.

Among his other books are *Hiroshima in America: Fifty Years of Denial* (written with Robert Jay Lifton), *Truth and Consequences,* and *Acceptable Risks* (coauthored by Pascal James Imperato). He is presently writing another book with Robert Jay Lifton on the current national debate over capital punishment.

Mitchell has written articles, essays, and book reviews for dozens of national magazines and leading newspapers, including *The New York Times, The Washington Post,* the *Los Angeles Times,* and the *San Francisco Chronicle.* He lives in Nyack, New York.

ABOUT THE TYPE

This book was set in Bembo, a typeface based on an old-style Roman face that was used for Cardinal Bembo's tract *De Aetna* in 1495. Bembo was cut by Francisco Griffo in the early sixteenth century. The Lanston Monotype Company of Philadelphia brought the well-proportioned letterforms of Bembo to the United States in the 1930s.